Oracle Press™

Oracle Performance Tuning 101

Gaja Krishna Vaidyanatha,
Kirtikumar Deshpande, and
John Kostelac

Dear Chris,
G'day mate.
Tune databases,
drink beer & Scotch
and hang loose.

Cheers,
Gaja
05/09/2001

Osborne/**McGraw-Hill**

New York   Chicago   San Francisco
Lisbon   London   Madrid   Mexico City
Milan   New Delhi   San Juan
Seoul   Singapore   Sydney   Toronto

This book is printed on recycled paper including 30% post-consumer waste material.

Osborne/**McGraw-Hill**
2600 Tenth Street
Berkeley, California 94710
U.S.A.

To arrange bulk purchase discounts for sales promotions, premiums, or fund-raisers, please contact Osborne/**McGraw-Hill** at the above address. For information on translations or book distributors outside the U.S.A., please see the International Contact Information page immediately following the index of this book.

Oracle Performance Tuning 101

1234567890 FGR FGR 01987654321

ISBN 0-07-213145-4

Publisher
Brandon A. Nordin

Vice President & Associate Publisher
Scott Rogers

Acquisitions Editor
Lisa McClain

Project Editor
Jennifer Malnick

Acquisitions Coordinator
Ross Doll

Technical Editors
Cary Millsap, Craig Shallahammer, Scott Gossett

Copy Editor
Lunaea Weatherstone

Proofreader
Carroll Proffitt

Indexer
Jack Lewis

Computer Designers
Carie Abrew, George Toma Charbak, Roberta Steele

Illustrators
Beth E. Young, Michael Mueller

Series Design
Jani Beckwith

This book was composed with Corel VENTURA™ Publisher.

To *Amma & Appa*, who created me and brought me into this world; to *my teachers*, who taught me how to learn and live; to *the force*, who has bestowed upon me everything in abundance; to *Savitha*, who chose to partner with me on the journey of *life*; and to our son, *Abhimanyu*, who truly personifies that *learning never really stops…*

—Gaja Krishna Vaidyanatha

To my family, who motivated me to write and kept my spirits up.

—Kirtikumar Deshpande

About the Authors

Gaja Krishna Vaidyanatha is currently the Director of Storage Management Products at Quest Software, Inc., providing technical and strategic direction for the storage management product line. He has more than ten years of technical expertise, with over nine years of industry experience working with Oracle systems.

Prior to joining Quest, Gaja worked as a Technical Manager at Andersen Consulting, where he specialized in Oracle Systems Performance Management and lead the Oracle Performance Management SWAT Team within the Technology Product Services Group. In a prior life, Gaja was also a Consultant and Instructor at Oracle Corporation specializing in the core technologies of Oracle.

His key areas of interests include performance architectures, scalable storage solutions, highly available systems, and system performance management for data warehouses and transactional systems. He holds a Masters Degree in Computer Science from Bowling Green State University, Ohio. He has presented many papers at various regional, national, and international Oracle conferences and is currently in the faculty of the IOUG-A Master Class University. He is also a contributor to the Oracle-L listserver and can be reached at gajav@yahoo.com.

Kirtikumar Deshpande (Kirti) has been working in the Information Technology field for over 20 years, including more than seven years as an Oracle DBA. Although trained as a Biomedical Engineer, he has chosen Information Technology as his career. He currently works with Verizon Information Services as a Senior Oracle Database Administrator and is a frequent contributor on the Oracle-L and LazyDBA listservers. He can be reached at kirti_deshpande@hotmail.com.

Contents

PART I
The Method

v

PART II
Application Tuning

Instance and Database Tuning

PART IV
Specialized Tuning

PART V
Environment Tuning

PART VI
Appendixes

Foreword

Is the performance of your Oracle system "abundantly successful"? Chances are good that your answer is no, especially since you've taken the trouble to open this book. You are not alone. Of the several hundred Oracle database owners that I've met since 1989, not one has come this far without enduring several weeks under siege as the victim of Oracle system performance misbehavior.

Even at sites where people are satisfied with their system performance, my colleagues and I routinely find application functions that consume 50 percent more hardware capacity than they should. I believe that virtually every Oracle system in the world works at least 20 percent harder than it needs to. The reason that this level of inefficiency is so pervasive is that there is a profound shortage of people who can competently optimize the performance of an Oracle system.

This particular labor shortage is well over ten years old. Of course, Oracle systems are complex, and they require talented, hard-working people to manage them. But the world has plenty of talented, hard-working people who enjoy abundant success in keeping airliners aloft, controlling disease, shipping packages overnight across geopolitical boundaries, and other complex jobs. Why, then, is it so hard to find someone who can competently optimize the performance of an Oracle system?

The shortage of competent labor exists because there is a desperate shortage of competent information published on Oracle performance topics. Yes, many database administrators' desks are stocked with thousands of pages of text devoted to Oracle performance topics. But, unfortunately, a lot of the Oracle performance information in print today actually inhibits your ability to improve the performance of an Oracle system.

The book you are holding is different. It is the first introductory textbook to describe an improved optimization method rather than encourage yet another generation of analysts to use the old ratio-based analysis methods that have guided Oracle database administrators down rat holes for over a decade. It is a long-overdue introduction to the subject of Oracle performance that breaks away from tuning myths that still dominates the market.

I like *Oracle Performance Tuning 101* for several reasons. It is the first book in print that gives top priority to the performance management tasks that I believe are the most important for the beginner to learn: how to identify bottlenecks, and how to activate Oracle tracing and begin to interpret the results. It also adds value to the Oracle bookshelf by providing relevant information for the beginning performance analyst about the workings of the Oracle kernel and its supporting technology stack. *Oracle Performance Tuning 101* confronts some deadly sins of performance management that many other books preach to be truth. Here, you'll finally begin to understand why rebuilding your database to eliminate fragmentation is a waste of time. You'll see that index effectiveness estimates that are based on row selectivity are unreliable. You'll read why your 99% database buffer cache hit ratio is usually not an indication that your system is running at peak efficiency. With *Oracle Performance Tuning 101*, good system performance managers will finally have a book that they can point to as an antidote for some of the inefficient (and sometimes downright wrong) advice that lives in so many well-established texts.

In the proposal phase of *Oracle Performance Tuning 101*, Gaja Krishna Vaidyanatha encouraged me to view this project as a piece in an Oracle system performance revolution that I hoped to stimulate by creating hotsos.com. We have all endured a culture of "performance by accident" for far too long. Since late 1999, Hotsos, our partner companies like Miracle A/S in Denmark, and several of our colleagues throughout the world have committed ourselves to creating a higher standard of information quality and accessibility for Oracle performance managers. I look for *Oracle Performance Tuning 101* to be a necessary early step in improving the quality of Oracle system performance around the world.

—Cary Millsap,
Founder and Manager, hotsos.com

Acknowledgments

**M**y first day on U. S. soil was the 26th of July 1990. It is a day that will be permanently etched in my memory. When I landed at the Los Angeles International Airport, I had just traveled more than 24 hours halfway around the world from my hometown in India and was ready to start a new chapter in my life. I was a kaleidoscope of emotions, feelings, and dreams; I had just joined a pool of many thousands of aspirants who come to the United States every year from every corner of the world, leaving their homes and families far behind, to pursue their academic dreams. And mine was to get a masters degree in Computer Science. I accomplished that at Bowling Green State University (BGSU) in Bowling Green, Ohio.

More than ten years since that first day and here I am summarizing the contributions of the people in who contributed to my growth, success, and to this book. I am what I am today as a result of the hard work and dedication of many people. This section of *thanksgiving* is for all those people.

First and foremost, my parents, Sarada Vaidyanatha Sharma & Krishnaswami Vaidyanatha Sharma, who continually believed in me, gave me strength, courage, and support in every endeavor I undertook. Words cannot express the amount of sacrifice, pain, and endurance they have undergone to raise and educate my sister and me. Hats off to you both for your contributions in our lives. I love you both very much. Always will!

Next on the list are my in-laws, Lakshmi & Kulathu Iyer Sankaran, who took a leap of faith and gave me their daughter's hand in marriage. What were you thinking?? Just kidding! Thank you for all your support and love in the past ten years. We couldn't have done it without you.

My dear sister, Durga Subramanyan; my brother-in-law, K.V. Subramanyan (Ishtan); and my niece, Sharanya Subramanyan, have been a perennial source of love, admiration, and warmth and has meant a lot to me.

Dr. Leland Miller and Dr. Ann Marie Lancaster are two individuals I cannot forget for their sensitivity, encouragement, and advice during those early days at BGSU. Thanks for keeping the faith in me. I also thank Dr. David Chilson, who taught me the VAX Assembly Language and much more. His orderliness and discipline were a true source of inspiration. Also, many thanks to Dr. Subramanian Ramakrishnan, who kept reminding me of my good writing skills (among other things), and told me that one day I should write a book. Your wish has come true.

My Oracle life began at Owens-Corning Fiberglas Corporation in Toledo, OH, in May 1992, with Oracle version 6.0.31 under the tutelage of Mark Amos. I hold Mark at very high esteem for his technical knowledge and his patience, while teaching me the rudiments of Oracle, client-server computing, TCP/IP, and networking. Mark hired me for my C programming skills, and on my first day at Owens-Corning told me that I was on an Oracle project. I could barely spell Oracle then. Thank you Mark for all of your contributions and literally laying the foundation for my career. This book would have been a distant dream without you. Thanks are also in order to Scott Highman, who saw my potential and hired me in the first place. Another individual I adored during those times was Charlie Mather. He was a great guy in many respects. Charlie inculcated in me the *fun aspect* of tuning and taught me some of the core essentials of application performance tuning, which I use to this day. You were awesome to work with and I thank you for your contribution in my life.

And to the many friends and technical cohorts I met during my tenure at Oracle Corporation. Mogens Norgaard, Chuck Muehlbrad, Inderpal Tahim, Robert Weitzel, Scott Gossett, Sue Jang, and David Austin are some of the few with whom I have had many *food for thought* discussions and learned a lot in the process.

Special thanks from the bottom of my heart to Scott Gossett of Oracle Corporation, Craig Shallahammer of OraPub, Inc. (http://www.orapub.com), and Cary Millsap of Hotsos, LLC. (http://www.hotsos.com), the dynamic trio that were entrusted the all important task of performing the technical review of this book. It felt wonderful being part of a great team; the quality of your work was fantastic. Thanks to Cary Millsap for taking the time to write the foreword. John Kanagaraj's contributions to some of the chapters were superb, and we wish we had your services for all the chapters, but understand that you had to *take care of life*. Thanks also to Susan McClain of Alliance Data Systems and Brian Spears, Database Consultant for Information Control Corporation, for sharing some real production system output of STATSPACK.

There can be one DBA Goddess in our world and that is Rachel Carmichael. We met on Jared Still's Oracle-L list in 1997 and have not looked back since then. I remember doing the *happy dance* with Rachel on the streets of Anaheim, CA, when we met for the first time in person at IOUG-A 2000. Rachel introduced me to Jeremy Judson, an Oracle Acquisitions Editor at Osborne/McGraw-Hill, and convinced me that I should undertake this project. Rachel later became the developmental editor of this book and provided invaluable input. Kudos for your contribution, and best of all, thanks for being such a great friend. Thanks also to Kris Austin for your incredible warmth and friendship.

The crew at Osborne/McGraw-Hill was great to work with. We started with Jeremy Judson, and then Lisa McClain took over the reins managing this project. Lisa and I have had countless hours of discussions ensuring everything was on track. Thanks for all your time, support, kind words, and humor during some crazy times in November and December 2000. Jennifer Malnick, Ross Doll, and Lunaea Weatherstone did a great job with keeping track of things through the various stages of this effort and copy editing the manuscript. You guys make us look very good! And to the many others at Osborne I did not encounter directly, thank you for making this book a reality.

My gratitude goes out to Jared Still for revitalizing the Oracle-L list during the 1997/1998 timeframe where I met Kirti, Rachel, and a bunch of other great people.

It was a great pleasure to work with Kirti on this project. You came into the project at a crucial juncture and delivered your share with outstanding colors. You also provided this book, the DBA facet, by bringing your in depth production experience. Plus, you are one of the primary reasons that I have my sanity in tact, as writing this book at night and managing the development and release of StorageXpert for Oracle (as part of my day job at Quest Software, Inc.) stretched me to my limit many times. Thanks also to Eyal Aronoff and Vinny Smith of Quest for giving me the opportunity to be part of one of the world's best open systems management solution companies.

When Kirti came on board, we also got another set of technical eyes in the form of Achala Deshpande (Kirti's wife). Thank you, Achala, for taking the time to review a ton of material in a short period of time, despite your very hectic schedule.

Many thanks are also in order to John Kostelac for his contributions to Chapters 1, 2, and 5–7. I wish you the very best in life.

Last but not the least, my heartfelt gratitude to my soul mate, Savitha, and our son, Abhimanyu. The sacrifice that you have made in the last six months during my travels and writing of this book is commendable. I could not have done it without your patience, support, and love. Thank you for understanding how important this book is to all of us. I promise to make it up to both of you. There is nothing more important in my life than you and your love. And that is a priority that will never change.

—Gaja Krishna Vaidyanatha

I do not have enough words to thank my parents, Srila Deshpande and Ekanath Deshpande, for their support and hard work in educating me to be what I am today. Both of them have been schoolteachers all their lives, working very hard with the goal to offer my brothers and me the best they possibly could. They not only taught me the importance of education, but also taught me to share with others what I have learned, to the best of my abilities. I love them both dearly.

My deepest thanks go to my in-laws, Vasant Joshi and Sulabha Joshi, for their love and trust in me, more like as their own son than a son-in-law. Mr. Joshi is an accomplished author himself, and naturally was very enthusiastic in supporting my decision to coauthor this book with Gaja. I've learned a lot from him when it comes to writing and expressing thoughts clearly.

My younger brother Krantikumar and his wife, Sadhana; and my youngest brother Sachin and his wife, Preeti, have been the source of love and kindness. Although we are thousands of miles apart, all of them are still very close to my heart. I love you all.

In January 1994, I left the mainframe and COBOL environment to join a company that dealt with Oracle and UNIX. Although I had never worked with Oracle before, I knew UNIX and the relational database PROGRESS. Steve Boley and Kathy Murphy offered me a job at Integrated Medical Networks (IMN). With them, I not only learned Oracle database administration but also UNIX system administration and network administration. If they had not given me the opportunity to work at IMN, I would not be writing this. I am very grateful to them and thank them sincerely.

I spend my spare time reading e-mails from the Oracle DBA e-mail list servers, Oracle-L and lazyDBA (http://www.lazyDBA.com), and offering help to others and sharing what I know with them. The people on both these lists have taught me a great deal more than I have to offer. My thanks to all of them who have helped me learn more and offered advice when I needed most. And in a timely manner, I must add.

My thanks go to Jared Still, the list owner and moderator for Oracle-L listserver. If it were not for Jared's Oracle-L list, I probably would not have met Gaja. Ever since we first exchanged e-mails back in 1997 via Oracle-L, Gaja and I have been in touch. All those e-mail exchanges have finally grown into a friendship and partnership. I owe this to Jared and the list. Not only did I find help on Oracle issues from the Oracle list, I have found a friend!

I would also like to thank Henry O'Keeffe, the list owner and moderator for the lazyDBA listserver. When I posted a message to the list, calling for material for possible inclusion in this book, Henry offered to open a discussion topic at his Web site, at no cost to us. Henry, thank you very much for your interest and generosity.

It was great working with all the people at Osborne/McGraw-Hill; they all have been very supportive. Ross Doll, Lisa McClain, Jennifer Malnick, and the rest of the staff—thank you for keeping this project on track and on time.

I want to thank my boss Paul Harrill for supporting and encouraging me in this effort. Paul is more like a coworker than a boss; he is always willing to help with his open-door policy.

And my sincere thanks to Gaja for giving me this totally unexpected opportunity to join him in writing this book. I have learned a lot from him via e-mails on Oracle-L listserver and from his popular presentations at IOUG-A Live! conference. However, it has been a great experience working so closely with him this book and for that, I consider myself very lucky and fortunate to be associated with him.

Finally, I must thank my wife, Achala, and our son, Sameer. Both of them have been the true source of support and motivation—Achala for taking on all the chores at the house, Sameer's school, and other activities while I was busy with the book. She even found time to read the drafts, suggest, and discuss a few things with Gaja and me. I am very grateful for her support in so many ways. Sameer has just been wonderful in understanding that often I was too busy to attend many of his activities, and wanted me to concentrate on completing the book on time, just as his grandfather did.

—Kirtikumar Deshpande

Introduction

The foundation for this book was laid from a paper on Oracle Performance Management, which was first presented at the International Oracle Users Group – Americas Live! 2000 conference and then updated for the Oracle OpenWorld 2000 conference. During that presentation, many of us agreed that any book written on Oracle Performance Tuning should be 40 pages or less. Well, not quite. When you take into consideration the publisher's required page format and figures and various tables, the page count went up by one order of magnitude—about 400 pages. Oops! But every section in every chapter has been carefully reviewed for its accuracy and relevance, not once but multiple times by many individuals. For us, writing this book felt like learning Oracle all over again, from scratch, because we took the time to verify everything we wrote on the present-day release of Oracle – 8.1.7.

We can honestly say that every line in this book has a purpose, including the humor and the stories. We consider humor a requirement for technical books such as these; without it they just become very boring slabs of information. This book is different in many aspects, and we urge you to explore and enjoy.

What Is so Different About this Book?

The key difference between this book and all other Oracle tuning books is that we deal with performance tuning using a proven methodology. We do this without providing you with a bunch of nifty scripts (which may highlight your problems without giving any relevant information about the cause or solution to the problems).

We use the term Oracle Performance Management, as we believe that tuning efforts in Oracle should be managed engagements, not arbitrary hunt-and-peck crusades. You will not find us making tuning recommendations based on some arbitrary cache hit ratios or any Myth and Folklore.

Every tuning effort suggested in this book is either based on identifying the current Oracle bottlenecks or proactively designing and implementing the Oracle database to prevent such bottlenecks. Everything written in this book has been implemented on one or more production systems or has been extensively tested on *real-life* tests and developmental databases. No tuning recommendation in this book is based on laboratory tests. After all, we will be the first to admit that we are engineers not scientists. Our combined experience (more than 70 years) is from real production databases on various platforms.

Also, we have performance tuning reachable to a DBA like you. You will not find a single reference to any X$ table in this book. What are those, anyway? *We have not made tuning simple; it was simple to begin with.* Nonetheless, we have removed the wizardry and witchcraft status from it and made it common sense material. Have a good read!

How to Use this Book

It is very rare that anyone would read a technical book from the beginning to end in one sitting. If you do that with this book, we will be very impressed. However, we urge you to read all the chapters in the book at some point in time. You will certainly find something new or different in each chapter, regardless of your level of experience. Please read Chapters 1 through 10 in order. Try reading Chapter 2 as many times as required, as it is the *sum and substance* of this book. Chapters 11 and 12 can be read at any time. Chapter 13 is a summary of every chapter in the book.

The book is divided in six parts.

Part 1: The Method

Part 1 defines the reason for the existence of this book and outlines the methodology to follow for Oracle Performance Management efforts. You will find invaluable information that can easily be used to identify bottlenecks in your Oracle environment after reading Chapter 2.

Part 2: Application Tuning

Part 2 discusses issues that the DBA must know when it comes to tuning or finding tuning opportunities in applications. Chapter 3 describes the optimizer, statistics, hints, SQL join methods, use of indexes, and so on, to arm the DBA with enough arsenal to attack ineffective SQL in applications. Chapter 4 offers more help to

DBAs as well as developers in tracing efforts ineffective SQL code by showing the use of **tkprof**, **explain plan**, and **autotrace**. We suggest you read both chapters for a thorough understanding about what it takes to tune an application.

Part 3: Instance and Database Tuning

Chapters 5 through 8 offer a wealth of information in tuning very specific areas of an Oracle instance. We suggest you read Chapters 5 and 6 to master the Oracle instance tuning, Chapter 7 for redo log buffer tuning and understanding some of the ways to tune the Oracle optimizer itself. Chapter 8 will help you tune the physical attributes for the database files, tables, indexes, and such.

Part 4: Specialized Tuning

Both the chapters in Part 4 deal with very specific tuning needs. You may read them as required and necessary. Chapter 9 discusses parallel query tuning issues. In Chapter 10 you will find what causes contention in your database and what measures you can take to avoid it.

Part 5: Environment Tuning

Part 5 deals with non-Oracle issues that affect Oracle performance. Chapter 11 is where you will find all the information you ever wanted on RAID and I/O configuration, as well as how Oracle works with RAID.

Chapter 12 introduces you to operating system tuning to affect Oracle performance. We discuss generic issues as applicable to UNIX and Microsoft Windows NT, as well as very specific issues as applicable to Solaris, HP-UX, AIX, and Windows NT operating systems. We suggest you read Chapters 11 and 12 before configuring your system to host an Oracle database.

Part 6: Appendices

Appendix A—Glossary: It is a collection of all the technical terms we used in this book.

Appendix B—More Tips & Resources: Here you will find some interesting information on tuning export, import, and SQL*Loader tools from Oracle. Also included is a list of initialization parameters grouped by their functionality for ease in understanding their role. Most of these parameters are discussed in various sections of this book. There is also a collection of Web sites that contain resources for more information on specific tuning issues.

Appendix C—References: It is a list of the material we referred to while writing this book. The Internet URL links that are provided were current at the time of writing this book.

PART
I

The Method

CHAPTER
1

Introduction to Oracle
Performance Management

Myth & Folklore
If you upgrade your system with faster CPUs, you will get better performance.

Fact
Upgrading your system with faster CPUs to gain better performance as an attempt to fix an existing performance problem (when the CPU is really not the bottleneck) will result in significant degradation in performance. This is because your CPUs got faster without a corresponding increase in the I/O system, resulting in an imbalanced system. For example, if you doubled the speed of your CPUs, jobs that were already hampered by I/O bottlenecks could potentially experience twice as much contention for I/O. More powerful CPUs will process jobs twice as fast, resulting in an increased demand for I/O resources. Do your homework before upgrading the CPUs.

elcome to the world of Oracle Performance Management. Performance tuning engagements with Oracle systems have developed a reputation as part science, part art, and part wizardry. The book you are holding—and if you are like most DBAs you are probably holding it over your head in bed—is a product of our passion for Oracle and our desire to share accurate and relevant information. If fact, we think the information is so important that you won't hesitate to give up your first born before giving up this book. This literary work is also a response to the misconception that tuning is a secret affair practiced by Oracle magicians under the cover of darkness. But you can count on us to ward off all aspects of magic and superstition and make sound principles of Performance Management available to everyone. Though you may not be working on the *multi-stage fuel propulsion system* for the Space Shuttle or the *docking interface module* of the International Space Station, you can apply all of these principles to all of your systems. After all, Oracle Performance Management is not rocket science.

Oracle Performance Management is a step-by-step process of iteratively investigating, determining, and implementing tuning solutions using a proven methodology. You will be convinced that this is the right way to address and fix an Oracle performance problem by the time you read this book from cover to cover. We want to steer you away from the bad habits of simply throwing more memory at Oracle's shared memory areas. Just because the instructor said to do something or a *tuning expert* told you so doesn't make it so.

We want to encourage a significant change in the way troubleshooting is done. We also want to encourage you into analysis of performance problems. At the end of the day, the goal is to remove the bottleneck, increase performance, and may be even spend some time with your family and have a life. The extra time might prompt you to ask questions like "What is Life? What is a family? Who are these people? Do I really have a family?" If you find yourself saying, "But I thought my co-workers were my family?" or "What is the meaning of life without an Oracle database?" we are just in time, as this book (along with some professional help) is probably required. But until you put these principles into action, you can at least start with some fresh air, water, sunlight, and sources of nutrition other than the ones from the vending machine. Then read on.

Our goal is to provide you with a way to optimize Oracle-based systems, not just tune a database or an instance. Additionally, we will debunk many common myths about system performance and tuning Oracle. Each chapter (like this one) will contain a section on the "Myth and Folklore" applicable to the content of that chapter. These are things that everybody "knows" but that aren't true. We will provide you with techniques to manage the various components of your entire system, not just arbitrarily increase the size of the Oracle shared pool area, database buffer cache, or the redo log buffer.

We will address issues specific to the major versions of Oracle, as well as common topics that are relevant to Oracle versions 7.3 and above. We will also look at the major platforms and provide information on areas of concern for each (when applicable). We will assist you with the dreaded chore of tuning applications, even in the cases where you can't quite get access to the SQL (as in packaged applications). We will show you things beyond just changing initialization parameters, simply creating additional indexes, or simply adding hints to change the execution plans of the queries.

One of the key differences between this book and other Oracle tuning books is the time-tested and field-proven methodology. This methodology looks at Performance Management as having a system-wide scope; it takes a holistic approach to Performance Management. While the New Age folks may have popularized the holistic approach, we can think of someone else who also approached helping people in a holistic manner by dealing with their body, soul, and spirit. For more information, visit www.orapub.com and read the paper "Total Performance Management (An introduction to the method)," by Craig A. Shallahammer.

By examining how Oracle, the operating system, and the application interact, it is possible to accurately pinpoint bottlenecks and identify *tuning avenues* that provide significant increases in performance. You need to alleviate the bottleneck(s) in your system to fix your problem, and the goal is to cure the disease, not just the symptoms.

Performance increases need to be measurable and perceptible by the user community. This book is dedicated to the idea that the bulk of possible performance gains can be achieved quickly and with minimal effort if you truly identify and understand the nature of your system, its constraints, and more importantly its bottlenecks. Managing performance on Oracle-based systems can be exciting, frustrating, and rewarding all at the same time. With the information in this book, you will be able to enjoy the exciting rewards of being a DBA while minimizing the level of frustration. And with this new job satisfaction, you will amaze your friends and confound your enemies.

What Is Tuning?

Tuning is a process of making a system meet one or more goals by purposefully changing one or more components of your system. More specific to Oracle performance, it is making purposeful component level changes to improve system performance—that is, increased throughput and decreased response time.

In its simplest form, tuning means providing the correct amount of resources to Oracle so that users are not kept *waiting* for data they need to do their jobs. All right, that seems straightforward enough. Let's just buy the biggest most robust server in the market. No, while that may forestall a problem, it will not prevent it. Again, you need to treat the disease not just the symptoms.

Sometimes supplying enough of the correct resources does not just mean throwing more memory or CPUs into a server. It may mean redesigning parts of the system or scheduling work and batch jobs appropriately to better utilize the existing resources in a uniform fashion. When tuning is done in the context of Performance Management, it takes into consideration all parts of the system and balances the needs of one part against others.

Needless to say, the list of tuning avenues is endless. That means you may have to think about all the issues in your environment. Some examples of such issues are how moving data files or striping a table will affect the utilization of your I/O controllers. Or, if you utilize NFS file systems to store some output files (say, from an export or a job), how will that impact network traffic? How does that in turn affect the network performance of data returned to interactive users? You must consider changes made to SQL statements and how they will affect the amount of data being manipulated at the client or at the server. Therefore, tuning in the context of Performance Management means maximizing the use of all system resources to improve performance.

Why Is Tuning Necessary?

So why tune? Consider an automobile. A manufacturer decides to create a really exciting high-performance car. He sends the specifications to a designer. The designer creates a blueprint calling for the finest composite materials and the most powerful lightweight engine. Now, between budget constraints and lack of availability of that lightweight engine, the builder has to use heavier materials and a different engine. The sales manager notifies the builder that two-seat sports cars or sport coupes are *in vogue*, so another change is made. Finally, the finished car is delivered. But does it perform the way it was conceived? No. As it ages, will it continue to perform as it did on the first day? No. When it is replaced with a newer car and if that car is used just for short trips within the neighborhood, can it be used as a racing car? No.

Information systems go through similar phases. Few systems are designed with a solid understanding of how they will be used and what is required of them. Fewer still make it through the build phase without significant change in design. Additionally, because of the changes a system undergoes through normal use or—in some cases due to dramatic use—more tuning may be needed. Just like an automobile, information systems need tuning, too. Things such as data distribution, modifying the ways of querying data, and increasing amounts of data change the performance characteristics of all systems.

As your car ages, it acquires deposits, some cylinders lose compression, and the fuel injector may not work as efficiently as it did when it was new. Similarly, as a database ages, indexes become imbalanced, and the distribution of data gets skewed. These things affect how quickly Oracle can get off the starting line and return data to a user. Over time, the very nature of the data can change. Applications that once worked great no longer work so well. Therefore, there is a need for a methodical process of tuning or Performance Management.

Using the automobile analogy, if you drive your car across the country in a road rally, you can expect that it will need a tune-up when you get to the other side. The same applies if you make wholesale changes to your database. If your system processes huge transfusions of data or goes through mass purges, you can expect some tuning opportunities to raise their heads. Clearly, tuning needs to be considered at all three distinct phases of a system's life: during design, at implementation, and then regularly during the production lifecycle, as the system matures.

Who Should Tune?

Who should be responsible for tuning? Well, that really depends on whom you ask. Many IT organizations are not organized optimally to handle potential performance tuning situations. This is due to the fact that the staff is compartmentalized into various departments, and they are usually are at odds with one another. The obvious requirement in this situation is the need for good synergy between departments. This should be done by promoting and championing a *lead person* who can work with all departments for any/and all performance tuning efforts.

Ideally, the person responsible for system tuning efforts needs to have experience with the system to be tuned. He or she should be knowledgeable about Oracle and have some understanding of the operating system in question. There is also a need for a good understanding of the application being used. That seems a bit much to ask of any one person, but most DBAs have other team members who can help. These include the operating system administrators, the application designers, and the network administrators. Of course, only one person can lead. And when it comes to Oracle systems, it is the DBA who has to exercise control over the process of tuning, if the desired results are to be achieved.

The DBA is usually in the best position to determine where the system bottlenecks reside, but even a DBA should expect some help with understanding the operating system–related issues. Let your structured analysis guide the entire process. Remember that typically if a user has a performance-related concern and there is a database involved, all fingers will point toward the database and the DBA.

How Much Should You Tune?

Many DBAs have gotten into the habit of tuning until they can't tune anymore. This not only drives them (and their customers) crazy with late hours and system downtime, but also it doesn't tend to result in much improvement in performance. We are absolutely convinced that there are a growing number of DBAs out there who suffer from the malady of Compulsive Tuning Disorder (CTD). We are pursuing all efforts to gain federal grants so that advanced studies and research can be performed on such individuals. If you or someone you know has CTD, help is on the way.

Joking aside, there is a dire need to prioritize tuning tasks and components that can be changed, based on the return on investment (ROI) of the effort. This needs to be done for your sanity and the sanity of the end user. You need to be able to *quantify* your tuning goals and your performance increase. At some point, however, every system experiences the law of diminishing returns and stops responding to performance tuning attempts.

The law of diminishing returns states that "as consumers consume additional units of a given product/service/resource, the additional benefit derived from consuming the additional unit increases at a decreasing rate." In common terms, this means that as you continue to consume something, the benefit or satisfaction you derive from consuming it progressively diminishes (of course, the exception to this is beer drinking during happy hour). Each unit consumed reduces the incremental benefit, and the benefit eventually tends to zero. Much before the benefit becomes zero, consumption should stop. In our discussion, the cost of tuning a given aspect or component of a system needs to stop when it ceases to generate any significant quantifiable benefits or performance gains.

Now, time for a trick question! How much of a "noticeable" difference in system performance would you be able to measure for an Oracle system with a cache-hit-ratio of 99.999 percent vs. 99 percent? The truthful answer: very little! In fact, you may be surprised to note that the system performance could be at perfectly optimum levels, even if the cache-hit-ratio is *low* (say 70 percent). The question you need to consistently ask yourself is this: "What is currently bottlenecking my system?"

If your system does not suffer any I/O or buffer block-related bottlenecks, the cache-hit-ratios are doing just fine. Experience dictates that if more performance increases are needed, you will need to look at other subsystems. Tuning is not a contest to see who can have the highest cache-hit-ratio or the lowest get/miss ratio. It is a concerted effort to improve the perceptible performance of the system.

Moral of the story

If you don't have a bottleneck, then don't tune that component. Or, as they say in Texas, if it ain't broke, don't fix it. When you tune a component on a system, you need to measure the performance difference and the cost of your efforts. Is the ROI worth your efforts? You are the best judge of that.

When Should You Stop?

As former Oracle instructors, we loved to start our tuning classes with the overhead projector (that was current technology at the time, so cut us some slack). We could demonstrate our point about setting tuning goals with this projector. Of course, those projectors had to be focused, or "tuned." Every night, the janitorial crew would clean the projector and in the process "un-tune" it; we would come in the next morning and find it in need of tuning again. This was a great way of showing how to over-tune a system. We would start with the slide completely out of focus. When the projected image was blurry, it represented a system that required tuning. Slowly we would adjust the knob, and soon the slide became clear. Though our goal was to *stop tuning* when the image came into focus, we often succumbed to our tendency to tweak just a little more. The result, of course, was that we made the image blurry again. If we had stopped when the image came into focus, we would not have had to refocus or retune.

The same applies to tuning any component of an Oracle system. In the context of an overhead projector, it was as simple as turning a knob. It is too bad that Oracle systems have yet to attain that level of sophistication, where tuning can be done using knobs. At least we will have stories to tell our children and grandchildren about how "Way back in the nineteen hundreds we had to tune using..." Some industry experts suspect that databases will eventually self-tune themselves, based upon a given set of performance objectives, using self-adjusting programs. We are so glad that we have the opportunity to write this book before that takes place. Our book will be radically smaller when that day dawns.

To avoid unnecessary tuning, you will need to establish clear goals. The goals should be quantifiable. Tuning takes on a different approach depending on whether you are trying to make the system faster or trying to return the results of a specific query in a reasonable time frame. If you focus on making the system faster, you may never be finished. However, if you are tuning with a specific and reasonable goal in mind, you will reach an end point, at which time you can celebrate by having a beer—no, make that two. (You are probably convinced, by this time, that we are a couple of incurable drunks who prefer beer to flow in our arteries instead of blood. We have decided to leave you wondering about that...at least for now!)

The core answer to the question "When should I stop?" depends on how well you can identify and measure the effect of your tuning efforts. When identifying a problem with a system, you may be faced with a set of configuration changes that help solve the problem. But it is extremely critical to ensure that the changes are made in a controlled and methodical fashion, preferably one at a time. Avoid the urge to change a bunch of initialization parameters all at once or the urge to build several indexes on a table all at once.

Be organized in your approach. Prioritize the things you want to change. Change them one at a time and evaluate the effect before changing the next one. Sometimes you will find that you can stop after just one or two changes. More importantly, by changing things one at a time, you avoid the risk of negatively impacting performance. Blindly increasing the size of the shared pool, the database buffer cache, and the log buffer all at once could cause adverse operating system problems (such as elevated levels of paging and sometimes even process deactivation and swapping).

Changing many things at once leaves you in a position of never really knowing what you did to fix a particular problem. Should the same performance problem arise again, you will be no better off before you solved the problem the first time. Using a surgical approach to Performance Management allows you to leverage your experience as you encounter more tuning challenges.

Keep in mind that it is possible to over tune. Since each component of your system is interdependent on each other, any changes to one may retard performance in another. This often means that tuning a 5-minute query to make it run in 15 seconds instead of 30 seconds might not always be a good idea. If running the query in 15 seconds causes an increase in response times for other operations (say some subsecond *mission-critical* transactions) you may create more problems than you solved by not stopping at the agreed-upon target.

Moral of the story

When you reach the agreed-upon performance goals, stop all tuning efforts. Remember to exercise control and avoid the temptation to tweak it just a little bit more. We know that may be a hard habit to break, but perseverance will prevail.

In a Nutshell

Oracle Performance Management is a step-by-step process of iteratively investigating, determining, and implementing tuning solutions using a proven methodology. While tuning a system it is important to know when to tune, what to tune, how much tuning it requires, and when the tuning efforts should stop. Specific goals need to be set and all tuning efforts need to cease when those goals are attained.

CHAPTER 2

The Method Behind the Madness

Myth & Folklore

Tuning the database always results in a better performing system.

Fact

Tuning a database may make the database perform more efficiently, but if the application, the I/O subsystem, and the operating system (OS) are not equally tuned, the user will not reap the benefits of your efforts. Users are the final measure of the success of your tuning efforts. If they don't see the performance gains, you might as well stay home. Enhancing system performance requires a methodical and holistic approach, not arbitrary hunt and peck efforts of just throwing more memory at the Oracle System Global Area.

Myth & Folklore

If the cache-hit ratios of the Oracle database are fine (99.999 percent), the performance of Oracle is at its best.

Fact

Not at all true. The cache-hit ratios could be inflated as result of a few correlated subqueries in the application, which iteratively accesses the same set of blocks. In this case, even though the cache-hit ratios may be fine, users could be waiting for their output for a long time. The wait for output/data (on further investigation), could be attributed to some significant I/O-related waits on the data and index segments stored in the data files of the corresponding DATA and INDX tablespaces. There are many aspects to tuning Oracle that do not involve ratios at all. The cornerstone of tuning Oracle-based systems should be wait events, not ratios.

n this chapter, you will learn about a holistic methodology and its associated technical details for tuning Oracle-based systems. Though the details pertain to Oracle, the process can be applied to any system. While Oracle Performance Management is not magic, there is some art to it and plenty of science. The science is easily quantifiable. The artistry is unique to each DBA, and you will surely develop your own as you gain experience. Every Oracle Performance Management effort is potentially tri-faceted: tune, schedule, and buy. The tune facet is the most important and the easiest facet to execute. However, it needs to be done in a proactive, iterative, and methodical fashion. That is what this chapter is all about.

The schedule aspect relates to the process of balancing the load on the system by running jobs at appropriate/meaningful times, rather than launching too many of them all in the same time window. The buy facet is the act of procuring more resources for your system, but there is a definite need to control this almost involuntary urge. Beware of reckless buying, as it is easy to execute (if you have the money), but it also holds the highest risk. When you upgrade one or more components of your system without doing a comprehensive impact analysis, you run the risk of putting yourself and your system in a worse state than you were before the upgrade. In addition, if you upgrade components that were not bottlenecks to begin with, you will push your system to a point of no return—for example, a wholesale CPU upgrade on your system, when the CPU is really not your bottleneck. For more information, visit http://www.hotsos.com/ and read "Performance Management: Myths & Facts," by Cary Millsap.

For practical purposes, Oracle Performance Management can further be classified into two types, proactive and reactive. Proactive Performance Management involves designing and developing comlpete systems with a high-performance architecture in mind. It also involves monitoring system performance on a regular basis, noting trends and proactively fixing potential issues before they become actual problems. But if you look at the guts of proactive Performance Management from the architecture perspective, it involves selection of the hardware, the operating system, performance and capacity planning, mass storage system selection, I/O subsystem configuration and tuning, including the selection and implementation of the appropriate level of RAID. And it also includes tailoring all the components to suit the complex needs of the application and Oracle.

From the scheduling aspect, proactive management may also involve logical and rational balancing of jobs on a system. This scheduling is done to prevent overloading the system within very finite time windows (the infamous batch window that we all are so fondly aware of). Needless to say, work done in a proactive manner costs the least and has the greatest impact on the final performance characteristics of all systems.

Reactive Performance Management involves performance evaluation, troubleshooting, tuning, and fine-tuning the environment within the limitations of the existing hardware and software architecture. It is the process of responding to a problem as it is unfolding. You tend to do this after the system has been built. The cost relative to the performance increase attained is often high. During this type of Performance Management you will often uncover needs for different hardware, software, or other basic components. This is also where you find out how well your applications were designed.

With the methodology and its associated technical details presented here, you will acquire a solid knowledge base for your reactive Performance Management efforts (the tune facet). Of course, the same principles apply when designing the system from the outset. This holistic methodology revolves around a core set of parameters and components that benefit from proper configuration and tuning. By focusing on these critical areas you will maximize the efficacy of your efforts in Oracle Performance Management and avoid tuning by trial and error.

Why Should You Care About a Tuning Methodology?

The amount of energy you expend to achieve a tuned database depends on your tuning methodology. Your own job satisfaction can be tied to your choice of tuning methodologies. As a DBA, you have to balance many responsibilities and therefore cannot spend time and energy on unrewarding pursuits. Developing a good approach to Performance Management will avoid wasted effort. Otherwise you may spend a lot of time tuning without actually improving performance. Your methodology should help determine when enough is enough.

The myths mentioned at the beginning of this chapter contribute to the failure of many tuning methodologies. The first one is predicated on the idea that system Performance Management is only a database issue. No consideration is given to limitations on the database imposed by the operating system, the storage system, the application, or even the network.

The second is based on ratios without consideration of what is the current state of the Oracle database. It does not take into consideration things like what the database is currently doing for the application. Both avoid the basic principle that good Performance Management must be based on avoiding adverse system activity. More importantly, one needs to tune those components that are causing the bottleneck, instead of making far-reaching global changes.

A tuning methodology is not random acts of change to a system in the hope of achieving the nebulous goal of better performance. Many a time, people who are engaged in the faculty of tuning, especially Oracle tuning, don't adhere to any kind of methodical approach. This results in haphazard efforts lacking repeatability. The number one offense committed in this style is how memory is just thrown at the Oracle System Global Area (SGA), in the hope that the system performance problem will cure itself. Haphazard increases in the amount of memory supplied to the major components of the SGA do little at best, and can cause severe performance degradation at worst.

Many of these kinds of efforts are based on the assumption that the database's cache-hit ratios should drive the tuning process. With this attitude, it is easy to get trapped into the swirling vortex of more memory, more CPU, more memory, more CPU... In one common example, in an effort to attain a high cache hit ratio (upper 90s), a significant amount of memory was configured for the database buffer cache. In doing so, the system began experiencing significant levels of paging and swapping.

Here is another classic example of ratios-based tuning. In some cases, when the size of the shared pool area is increased beyond reason, it is possible for parsing hiccups to occur. Oracle can encounter difficulties managing unduly large memory segments associated with the shared pool area. In some production environments, it has been observed that an excessive amount of memory for the shared pool area caused increased parse times, hanging of SQL statements, and in some cases a serious case of library cache latch (an internal resource used within Oracle to manage the library cache, which is a component of the shared pool area) contention.

Now, if the action was taken just to attain high cache-hit ratios for the shared pool area (because we all know that high cache-hit ratios are good for the physical, emotional, and mental happiness of a DBA!), suddenly there exists a problem situation, where performance begins to wave a red flag, when there was no problem to begin with.

This is one scenario, where everything was fine, but the *must have 99.999 percent* cache-hit ratio disease took over. Remember Compulsive Tuning Disorder (Chapter 1)! To make matters worse, when such symptoms are noticed, some DBAs resort to extreme measures, such as flushing the shared pool frequently. Instead of engaging in a managed effort, tuning operations become hunt and peck or trial and error fiascoes.

These examples highlight additional reasons why you should care about the discipline of a sound and proven tuning methodology. The kind of tuning explained in this section is best described as madness without a method. Good Performance Management depends on having a method to the madness. And you have two raving lunatics (us) who have been there, used the method, and done that!

What Is a Good Tuning Methodology?

So what is the method behind the madness? The method is a prioritized, orderly, goal-oriented, holistic approach to Oracle Performance Management. The process can be as simple as reacting to calls from users who say there is a problem or as complex as calling in teams of experts to evaluate a system from top to bottom. But to be effective it must consider the entire system in all phases. Any reliable tuning methodology must include:

- Baseline readings

- Established performance goals

- Structure and tracking of changes that are made (some change-control mechanism)

- Evaluation of the effects of those changes

- Comparison of the performance with the established goals

- Reiteration until the goals are met

If the process is complex, it is less likely that anyone will adhere to it. A good methodology should be simple yet have all the core components of problem solving. It must focus on specific issues and must have a definite end point. Too many efforts fail because no definite end point is set. The very best methodology also considers the effect that changing one component has on the other related components. It must be holistic. You cannot increase the size of the database buffer cache of one instance on a host without expecting to impact performance of other instances as well as the operating system itself. You cannot add several indexes to a table to improve data retrieval operations and not consider the impact on DML (Data Manipulation Language) in the form of insert, update, or delete.

A good tuning methodology should allow you to quantify work and the desired results in such a way that you can design changes that will achieve those results. It allows you to reliably track the changes made to systems for repeatability and even reversibility. And it allows you to say "I'm done" when the goals are achieved.

The Oracle Performance Tuning 101 Methodology

Now is the time to share a tried and true, reality test approach to Oracle Performance Management that has stood the test of time. It is what we call the two-pronged tuning approach. And it is very simple. Begin your troubleshooting efforts with the operating system (OS) on one hand (first prong) and Oracle on the other (second prong). Then consciously drive your research on each prong, and move toward the other. When the information derived from the two prongs meets, you will have your finger on the problem. Done. In fact, you might have a lot more than just your finger on the problem when you use our approach. Remember, your research efforts should be wait event driven, *not* cache-hit ratio driven. Keep this in mind as you follow the steps below to setting goals and selecting your tuning targets:

1. Set reasonable performance tuning goals.

2. Measure and document current performance.

3. Identify the current Oracle performance bottlenecks (what Oracle is waiting for, which SQL statements are part of that wait event).

4. Identify the current OS bottlenecks.

5. Tune the required component (application, database, I/O, contention, OS, and so on).

6. Track and exercise change-control procedures.

7. Measure and document current performance.

8. Repeat steps 3 through 7 until the tuning goal is met.

Do not tune a component if it is not the source of the bottleneck. Doing so may cause serious negative repercussions. Remember, "If it ain't broke, don't fix it." And more importantly, cease all tuning efforts when the tuning goals are met. Besides, if you overachieve today, what will you do tomorrow? Just kidding!

If some aspect of the systems hit ratios does not meet with your approval, but is not a part of the current problem, addressing it now only makes the water murkier. You can always establish a tuning effort to investigate that issue after you have resolved the current issue. Tuning a system is a lot like white-water rafting. There are backwashes, currents, and eddies, all trying to pull you toward them and into wasted effort and danger. So it is important for you to stay on course, with your eye on the goal of getting safely downstream, and you will live to tune another day.

Let's talk about each of the steps in this process.

Set Reasonable Performance Tuning Goals

The major feature lacking in most methodologies and definitely lacking in haphazard tuning is establishing specific, reasonable, attainable goals. Without a reasonable goal you won't know if you have met your customer's expectations and you won't know if you have finished and therefore have time to have a drink.

Before launching into any tuning effort you will need to meet with your customer/user and agree on specific and reasonable performance goals. Not only does this signify when you are done, but also it facilitates benchmarking and consistent performance measurement. The most important thing about setting goals is that they must be quantifiable and attainable. It is meaningless to say, "This query runs poorly and it needs to run faster." You need to know that the query runs in one hour and twenty minutes now, but needs to run in ten minutes or less. Or you need to know that a given operation is performing ten sorts to disk, but should not perform any.

If you can't make a similar statement, you don't really know what your goal is. Tuning without a goal can be compared to driving your car without having a specific destination in mind. If you drive around the neighborhood in the middle of the night just to put your kid to sleep on a very rough night (some of us have done that), there is still a goal behind your driving exercise. But if you got into the habit of driving your car around your neighborhood without any rhyme or reason, all you would have achieved is to make some gas station in your neighborhood rich and voluntarily contribute to the warming of our planet.

NOTE
Your goal should be in the form of a statement that defines the current performance and the desired performance. Just fill in the blanks in the following box.

The _____ takes _____ (hours/minutes/seconds), but we need it to run in _____ (hours/minutes/seconds).
The _____ uses _____ (amount of resource), but it can't use more than _____ .

Now you know your target. Take aim and fire away!

Quantifying the required performance values gives direction on what to tune, how to tune, when to tune, how much to tune, and more importantly when to stop tuning. Failure to set specific goals results in unnecessary time spent on tuning the system, without significant and measurable gains.

Now, please take our word of advice while working with customers to set performance goals. The customer may need help in uncovering the real business need. How do you recognize or handle unrealistic performance goals or unrealistic business requirements? In a real-life example, a power user wanted an eight-hour batch job to complete in half an hour or less, based on a business requirement. Tests showed that the third-party application that contained the batch job could be reduced to three stages:

1. A database read which loaded some tables in memory

2. A calculation part (entirely CPU) that processed these tables

3. A database write-back

When it was shown how this unrealistic goal cannot be achieved even with the best-of-breed systems (due to its inherent workload), the user's expectations were realigned. Projected improvements trimmed the database part to about half an hour, but there was no way to bring down the calculation to less than two hours. It was important to show *why* the job in its entirety could not be run in half an hour or less, and breaking the job down to its logical parts helped in resetting the user's expectation.

Many customers push their DBAs to have high hit ratios and incredible response times that simply can't be met. This is one of those backwater eddies that will eat your lunch. You must dig down and understand what they are trying to accomplish and then help them to help you set a reasonable goal. Not all operations performed by a system must be performed with subsecond response times. Okay, you have your tuning goals...let's move on.

Measure and Document Current Performance

This section (step 2) in the performance tuning methodology, and the next couple of sections (steps 3 and 4) is where we will cover the technical aspects of the methodology. While this might seem like a detour from a pure methodology perspective, our goal is to provide the relevant technical details that go along with the various steps in the methodology, and we could not think of another place to put them but here. Ultimately, it is the underlying technical details that make or break a methodology. In our view, it is important for you to be able to get a packaged view of the methodology with its associated technical details. This detour will cover all the vista points in our road trip to optimal Performance Management.

Before you can be expected to achieve a goal, you have to know where you are in relation to that goal. Imagine trying to fill your pantry for the holidays without knowing what you have and don't have. Can you do it? Sure. Will you end up with a lot of duplicate items and thus wasted effort? Sure. You will agree that it would be better to know that you already have twelve cans of tuna (or kidney beans for us vegetarians) before going to the store. The same applies to Oracle-based systems. You have to know what it does well and what it does not do well before you start hammering on it, trying to beat it into shape.

So the next step has to be to find out where the system is in relation to the goal of subsecond responses and 100 percent uptime. Start by getting a good picture of your system's performance. Performance snapshots, benchmarks, before and after images, or whatever you call them, need to be captured during peak activity periods. Most businesses, and thus the databases that support them, have very predictable load cycles.

In the course of the day in most business environments, things are slow at 8:00 A.M. and start to really hop around between 10:00–10:30 A.M.. Then it comes to a screeching halt from 11:30 A.M. until about 1:00 P.M. It then starts to pick up again, achieving peak load around 3:30 P.M. and starts to trail off around 5:00 P.M. Additionally, the days at the end of the month and the very beginning of a month tend to be busier. Therefore, taking snapshots of a database in a business like this around 12:00 midnight is not very useful. Those statistics aren't going to be very helpful. Of course, many companies perform reporting and batch jobs at midnight. So if those are the areas of concern, you would be right on target. The point is that you need to gather information from the time period in which the questionable performance occurs.

Another important note about gathering evidence for your investigation: don't try to get these statistics immediately after instance startup. When an instance has just started, there is nothing in the SGA and you will have to give it some ramp-up time. Statistics are only valuable over a large number of things or over a reasonable period of time. Measuring statistics five minutes after the start of an Oracle database is not only meaningless but also a waste of your precious time. It may also result in misdirected efforts to tune your database. Your instance will appear to have all kinds of problems it doesn't, and you are not likely to see evidence of the problems it does have.

Still another issue to keep in mind when gathering statistics is that they have to be gathered over a reasonable period of time. Collecting statistics over a period of many hours is not reasonable, as the problems with your system may get buried in the depths of time. Many a time DBAs gather statistics starting at eight in the morning and end at five in the afternoon. Then, based on those reports, they can say the database performs well or it looks like the whole thing is going down the drain.

The smoothing effect of too much time can make poor performers look great and cause some things like "log buffer space" to seem unreasonable. Our method of gathering statistical information on Oracle is to take several snapshots of 15-minute duration during peak periods. What will be of real use to you is if you can identify the process or program that is suffering and gather statistics while it is running.

For the information that you are going after in the dynamic performance views to have any significance, your instance needs to have the initialization parameter TIMED_STATISTICS set to TRUE. This is accomplished in either of two ways in Oracle 8.0 or above (this may be back-ported on some platforms for release 7.3). You can dynamically set this with the SQL command **alter system set timed_statistics = true**. Execute this as the user SYS. Here is how:

```
Oracle Server Manager Release 3.1.5.0.0—Production
(c) Copyright 1997, Oracle Corporation.  All Rights Reserved.
Oracle8i Enterprise Edition Release 8.1.5.0.0—Production
With the Partitioning and Java options
PL/SQL Release 8.1.5.0.0—Production
SVRMGR> connect / as sysdba;
Connected.
SVRMGR> alter system set timed_statistics=true;
Statement processed.
```

The second method is to keep the TIMED_STATISTICS initialization parameter set permanently to TRUE in the Oracle initialization file (init.ora). On most versions of Oracle across multiple operating system platforms, there is no *measurable* overhead in setting this permanently at the instance level.

CAUTION

Before setting this or any other initialization parameters that we recommend, you should take the time to do your homework and ensure that there are no "undocumented features" that crop up by setting that parameter on your version of Oracle and your OS platform. Please take the necessary steps to check Metalink or open a "tar" with Oracle to accomplish this. One test is worth a thousand speculations!

NOTE
All references to $ORACLE_HOME is specific to
Oracle on a UNIX platform. The equivalent on
Windows NT is %ORACLE_HOME%. Also, in UNIX,
subdirectories are indicated using the forward slash
(/) and on Windows NT they are indicated using the
backward slash (\). Please make the appropriate
changes depending on your operating system platform.

Running utlbstat.sql and utlestat.sql

To create a statistical picture of an instance, you can use the scripts provided with
every Oracle installation. There are two scripts located in the $ORACLE_HOME/
rdbms/admin directory. The first is utlbstat.sql. It is run as the user INTERNAL and
is run from Server Manager or SQL*Plus (Oracle8i and above). It creates a number
of interim tables that are snapshots from the various dynamic performance (V$)
views. Running this script begins the snapshot period and provides the beginning
point in statistics.

To end the snapshot period, you will need to run utlestat.sql. This script takes
another snapshot from the same dynamic performance views. It subtracts the original
values stored in the interim tables from the new values and saves the differences
to a file called report.txt. It then drops all the interim tables. This report gets written
to the directory from which you ran Server Manager or SQL*Plus. This report
contains all the relevant metrics that were captured for that Oracle instance during
the time interval that elapsed between utlbstat.sql and utlestat.sql. It also contains
a bunch of stuff you don't even want to know about. But don't worry—you'll know
the important stuff after you have digested this book. Be sure to rename the report
before running utlbstat.sql/utlestat.sql again if you want to keep a history of
performance statistics. Consider appending the date/time to the file name, such as
report.txt.20011031-11:15. The following is a sample utlbstat/estat run. The output
has been formatted to provide you with the highlights of what Oracle does when
you run the two scripts:

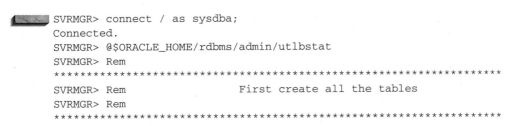

```
SVRMGR> connect / as sysdba;
Connected.
SVRMGR> @$ORACLE_HOME/rdbms/admin/utlbstat
SVRMGR> Rem
*********************************************************************
SVRMGR> Rem                    First create all the tables
SVRMGR> Rem
*********************************************************************
```

```
SVRMGR>
SVRMGR> Rem
********************************************************************
SVRMGR> Rem                    Gather start statistics
SVRMGR> Rem
********************************************************************
SVRMGR> Rem                    Wait for 15 minutes
SVRMGR> Rem
********************************************************************
SVRMGR> @$ORACLE_HOME/rdbms/admin/utlestat
SVRMGR> Rem
********************************************************************
SVRMGR> Rem                    Gather Ending Statistics
SVRMGR> Rem
********************************************************************
SVRMGR>
SVRMGR> Rem
********************************************************************
SVRMGR> Rem                    Create Summary Tables
SVRMGR> Rem
********************************************************************
SVRMGR>
SVRMGR> Rem
********************************************************************
SVRMGR> Rem                    Output statistics
SVRMGR> Rem
********************************************************************
SVRMGR>
```

NOTE
Since Oracle8i, these scripts can be run in SQL*Plus by **connect internal** *or* **connect / as sysdba***. The Server Manager tool is not part of the Oracle9i database toolset. Hence, all DBA and development tasks from Oracle8i and up should be performed just using SQL*Plus.*

The customary way to review report.txt is to grab a calculator, go down and gather your favorite statistics, and see how they add up. This is a perfectly good time to find out about such things as all the different cache-hit ratios. But more importantly, you will want to look at the wait events described in the file. The report also gives great information about I/O characteristics of the data files. You can definitely find the hot spots here.

If you support multiple databases, you might want to take the easier road to analyzing your report.txt. At the time of writing this chapter, there was an online report.txt analyzer available at http://www.oraperf.com/. This Web site—Yet Another Performance Profiling (YAPP) Method—has expert analysis information on the contents of your report.txt from some of the performance-tuning experts in the industry. All you need to do is to point the tool to the location of your report.txt on your PC and it will do the rest. It also provides additional information on the meaning of some of the values and parameters listed in the file. It is a great tool to learn the core elements in the report.txt. Within a short time after you submit the report.txt, you will be presented with useful interpretations and recommendations right on your screen.

When we last checked, this Web site also allowed comparison of two report.txt files, and supported analysis and comparison of report files generated by STATSPACK (covered in the next paragraph). Save this information for use later to see if you are making progress in your tuning efforts.

Running STATSPACK (Available in Oracle 8.1.6 and Above)

With Oracle8i (8.1.6) comes a brand new package called STATSPACK, which promises to be the new and improved version of utlbstat.sql/utlestat.sql. It is considered the replacement for the age-old BSTAT/ESTAT method.

STATSPACK collects more relevant performance data than BSTAT/ESTAT, precalculates some of the performance ratios, stores them in a schema for future use, and provides the capability to refer data from prior runs by supporting history.

NOTE
Even though STATSPACK is shipped with 8.1.6 and above, it can be run on Oracle 8.0 databases.

The following table lists the major differences between BSTAT/ESTAT and STATSPACK:

Underlying Characteristic/Feature	BSTAT/ESTAT	STATSPACK
Data capture is configurable	No	Yes
Summary page for report	No	Yes
Identify SQL that consume a lot of resources	No	Yes
Ability to store performance snapshots in a database	No	Yes

STATSPACK can be installed by running the script statscre.sql(spcreate.sql in Oracle 8.1.7), which is located under $ORACLE_HOME/rdbms/admin directory, within a SQL*Plus session logged in as **Connect / as SYSDBA**. This script creates a user called Perfstat, a set of tables, and a package. All commands and procedures mentioned as follows need to be run as user Perfstat.

NOTE
*This script should be run with SQL*Plus and not under Server Manager. Also, it must be noted here that a STATSPACK report should be run in the same recommended frequency as a BSTAT/ESTAT report—15 minutes. Also, it is recommended that the tables created under this user not be created in the SYSTEM tablespace, as the size of the tables owned by Perfstat is dependent on the number of snapshots you save.*

To capture performance data, use **execute statspack.snap**. This should be done when the system supports peak loads and across various workloads in the environment (OLTP, Batch etc.). It may be advisable to schedule the execution of this via DBMS_JOB or an operating system scheduler like cron on UNIX. There is an example file—statsauto.sql (spauto.sql in Oracle 8.1.7) that can be used as reference.

The relevant parameters are:

- i_snap_level takes values such as 0 for instance statistics, 5 for information about SQL statements (default), and 10 for determining child latch information and some low-level investigative purposes (turn on only upon Oracle Support's request).

- i_executions_th, i_buffer_gets_th, i_disk_reads_th, i_version_count_th, i_parse_calls_th, and i_sharable_mem_th are all parameters that are relevant for setting thresholds for identification of high-resource SQL statements.

- i_ucomment allows you to name a given snapshot.

- i_session_id provides capture of session-level information (not done by default).

All default values of the aforementioned parameters are stored in a table and can be changed by executing the statspack.modify_statspack_parameter procedure.

The report on performance snapshots is generated by executing statsrep.sql (spreport.sql in Oracle 8.1.7). The data for the report is stored in the database, and it is useful to note here that these reports cannot span to remote databases nor can they currently span across an instance/database startups. This script takes runtime arguments of beginning and ending snap_ids. Each run of a performance snapshot will generate a value for snap_id. The value for snap_id is populated using an Oracle sequence generator.

The report itself should be read sequentially and is similar to the output generated by BSTAT/ESTAT. The summary page does include information about the top five wait events (hello there…this what you need to tune), shared pool cache usage, the profile of the load on the system, general environment information, and the level of efficiency of the instance.

The following is a sample report generated from a STATSPACK report run of a production environment. This report is formatted to display only the summary page. Realistically, the summary page should provide you with the state of the union. Again, your primary goal should be to investigate the *top five wait events* in your database. Once that is done, you may want to tackle the next five top events by another run of STATSPACK. The database and instance names in the sample run below have been modified to maintain customer confidentiality.

```
STATSPACK report for
DB Name        DB Id      Instance     Inst Num  Release     OPS   Host
----------     ----------  ----------   --------  ----------  ----  ----------
ACME           708513117  acme               1  8.0.5.0.0   NO    hp6
                                                                  Snap Length
Start Id   End Id      Start Time            End Time            (Minutes)
--------   --------    --------------------  --------------------  -----------
      3        4  30-Oct-00 13:12:15    30-Oct-00 13:27:39         15.24
Cache Sizes
~~~~~~~~~~~
          db_block_buffers:       40000
            db_block_size:       16384
             log_buffer:    13107200
        shared_pool_size:   100000000
Load Profile
~~~~~~~~~~~~
                                Per Second       Per Transaction
                                ---------------  ---------------
                Redo size:       12,924.49          5,739.29
            Logical reads:        2,901.46          1,288.43
            Block changes:           51.98             23.08
           Physical reads:          313.53            139.23
          Physical writes:            4.71              2.09
               User calls:           88.15             39.14
```

```
                Parses:                    8.76              3.89
           Hard parses:                    0.08              0.04
                 Sorts:                    3.46              1.54
          Transactions:                    2.25
         Rows per Sort:         691.26
Pct Blocks changed / Read:        1.79
       Recursive Call Pct:      11.13
   Rollback / transaction Pct:    8.54
Instance Efficiency Percentages (Target 100%)
~~~~~~~~~~~~~~~~~~~~~~~~~~~~~~~~~~~~~~~~~~~~~
       Buffer Nowait Ratio:    100.00
       Buffer  Hit  Ratio:     89.19
       Library Hit  Ratio:     99.70
       Redo   NoWait Ratio:   100.00
       In-memory Sort Ratio:  100.00
           Soft Parse Ratio:   99.05
           Latch Hit Ratio:   100.00
Top 5 Wait Events
~~~~~~~~~~~~~~~~~~                            Wait     % Total
Event                            Waits    Time (cs) Wt Time
-------------------------------- --------- --------- ------
slave wait                          7437    720443  55.3
library cache pin                   1204    362531  27.8
Parallel Query Idle Wait - Slaves    662    121720  9.35
db file scattered read             99776     51846  3.98
db file sequential read            18386     11504   .88
Wait Events for DB: PKMS  Instance: pkms  Snaps:      3 -          4
->cs - centisecond -  100th of a second
->ms - millisecond - 1000th of a second (unit often used for disk IO timings)
```

More information about STATSPACK can be acquired by accessing the Oracle Technology Network at http://technet.oracle.com/deploy/performance/ and the documentation that is supplied with Oracle release (statspack.doc in 8.1.6 and spdoc.txt in 8.1.7). This file is also located in the $ORACLE_HOME/rdbms/admin directory.

NOTE

It is our recommendation that you use STATSPACK instead of BSTAT/ESTAT, if your database version is 8.0 or above. STATSPACK provides the same numbers as BSTAT/ESTAT in a more meaningful fashion, with a good Load Profile and Instance Efficiency section. Also please note that there have been many changes to the names of the scripts in Oracle 8.1.7. You can find the complete list of changes in the spdoc.txt file.

Identify the Current Oracle Performance Bottlenecks

In addition to what you will find in the report.txt and STATSPACK, there is a wealth of information about Oracle's current health in V$SYSTEM_EVENT, V$SESSION_EVENT, and V$SESSION_WAIT. In some circles, these three dynamic performance views are referred to as the "wait interface". In fact, when dealing with a performance problem, these should be among your first stops in understanding where the bottleneck really is. If you don't spend time on these three V$ views, you really are not looking in the right place. Not a good use of your time. Not convinced? Read what Craig Shallahammer has to say in his paper "Direct Contention Identification Using Oracle's Session Wait Tables," available at http://www.orapub.com/. To get another perspective of the wait-event-based method, check out a presentation titled "Oracle Performance Problem Diagnosis," by Cary Millsap, available at http://www.hotsos.com/, under the OAUG 2000 Database SIG Meeting link. Both of the aforementioned Web sites have a variety of tools that will assist you in bottleneck detection and analysis.

What Is a Wait Event?

A *wait event* is a named section of the Oracle kernel code. The concept of wait events was introduced in Oracle 7.0.12. With Oracle 7.3, there were approximately 100 wait events. This number increased to approximately 150 in Oracle 8.0 and is now at approximately 200 events in Oracle8i.

There are two categories of wait events, namely i*dle* and *non-idle*. The idle events indicate that Oracle is waiting for some work. Some common idle events are client message, NULL event, pipe get, pmon timer, rdbms ipc message, smon timer, SQL*Net message from client, and so on.

Non-idle wait events are actions that are specific to Oracle. Some common non-idle wait events are buffer busy waits, db file scattered read, db file sequential read, enqueue, free buffer waits, latch free, log file parallel write, log file sync, and so on.

Where Is the Bottleneck?

Performance may be slow, but if you don't know what the user processes are waiting for, you will only be guessing as you make arbitrary changes. Once you become familiar with the wait events for your system, you will be able to get right to the crux of the matter. You will be able to use your resources to tune the component that is bottlenecking the system. You will not engage in arbitrary tuning efforts.

What Can Be Learned from V$SYSTEM_EVENT?

To get the best possible understanding of what things are keeping your system from optimal performance and thus keeping you from that beloved beer, get familiar with the V$SYSTEM_EVENT dynamic performance view. The V$SYSTEM_EVENT view provides a bird's eye view of all the events in an Oracle system. Even though it does not contain session-level specific information (current or past), it does sum up all the waits since the last time the instance was started. The statistics in this dynamic performance view are reset to zero on instance startup. For that reason, the information in this and all the V$ views must be sampled over time.

The columns in the V$SYSTEM_EVENT dynamic performance view are

- **Event** This is the name of an event. Some of the more common meaningful events are enqueue, buffer busy waits, latch free, db file scattered read, db file sequential read, and free buffer waits.

- **Total_Waits** This is the total number of waits for a given event since the time the instance was started.

- **Total_Timeouts** This column provides the total number of wait timeouts for the specific event since the time the instance was started.

- **Time_Waited** This is the total wait time (in 1/100ths of a second, also known as centiseconds) by all sessions for a given event since the time the instance was started.

- **Average_Wait** This is the average wait time (in 1/100ths of a second) by all sessions for a given event since the instance was started. Average_Wait = (time_waited/total_waits).

The following script will assist in determining the delta for the current waits within a time interval (T2–T1) for each of the wait events on the system, if you are looking for the "delta":

```
drop table BEGIN_SYS_EVENT;
drop table END_SYS_EVENT;
/* Create Begin Table at Time T1 */
create table BEGIN_SYS_EVENT as
    select * from V$SYSTEM_EVENT;
/* Wait n seconds or n minutes */
/* Create End Table at Time T2 */
create table END_SYS_EVENT as
    select * from V$SYSTEM_EVENT;
/* View delta numbers for wait events between Begin (T1) and End (T2) */
```

```
select T1.Event, (T2.Total_Waits—T1.Total_Waits) "Delta Waits",
       (T2.Total_Timeouts—T1.Total_Timeouts) "Delta Timeouts",
       (T2.Time_Waited—T1.Time_Waited) "Delta Time Waited",
       (T2.Average_Wait—T1.Average_Wait) "Delta Average Wait"
  from BEGIN_SYS_EVENT T1, END_SYS_EVENT T2
 where T1.Event = T2.Event;
```

After reviewing this information, it is easy to pick out the areas of concern. Look at the items with the most time waited and try to categorize them. Are they I/O-based events like db file scattered read, db file sequential read, or free buffer waits? Or are they memory-based events like buffer busy waits? Now you can zero in on the system resources that need augmentation. No time is wasted on areas that are doing well. But before you run off and start changing things, it behooves you to drill down further by visiting additional V$ views.

Drilling Down Further: V$SESSION_EVENT

The V$SESSION_EVENT view provides the same information as V$SYSTEM_EVENT, but at the session level. Of course, it also includes session information, such as the SID. Use this information to join with V$SESSION and you can see how individual sessions are performing. It's a good idea to look for the same events in V$SESSION_EVENT that were observed to be problematic at the system level. Sometimes you will find that many of the system-level events can be tied back to a single session or just a few sessions doing the same or similar work. The following is a sample query for drilling down into the sessions:

```
select S.Username, S.Program, S.Status,
       SE.Event, SE.Total_Waits, SE.Total_Timeouts,
       SE.Time_Waited, SE.Average_Wait
  from V$SESSION S, V$SESSION_EVENT SE
 where S.Sid = SE.Sid
   and SE.Event not like 'SQL*Net%'
   and S.status = 'ACTIVE'
   and S.Username is not null;
```

NOTE
The previous query excludes information where the username in V$SESSION is NULL. Remove this line if you want to see what events are associated with background processes such as PMON and SMON. After reviewing the output from V$SESSION_EVENT and comparing it to V$SYSTEM_EVENT, you will want to drill down even further.

Formatted sample output from the preceding query without the Program Name and TimeOuts columns:

USERNAME	STATUS	EVENT	TOTAL_WAITS	TIME_WAITED	AVERAGE_WAIT
UREG	ACTIVE	db file scattered read	15	10	.66666667
AREG	ACTIVE	latch free	12	27	.44444444

Cutting to the Chase: V$SESSION_WAIT

The V$SESSION_WAIT view provides the lowest-level information for each event. As the name implies, it is based on waits at the session level. Unlike some of the other views, which display totals, this view displays session-level wait information in real time. This is the real stuff, as it unfolds. Because the information in V$SESSION_WAIT is real time, it may show different results each time you query it. Since the needs of each process change from time to time, it is easy to see that the differences in output are based on the activity on the database at the time of the query. Repeatedly querying V$SESSION_WAIT can reveal patterns in events and processes as well as point out who is using a given resource and which other processes are waiting for the same resource. Most importantly, since this view displays the drill-down information for the wait events and the associated resource, you can definitively identify the areas to tune.

For example, if a session is waiting on an index scan, denoted by the event *db file sequential read* (yes, we know…whoever named this was not smoking the right stuff and had it all backwards), the file number and data block number where the wait is occurring will be provided. This is the actual location from which the process needs to get its data. Now, that is useful information! Let's get to the heart of this by defining the important columns in V$SESSION_WAIT:

- **SID**   This is the session identifier number.

- **Seq#**   This number is an internal sequence number for the wait event related to this session. Use this value to determine the number of waits for a given event that a session has endured.

- **Event**   This is the name of the event. Some of the more common events are enqueue, buffer busy waits, latch free, db file scattered read, db file sequential read, and free buffer waits. Look for recurring events, but avoid concern over events such as PMON Timer, RDBMS timer, and so on. These are normal and indicate that the instance is waiting for things to do.

- **P[1-3]**   Here it is folks! This is the treasure we have been digging around for. These three columns contain the detail information that really tells us what a given wait event means. The values in these columns are the logical relationships (foreign keys) to other V$ views. This is also where you have to really pay attention, because the interpretation of a value here is wait-event dependent.

For example, for the wait event db file scattered read (which denotes a full table scan in progress...yes, we know), P1 contains the file number, P2 contains the block number the process is waiting for, and P3 contains the number of blocks to be read from the block number specified in P2. By using P1 to query V$FILESTAT or DBA_DATA_FILES and P2 to QUERY DBA_EXTENTS or SYS.UET$, you can determine the object this session is waiting for. If you have several processes waiting for the same file or files on the same file system, you can start looking at I/O distribution as a way of fixing the problem.

But wait, what if the event is a latch free? Well, then P2 is the number of the latch, which points to V$LATCH. So query V$LATCH and you will see which latch is the problem. Instead of running around tuning every little thing, you can now tune what needs to be tuned. For the complete list of the waits with their associated parameters, please refer to Appendix A in the Oracle Reference Manual.

NOTE
*An I/O request in this context is for a set of blocks,
not just one block.*

■ **State** The state of given event is a very important indicator, as it provides details for interpreting the following two columns, wait_time and seconds_in_wait. Without fully understanding the state, the wait_time and seconds_in_wait numbers can be worthless. There are four possible states (not counting Texas, of course):

  ■ **WAITING** The session is currently waiting for the event. That was not so tough.

  ■ **WAITED UNKNOWN TIME** This is true if TIMED_STATISTICS is set to FALSE.

  ■ **WAITED SHORT TIME** This value means the session has waited for an insignificant amount of time. Don't worry about these events, unless they occur very frequently.

  ■ **WAITED KNOWN TIME** When and if a process acquires the resource it has been waiting for, the value in the STATE column will change to WAITED KNOWN TIME.

■ **Wait_time**   The value of this column is STATE dependent and is measured in seconds:

```
If STATE in ('WAITING','WAITED UNKNOWN TIME','WAITED SHORT TIME') then

  WAIT_TIME = Irrelevant;

End If;

If STATE = 'WAITED KNOWN TIME' then

  WAIT_TIME = Actual wait time, in seconds;

End If;
```

Okay, now to explain the previous text in plain English. If you have WAITED_SHORT_TIME, the wait event is really not a problem, unless the wait event keeps occurring over and over again. If you are currently WAITING, you really don't know what your final WAIT_TIME is, hence WAIT_TIME is currently not useful (look at SECONDS_IN_WAIT). If you have WAITED UNKNOWN TIME, it is because TIMED_STATISTICS is not set to TRUE, hence not relevant. Got it?

But one thing to note here is that if the system is very busy, and the session is waiting on multiple resources and begins to wait for another resource, the STATUS for a wait event will change back to WAITING, and WAIT_TIME = Irrelevant again, per the first If condition. You might want to read the last couple of pages again to get a better understanding.

■ **Seconds_in_wait**   The value of this column is also STATE dependent.

```
If STATE in ('WAITED UNKNOWN TIME','WAITED_SHORT TIME','WAITED KNOWN TIME') then

  SECONDS_IN_WAIT = Irrelevant;

End If;

If STATE = 'WAITING' then

  SECONDS_IN_WAIT = Actual Wait Time in seconds;

End If;
```

Wow! Did you catch the difference between SECONDS_IN_WAIT and WAIT_TIME? Okay, let's try that in another way. We are trying to find out the current value for SECONDS_IN_WAIT. If the process has WAITED_UNKNOWN_TIME, again TIMED_STATISTICS is not set, hence it is irrelevant. If the process has WAITED_SHORT_TIME, it is really not currently waiting, hence SECONDS_IN_WAIT is meaningless. Lastly, if the process had WAITED_KNOWN_TIME, SECONDS_IN_WAIT is again meaningless (look at WAIT_TIME instead), as it is currently not waiting.

Values in this column may not reappear on multiple iterations of querying. Now you have got it...right?

If the values do reappear, the session is waiting for a long time for the given event. Multiple queries against this view provide information about the duration of the wait by a session for a given event. Now you really know what is important.

The following code examples illustrate the wait_event–based performance tuning methodology.

First we run the following query to check some common wait events in the database using V$SYSTEM_EVENT view:

```
SQL> select *
  2      from V$SYSTEM_EVENT
  3    where Event in ('buffer busy waits',
  4                    'db file sequential read',
  5                    'db file scattered read',
  6                    'enqueue',
  7                    'free buffer waits',
  8                    'latch free',
  9                    'log file parallel write',
 10                    'log file sync');
EVENT                       TOTAL_WAITS TOTAL_TIMEOUTS TIME_WAITED AVERAGE_WAIT
--------------------------- ----------- -------------- ----------- ------------
latch free                       236563         230494       41893  .177090247
enqueue                             424             40         343  .808962264
free buffer waits                  4232           3561       28201  6.66375236
buffer busy waits                894377           2502      181907  .203389622
log file parallel write         3938548              0      804870  .204357037
log file sync                   1890409            890      544425  .287993233
db file sequential read        62769635              0   311819246  4.96767658
db file scattered read         17928634              0     3843986  .214404845
8 rows selected.
SQL>
```

Next, we drill down to the sessions with wait events that are contributing to the above display using the following query against the V$SESSION_EVENT and V$SESSION views:

```
SQL> select SE.Sid, S.Username, SE.Event,
  2         SE.Total_Waits, SE.Time_Waited, SE.Average_Wait
  3    from V$SESSION S, V$SESSION_EVENT SE
  4    where S.Username is not null
  5      and SE.Sid = S.Sid
  6      and S.Status = 'ACTIVE'
  7      and SE.Event not like '%SQL*Net%';
```

```
    SID USERNAME    EVENT              TOTAL_WAITS TIME_WAITED AVERAGE_WAIT
    --- ----------  ------------------ ----------- ----------- ------------
     29 OLUSER14    latch free                 108         206  1.90740741
     29 OLUSER14    file open                   16           1       .0625
     29 OLUSER14    db file scattered read    7241       36357  5.02099158
     29 OLUSER14    db file sequential read 1010122     4611646  4.56543467
     29 OLUSER14    buffer busy waits         6509        2592  .398217852
     32 ID2USER     latch free                  49          63  1.28571429
     32 ID2USER     file open                    9           1  .111111111
     32 ID2USER     db file sequential read   8755       10056   1.1486008
     32 ID2USER     db file scattered read       3          10  3.33333333
     32 ID2USER     log file sync            72739       47177  .648579167
     32 ID2USER     buffer busy waits            1           0           0
     51 VENDOR1     latch free                 214         338  1.57943920
     51 VENDOR1     file open                   20           1         .05
     51 VENDOR1     db file scattered read   57469      207155  3.60463902
     51 VENDOR1     buffer busy waits         3091        1221  .395017794
     51 VENDOR1     db file sequential read 656434      245814   .37446872
16 rows selected.
SQL>
```

To find the current wait events associated with the connected sessions, we use the following query. This is very dynamic information and the query will need to be run multiple times to see what the most waited events for a session are.

```
SQL> select SW.Sid, S.Username, SW.Event, SW.Wait_Time,
  2         SW.State, SW.Seconds_In_Wait SEC_IN_WAIT
  3    from V$SESSION S, V$SESSION_WAIT SW
  4   where  S.Username is not null
  5     and SW.Sid = S.Sid
  6     and SW.Event not like '%SQL*Net%'
  7   order by SW.Wait_Time Desc;
SID   USERNAME EVENT                    WAIT_TIME STATE                SEC_IN_WAIT
---   -------- ----------------------   --------- ------------------   -----------
 29   OLUSER14 db file sequential read     12 WAITED KNOWN TIME              1
 32   ID2USER  db file scattered read       0 WAITING                        0
 51   VENDOR1  log file sync                0 WAITING                        0
3 rows selected.
SQL>
```

Session 29 is waiting for *db file sequential read.* In our testing that event showed up quite a few numbers of times, and got our attention. Following query shows additional information related to its wait event. We have restricted the query to show only a few sessions of our interest.

```
SQL> select Sid, Event, P1text, P1, P2text, P2, P3text, P3
  2      from V$SESSION_WAIT
  3    where Sid between 28 and 52
  4      and Event not like '%SQL%'
  5      and Event not like '%rdbms%';
```

```
 SID EVENT                        P1TEXT       P1 P2TEXT           P2 P3TEXT     P3
---- ----------------------- ------- ------- ---------- -------- ------- -----
  29 db file sequential read  file#       67 block#      19718 blocks     1
  32 db file scattered read   file#       67 block#      17140 blocks    32
  51 db file sequential read  file#       63 block#       7556 blocks     1
3 rows selected.
SQL >
```

Here it is folks! Two sessions are accessing the same data file and possibly the same segment. P1 shows this fact clearly. One session is performing a full table scan whereas other is using an index scan. With the information from P1 and P2, it is easy to find out what this segment is. Following query does just that.

```
SQL> select Owner, Segment_Name, Segment_Type, Tablespace_Name
  2      from DBA_EXTENTS
  3    where File_Id = &FileId_In
  4      and &BlockId_In between Block_Id and Block_Id + Blocks - 1;

Enter value for fileid_in: 67
old   3:  where File_id = &Fileid_In
new   3:  where File_id = 67
Enter value for blockid_in: 19718
old   4:  and &Blockid_In between Block_Id and Block_Id + Blocks - 1
new   4:  and 19718 between Block_Id and Block_Id + Blocks - 1

OWNER        SEGMENT_NAME             SEGMENT_TYPE      TABLESPACE_NAME
---------- ------------------------ ---------------- --------------------
MARKET       ITEM_MASTER_INFO         TABLE             ITEM_MASTER
1 row selected.
SQL>
```

There you have it! Queries accessing table ITEM_MASTER_INFO are causing some waits. Let us see what SQL queries session 29 is running at the moment.

We have created a small function to retrieve the SQL text for the session from view V$SQLTEXT. Following is that function:

```
-- GetSQLtext.sql
-- Simple function to access address, hash_value and return
-- SQL statement (will fail if stmt size > 32 k)
--
CREATE OR REPLACE
FUNCTION GetSQLTxt (HashAddr_In IN V$SQLTEXT.Hash_Value%TYPE
                   ,Addr_In IN V$SQLTEXT.Address%TYPE)
RETURN VARCHAR2
IS
    Temp_SQLTxt varchar2(32767);

    CURSOR SQLPiece_Cur
    IS
```

```
    select Piece, Sql_Text
      from V$SQLTEXT
     where Hash_Value = HashAddr_In
       and Address    = Addr_In
     order by Piece;
BEGIN
  FOR SQLPiece_Rec IN SQLPiece_Cur
  LOOP
     Temp_SQLTxt := Temp_SQLTxt || SQLPiece_Rec.Sql_Text;
  END LOOP;
  RETURN Temp_SQLTxt;
END GetSQLTxt;
/
```

Here is a simple SQL query to use the above function to get the SQL Text:

```
SQL> select Sid, GetSQLtxt(Sql_Hash_Value, Sql_Address)
  2    from V$SESSION
  3    where Sid = &Sid_In;

Enter value for sid_in: 29
old   2: where Sid = &Sid_In
new   2: where Sid = 29

  SID  GETSQLTXT(SQL_HASH_VALUE,SQL_ADDRESS)
  ----- --------------------------------------------------------------
   29 select  sum(decode(im.action_code,'A',1,'I',2,'P','1',0) * im.disc_amt),
      sum(im.last_amt),  sum(decode(im.action_code,'A',1,'I',2,'P',1,0) * im.m
      isc_amt) - sum(im.last_amt)  from  items_detail_info id, item_master_in
      fo@INVP im where id.period_num in ('00','02','04') and id.item_flg = '1'
      and im.action_code in ('A','I','P') and (im.suff_code_id <> 0 or im.stat
      us in ('R','S')  or im.type in ('C','S'))
SQL>
```

We have found the culprit!

So, from knowing that event *db file sequential read* was experiencing some waits, we have identified not only the sessions contributing to those waits, but the exact SQL.

Some Common Events

It is very important for those of us who are involved in tuning engagements to become familiar with the common wait events that occur on most systems. A very good source of information for all the events on the system is available in Appendix A of the Oracle Reference Manual. We urge you to study that reference, as it is essential to understanding what each wait event means. Table 2-1 lists some common events that we have encountered across many systems over the past years. The Meaning/Relevance section for this should not be considered as the *end-all* for a given wait event. Table 2-1 is meant to be a general overview of the events, not necessarily a comprehensive description of every event and is *not* intended as a checklist.

Wait Event Name	Meaning/Relevance
buffer busy waits	Indicates wait for buffers in the database buffer cache. This indicates that a session is reading this buffer into the cache and/or modifying it. Can also be a symptom of lack of enough free lists on tables that support many concurrent INSERT operations.
db file parallel write	Indicates waits related to the DBWR process. May be related to the number of DBWR processes or DBWR I/O slaves configured. May also indicate slow or high contention devices.
db file scattered read	Indicates waits associated with a full table scan. May indicate I/O contention or an excessive amount of I/O.
db file sequential read	Indicates (among other things) waits associated with an index scan. May indicate I/O contention or an excessive amount of I/O.
db file single write	Indicates waits associated with header writes during a checkpoint. Typical in an environment with an inordinate number of data files.
direct path read	Indicates waits associated with direct I/O enabled. Usually indicates I/O contention on devices.
direct path write	Same as above. Relevant to writes.
enqueue	Indicates waits associated with internal queuing mechanism for locking various resources and components of Oracle. Please refer to Appendix B of the Oracle8i Reference Manual for the complete list of enqueues in Oracle.
free buffer inspected	Indicates waits associated with the process of identifying a free buffer in the database buffer cache to bring data into the cache.

TABLE 2-1. *Some Wait Events and Their Relevance*

Wait Event Name	Meaning/Relevance
free buffer waits	Indicates lack of free buffers in the database buffer cache. This could mean either the database buffer cache is too small or the dirty list (list of modified blocks in the cache) is not getting written to disk fast enough. If that is the case, configure more DBWR processes or I/O slaves, as the case may be. This event occurs when the free buffer inspected event does not find any free buffers.
latch free	Indicates latch contention for the latch# that is being waited on. Ensure that you already have tuned the number of latches to their allowed maximums by setting the relevant init.ora parameters. If the problem persists, you should determine what is causing the contention for the latch and fix the underlying problem. Your goal should be to cure the disease not the symptom. A latch free event is a symptom of a bigger problem. For example, if the latch# derived from this is a library cache latch (assuming that the shared pool is configured appropriately), it may indicate a significant amount of hard parsing. This usually is a problem with applications that have hard-coded values in them. Either rewrite them with bind variables or upgrade to Oracle8i and use CURSOR_SHARING=force (or just look the other way).
library cache load lock	This is required to load objects into the library cache. This wait event can occur when a significant amount of reloads/loads are occurring (normally caused due to either lack of reuse of SQL statements or a improperly sized shared pool area).
library cache lock	Indicates waits associated with concurrency of multiple processes accessing the library cache. Can indicate an improperly sized shared pool area, as this lock needs to be acquired to locate objects in the library cache.
library cache pin	This wait event is also associated with library cache concurrency and can occur when a given object needs to be modified or examined in the library cache.

TABLE 2-1. *Some Wait Events and Their Relevance* (continued)

Wait Event Name	Meaning/Relevance
log buffer space	Indicates a potential problem of LGWR not being able to keep up with the rate of writes into the redo log buffer by server processes. Usually indicates a log buffer size problem (too small) or slow device(s) or contention where the online redo logs are located.
log file parallel write	Indicates waits associated with the writing of redo records from the redo log buffer to disk. Usually indicates slow device(s) or contention where the online redo logs are located.
log file single write	Indicates writing to the header block of the log files. May indicate waits during checkpoints.
log file switch (archiving needed)	Waits indicate ARCH is not keeping up with LGWR. Could be because of online redo logs being too small, slow devices, or high contention on devices (usually caused by the log files placed on the devices where data files are). May also want to investigate the possibility of multiple ARCH processes or I/O slaves, as the case may be.
log file switch (checkpoint incomplete)	Indicates waits associated with improperly sized online redo log files (usually too small).
log file sync	Indicates waits associated with the flushing of the redo buffers on a user commit. If the waits are persistent, it may indicate device contention where the online redo log files are placed and/or slow devices.
SQL*Net message from/to client	Indicates elapsed time during communication between the user process and the server process. In some rare cases can shed light on a network transmission problem, but for the most part can be ignored. If the application supports the configuration of ARRAYSIZE (for example, Oracle Forms, SQL*Plus, Pro*C, and so on), configuring ARRAYSIZE to a value greater than its default value can potentially decrease the waits for this event.

TABLE 2-1. *Some Wait Events and Their Relevance* (continued)

Wait Event Name	Meaning/Relevance
SQL*Net message from dblink	Indicates wait associated with distributed processing (SELECTs from other databases). This event occurs when online lookups to other databases are done via DBLINKS. If the data being looked up is mostly static, moving the data to a local table and refreshing it as needed can make a significant performance difference.
timer in sksawat	Again indicates a slow ARCH process, either due to contention of multiple components of the database or not enough I/O processes/slaves to perform the archival.
transaction	Indicates waits associated with a blocking transaction to a rollback operation.
undo segment extension	Indicates dynamic allocation of extents and extension of rollback segments. This may indicate the lack of the optimal number of rollback segments or the lack of the optimal number of MINEXTENTS for those segments.
write complete waits	Indicates waits associated with buffers to be written down to disk. This write may be caused by normal aging of blocks from the database buffer cache.

TABLE 2-1. *Some Wait Events and Their Relevance* (continued)

NOTE
It is useful to note here that the Oracle Wait Interface does not directly identify wait events associated with memory operations, CPU operations, or even logical I/O calls. But the list of such events is very finite and this should not in any way deter you from using the Oracle wait interface. This is because if you don't see the event in the wait interface, it should indirectly lead you to the potential problem areas. Given that what we have described here is a two-pronged approach, where the second prong is operating system statistics and monitoring, the culprit will be found either in Oracle or in the operating system. It is very rare that the culprit will fall through the cracks and go undetected in either prong.

VIP
Although your primary goal should be to take corrective action for the wait events with the STATE of WAITED_KNOWN_TIME, it should be noted here that if there are a significant number of sessions in your system that wait for an event with the STATE of WAITED_SHORT_TIME (less than 1/100ths of a second), you need to calculate the weighted average of the amount of time waited by those sessions. If the resulting number is greater than 1/100ths of a second, you need to pay attention to those events, which you may have originally ignored due to the event's WAITED_SHORT_TIME value in the STATE column.

Miscellaneous Sources of Performance Clues

More clues for the Oracle Performance Management sleuth can be found in the Oracle trace files and the alert log. These files may actually serve as the first warning that something is not going exactly the way it should. In particular, monitoring the alert log should be a routine part of the daily care and feeding of a database. Look for any kinds of errors. Things like deadlocks will be noted in the alert log. Space allocation errors and the infamous ORA-00600 errors are all listed here. Some of these errors do appear once in a while and can be considered normal. Repeated occurrences are grounds for suspicion.

Adding the parameter LOG_CHECKPOINTS_TO_ALERT = TRUE will cause checkpoint events to be written to the alert log. If a checkpoint doesn't finish before the next one starts, there will be some notice. Routinely reviewing these files can provide a heads-up that the instance is starting to go astray or that developers are writing code that doesn't take best advantage of Oracle's locking mechanism.

Trapping Wait Events to a Trace File

If you are having trouble tracking down the wait events on your system (for whatever reason), you can trace these wait events and trap them to a trace file. Here are the steps.

For your current session:

```
alter session set timed_statistics=true; /* If not already set */

alter session set max_dump_file_size=unlimited; /* Just to make sure your
trace file does not get truncated, due to current setting in the database */

alter session set events '10046 trace name context forever, level X';
/* Where X = (1,4,8,12) */
1   = Statistics
```

```
4  = Statistics, Bind Variable Values
8  = Statistics, Wait Event Information
12 = Statistics, Bind Variable Values, Wait Event Information
```

1. Run your application and then look for the trace file in the directory location pointed by USER_DUMP_DEST.

2. Scan the file for all lines that begin with the word WAIT.

For someone else's session:

1. Identify the session's process ID (SPID). The following query identifies the session process ID of all users whose name begins with A:

```
select S.Username, P.Spid
   from V$SESSION S, V$PROCESS P
 where S.PADDR = P.ADDR
   and S.Username like 'A%';
```

2. Launch SQL*Plus or svrmgrl and connect as internal or connect / as sysdba:

```
alter system set timed_statistics=true; /* If not already set */

alter system set max_dump_file_size=unlimited; /* Just to make sure your trace
file does not get truncated, due to current setting in the database */

oradebug setospid <SPID>

oradebug unlimit

oradebug event 10046 trace name context forever, level X   /* Where X = (1,4,8,16) */
```

3. Trace session application for some time interval.

4. Look for the trace file using the SPID in the directory location pointed by the value of USER_DUMP_DEST.

5. Scan the file for all lines that begin with the word WAIT.

Identify the Current OS Bottlenecks

Now that you have taken the time to gather information about the database, you will want to compare those with statistics for the operating system during the same period. What? You didn't gather any? Well, now is the time. On UNIX and Windows NT, some of the core system metrics that need to be measured include CPU utilization, device utilization, and virtual memory statistics.

NOTE
We'd like to make a special mention here for our readers using Oracle on Windows NT. Although the following sections are UNIX-heavy, the issues and the key metrics that you deal with on Windows NT are no different on UNIX. We have provided the relevant equivalents on the Windows NT Performance Monitor when discussing the UNIX commands/tools. Please realize that the UNIX commands need to be explained in far more detail, due to their inherent complexity. We sincerely apologize for not incorporating sample outputs from the Windows NT Performance Monitor.

Monitoring on Windows NT

On Windows NT, monitoring the operating system is as simple as launching the Windows NT Performance Monitor (Start | Programs Administrative Tools (Common) | Performance Monitor). When you see the blank chart or an existing chart, you can Edit | Add to Chart, and a whole slew of options and information is at your fingertips. The Explain button details the meaning of each option/value. We urge you to read on and understand the issues you need to deal with, even though the following sections are UNIX-heavy. Look for the comparable Windows NT equivalents in each section. For a very high-level overview of your Windows NT system performance, you can use the Task Manager (right-click on your taskbar and order your applications by either CPU or memory, by clicking the header buttons).

Also, when you feel you do not have the time or the patience to build your Windows NT monitoring toolkit, you might want to check SysInternals Inc.'s Web site at http://www.sysinternals.com/. There is a wealth of Windows NT–specific free tools and information available.

Monitoring on UNIX

All right, you UNIXoids. Your life is not as easy as that of your Windows NT compatriots. There are several tools you can use on UNIX to provide some interesting information on the OS for the same period. These tools are available on most flavors of UNIX and we have tried to keep them as generic as possible. They include **sar**, **vmstat**, **iostat**, **cpustat**, **mpstat**, **netstat**, **top**, and **osview**. Please note that these commands display varied output, depending on the flavor of UNIX you use, hence we recommend that you get more information about the various tools mentioned above in the manual pages of your UNIX (a.k.a. man pages). The sample commands and their relevant switches, along with their outputs in this chapter, were produced from a Sun Solaris system (version 2.61).

Many operating systems offer more advanced tools such as PerfMon and Glance Plus, and many companies purchase tools for the express purpose of monitoring the operating system. You will also want to be aware of how the hardware and operating system is configured. How much memory does it have, how many CPUs, controllers, disks, disk groups, and so on. After you have this and the previous Oracle reports, you can move on to the next task: identifying the bottlenecks.

CPU Utilization   CPU utilization can be measured on most flavors of UNIX, by executing the **sar -u 5 1000** command. The command *sar* is short for *system activity reporter*. The switch **-u** is for CPU numbers. The first number represents the measurement frequency (in seconds), while the second number represents the number of iterations of measurement for each elapsed measurement frequency.

One of the classic myths about CPU utilization is that a system with 0 percent idle is categorized as a system undergoing CPU bottlenecks. The real issue here is, how many processes are waiting for the CPU? It is perfectly okay to have a system with 0 percent idle, so long as the average runnable queue for the CPU is less than (2 x number of CPUs).

NOTE
This number (2 X number of CPUs) has been used for a few years now, based on current processor architectures and speeds, personal experience, and recommendations from some of the UNIX experts in the industry. It is a yardstick, not a high-precision measurement tool.

If your runnable queue is less than the mentioned threshold and your %idle is 0, go ahead and pat yourself on your back, as you are utilizing 100 percent of the system you purchased. You are getting your money's worth. In the coming pages, we will help you determine the runnable queue on your system using the **vmstat** or **sar -q** commands. On Windows NT, if you launch the Task Manager and select the Performance tab, you can view your overall CPU utilization numbers, under the Processor Object. You can also break down the CPU numbers into %Privileged Time, %Processor Time, %User Time, as well as get queue information such as DPC Queued per second and so on. A sample **sar -u** output is as follows:

```
SunOS ganymede 5.7 Generic sun4u    10/30/00
18:58:12   %usr    %sys    %wio    %idle
18:58:17    68      4       22       4
18:58:22    61      2       22      15
18:58:27    57      4       11      28
18:58:32    46      5       23      27
18:58:37    67      2       10      21
18:58:42    67      4       20       9
18:58:47    73      3       15       9
18:58:52    75      5        4      16
18:58:57    79      4       18       0
18:59:02    69      3       12      17
Average     66      4       16      14
```

The CPU utilization is broken down into various components: %usr, %sys, %wio, and %idle. The first component, %usr, refers to the percentage of the CPU that is utilized by user processes (mind you, the term "user processes" here is from the perspective of the operating system). Oracle is considered a user of the operating system. The second component, %sys, measures the amount of CPU utilized by the operating system to do its job (context switches when a process needs to perform I/O and currently has the CPU or vice versa, servicing of interrupts, servicing signals, and so on). The third component, %wio, is a measure of processes that are currently utilizing the CPU, but are waiting for I/O requests to be serviced and hence are not making prudent use of the CPU. Depending on the amount of I/O and the load on the system, any time a process currently holding the CPU has to perform I/O, will cause the operating system to perform a context switch by de-assigning the CPU from the process and giving it to another process in the runnable queue. When the original process has completed the I/O operation, it will get back into the runnable queue to get a slice of the CPU time. Depending on which school of thought you are from, you may consider %wio a wasteful use of CPU or potential idle time. The fourth and final component, %idle, refers to the percentage of available CPU or in simple terms the amount of idle CPU capacity.

Everything remaining constant, the numbers that come out of the %sys and %wio should be less than 10–15 percent. If you consistently notice numbers higher than that, it is pretty obvious that your system is experiencing a very high number of context switches and interrupts (%sys) and also experiencing a significant amount of wait-for-I/O (%wio). If you do observe high numbers, you need to get to the bottom of it and find out what is causing it. It is an application problem 9.9 out of 10 times.

Device Utilization   Device utilization numbers can be acquired by executing **sar -d 5 1000**. This command provides useful information such as the device name, the %busy for a given device, the average length of the device queue (avque), the number of reads+writes per second (r+w/s), blocks transferred (blks/s measured in 512 byte chunks), the average wait time for each I/O operation during that period of five seconds (avwait, in milliseconds), and the average time it took to service I/O operations (avserv). Again, comparable settings and values are available in the Windows NT Performance Monitor under the Logical Disk Object.

Optimal device utilization starts to degrade when the %busy exceeds 60 percent. There is also a direct correlation between an increase in %busy and the average device queue length, average wait time, and average service time (avque, avwait, avserv). On current disk systems (with significant amounts of disk cache), a value of 100 milliseconds for avserv is considered very high. If you see such high numbers, you should start an investigation to unearth the cause.

NOTE
*When using third-party storage systems, investing in a tool that will provide you with the necessary information (inside the storage arrays) is not only useful but required. This is due to the fact that the numbers from the **sar -d** output have been observed to be bogus. It will make you believe that there is no real I/O contention or bottlenecks when such beasts exist in your I/O subsystem. You will see evidence of that in the wait events of Oracle. This phenomenon is due to multiple levels of cache between what the operating system views as a device and what really ends up being a disk on a storage system.*

Sample output from a **sar -d** command:

```
SunOS ganymede 5.7 Generic sun4u    10/30/00
19:09:51    device       %busy   avque   r+w/s   blks/s   avwait   avserv
19:09:56    dad1            30     0.5      59      964      0.6      7.3
            dad1,d          21     0.2      21      350      0.7     10.4
            dad1,f          18     0.2      34      543      0.6      5.4

19:10:01    dad1            25     0.4      46      735      0.3      8.0
            dad1,d          22     0.2      23      377      0.0      9.3
            dad1,f          14     0.1      16      259      0.0      8.4

19:10:06    dad1            28     0.5      50      814      1.1      8.4
            dad1,d          22     0.2      15      249      1.1     14.3
            dad1,f          18     0.2      29      469      0.5      6.1

Average     dad1            29     0.5      61      750      0.5      6.9
            dad1,d          23     0.3      30      249      0.2      8.2
            dad1,f          15     0.2      25      348      0.4      5.9
```

Virtual Memory Utilization   Virtual memory statistics can be acquired by executing **vmstat -S 5 1000**. This command provides in-depth information not only about various virtual memory statistics but also on any current CPU bottlenecks that the system is experiencing. The preference of **-S** is to focus on processes that are swapping rather than the ones that are just paging. The output from this command is very comprehensive and is divided into six distinct sections: process information, memory usage, paging activity, some rudimentary disk usage numbers (not very useful), system-wide traps/faults, and CPU utilization. On the Windows NT Performance Monitor, you need to focus your attention on the memory object. The following is a sample output from a **vmstat -S** command:

```
procs     memory            page            disk          faults      cpu
 r b w   swap  free  si  so pi po fr de sr dd dd f0 s0   in   sy   cs us sy id
 1 0 0   1864   168   0   0 124 72 93 0 11  2 17  0  0  471  554 1208 23  9 68
 0 0 0 1906800 10808   0   0   0  0  0 0  0  0  2  0  0  191 13616 201 98  2  0
 2 0 0 1906800 10800   0   0   0  0  0 0  0  1  2  0  0  172 13671 175 96  4  0
 3 0 0 1907288 11112   0   0   0  0  0 0  0  0  2  0  0  174 13584 170 96  4  0
 2 0 0 1907288 11112   0   0   0  0  0 0  0  0  2  0  0  172 13630 164 97  3  0
```

In the output for virtual memory statistics, **r b w** belongs to process information, **swap free** belongs to memory usage for these processes, **si so pi po fr de sr** belongs to paging activity of the processes (also related to memory), **dd dd f0 s0** relates to rudimentary disk usage information, **in sy cs** belongs to system-wide traps/faults, and last but not least, **us sy id** belongs to CPU utilization (the only difference between **sar -u** and this output is that this output combines %wio and %idle into one bucket). Table 2-2 summarizes and explains the output from a **vmstat -S** command.

The key things to look for here is the size of the runnable and blocked queues (**r** and **b**), the rate of swapping, if any (**si** and **so**), the amount of short-term memory shortfall (**de**), and the scan rate of the clock algorithm (**sr**). The value of **r** should definitely average less than (2 x number of CPUs), failing which your system could be experiencing CPU bottlenecks. The value of **b** should indicate the number of processes blocking (usually for I/O), and this should again provide insight into the performance of the system from the operating system's perspective. **si** and **so** provide swapping information (ideally this should be always 0 if you have not gone overboard on memory allocation for the Oracle SGA or components of the PGA). **de** and **sr** provide any indications of memory starvation in kilobytes and also in the form of whether the clock algorithm is scanning the memory freelist for available pages. On more recent versions of some operating systems (Solaris 2.8), **sr** should be 0 or very close to it. In prior releases of Solaris, you may see some high numbers for **sr**, but that by itself should not cause any alarm.

vmstat -S (Output Information)	Meaning/Relevance
Procs (**r b w**)	**r** refers to processes in the run queue (waiting to run with the CPU). **b** refers to processes that are blocked for resources such as I/O, paging, and so on. **w** refers to processes that are runnable, but are currently swapped (possibly due to extreme memory starvation).
Memory (**swap free**)	**swap** refers to the amount of swap space currently available in kilobytes. **free** refers to the size of the freelist of memory (also in kilobytes).
Page (**si so pi po fr de sr**)	**si** and **so** refer to the number of kilobytes of memory swapped in and out. **pi** and **po** refer to the number of kilobytes of memory paged in and out. **fr** refers to the number of kilobytes freed. **de** refers to the anticipated short-term memory shortfall in kilobytes. **sr** refers to the number of pages (sized in pagesize) scanned by the clock algorithm.
Disk (**dd dd f0 s0**)	Up to four devices worth of information is provided. The numbers indicate the number of I/O operations per second. Not very useful, can get better information from the **sar -d** command.
Faults (**in sy cs**)	**in** refers to the number of device interrupts. **sy** refers to the number of system calls. **cs** refers to the number of CPU context switches.
CPU (**us sy id**)	**us** refers to the percentage of time utilized by user processes. **sy** refers to the percentage of time utilized by system processes. **id** refers to the percentage of time not currently utilized (includes all wait-for-I/O numbers).

TABLE 2-2. *Keys to Understanding Vmstat –S Output*

It is also useful to run commands such as **top** and **osview** or any other operating system performance monitor that provides information and metrics about the health of the system. The **sar** command itself has many switches that provide various information such as rate of paging (**-p** option), size of the CPU run queue (**-q** option), and so on. It is useful to understand the various options that the **sar** command provides, as it is more readily available across all flavors of UNIX, when compared to commands such as **vmstat** that may not be readily available. For example, the output of a **sar -q 5 1000** command has two important columns of information, *runq-sz* and *runocc*. The first column provides information on the number of processes awaiting the CPU (run queue) and the second column provides information on the percentage of time the CPU is occupied or busy. There are two other columns of output (*swpq-sz* and *swpocc*), and they provide information related to the swap queues.

The commands **netstat -v** and **netstat -s** provide detailed network statistics, including information about various open sockets and some basic routing information. Please refer to the man pages to get a better understanding about this and other OS commands used here. On Windows NT, there are scores of graphical tools that provide network performance analysis. Hang out with your network administrator for a few hours and you will become familiar with the tools he or she uses.

There are many ways to find out the health of your operating system; what we have described here is a subset of the various methods. We have shared with you the methods we have used at various sites and that have worked for us.

Tune the Required Component

What does that mean? It means change the one thing that will cause the wait event to become insignificant or just go away. But be careful. This is the point at which self-control comes into play. Now you have to resist all temptation to do more than your well-reasoned, well-researched study indicates.

If you have identified that you have a serious resource shortfall in the allocation of memory to the shared pool, now is the time to change the value of SHARED_POOL_SIZE. But if the research did *not* indicate a need for more database blocks to be cached, don't even think of increasing the value of DB_BLOCK_BUFFERS.

If you find that your application is joining a local table with 10,000 rows with a remote table with 10 million rows, adding anything to either of those areas isn't going to help. So don't. Believe it or not, nine out of ten times, if you tune or rewrite the SQL statements that were causing the problem, the problem goes away. There is no substitute to optimal SQL statements. No amount of memory, CPU power, and disk storage can replace good old-fashioned, reasonable, decent SQL code. You might want to take your developers out to happy hour and try teaching them SQL optimization techniques. You may be surprised at their problem-solving techniques when the level of inebriation goes up and the creative juices start to flow. Insurmountable problems and issues will get solved faster than you can imagine.

Also, understand the options and limitations of the version of Oracle you are working on, and get to know what it has to offer with respect to the situation you are in and the solution you are trying to implement. Research implementation options on Oracle forums, such as list servers on the Internet, access forums like Oracle Metalink, the Oracle Technology Network (OTN), and such, to find out how someone has fixed the same problem you are having. But before you post any queries, please Read The Fine Manual.

You may find there is something amiss with the operating system. If that is truly the case, then say so. Tell the system administrator you don't have enough independent devices to separate your hot files that are experiencing the maximum amount of I/O. But don't just add more memory or even start rearranging files when you know that it won't help.

Figuring out which component to tune is accomplished by comparing information from the investigation of the OS and the investigation of the Oracle instance. The primary goal is to see where the two overlap. For instance, if the V$ views show wait events associated with index scans, you should drill down to the file and the segment on that file that is causing the wait event. Look at what the OS is doing— do you see significant %wio numbers in your **sar -d 5 1000** output for the specific device where that file system is mounted (in which the specific file and segment are housed)? If that is the case, congratulations, you might have your finger on your problem. The index scan-related wait event could be a case of poor disk layout, poor application design, or poor SQL. Once you have made the few controlled changes that were defined by your analysis, it's time to go to the next step. You have to see if you hit your target.

Track and Exercise Change-Control Procedures

It is extremely important to track the changes you make in your environment, so that if things do not go according to your grand plan, you at least have a fallback option. Having your Plan B ready to deploy when you need it is the sign of a good DBA who plans for Mr. Murphy being in your neighborhood. Deploying change-control procedures that will work for your environment is your responsibility and your first order of business. You should not attempt any tuning efforts before setting up your change-control procedures. Said in another way, you need some method of doing a rollback of your tuning efforts. Your tuning efforts should not be similar to operations that cannot be rolled back, such as the **truncate** operation on a production table. Don't make us say "We told you so!"

Measure and Document Current Performance

This part of the process looks a lot like the first part. That's because it is. It's time to gather statistics all over again. Get them from the same time frames as before, otherwise you will be comparing apples and oranges. The idea is to see if the things that were a problem are still a problem and to what degree. If there were lots of "redo space wait requests" before, do you have fewer now? Of course, statistics such as these won't answer the ultimate question: is the customer satisfied? Does the query run in the time required? If so, you are finished. If not, go to the next step.

Repeat Steps 3 Through 7 Until the Tuning Goal Is Met

This one is pretty self-explanatory. Since tuning is known to be an iterative process, now is the time to go to the next iteration. Be prepared to go through the process several times before hitting your target. And, of course, when you do hit that set of targets and your reputation for success spreads, you will have many other systems to tune.

In a Nutshell

Every Oracle Performance Management effort is potentially tri-faceted: tune, schedule, or buy. Ultimately, the point we are trying to make regarding the tune facet is very simple: don't bet your professional life on performance tuning systems based solely on cache-hit ratios. By following the process of setting attainable goals, measuring current performance, making deliberate, well-considered changes, and reevaluating and reiterating the process, you can be assured of making positive progress in your tuning effort. Taking the two-pronged parallel approach to monitoring the operating system for resource bottlenecks, and using session wait statistics within Oracle to determine the exact nature of the performance difficulties, allows for a very productive Performance Management effort. The key to this method is drilling down to the heart of the problem. So, here we go again:

1. Start with V$SYSTEM_EVENT and determine what resource is in highest demand, such as db file sequential read (the wait event for index scans—really, it is for index scans even though it sounds like it is for full table scans), and so on.

2. Drill down further to V$SESSION_EVENT and see which and how many sessions are involved for any given wait event.

3. Next, look at V$SESSION_WAIT to find the details of the resource contention, for example, which files, tables, latches, and so on.

4. Check the values for P1–P3 to find the relationships to other views.

5. Consider the time waited for these and other events. Pick the top five events.

6. Continue this process until all of the contention-related events are unearthed.

7. At the same time, determine which SQL statements are contributing to these wait events. Is it the same statement repeated? Remember that a large percentage of tuning problems originate with SQL that has not been optimized for the current architecture.

8. In a parallel effort, analyze the OS statistics. Perform this operation focusing on the issues that confront the Oracle environment. That means you should read the OS statistics as they relate to Oracle. For example, nine times out of ten, if you have an index block or full-table scan related wait, the I/O statistics at the OS will show their equivalent event "wait of I/O". Figuring out which device is the problem is then just a matter of drilling down using the OS tools described earlier. Also, the values in P1 and P2 will provide the perspective from Oracle's side.

9. Once you have determined the problem area, decide on a solution and implement it.

10. Deploy adequate change-control mechanisms so you can track what changes you have made and what effect they have had on the system.

After the solution is implemented, reevaluate to see if you have met your goals. If so, well, you know what to do. Cheers!

NOTE
If the source of a system performance problem is created by a user because of an application that he or she is running, it is okay to start from step 2 of the above checklist, as the problem is specific to a user's session. This is relevant when a user says that "Query X is running slow."

Just to recap, if the database buffer cache-hit ratio is low and you are beginning to get alarmed, stop and look at the wait events for the sessions. If there are no I/O-related wait events, your suspicion of a performance problem is unfounded. On the flip side, if your cache-hit ratios are in the upper 90s, don't just sit back thinking that everything is fine, because in reality it may not be. All you have to do is check for the wait events. Don't assume that a 99.999 cache-hit ratio implies that your Oracle database is performing at its peak efficiency, because even with that kind of cache-hit ratio, something nasty could be brewing. The cornerstone of tuning Oracle-based systems should be wait events, *not* ratios. If you were on a desert island with no documentation, without any of your tuning tools, and you were asked to troubleshoot an Oracle performance problem using five V$ views or less, you should pick V$SYSTEM_EVENT, V$SESSION_EVENT, and V$SESSION_WAIT (in that order). Have we made our point?

One more thing: This chapter is the core of this book. Our primary goal behind this book rests on the number of times you reuse this chapter in your tuning efforts. Well, the other chapters also contain valuable information, but this chapter is key to your continued success in performance engagements. So go ahead, enjoy your tuning efforts, and, please do take the time for your family and loved ones. Ultimately, they are paramount to everything. And, by engaging in methodical and organized tuning efforts, you might actually find the time to spend with your family and loved ones.

PART II

Application Tuning

CHAPTER
3

Application
Tuning—Issues that
Concern a DBA

Myth & Folklore

Index scans are always the preferred method of executing a SQL statement, as it will perform much less I/O than a full table scan, and thus execute better.

Fact

Time and time again, real-life applications have proven that a SQL statement loses the efficiency of using an index when the number of blocks that are visited by it exceeds the number of blocks from a full table scan. A couple of exceptions to the above rule are columns in tables that contain redundant and low-cardinality data and are supported by bitmapped indexes or fast-full index scans. The point we are trying to make here is that the overhead related to reading the root, intermediate, and leaf blocks of an index, plus the data block reads for each row returned by the query, should not outweigh the cost of a full table scan. If an index scan performs more I/O than a full table scan, it will actually hurt performance, rather than help. Ironically, if the rows that are being retrieved are splattered across numerous blocks of the table and are not clustered or located next to each other, the use of an index in the query's execution plan will result in the query *not* performing at optimal levels (even if the number of rows processed or retrieved is less than the mythical level of 15 percent), due to the excessive amount of I/O generated by it. This excess I/O generation can potentially strain the storage subsystem. It thus makes performing a full table scan a much more viable option. If the table in question is of significant size (definition of significant is left to you), you should even consider a parallel scan on the table.

riends, cosmic earthlings, and die-hard DBAs, lend us your ears. Allow us to be your tuning psychiatrics (also known as tuning shrinks in some parts of the world) and hear us out. Yes, this is all happening backwards—even though you have come to us for tuning therapy, we do all the talking and you do all the listening. We promise, in the end, you will feel much better, and you will go home feeling much lighter, so much that your loved ones will wonder what has come over you. If you don't, try reading this chapter again. Your exit condition for this chapter should be **(REPEAT UNTIL Happiness = TRUE)**.

VIP

Did you know? Eighty percent of the performance problems on your system actually have nothing to do with you or your Oracle Database configuration.

Well, given that a significant portion of your performance problems is related to SQL, it is important for us to talk to you about SQL and application tuning issues. When we set out to write this book, our goal was to focus on the database tuning aspects (the remaining 20 percent we plan to cover in good detail), but given that 80 percent of the problems that you inherit have nothing to do with the database configuration, we thought you might need some help.

In most environments, the DBA ends up inheriting someone else's incredible programming skills or I/O subsystem design and has to either live with it or go find another job. But the bad news is that this knack of inheriting someone else's work does not just go away. The more years you spend working with this technical beast we call Oracle, the higher your propensity to attract with uncanny frequency those works of art SQL programs. We have a name for it: SQL from the Dark Side.

To make things even more complicated, someone or the other keeps inflating your ego with terms like expert, guru, or flippant quotes like, "You da man," "Oh, she walks on water," "Could you please wave your DBA magic wand?" "She is the goddess," (now, where have I heard that one before?), and so on. Don't let that stuff go to your head, as the upper part of your body will start defying gravity. Please do not put Sir Isaac Newton and his three laws of motion to shame!

On the bright side, it is only natural for people to frequently beseech you to undertake the work of a SQL janitor. Yes, in very simple terms you will have to clean up the…well, you know what we mean! And the more you clean up, the better you will get at it, and the more stuff you will be given. Your life might seem like a PL/SQL loop with no exit condition in sight.

If you are a novice DBA, it is absolutely normal to experience body shivers, cold sweats, and nightmares if you go to bed thinking of those SQL statements that need tuning. Some of us get technical nightmares, and the concept of rapid eye movement sleep becomes a thing of the past. Yes, believe it, you are the chosen one to fix all the performance issues that arise in your environment, even though you had nothing to do with it. Over the years, you will also have your own armory of horror stories to tell: *SQL from the Crypt*. Now that's a fascinating book to write. Maybe there is even hope for a television series. Okay, we will be right back, need to talk to our acquisitions editor!

A day after speaking with the acquisitions editor, SQL tuning is of paramount importance to your system's health and performance. No amount of database tuning is going to provide you with the quantum of benefit that an optimal SQL statement will. We are literally talking about the potential for many orders of magnitude of performance increase here. No book on database tuning (including ours) or any database-tuning expert (regardless of how many years they have tuned Oracle databases) can provide that kind of performance increase. Remember that 80 percent of your Oracle system performance problems arise from badly designed and badly implemented SQL statements. Does that make sense?

Now it's time to set some expectations. When we talk about application tuning, we are not talking about every minute detail of SQL programming, we are talking about the issues most DBAs face when confronted by an application problem. But if you are in need of the minutest details of SQL programming, allow us to recommend three books that will provide almost everything you need. Please realize that we are doing this in an effort to avoid reinventing the wheel and to save some trees.

The books we recommend for application tuning (in no specific order of preference) are *Advanced Oracle Tuning and Administration*, by Eyal Aronoff, Kevin Loney, and Noorali Sonawalla, *Oracle SQL High Performance Tuning*, by Guy Harrison, and *Oracle Performance Tuning*, by Peter Corrigan and Mark Gurry.

Our primary goal for this chapter is to make you aware of the issues that we know are significant and provide you with tips about facilitating optimal SQL. More importantly, we want to bring to light what *not* to do. Knowing your enemy is the first step toward winning a battle. And that is exactly our focus: to tell you more about the number one performance enemy: bad SQL. Once you know your enemy in your own environment, you will be more than able to build your own battle plan. Get ready, action stations!

NOTE
Sometimes bad SQL is the result of a bad data model. In that case, you may have to address the data model issues first.

The Story of the Oracle Optimizer

Before talking about SQL, it is appropriate to talk about how SQL statements get optimized, and we intend to share that information with you by telling you a story. This story of the Oracle optimizer will provide you insight into your application and SQL tuning efforts.

The Older Sibling: The Rule-Based Optimizer

Long ago in Oracle-land, prior to version 7.0, there were no flexible options for SQL statement optimization within the Oracle optimizer. The optimizer just optimized SQL statements using a set of fixed internal rules. It was that simple. Now, we really don't need to know what those rules were, but you will appreciate some of the optimizer's limitations, if you know what they are and how they worked. Here are four sample rules:

- **Rule #1** Single row by ROWID. For applications that utilize the actual ROWID numbers in the *where clause*. Oh, did they pay dearly when their table(s) had to be reorganized. Or even worse, when their database was migrated to Oracle8 and the ROWID format changed. Ouch…that hurt!

- **Rule #8**   Access by a composite index (an index with more than one column).

- **Rule #9**   Access by a single-column index.

- **Rule #15**   Full table scan.

So now you know how it acquired the name "rule-based optimizer." Basically, when the optimizer had a SQL statement to process, it started at the bottom of the list—say, Rule #15—and worked its way up. If it found an index (based on *where clause* conditions), it opted to use it as an index (depending on which kind) qualified for either Rule #8 or #9. Given that Rule #8 or Rule #9 had a higher precedence than Rule #15 (because it was a rule with a smaller number), it executed the query with 8 or 9, assuming that there were no further rules that qualified potentially to provide the optimizer with better precedence to run the SQL. The basic assumption that the rule-based optimizer made was that as a SQL statement qualified for a given rule and as the rule number got smaller, the execution plan allegedly got better. Which it did...most of the time!

Well, that was exactly where the rule-based optimizer started to falter. It could not determine the "least expensive method," as it did not utilize any kind of cost function or statistics. It optimized SQL statements, for example, to use an index or to perform a full table scan, based on the existence of one or more indexes and the bunch of rules. The optimizer was thus reduced to an engine that blindly (yet many times quickly) implemented a set of rules, whether or not it made sense to implement a given rule. The lack of flexibility and adaptability are quite possibly the biggest disadvantages of the rule-based optimizer. It is important to note that the cost-based optimizer was initially designed for online transaction processing (OLTP) databases. Data warehouses were nonexistent in the early days of the rule-based optimizer.

What Was the Impact of the Rule-Based Optimizer's Inflexibility?

The only way to work around the optimizer's inflexibility was to deliberately modify the application and do some not-so-smart things, such as wrap a function around the leading column of an index column like *upper*(Last_Name), *round*(price), and so on, in the *where clause* of the SQL statement to force a full table scan. The following queries will illustrate the inflexibility we are talking about:

```
select Last_Name, Hire_Date, Salary
   from EMP
 where Mgr_Id = 123;
```

This query, by default, was executed using an index (because there existed an index called Mgr_Id_Idx on the Mgr_Id column). Over time, if a significant number of employees in the EMP table reported to 123, and if the index scan did not provide the needed performance, the query had to be rewritten as shown below to prevent it from using the Mgr_Id_Idx index. This is because an index usually fails to serve its purpose when the number of blocks visited to execute the query exceeds the number of blocks from a full table scan.

```
select Last_Name, Hire_Date, Salary
   from EMP
 where round(Mgr_Id) = 123;
```

Like this example, many SQL statements had to be recoded, and in many cases, this resulted in multiple versions of the same SQL statement, with minor modifications, maintained within the same application. This was because one version of the SQL statement had the function wrapped around the indexed column and another version of the same SQL statement was without the wrap. Many of us had to take such not-so-smart measures to cater to the varying performance needs of the same SQL statement. Ultimately, this often resulted in poor utilization of the shared pool area memory structure (which we will discuss in good detail in the chapter "Instance Tuning—The Shared Pool Area"), as multiple versions of similar SQL statements had to be stored and maintained in memory, even though they functionally performed the same operation.

The Rule-Based Optimizer and the C Compiler: An Expert's View

We added this section to this chapter because we felt a significant message needed to be relayed, and the discussion of application tuning would not be complete without it. This was a direct result of an interesting discussion with one of the industry's experts in Oracle Performance Tuning, Cary Millsap. The perspective that Cary provides on this topic is pretty amazing. He says that the rule-based optimizer was formerly an operator precedence list, *not* a list of how fast Oracle's execution plans are. He adds that when he figured out that the rule-based optimizer precedence list was *exactly* like the operator precedence list in the book on C language by Kernighan and Ritchie, he crossed a major threshold of understanding about SQL optimization. An analogy he shared with us was that "exponentiation is not always faster or better than multiplication, although it has a higher precedence in most computer languages." Amazing stuff indeed, and we could not agree more.

In particular, there are three rules of precedence in which this thinking makes a huge difference:

- **Rule #8** Composite index, all keys listed in the *where clause* (the entire key).

- **Rule #9** AND-EQUALS merge (single index or index merge).

- **Rule #10**   Composite index, prefix of keys listed in *where clause* (bounded range search on indexed columns, including the key prefix).

Rule #9 is never faster than Rule #10, but it is always executed at higher precedence. This hurts customers who use the General Ledger module of Oracle Apps, and who attempt to optimize the following query by appending the primary key to the composite index:

```
select Code_Combination_Id
  from GL_CODE_COMBINATIONS
 where Segment1=:v1
   and Segment2=:v2
   and Segment3=:v3
   and Segment4=:v4
   and Segment5=:v5;
```

If you have an index that is structured in the following manner, the rule-based optimizer will use it to execute this above query: glcc_n1 (Segment3, Segment1, Segment2, Segment4, Segment5) /* Good */. This index will cause execution to take place with less than a half dozen logical I/Os, and the result set will appear instantaneous on most systems.

However, if you append the Code_Combination_Id to this index (shown below), in an attempt to cleverly eliminate data block access, you'll motivate an AND-EQUALS merge (Rule #9), which will take several seconds even on fast systems: glcc_n1 (Segment3, Segment1, Segment2, Segment4, Segment5, Code_Combination_Id) /* Bad */. This is a classic scenario where the rule number is better (lower rule number but higher order of precedence, Rule #9), but the performance would have been better with a rule number (with a higher rule number but lower order of precedence, Rule #10).

The Newborn: The Cost-Based Optimizer

In Oracle 7.0, the cost-based optimizer was born, and there was joy in Oracle-land. This was way back in the early 1990s. Good grief, we are starting to sound like grumpy old men. Anyway, the fundamental rationale behind the cost-based optimizer was to allow more options in building execution plans for SQL statements. It was supposed to infuse badly needed flexibility into our world of optimization. This was because the rule-based optimizer ran its life with a bunch of rules, regardless of whether it made sense to use a rule or not.

With the advent of the new optimizer, there was magic in the air. People rejoiced and made merry to celebrate its birth, as it was supposed to literally change the face of Oracle SQL optimization and eventually replace its older sibling—the rule-based optimizer, which had served us well for many years. But the joy of the newborn was short-lived. As much as people loved the cost-based optimizer conceptually, it was still a baby. In many cases it did not do a good job of optimizing SQL. As a result, people went right back to the older sibling, who was much more reliable. As weird as it sounds, the cost-based optimizer, for some of us, was a precursor to parenthood.

The Maturing Process of the Cost-Based Optimizer

The biggest drawback of the cost-based optimizer (in the early days of Oracle versions 7.0–7.2) was that it was naïve. It assumed that the world was a perfect place to live in, and it truly believed in fairy tales such as even distribution of data. What did that mean? We'll give you an example. Assume a table named Car, having 100,000 rows in it and having an index on the Color column. As part of routine administration, statistics need to be calculated and stored in the data dictionary of the database so the cost-based optimizer can use the statistics when needed to help in the determination of the cost of a given optimization plan.

Let's say after one such collection of statistics (which took many hours if the environment contained large tables), the data dictionary was populated to reflect 100 distinct values for the index on Color. At runtime, when the optimizer was building a plan for a SQL statement on that table, it would wrongfully deduce that each color in that table occurred (100,000/100) = 1,000 times. If you have been around real production systems, you know that such assumptions could leave you in the dust. Do you see what we mean by lack of maturity?

Golden Oldie: The Rule-Based Optimizer

The many attempts made to speed up the education process of the cost-based optimizer were in vain. It had to take its time to learn and grow. As a result, many of us took deliberate steps to sidestep the cost-based optimizer, but promised to come back and look it up when it had grown up. This was because the older sibling performed and dealt with real-life systems with much better reliability and predictability. But the fact remained that the older sibling, albeit reliable and predictable, was inflexible...funny how we acquire that characteristic as we age!

The Return of the Cost-Based Optimizer

They say that time is the best teacher. That surely was true in the case of the cost-based optimizer, as it took a good seven years before it could deal with the real world. The growing process was assisted and in some cases facilitated by the adoption of Rdb into the Oracle family in the 1996–1997 time frame. Given that the Rdb Optimizer had seen many years of research and work, it had aged and mellowed graciously, as smooth as a Cabernet from the Napa Valley. The experience, wisdom, and maturity that the Rdb Optimizer brought to the Oracle cost-based optimizer was incredible, so much so that, in Oracle 7.3, the cost-based optimizer turned a new leaf. It actually felt like it had actually turned a new tree (if you would allow us to use that idiom). It seemed as though the optimizer had been transformed overnight into an incredible powerhouse of optimization functions. It was quite a metamorphosis.

The Cost-Based Optimizer Grows Up

Beginning in Oracle 7.3, the ability to generate and store column-level histograms (statistical functions that allow sampling and storing data distribution) was supported. This made a huge difference to the cost-based optimizer, as it was accurately able to determine the distribution of data for a given column, based on the histograms that were generated. It had learned that even distribution of data was indeed a fairy tale.

NOTE
The use of histograms is relevant only for SQL statements that utilize hard-coded values and not bind variables. There is a new twist to this feature in Oracle 8.1.6, with the introduction and forcing of CURSOR_SHARING. Histograms are not used when CURSOR_SHARING is set to FORCE in Oracle8i.

Since then, the cost-based optimizer has never looked back. With every new release, more functionality has been added to it to recognize partitioning, parallel DML, index organized tables, and other new features. The waiting was really over. The cost-based optimizer was ready for the real world. According to undisclosed sources, the rule-based optimizer could be retired sometime in the near future. (We know you have been hearing this for a while, but that day may be nearing.)

Initialization Parameter Settings for the Oracle Optimizer

OPTIMIZER_MODE is the parameter that configures the Oracle instance for either rule-based or cost-based optimization. The default value (when not explicitly set in the init.ora) of this parameter is CHOOSE, and that is the required setting for cost-based optimization. The value setting of RULE is meant for rule-based optimization. There are two other values that it supports—ALL_ROWS and FIRST_ROWS—and we strongly recommend that you *do not set* those values in your initialization file, as they may not be appropriate for all of your applications.

If you need the FIRST_ROWS or ALL_ROWS optimization functionality, you have the option of setting OPTIMIZER_MODE either at the session level or incorporating a /*+ *hint* */ at the statement level. First, let us show you how to change the OPTIMIZER_MODE value at the session level:

```
SQL*Plus: Release 8.1.5.0.0 - Production on Fri Nov 3 16:04:31 2000
(c) Copyright 1999 Oracle Corporation.  All rights reserved.
Connected to:
Oracle8i Enterprise Edition Release 8.1.5.0.0 - Production
With the Partitioning and Java options
PL/SQL Release 8.1.5.0.0 - Production
SQL> alter session set OPTIMIZER_MODE=FIRST_ROWS /* Modifying OPTIMIZER_MODE just
for this session */;
Session altered.
```

What on Earth Is a Hint?

Well, it is pretty easy to explain a hint. Remember back when you were a kid and your birthday was coming and you *really* wanted that new bike or those new roller skates (we did not have cool rollerblades in those days)? You didn't come right out and ask your parents for them (well, those of you who were bolder may have). Instead, you started saying things like, "Gee, my skates are starting to hurt my feet," or "Mom, my knees are bent when I sit on my bike and my feet are on the ground." You were dropping some pretty strong hints. And, if your parents were like Oracle, they listened to what you wanted, and most of the time they made sure that it happened.

Believe it or not, that is exactly what the Oracle optimizer does, when you embed a /*+ *hint* */ in the SQL statement. Please observe that a hint looks very similar to a comment, with the exception of the + after the /*. It is important that you place the hint in the right location of a SQL statement for the Optimizer to recognize it. It should ideally be placed before the reference of the first column in the SQL statement.

The following example illustrates how to incorporate a statement-level hint. Please notice the location of the /*+ *hint* */ in the SQL statement:

```
SQL*Plus: Release 8.1.5.0.0 - Production on Fri Nov 3 16:04:31 2000
(c) Copyright 1999 Oracle Corporation.  All rights reserved.
Connected to:
Oracle8i Enterprise Edition Release 8.1.5.0.0 - Production
With the Partitioning and Java options
PL/SQL Release 8.1.5.0.0 - Production
select /*+ FIRST_ROWS */ Last_Name, Hire_Date, Salary
  from EMP
 where Mgr_id = 123;
```

NOTE
If you specify an invalid hint, the optimizer will ignore it, just like your parents did when you asked for something totally unreasonable (invalid). The optimizer will not notify you that your hint is incorrect, because an invalid hint is treated like a comment. It is your responsibility as the performance caretaker of your system to check the execution plan of your SQL statement and verify whether the hint was recognized and processed.

Many hints can be specified to control the execution plan the Oracle optimizer builds for SQL statements. A full list of the hints and their explanation can be found in the Oracle8i Tuning section of the Oracle documentation (mostly electronic these days) supplied with your Oracle software. If you are not running on Oracle8i, please refer to the appropriate Tuning section of your Oracle database version.

Which Optimizer Are You Running?

If the OPTIMIZER_MODE parameter is set to CHOOSE, the existence of statistics in the dictionary is what determines whether the cost-based optimizer will be used. In the absence of statistics for all objects in a SQL statement, rule-based optimization will be performed for that SQL statement. If statistics are generated, true cost-based optimization is possible, unless the OPTIMIZER_MODE setting is reset at the session level or is overridden by a statement-level /*+ *hint* */.

NOTE
If the table has a degree of parallelism on it, the cost-based optimizer will be used even if there are no statistics.

Be careful! It is important that statistics be generated for all objects in all of the application schemas (unless your third-party application does not support the cost-based optimizer). This is because the presence of partial statistics—say, for a *select* statement—could cause the server process servicing the SQL statement to *estimate* statistics on the objects without statistics only for the execution of that SQL statement. Such dynamic runtime sampling of statistics is not permanently stored in the data dictionary, and hence is repeated for every run of the same query. This can and will cause significant performance degradation. If your third-party application does not support cost-based optimization (that is, your application vendor has rule-based optimization and you really need to question their long-term vision), ensure that all statistics in your application's schema are deleted. It is easy to determine that by querying the *num_rows* column in the USER_TABLES view. If you see values for any tables, that implies there are statistics calculated for those tables. If partial statistics are present, the performance you will observe will be very unpredictable. This may annoy users more than consistently poor performance (the user may not be sure whether he can take a coffee break or just peek at his calendar while a given transaction is running). You definitely run the risk of runtime statistics calculation, which will significantly slow down the execution time of your application. So either calculate statistics for all objects or do not have any statistics for any of the objects, so that rule-based optimization will take effect.

NOTE
To determine the last time statistics were calculated for the objects in a given schema, you can query the Last_Analyzed *column in DBA_TAB_COLUMNS data dictionary view. You might want to run the query with the DISTINCT keyword, because the results returned are one row for each column in each table.*

Calculation of Object Statistics

In this section, you will get familiar with most of the aspects and issues you need to deal with when collecting object statistics. We will talk about why calculation of object statistics is important, how to go about collecting statistics, how much, how often, and the various issues you need to be aware of in collecting statistics.

Why Do You Need to Calculate Statistics?

The calculation of object-level statistics is a core performance-related administrative function of a DBA, as it is statistics that controls the behavior of the cost-based optimizer. Without the calculation of object statistics, the process of determining the cost of a SQL statement is done by Oracle using some internal hard-coded values.

How to Calculate Statistics

The calculation of statistics is accomplished via the **analyze** command. It is enough to run the **analyze** command for a table, as this command will calculate not only statistics for the table, but also for all indexes that are based on columns of that table. The calculation of statistics can be done in a couple of ways: you can either *estimate* the statistics based on a *sample* size, or you can just *compute* statistics for the entire object. The *estimate* should be the preferred method for databases with very large tables or environments that cannot afford the time or resources to perform a *compute*.

CAUTION
It is highly recommended that you do not generate object statistics for the user SYS, as you run the risk of deadlocking your database during this process. You also run the risk of having arbitrary performance degradation due to the existence of statistics in SYS's objects. Don't do it!

In Oracle8i, a new package called DBMS_STATS has been provided to perform and supplement the operations supported by the **analyze** command. Among operations that are supported are preparing for collection of statistics, improved calculation of statistics (parallel collection), transfer of statistics between the data dictionary and your *own* statistics tables, and getting information on statistics. Depending on your environment, you might want to use your own statistics tables (which are outside the data dictionary and hence do not affect the cost-based optimizer) to experiment with various statistical collections and optimization plans without running the risk of permanently replacing dictionary statistics and thus potentially degrading performance.

CAUTION
The direct use of DBMS_STATS is not supported and not advised on Oracle Application databases. Oracle Apps supplies its own statistics package (FND_STATS), which calls DBMS_STATS and also updates important statistics in the Application Object Library Schema as well.

In Oracle8i, the execution plans of your SQL statements can also be stabilized, so that they remain static. This concept is called *plan stability*. This is especially relevant for environments that cannot risk the change in execution plans of their applications, with changes in database version, changes in initialization parameters, data volumes in tables, and so on. Oracle supports plan stability using *stored outlines*, which allow you control over the execution plans of your applications.

The DBMS_STATS package and the Stored Outlines functionality contain considerable detail, and the discussion of the detail is beyond the scope of this book. For more information on the various features and syntax of the aforementioned two features, please refer to the Oracle8i Tuning section in the Oracle documentation.

How Much Statistics Is Enough?

If you *estimate* statistics on your objects based on a sample size, you need to ensure that your sample size is adequate so that the statistics will hold reasonable confidence for its accuracy. The sample size for statistics is important as it provides the optimizer with statistics that have a good confidence interval and hence statistical relevance. "Confidence Interval" is a term used in the field of Statistics to describe the level of confidence that one has in the accuracy of the statistics. This confidence interval is very much tied to the size of the sample population.

A sample size of 20 percent for *estimate* operations has been used many times and seems adequate. But there are some applications where a higher sample size is required. There are no hard and fast rules in this. You really need to determine what is the optimal minimum sample size that your application and database environment require. Obviously, if you *compute*, your confidence in your statistics is 100 percent, as it is truly accurate. But for environments that support very large tables, or that can't sustain the resource cost and time taken by a *compute*, *estimate* will be the viable option. Use your judgment to determine whether or not *compute* is right for you, based on the size of your objects, available downtime, and so on. Also, if your database version is Oracle8i, the DBMS_STATS package will allow you to analyze your tables in parallel, which can considerably reduce the amount of time it takes to perform a *compute*.

NOTE
You should be aware that performing an **analyze** *with the* estimate *option and a* sample *size that exceeds 49 percent of the table will cause a* compute *of the statistics on the table.*

NOTE
There may be some specific applications that are influenced by some unique data distributions, where an increase in the sample *size for an* estimate *operation may provide better plans and performance. However, the previous note should be kept in mind when increasing the* sample *size.*

Various Methods of Calculating Object Statistics

The following examples illustrate the various methods of calculating object statistics:

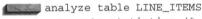

```
analyze table LINE_ITEMS
    compute statistics /* This calculation computes full
statistics for the LINE_ITEMS table and all of its indexes */;
```

or

```
analyze table LINE_ITEMS
   compute statistics
   for all indexed columns size 254 /* This calculation computes
histograms for all columns of all indexes on the LINE_ITEMS table.
The Size 254 is for the number of buckets utilized during the
calculation of the distribution of data */;
```

or

```
analyze table LINE_ITEMS
   estimate statistics
   sample size 20 percent  /* This calculation estimates statistics
for the LINE_ITEMS table and all of its indexes using a sample size
of 20 percent of the number of rows in the table */;
```

NOTE
*The **analyze** command also has options to analyze
a specific partition of a partitioned table or index.*

The *analyze_schema* procedure in the DBMS_UTILITY package allows calculation of statistics for an entire schema. The following sample execution calculates statistics for the BENCHMARK schema, with the *estimate* option, using 20 percent *sample size* on all objects. The \ character at the end of the first line in the following code sample is a "continuation" character:

```
SQL*Plus: Release 8.1.5.0.0 - Production on Fri Nov 3 16:07:33 2000
(c) Copyright 1999 Oracle Corporation.  All rights reserved.
Connected to:
Oracle8i Enterprise Edition Release 8.1.5.0.0 - Production
With the Partitioning and Java options
PL/SQL Release 8.1.5.0.0 - Production
SQL> execute dbms_utility.analyze_schema('BENCHMARK',\
'estimate',estimate_percent=>20);
PL/SQL procedure successfully completed.
```

The new object statistics package in Oracle8i, DBMS_STATS, allows calculation of statistics with various options. The following is an example that illustrates how to *estimate* statistics only on the tables of the BENCHMARK schema, with a sample size of 20 percent and with the default degree of parallelism on the tables. This command will not calculate statistics for indexes, as the cascade argument for the *gather_schema_statistics* procedure is set to *false* by default. Setting *cascade* to *true* allows calculation of statistics on *indexes* at the same time when statistics are calculated on tables. However, it should be noted that if indexes are analyzed along with the tables, any parallelism set on the collection of statistics for the tables does not apply to the indexes. If the indexes need to be analyzed in parallel, it is recommended to issue independent **gather_index_stats** commands to calculate statistics on those indexes in parallel. In the final analysis, make sure that statistics on all indexes are calculated, as you do not want partial statistics on your database.

```
SQL*Plus: Release 8.1.5.0.0 - Production on Fri Nov 3 16:08:12 2000
(c) Copyright 1999 Oracle Corporation.  All rights reserved.
Connected to:
Oracle8i Enterprise Edition Release 8.1.5.0.0 - Production
With the Partitioning and Java options
PL/SQL Release 8.1.5.0.0 - Production
SQL> execute dbms_stats.gather_schema_statistics('BENCHMARK',\
20,estimate_percent=>20);
PL/SQL procedure successfully completed.
```

NOTE

The gather_schema_statistics *procedure performs two operations. It first performs an* export_schema_stats *and then gathers the statistics for a schema. It is useful and important to know this, as your efforts to implement new statistics may sometimes cause a sudden degradation in performance (for whatever reason), and you should have a back-out plan. The running of the* import_schema_stats *to replace the new statistics with the old statistics should be part of your back-out plan. Also note that the* export_schema_stats *facilitates importing of these statistics using the* import_schema_stats *across databases. This is relevant when setting up test environments that are identical to the production environment (at least from the point of view of statistics). It is also relevant when the target database cannot afford a* gather_schema_stats *or gather_database_stats to be performed on it.*

The following SQL-generating-SQL script builds another script to automatically *analyze* the BENCHMARK schemas for all tables that begin with the letter A. This script is meant to be run as the user—SYS in SQL*Plus. You may want to use this script if your database version is not Oracle8i and you need to calculate statistics on specific objects within a schema, and the list of objects is dynamic.

"Job Security" Tips

The following tips can be classified under "job security." The more you know, the more secure your job will be!

- When you export one or more objects, ensure that the STATISTICS parameter is set to NONE, so that the import operation does not overlay the statistics you have already calculated. The default value for STATISTICS is ESTIMATE and some releases of Oracle have used a sample size of 1,064 rows. You need to be aware of this, as not setting *statistics=none* during the export operation or specifically recalculating the statistics after the import is done can result in significant performance degradation after the reorganization of the table is complete.

- When you *rebuild* your indexes, it is required that you reanalyze those indexes. Failure to do so can result in significant performance decrease, because the **rebuild** command will *estimate* statistics on the index with an internal sample size, which may be inadequate, replacing your previous statistics on that index. The automatic calculation of statistics during the rebuild can be done by incorporating the *estimate* or *compute* clause in the *rebuild* command (if your database version supports that feature). Please also note that any time you add a new index, you should immediately follow it with an *analyze* of that index. Otherwise the lack of statistics on the index will cause runtime performance problems until that index is analyzed.

- On some versions of Oracle (7.3.X, 8.0.4, 8.0.5, and others), a weird phenomenon has been observed with the *estimate* operation. From time to time, it has been noticed that the *estimate* operation does not fully *delete* the old statistics before calculating new statistics on the objects and this leaves the statistics in the data dictionary in a questionable state. A classic symptom of this problem is noticed when the same query is run on two databases (such as test and production) with the same amount of data and similar setup, but the performance of the same query is radically different in the two databases. If you experience such a weird phenomenon, it is recommended that you explicitly *delete* the statistics on the objects first, then *estimate* the statistics. Rerun the queries to use new statistics. That usually fixes the problem.

```
/* Set up environment for script file generation */
set echo off
set feedback off
```

```
set verify off
set pagesize 0
spool analyze_script.sql
/* Run query for script file generation */
select 'analyze table '||Owner||'.'||Table_name|| ' estimate
statistics sample size 20 percent;'
  from DBA_TABLES
 where Owner in ('BENCHMARK')
   and Table_Name like 'A%';
spool off

/* Run query script file to calculate statistics on all tables
based on a sample size of 20 percent */
@analyze_script.sql
set echo on
set feedback on
set verify on
set pagesize 23
```

How Often Should the Statistics Be Calculated?

The frequency of calculation of statistics is application and environment dependent. It solely depends on the rate and quantum of data change in your databases. If your databases encounter a significant change in the volume of data (application specific), combined with a potential change in the distribution of data, it is advisable to *analyze* your application schemas at the same frequency as the change of data. It is okay to have different schedules to analyze different sets of tables and indexes. Some could be analyzed daily, some weekly, and others monthly. Care needs to be taken that any unusual bulk insert or bulk purging of data is immediately followed by an *analyze*. This will ensure that the statistics in the dictionary match the actual number and distribution of rows in the table. If your table currently has 10,000,000 rows and your statistics reflect 5,000,000 rows, it is possible that the execution plan the optimizer builds may not be optimal.

With DBMS_STATS, you also have the option of *automatic* calculation of statistics on specific tables. This can be done by setting the *monitoring* option at the table level for the list of tables that require this feature. The tables you wish to monitor need to be *altered* and the *monitoring* attribute should be set to *yes*. The actual calculation of statistics on these tables can be done using the *dbms_stats.gather_ schema_stats* or *dbms_stats.gather_database_stats* procedures. These procedures have the capability to track the state of statistics for a given table and determine whether statistics for a given list of tables is *stale* or *empty*.

An object's statistics become *stale* when there has been a considerable amount of DML activity on the table. This is similar to the cross-country rally example that we shared with you in the chapter "Introduction to Oracle Performance Management." If your car has been on a cross-country rally covering thousands of miles, it is only fair that it gets an inspection, a tune-up, and an oil change after the rally. To expect a car to perform at optimal levels without any maintenance after such a long and arduous trip is being unrealistic (regardless of the car's manufacturer). The same applies to Oracle databases. When a significant amount of data purging, insertion, or update activities have been performed, the statistics of the tables in question will become *stale* and need recalculation. Expecting optimal performance without recalculation of statistics is far from being realistic.

Issues with Calculating Object Statistics

Depending on the release of your Oracle database, the **analyze** command does perform some level of locking during the calculation of object statistics. Although the locking was significantly more restrictive in early releases (if we recall correctly, in Oracle 7.2 the entire table was locked), the locking in newer releases is not that restrictive. But you should be aware of the locking and plan accordingly. You should also be aware that there may be some loss of performance for queries that access a given table that is currently being analyzed. This is because the execution plan for those queries could have been built during the time interval between deletion of old statistics and the calculation of new statistics, as part of an **analyze** operation. This means the statistics for the table in question were not present, hence the process running the query would have to calculate statistics at runtime. And don't forget that collecting statistics consumes CPU, memory, and I/O resources.

Optimal Indexing Strategies

As part of discussing the various issues that affect you in application tuning, the issue of formulating and implementing a meaningful indexing strategy has very high importance. This one aspect of your application in itself has great impact on the performance of your applications. So here is our take on indexing.

What Is an Index?

An index is a supplementary object that is created on one or more columns of a table to facilitate fast access to the data in the table. An index, by nature of its inherent structure, has some built-in overhead, and this overhead will outweigh the cost of doing a sequential full table scan, depending on the number of blocks visited in the table to retrieve the rows pointed by the ROWID in the index.

The data structure utilized by Oracle to store an index is a B*-*tree*. This is true even for bitmap indexes, although in the case of bitmap indexes, the content of the leaf node is different than that of a regular index.

The top node of an index is called the root node. The second-level nodes are called branch nodes, and the lowest-level nodes are leaf nodes. The upper blocks (branch nodes) of an index contain index data that points to lower-level index blocks. The lowest-level index blocks (leaf nodes) contain index data for every value and a corresponding ROWID used to locate the actual row. The leaf nodes themselves are connected using a double-linked list, which allows two-way traversal of the leaf nodes. Indexes in columns containing character data are based on the binary values of the characters in the database character set.

When a SQL statement uses an index, it is the root node that determines the side of the tree where the value is present, and the intermediary nodes provide location information on the values stored in the leaf nodes of the index. For those of you who are algorithm fans, the B*-*tree* search algorithm is similar to a binary tree search algorithm, with the exception that a B*-*tree* can have up to "n nodes" as children versus a binary tree, which can only have up to two children.

When to Use Indexes

Given that the sole purpose of an index is to reduce I/O, as a query performs more I/O using the index versus performing a full table scan, the usefulness of using an index diminishes significantly. For example, let us assume a table with 1,000,000 rows stored in 5,000 blocks, and further assume that the rows matching a given value of a column are disbursed over 4,000 blocks. In this case, it is definitely not optimal to create and use the index on that column. This is true even if the raw percentage of rows retrieved from the table is less than 1 percent, given that 80 percent of the total blocks in the table have to be visited to retrieve the data. When you add the index blocks that have to be visited to read the ROWID information from the index, the cost of using an index skyrockets and performance plummets. Hence, in this case it makes absolutely no sense to use an index.

Now for the flip side! If a table with 1,000 rows has undergone a significant amount of repetitive *insert* and *delete* operations, the high-water mark of the table will be high, as it does not get reset on *delete* operations. If the high-water mark is 1,000 blocks, but the 1,000 rows are physically located in 100 blocks, even though a query may be retrieving 100 percent of the rows in the table, it makes sense to use the index, as the number of blocks visited and I/O done will be significantly less than performing a full table scan. The obvious problem here is a fragmented table, but from a pure I/O perspective, the use of the index is still useful.

The Moral of the Story

The flaws of row selectivity while using indexes were first identified in a little-known article "Predicting the Utility of the Nonunique Index," by Cary Millsap, Craig Shallahamer, and M. Adler (*Oracle* magazine, Spring 1993, pages 48–53). The usefulness of an index was questioned from a pure row selectivity perspective. It is pretty clear that the use of an index for a query should *not* be determined by some arbitrary percentage of the rows processed or selected from the table, instead it should be determined by the number of blocks visited to retrieve the data. If the number of blocks visited for an index, is lower than a full table scan, then an index will be useful. Otherwise, a full table scan will provide much better performance. The criteria to use an index should not be based on row selectivity percentages, as it is impossible to set a specific percentage for all applications. Every application and database has its own idiosyncrasies, and generalizations on row selectivity and its relevance to indexes should be avoided, as no two applications behave alike. The needs of each application are unique and Performance Management should be tailored to those needs.

How to Build Optimal Indexes

Building optimal indexes is not one of the easiest to perform, because it is totally dependent on the application's data querying patterns. If you know your application, the problem is less complex. Can you summarize the most commonly utilized method of access of data from the LINE_ITEMS table? If the answer is yes, there lies your answer on how to build optimal indexes. You basically have to go through the list of columns that are used most often and make decisions as to the number of indexes you will build, the required column combinations, and the type of index you will build. You also need to consider availability needs, which will determine the type of index, especially when creating partitioned indexes. Here is a partial list of some fascinating indexing options:

- Non-unique index
- Unique index
- Bitmap index
- Local prefixed partitioned index
- Local nonprefixed partitioned index
- Global prefixed partitioned index
- Hash partitioned index
- Composite partitioned index
- Reverse-key index
- Function-based index
- Descending index
- Index-organized table
- One or more legal combinations of the above list

Answers You Need Before You Build Optimal Indexes

The answers to the following questions will also assist you in building optimal indexes:

1. How many blocks of I/O need to be performed for an index scan versus a full table scan?

   Answer If you know the answer to this, you will immediately know whether building and using an index makes performance sense.

2. What is the most common set of column combinations that are used for data access from a given table?

   Answer Dig into the application code. If it's not easily accessible, take a look at V$SQLAREA or V$SQLTEXT and analyze the most commonly used SQL statements. Look for the ones with a high number of *executions* in V$SQLAREA and find out what is the composition of their *where clause*.

3. What is the selectivity of a given set of columns on which you are planning to create an index?

   Answer If some columns will always have values and they are relatively unique, they should be the leading column or cutting-edge of your index. Order your columns for your index creation in decreasing order of the probability that it will have a unique value.

4. Do all the columns referenced in the *where clause* need indexing?

   Answer Not necessarily, if columns have very poor data cardinality and/or could have *null* values. You need to consciously eliminate such columns from your indexing list. Having such columns in your index does not do your query any good.

5. Is the table on which the index is created used for transactions or is it predominantly queried?

   Answer If you don't know this, you should find out! If it is a transactional table, you need to determine the potential negative impact to transaction times by the existence of that additional index. What is the trade-off between better query performance and the negative impact of transaction time? If it is a table predominantly used for queries, then it's okay to create the index, but you need to be aware of space-related issues in your INDX tablespace(s).

6. If the data in the table is updated, is it done in a batch process (one user and one massive update) or is it transactional (with many users and many small updates)?

Answer You should know; if not, spend some time finding out. This will assist you in making decisions on when to drop an index or make it unusable.

7. Do you need to keep the index for the batch process or can you *drop* it or make it *unusable*?

Answer You should know; if not, find out!

8. What are the storage implications of creating this new index (number of partitions if applicable, tablespace sizing, space utilized, and so on)?

Answer Plan for this, keeping your bigger storage, capacity planning, and storage budget picture in mind.

9. What downtime implications does this index have for the application?

Answer If you configure a global prefixed index on a partitioned table and if this table needs frequent online partition administration, the global index will be *unusable* for the time period between the partition maintenance operation and the rebuild of the entire global index. Is that okay?

10. How much downtime do you have to rebuild your indexes? (Not an issue in Oracle8i, as indexes can be built online, but for those of you not in Oracle8i, this is relevant.)

Answer If you have indexes on columns that are fed by an Oracle sequence, by design you will have monotonically increasing values in that column and also in the index. All new values will be stored to the right side of the B*-*tree* and you will need to rebuild those indexes periodically to rebalance the tree. How often can you do that? How many new records are inserted into that table every day? You'll have more questions as you answer this question.

NOTE
Since Oracle8, when entries into the index blocks are done with monotonically increasing values (inserts), the blocks are filled completely instead of leaving them 50 percent full as in prior versions. Also consider the use of reverse-key indexes for better random access. Beware of using reverse-key indexes for range scan; you will incur much more I/O than a normal index.

As you can see, answers do not come easily; they are quite complex. But the aforementioned guidelines will put you on the right path. One thing you should be aware of and work toward, from a performance standpoint, is how you minimize the overhead of using an index, so that it actually assists in performance rather than hinders. Bottom line: get to the leaf node of the index (which contains the data and their corresponding ROWIDS) in the quickest way you can. It will all boil down to questions 1 and 2.

Single-Column versus Composite Indexes

If you know that in your application the Ord_Id, Ord_Status, and Ord_Date columns are frequently used together, creating a composite index is much better than creating three individual single-column indexes. Also, be advised that any combination of usage of the Ord_Status and Ord_Date columns will still require only the following index. The following index will also suffice for SQL statements that use the Ord_Id column in their *where clause*. So your index creation should be something like this:

```
create index U_ORD_ID_STATUS_DATE on ORDERS
( Ord_Id,Ord_Date,Ord_Status)
tablespace INDX;
```

Function-Based Indexes

Function-based indexes are new to Oracle8i and involve creating the index with one or more functions such as *upper, lower, round* and so on, as part of your index creation. This allows the query to utilize this index rather than performing a full table scan. Prior to Oracle8i, any function or expression applied on an index column would cause the index to be ignored. Here is an example of how to create a function-based index:

```
create index U_ORD_ID_STATUS_DATE ON ORDERS
( upper(Ord_Id),Ord_Date,Ord_Status)
tablespace INDX;
```

A function-based index can also be created with a PL/SQL function embedded in it. Here is an example of creating an index with the *calc_profit* PL/SQL function embedded in it:

```
create index LINE_ITEM_CALC_PROFIT on LINE_ITEMS
(Calc_Profit(Item_Id, Item_Cost, Sticker_Price))
tablespace INDX;
```

The following query utilizes the *line_item_calc_profit* function-based index to determine the LINE_ITEMS that generate more than $1,000 in profit:

```
select Ord_Id, Item_Id, Item_Cost, Sticker_Price
  from Line_Items
 where Calc_Profit(Item_Id, Item_Cost, Sticker_Price) > 1000;
```

When Do You Need to Rebuild Your Indexes?

Since an index is stored in a B*-*tree*, and the ultimate goal of an index is to provide quick access to the data in a table, it is pretty obvious that any index lookup needs to occur with the fewest possible node/block reads (reduction of I/O is key to an index's usability). The single most relevant factor here is the number of leaf blocks that need to be accessed. The smaller the number of leaf blocks in an index, the fewer I/O operations a index will impose and the faster you can retrieve the rows from the table. Having said that, it should be noted that indexes on tables that undergo repeated insert and delete operations face the highest risk of fragmentation.

Now the question is, how fragmented are the leaf blocks in a given index? Is there a significant number of leaf blocks that are read and empty? So it is extremely important to determine the *leaf block density* of an index. The denser the contents of the leaf blocks, the better health the index is in. It is very useful to determine the density by running a script that retrieves the number of row values in the column(s) of the index and number of leaf blocks present in the index.

For example, if there are 1,000 row values and 10 leaf blocks today, the leaf block density is equal to 1,000/10 = 100 rows. If a week from today the number of rows is 1,200, but there are 20 leaf blocks, the leaf block density is equal to 1,200/20 = 60 rows. In raw numbers, there has been a 20 percent increase in the number of rows, but a 40 percent decrease in leaf block density. It is time to rebuild this index, and it potentially contains a lot of empty blocks.

Another data dictionary view that provides detailed information about indexes is INDEX_STATS. This data dictionary view is populated when an **analyze index index_name validate structure** command is executed. You can run this command for a specific index on which you are trying to get more information. INDEX_STATS also contains a column called *Height*, and this column starts counting from 1. Don't ask why—it is part of your job security. You might also observe, based on the data distribution of the underlying table, that some rebuild operations do not decrease the height of an index. Don't try to fight that phenomenon, unless there are plans to significantly change the underlying table or application design.

NOTE
*The **analyze index index_name validate structure** command populates INDEX_STATS with one row, but does not retain the row in INDEX_STATS across multiple sessions. The row in this view will be removed when you exit your session. If you need to save this information, please do so in a table of your choice. This "feature" has been observed since Oracle 7.3.0 and still exists even in Oracle 8.1.7.*

It is obvious here that planning downtime for rebuilding your indexes (unless you are in Oracle8i, which supports online rebuilds) is a required component of your job description. And when you rebuild, you need to do it quickly and efficiently. The two factors that assist you in your rebuilding efforts are parallelism and prevention of redo generation. The first can be achieved by setting the *parallel clause* in the ALTER index...**rebuild** command. The second can be achieved by using the *unrecoverable clause* (prior to Oracle 8.0) or the *nologging clause* (Oracle 8.0 or above). Please note that the relevant parallel query initialization parameters need to be set in the init.ora before any parallel operations are attempted. This is covered in detail in the chapter "Parallel Query Tuning."

```
alter index U_ORD_ID_STATUS_DATE rebuild
   parallel (degree 4)
   nologging
   tablespace INDX
/* You can use the ONLINE clause for the above statement if your
database version is Oracle8i or above */;
```

NOTE
It usually makes no business sense to generate redo logs when you rebuild your indexes. Not generating redo logs and rebuilding your indexes using the parallel clause *will facilitate quick and efficient rebuilding of your indexes. For that reason, it is customary to schedule a backup of the index tablespace(s) after the rebuild operation, to reduce the risk of downtime if a media failure were to occur in the index tablespace(s) before the next full backup.*

You should also compact or coalesce the leaf nodes of an index by using the *coalesce* option in the *alter index* statement. This facilitates combination of leaf blocks and/or levels in an index, so that free blocks could be reused. Realize that an empty index block does not get reused until the index is coalesced or the index is rebuilt. Over time, leaf blocks can get fragmented due to block splits. All in all, the height of an index is one of the keys to reducing the amount of I/O on that index and thus should be closely monitored. Use this option on those indexes that undergo a significant amount of repetitive *insert* and *delete* operations.

Which Join Method Should You Use, and When?

Monitoring and choosing the type of join operation can provide good performance improvements. Actually, choosing the right join mechanism and the right index can provide the some of the greatest positive impacts on SQL performance. There are three join methodologies available since Oracle 7.3. These are sort merge join, nested loops join and the newest, hash joins. Each offers different performance characteristics and is suitable for different situations. The challenge, as usual, is to evaluate the requirements and structure the SQL to provide the best access path for the operation.

A *sort merge* join is a set operation. This means that each step of a sort merge join must be completed before the data can be passed on to the next step. A set operation works on all rows as a single unit. Sort merge joins should be considered when indexing is not available to the query. Inability to use an index could be caused by the lack of an appropriate index that supports the *where clause* or perhaps a function was used on the indexed column in the *where clause.*

A *nested loops* join is a row operation and is often preferred for transactional processing. It can send processed rows from one step to the next step before having completed all processing in the previous step. The nested loops join methodology reminds us of the first programming class we took many years ago. Notable in that class was the assignment where we had to write a Pascal program to manipulate a two-dimensional array. We had to use a loop within a loop—nested loops—to accomplish that.

A *nested loops* join is the most commonly seen join operation for OLTP applications and is usually fairly efficient. This is because this join methodology makes use of indexes to a high degree and, given that every application vendor seems to be indexing their tables to death, this join method works. Unfortunately, if your system has too many wacky indexes on its tables, you could end up with the nested loops method when full table scans with merge or hash joins could give better performance. Watch out for that!

A *hash joins* is quite different because the implementation is mostly done using full table scans of the tables that are joined. Oracle performs a full table scan on each of the tables and splits each into as many hash partitions (not to be confused with table and index partitioning) as necessary based on the available memory. Oracle then builds a hash table from one of the hash partitions. If possible, Oracle will select a partition that fits into available memory. It then uses the corresponding partition in the other table to probe the hash table. For each pair of partitions (one from each table), Oracle uses the smaller one to build a hash table and the larger one to probe the hash table. All partition pairs that do not fit into memory are written to disk.

Hash joins were introduced in Oracle 7.3. To make the best use of them, you need to configure the initialization parameters *HASH_AREA_SIZE* and *HASH_MULTIBLOCK_IO_COUNT*. Hash joins are useful for joining large tables to each other or when a small table is joined with a very large table and the *where clause* predicates process of a significant portion of the large table. Even though Oracle will incur a lot of I/O doing full table scans on both tables, it will more than make up for it with the speed of joining the rows in memory and moving rows from and to the disk. One caveat, though: if the tables are large, you should expect a certain amount of physical I/O as Oracle writes the hash segments that it created in memory to disk for further processing. You can set *hash_area_size* appropriately to minimize this, and this parameter can be set at the session level.

NOTE
Setting HASH_AREA_SIZE *and* HASH_MULTIBLOCK_ IO_COUNT *to very high values can cause the Oracle optimizer to prefer and pick hash joins as the default optimization plan. Care needs to be taken to balance the setting of these parameters with the transactional needs of your system. We will cover this in more detail in the chapter "InstanceTuning—The Redo Log Buffer and Miscellaneous Tuning."*

When selecting a methodology, consider the size of the tables, the selectivity of the indexes, and the availability of the tables. Most importantly, test the choices and see which returns data in the least elapsed time and/or with the least physical I/O. These last two points are what define a well-tuned SQL statement.

How Not to Write SQL

The focus of this chapter is to prep you, the DBA, for the application-tuning challenges ahead of you. In doing so, it is relevant to document some bad SQL programming practices that we have encountered, which have been observed to kill application performance on a consistent basis. This is by no means a comprehensive list. Some of the pitfalls (where applicable) contain code examples that show you the before and after. These are things to avoid and/or rewrite. Here are some not-so-best practices for writing SQL statements that should be avoided:

- Disallow the use of indexes when the *where clause* predicates for SQL statements visit more data blocks when using an index, rather than performing a full table scan. This can be done either by applying a harmless expression on the indexed column (such as +0 for a numeric column, or concatenate a null string '' for an alphanumeric column) or by hinting the SQL statement with a FULL hint (if you are using the cost-based optimizer).

  Consider the following:

  1. The LINE_ITEMS table has 1,000,000 rows in it.

  2. There is an index on the Shipped_Date column and it is used by the following query.

  3. The distribution of data on the Shipped_Date column is such that the rows are disbursed across a significant number of blocks in the table.

  4. The selectivity of the index is good.

  Before:

  ```
  select *
    from LINE_ITEMS
   where Shipped_Date between SYSDATE
     and (SYSDATE - 30);
  ```

  The preceding query uses the index on the Shipped_Date column, even though it is not optimal to do so. Hence, the above query needs to be hinted with a FULL (to force a full table scan) and may be even a PARALLEL hint (need to set init.ora parameters for this before you use it), given the size of the LINE_ITEMS table. The query is rewritten as:

  After:

  ```
  select /*+ FULL(LINE_ITEMS) PARALLEL(LINE_ITEMS, 2) */ *
    from LINE_ITEMS
   where Shipped_Date between SYSDATE
     and (SYSDATE - 30);
  ```

- Disallow full table scans, when the *where clause* predicates for SQL statements process or return a very small portion of the table, unless the table is highly fragmented (small number of rows in a few blocks, but the high-water mark is very high). An obvious exception to this rule is if the table itself is very small (the definition of small is relative to the size of your database). This can be done by explicitly providing an INDEX hint or by creating appropriate indexes for the table. Be cautious when creating additional indexes, especially on tables that are transactional in nature, as they will impact the time it takes to *insert, update* or *delete* rows into that table. Consider the following:

1. The ORDERS table has 1,00,000 rows in it.

2. The Ord_Id column can contain alphanumeric values (combination of numbers and alphabetic data) and the values are stored in uppercase. But the application allows entry of the Ord_Id in upper- or lowercase.

3. There is a composite index on the Ord_Id, Ord_Status, and Ord_Date columns.

4. The selectivity of the index is good.

Before:

```
select *
  from ORDERS
 where upper(Ord_Id) = ':b1'
   and Ord_Status = 'Not Filled'
   and Ord_Date = SYSDATE;
```

The preceding query does not use the index, because the *upper* function has been applied on the leading column of the index, thus preventing the use of the index. The bind variable ':b1' is on the right side of the expression. Removing the *upper* function from the leading column of the index and moving it to the right side of the expression allows the index to be used. The query is rewritten as follows:

After:

```
select *
  from ORDERS
 where Ord_Id = upper(':b1')
   and Ord_Status = 'Not Filled'
   and Ord_Date = SYSDATE;
```

If the values in the Ord_Id column are not stored in any predetermined format—such as uppercase—and the database version is Oracle8i, function-based indexes could be created to prevent the full table scan. If your database version is prior to Oracle8i, consider storing the values for this column in some standard case (*upper, lower,* or *initcap*). Yes, you are denormalizing your data, but the founding fathers of relational databases and normalization rules will understand your predicament and forgive you.

- Do not mix and match values with column data types. This will result in the optimizer ignoring the index. For example, if the column data type is a *number, do not* use single quotes around the value in the *where clause.* Likewise, do not fail to use single quotes around a value when it is defined as an alphanumeric column. For example, if a column is defined as a *varchar2(10)* and if there is an index built on that column, reference the column values within single quotes. Even if you only store numbers in it, you still need to use single quotes around your values in the *where clause,* as not doing so will result in a full table scan.

- Do not use the *is null* operator on a column that is indexed, as the optimizer will ignore the index.

- Do not build applications that contain SQL statements that are identical except for their hard-coded values for their *where clauses.* This effect is normally observed in applications that build dynamic SQL. By their inherent design, hard-coded values in the *where clause* prevent reusability of the SQL statements in the shared pool area. Supporting multiple SQL statements with hard-coded values in the shared pool area begs the issue of huge amounts of memory allocation for that memory structure. This is because the application that you support is designed in such a way that it prevents anything from being shared.

  Before:

  ```
  select First_Name, Last_Name, Hire_Date
    from EMP
   where Empno = 1234;

  select First_Name, Last_Name, Hire_Date
    from EMP
   where Empno = 9876;
  ```

  After:

  ```
  select First_Name, Last_Name, Hire_Date
     from EMP
   where Empno = :b1;
  ```

  If the application *cannot be recoded* with bind variables, and if the database version is Oracle8i (8.1.6), using the init.ora parameter *CURSOR_SHARING=force* will help significantly. Not only will you introduce the novel concept of SQL sharing, but you will also reduce the amount of library cache latch contention. The parameter

CURSOR_SHARING can also be set at the session level. You should know that setting CURSOR_SHARING=force can cause some significant parsing delays, so ideally rewriting the application should be the preferred method.

■ Do not code iterative single *insert, update,* or *delete* statements on a table within a PL/SQL loop when they can be done in bulk. This is a classic iterative PL/SQL application design performance problem. For example, if a bulk *insert* is feasible and the operation does not need recovery, it can be performed with the /*+ APPEND */ hint, which will provide direct-load capability and virtually eliminate redo generation for that operation. Unfortunately, this option is not available for the *delete* and *update* operations. At any rate, operations that can be done in bulk should not be done in an iterative fashion, as the operations themselves will not scale, when the number of rows iteratively processed increases in a significant manner. Following is one example:

Before:

```
declare
   Ord_Struct ORDERS%ROWTYPE;
   Cursor c_ord  is
      select *
        from ORDERS
       where Ord_Status = 'Not Filled'
         and Ord_Date = SYSDATE;
begin
open c_ord;
loop
   fetch c_ord into Ord_Sturct;
   exit when c_ord%NOTFOUND;
insert into TEMP_ORD values (Ord_Struct.Ord_Id, Ord_Struct.Ord_Date,
(Ord_Struct.Ord_Price * 1.1),Ord_Struct.Ord_Status);
commit;
end loop;
close c_ord;
end;
/
```

The preceding PL/SQL block of code is a simplified example that uses the classic iterative technique to input and calculate values for processing. It calculates the new price for TEMP_ORD by increasing it by 10 percent. The equivalent code below will accomplish the same in a fraction of the time and cost it would take to run the above code. This is true even if the /*+ APPEND */ hint cannot be used.

Please note that the *nologging* attribute on the TEMP_ORD table should be set before the following is attempted. This can be accomplished by executing an **alter table** command. And, yes, that means Oracle will not perform full-fledged logging for your *insert* operations, which implies that if the job gets terminated due to any kind of failure, the data in TEMP_ORD is unrecoverable. But given the temporary nature of the job, all you will have to do is to restart it after the failure is resolved. Also note that the commit in the tuned version is done once for the entire operation, instead of once per iteration of the loop.

After:

```
declare

begin

insert  /*+ APPEND */ into TEMP_ORD
  select Ord_Id, Ord_Date, (Ord_Price * 1.1),Ord_Status
    from ORDERS
   where Ord_Status = 'Not Filled'
    and Ord_Date = SYSDATE;
commit;
end;
/
```

■ Do not code correlated subqueries in your applications, as they will adversely impact system performance, consume significant amounts of CPU resources, potentially cause CPU bottlenecks, and disallow application scalability. This means if the number of rows in your table in your correlated subquery increases, you are personally writing the death certificate of your CPUs. Alternatively, use *inline views* (subqueries in the *from clause* of your *select* statements which have been available from version 7.3), which perform orders of magnitude faster and are much more scalable. The query below displays all employees who make more than the average salary of the department that they work in. Watch the fun!

Before:

```
select OUTER.*
  from EMP OUTER
 where OUTER.Salary >
   (select Avg(Salary)
       from EMP INNER
     where INNER.Dept_Id = OUTER.Dept_Id);
```

The preceding query contains a correlated subquery, which is extremely inefficient and is very CPU intensive. The subquery will be run for every employee record in the EMP table. As the number of records in EMP increase, the performance can degrade exponentially. This query will artificially increase the database buffer cache-hit ratio to such heights that you will think that your database is performing well, when in reality it is not. The query when rewritten with inline views is functionally equivalent, but is significantly more scalable and is guaranteed to outperform its predecessor.

After:

```
select E1.*
    from EMP E1, (select E2.Dept_Id Dept_Id, Avg(E2.Salary) Avg_Sal
                    from EMP E2
                  group by Dept_Id) DEPT_AVG_SAL
  where E1.Dept_Id = DEPT_AVG_SAL.Dept_id
   and E1.Salary > DEPT_AVG_SAL.Avg_Sal;
```

■ This one is a no-brainer, but we have to mention it for the sake of completeness. Do not build the *where clause* predicates for a *select* statement without having all the join conditions for all tables in your *from clause.* You do not want Mr. Descartes around to assist you with a Cartesian product in your query execution plan. You will be surprised how many SQL statements we've found that did not have this critical component.

■ Do not code the transaction logic of your applications literally in the sequence that is specified in the design document. That sounds pretty radical, but let us explain. Realize that both SQL and PL/SQL allow combination of multiple operations into one. Let us provide you an example. The design document defines the transaction logic as follows: 1 million rows should be inserted into a temporary table, followed by 12 updates on all of those rows in sequence. But you really don't have to do exactly that. Investigate the use of the *decode* function (it supports *if..then..else..end if* logic within the SQL statement) in your *insert* statement to avoid as many *update* statements as possible. In fact, *decode* is amazingly powerful and, if treated just so, can be used to do *greater than* or *less than* operations. Investigate the use of the outer join (+) operator; it is useful in quite a few applications and facilitates multiple operations to be combined into a single operation. Remember that it is okay to perform some additional computation for the *insert* operation, thus making it slower. On the other hand, the resource and computational savings of not performing one or more *update* statements will justify the additional cost on the *insert* operation. Just trying to optimize the response time of each SQL statement without focusing on the total response time of the batch job makes no computational and resource management sense. The following pseudo code is for a *create table* statement that combines multiple operations into one and optimizes the use of resources:

```
create table DM_SUMMARY_TBL
     ( Fact_Id
      ,D2_Key
      ,D1_key
      ,Datekey
      ,D2_Col
      ,D1_Col1
      ,D1_Col2
     )
parallel (degree 12)
nologging
partition by range (datekey)
 (P1 values less than…P36 values less than NOMAXVALUE)
as
select /*+ FULL(F) FULL(D1) FULL(D2) */
       F.Fact_Id,
       F.D2_Key,
       F.D1_Key,
       F.Datekey,
       D2.D2_Col,
       D1.D1_Col1,
       D1.D1_Col2
   from FACT F, DIMENSION1 D1, DIMENSION2 D2
 where D1.D1_key(+) = F.D1_Key
   and F.D2_key = D2.D2_Key(+);
```

■ Do not force every SQL statement to be executed using the nested loops join methodology. While most transactional SQL statements do perform optimally using this methodology, certain batch jobs definitely will benefit from the use of hash joins. For example, if your *select* statement joins two or more tables and the join pairs in the *where clause* are such that one of the tables is very small (say, 1,000 rows) and the other is very large (say, 1,000,000), and if the *where clause* predicates are such that a significant portion of the large table will be processed, hash joins should be the preferred join methodology for that join pair. If you religiously attempt to eliminate full table scans by forcing every SQL statement in your environment to use nested loops, you will end up with an Oracle database with a fantastic 99.999 percent buffer cache-hit ratio, but whose performance would leave a lot to be desired.

■ Avoid the use of **select *x* from DUAL;** wherever possible. As innocent as this looks, it can eat up system performance in a hurry. For example, if a numeric column needs to be populated by a sequence generator, do not code an independent *select* statement to select its *nextval* into a PL/SQL variable and then use the value of the variable in the *values clause* of the *insert* statement. Alternatively, use the *nextval* operation on the sequence (*sequence_name.nextval*) in the *values clause* of the *insert* statement. Observe the key difference between the before and after code shown below. The after code has the unnecessary references to the table DUAL removed.

Before:

```
declare
   Ord_Seq_Val ORDERS.Ord_Id%TYPE;
begin
for i in 1..10000
loop
   select Ord_Seq.NEXTVAL
     into Ord_Seq_Val
     from DUAL;
   insert into TEMP_ORD(Ord_Id)
     values (Ord_Seq_Val);
/* Do more misc. processing */
end loop;
/
```

After:

```
declare
begin
for i in 1..10000
loop
   insert into TEMP_ORD(Ord_Id)
     values (Ord_Seq.NEXTVAL);
/* Do more misc. processing */
end loop;
/
```

■ And lastly (this one is not for Performance Management, but rather, for sanity management), do not design table/column names and write SQL statements in a foreign language (such as Pali or Prakrit). Use meaningful aliases, consistent naming conventions, and for the sake of Jamba, please desist from using your native language if you want any one of us to help you out when you have a problem. We have one ERP vendor who forces us to be bilingual. Enough already!

The Basics of Optimal SQL

Now that we have been through the list of what not to do, allow us to introduce you to the things we think you should consider while designing, rewriting, and tuning SQL statements. If you avoid the potholes described in the previous section, you will be closer to the desired path of coding optimal SQL.

The ultimate goal in writing any SQL statement has three facets: quick response times, the least usage of your CPU's resources, and the fewest number of I/O operations. But many a time, you may have to compromise on one of the three facets. While quick response times of individual SQL statements are often a required component, it is not the end of all SQL statements. The key thing to remember here is *system throughput*. How successful are you in getting through your day, doing everything you need to get done in a timely and accurate fashion?

For example, if it makes sense for a given SQL statement to do a full table scan from the perspective of processing, you may end up reading more blocks than, say, an index lookup. But if the index lookup takes twice as long to complete, even though from the pure sense of I/O it is better, it actually hinders system throughput. This is because your system could have been utilized to process other operations if the job had been completed in half the time.

Tips for Facilitating Optimal SQL

The following are a few tips, in no particular order, for optimizing SQL performance. These tips are not restricted to just queries:

- Encouraging full table scans when using an index does not make sense from an I/O perspective. Keep in mind that a full table scan will be very effective when using an index is counterproductive, such as when the index scan performs more block visitations than a full table scan.

- If your SQL contains subqueries, tune them. In fact, tune them first. The main query will not perform well if the subqueries can't perform well themselves. If a join will provide you with the functionality of the subquery, try the join method first, before trying the subquery method. Pay attention to correlated subqueries, as they tend to be very costly and CPU-intensive.

- Use *not exists* instead of *not in* in the *where clause* predicates of your SQL statements.

- Use the *like* operator with a leading character instead of a *substr* function. The *like* operator with a leading character such as 'A%' in the value that is compared will use the index. The *substr* function will invalidate the index, unless your database version is Oracle8i and you have created a function-based index.

■ Use the *nvl* function wherever appropriate, as it does not require you to know the data type of the column on which the function is applied and hence greatly reduces the probability of accidental typecasting. Secondly, *nvl* was observed to be microscopically faster than concatenation (if you have a choice to do a concatenation versus an NVL) by some performance analysts in the early 1990s.

■ For very complex queries with many OR conditions, consider rewriting them using *union all*. By doing so, you will break down the query into good-size chunks and will be able to optimize better. This works on the concept of divide and rule.

■ Use appropriate indexes. That means only create and use the most selective indexes possible. Data selectivity is the ratio of distinct keys to rows. The closer it is to 1.00, the better it is, and the more sense it makes to consider creating an index on that column. Appropriate indexes will not only improve access, but also eliminate the overhead of updating many useless indexes when the data in the table is updated.

■ Create indexes on foreign key columns if the queries always retrieve master-detail relationship-based rows.

■ Make use of composite indexes (indexes with two or more columns). These need to be ordered in the decreasing order of selectivity. Fewer indexes used within a specific query imply fewer physical I/O operations in most cases, which in turn translates to better performance.

■ Consider using non-unique indexes to support the *unique* constraint. This is supported in Oracle8 and above and is very powerful. The greatest advantage here is that the index is not dropped when the constraint is *disabled*. This also eliminates redundant indexes. For example, if a *primary key* constraint needs to be created on the Ord_Id column in the ORDERS table, it does not require an independent *unique* index if another composite index with Ord_Id as the leading column already exists.

■ Consider using the *enable novalidate clause* while enabling constraints, as they do not perform a data check of your data. This is especially true if you have summary tables that contain data from one or more base tables, and the integrity of the data is already checked in the base tables.

■ Consider bitmap indexes when the *where clause* predicates contain low-data-cardinality columns, contain logical operations such as *or, and,* or *not* on those columns, or return a large number of rows from a table with a large number of rows. Bitmap indexes are usually avoided on tables with heavy concurrent DML operations, due to their inherent locking behavior, which is based on a range of *rowids*, even if the number of rows that need to be updated is only one.

■ Consider single-table hash or index clusters (depending on your application), as they provide excellent performance on those tables that are relatively static, but are normally queried for a range of values. Given that a cluster stores the data within a block in an ordered fashion, a range scan using an index on this cluster will perform fewer I/O operations to service the query.

■ Beware of SQL statements with views in them. Odd as it may seem, Oracle does not necessarily execute a view the same way by itself as it does in a complex SQL statement containing tables. Consider including the view definition in the main query by actually including its code without the actual view name. In some cases, we have observed significant performance improvement, as there were documented problems with how the optimizer dealt with the views and tables when faced with a complex multitable and multiview join.

■ Avoid remote access when possible. Be particularly careful when joining a local table to a remote table or view. Oracle (depending on your version) can end up sending the entire remote table to the local database to resolve the join. This can foul up performance of not only the query, but also the network.

■ Proactively decide on nested loops, merge joins, or hash joins. When doing a join of three or more tables, try to structure the query to do the greatest elimination on the first join. This can often be done by incorporating all of the restrictive *where clause* conditions on one table. The result is a smaller driving set.

■ Identify and use array processing and bulk collections whenever relevant and wherever possible. This is true even if your processing environment is PL/SQL. Here is an example of how to set up array processing in PL/SQL. This example retrieves a significant portion of the values in the Product_Id column (using the new *bulk collect* feature in Oracle8i) and then utilizes those values to decrease the Reorder_Level column values of those PRODUCTS table by 20 percent. The reduction in reorder levels has been initiated due to some recent inventory management process re-engineering that has been implemented.

```
declare
TYPE Ord_Id_Tab IS TABLE OF PRODUCTS.Product_Id%TYPE;
begin

/* Retrieve all values of Product_Id that are relevant /
select /+ FULL (PRODUCTS) */ Product_Id BULK COLLECT into
Product_Id_Tab;
    from PRODUCTS
  where Product_Name like 'A%';
```

```
forall i in 1..Product_Id_Tab.LAST
  update PRODUCTS
    set REORDER_LEVEL = (REORDER_LEVEL * 0.8)
  where Product_Id = Product_Id_Tab(i);
/* Do more processing */
end;
/
```

NOTE
Although there may be other methods to implement this functionality, the goal here is to provide some insight into these new powerful processing capabilities of PL/SQL.

■ If the database version is Oracle8i and the application contains a lot of dynamic SQL generation (using DBMS_SQL), consider using the new PL/SQL feature *execute immediate*, which performs significantly better than DBMS_SQL. The following is a simple PL/SQL block that uses *execute immediate* to increase the column width of the Ord_Id column in the ORDERS table from its current size of 8 to 10. This new feature also supports DDL commands within PL/SQL without having to write many lines of code to accomplish something really simple:

```
declare
begin
execute immediate 'alter table ORDERS modify (Ord_Id VARCHAR(10))';
end;
/
```

■ For very large tables, consider taking advantage of table and index partitioning. Very large tables pose special challenges because of the way they impact the consumption of space in the database buffer cache of the Oracle SGA. Partitioning should be designed and planned keeping in mind the requirements of the application.

■ If you are still using the rule-based optimizer (you really should not be using this for much longer), structure your *from clause* so that your smallest table is the last one defined in the list of tables.

■ If you need to speed up the time it takes for an index build, you can modify the *sort_area_size* parameter at the session level to a large value, so that most of the sorting for the index build will occur in memory.

■ Last but not least, you need to continually test all of your queries. Keep in mind that as the data changes, the execution plan may change and not necessarily for the better. What worked well six months ago may be a real mess now. Remember, you need to perform maintenance inspections on your car frequently. The whole key to Performance Management is the management aspect.

NOTE
In the cost-based optimizer, there is really no relevance of the order of the tables in a from clause, *unless you use the /*+ ORDERED */ hint, in which case the driving table for your join will be the first table in your* from clause. *Also, in the cost-based optimizer, there is really no relevance to the order of the* where clause *predicates. As long as you reference the leading column of an index in your* where clause, *it will be considered for the execution plan.*

In a Nutshell

Eighty percent of your performance problems arise due to bad SQL. Designing and developing optimal SQL is quintessential to scalable system performance and consistent response times. As a DBA, you need to be aware of the type of optimization methodology you are using, the method and frequency of calculating statistics, optimal indexing strategies, and selecting the right join methodology for a given SQL statement. Remember, it is not always beneficial to use an index. Care needs to be taken to identify this on a case-by-case basis.

While we identified some commonly observed pitfalls of SQL programming, there is more to optimal application design and tuning than what we or anyone else can write. It is like an endless ocean. What we have shared with you here is a few buckets and what we all need to know far exceeds what we currently know. Isn't life wonderful when you learn something new every single day? But knowing that you can dramatically transform system-wide performance by just adding an index, changing the join methodology of a SQL statement, or providing a /*+ HINT */ is very powerful. Again, we are talking about many orders of magnitude in potential performance increase. Go get those bad SQL and fix them. Make it a habit...and stick with it.

CHAPTER
4

Application Tuning—
Tracking Down Bad SQL

Myth & Folklore

If a job runs for eight hours, you really need to trace it for the entire duration to get complete information on the badly performing SQL statements.

Fact

You do not need to wait eight hours to find out what is wrong with the job, especially if the job is *iterative* in nature. A trace file with, say, an hour of information will provide you plenty of insight into the culprit SQL statements that are causing the job to run that long. If a job has 16 SQL statements in it, chances are that if you fix the top three or four SQL statements, you probably would have fixed the performance problem of the entire job. We have walked into performance troubleshooting engagements where the culprit jobs allegedly ran for two and a half days. We would have been fired on the spot, if we had even suggested that we had to wait for two and a half days before we could begin suggesting corrective action for the performance problem. An hour or so does the trick most of the time; some unique situations may need more time.

ans of Sherlock Holmes, get ready. We are going on an investigative mission. Tracking down bad SQL that makes your applications run like snails requires perseverance just like finding out the details in a crime scene. And since you are the DBA, it is your job to get to the bottom of those SQL statements that can potentially leave your system in a crippled state and have you wondering why on earth you aren't sipping mai tais on an exotic beach in the Caribbean instead. Make no mistake, you need the right tools in this effort, you need to understand how to use these tools, but most importantly you need the *right mindset*. You need to look out for those clues that are particularly elusive. Everything may look perfectly normal on the outside, but when the numbers don't add up, you know there is something else lurking out there. Another important decision you will have to make is whether you tune a query performing 1,000,000 logical I/Os that is run once a day or tune a query that performs one logical I/O, but is run 1,000,000 times a day. Which one should you work on? Are there any systemwide differences in tuning one versus the other? Your application, the environment, the load on the system when the queries are run, and the time of day when the queries are run will all provide you with the answers to the above questions.

The SQL Statement Tuning Process

Following are the steps in the SQL statement tuning process:

1. Ensure TIMED_STATISTICS is set to TRUE at the instance level (set it permanently in the init.ora or set it temporarily by executing an **alter system** command).

2. Ensure MAX_DUMP_FILE_SIZE is set high enough. This controls the size of your trace file.

3. Determine the location pointed to by USER_DUMP_DEST, and make sure there is plenty of free disk space. This is the home of your trace files.

4. Turn on SQL_TRACE for the session in question.

5. Run the application.

6. Locate the trace files.

7. Run *tkprof* (transient kernel profile) on the trace file that was located in step 4, to generate a trace output file.

8. Study the trace output file.

9. Tune the most expensive SQL statements.

10. Repeat steps 4 through 9 until required performance goals are achieved.

How to Trace SQL?

Tracing SQL statements can be compared to tracing or tapping into a suspect's telephone call not only to get all the details about the conversations, but also to determine the originating point of the call (probably to find out the accomplices to the crime).

NOTE
It is important to note here that running the application with meaningful and relevant data is essential to the information that will be collected by the tracing facility. If the data retrieved or manipulated is not realistic, the trace output will also not be realistic. Also, if you are running the cost-based optimizer, ensure the validity of your statistics. When was the last time you analyzed tables and indexes? How much data has been infused into your tables since then? Are your statistics even valid today? Further, ensure that all relevant init.ora parameters are set. If you have configured Oracle in MTS mode, ensure that your current connection (for SQL tracing) is in the dedicated mode, so the trace output will not be split across multiple files.

The tracing of SQL statements can be done in several ways. It basically involves setting the SQL_TRACE parameter at the session level. But before you start tracing

SQL statements, the following Oracle initialization parameters (if applicable) need to be set or modified:

■ USER_DUMP_DEST = <$ORACLE_ADMIN>/<$ORACLE_SID>/udump

Use this setting for OFA compliance. This parameter cannot be changed dynamically and any change will require you to bounce the database. Look up its current value to determine where your trace files are currently located.

■ TIMED_STATISTICS = TRUE

It is better to set this permanently in the init.ora, unless your version of Oracle suffers from some *undocumented feature* associated with setting this permanently. As always before modifying any initialization parameter, you will need to determine that there are no bugs logged against this parameter for your version of the database. TIMED_STATISTICS can be modified dynamically by issuing an **alter system** or **alter session** command to set this at the system level or session level and can be turned off later. This is an option if you have problems keeping this parameter permanently set in the init.ora.

■ MAX_DUMP_FILE_SIZE = 1024

This parameter determines the maximum size of the trace files on your system. For trace efforts that need larger files, you can modify this parameter at the session level, using an **alter session** command and set it to UNLIMITED to avoid running the risk of potentially truncating the trace file.

CAUTION
Do not set SQL_TRACE to TRUE in the init.ora, as it will trace every SQL statement that is executed. This will cause noticeable delays and will also fill up the file system where USER_DUMP_DEST points to, with potentially unnecessary trace files. We recommend that you keep this set to FALSE in your init.ora (default). This should be a last-resort option only when you have determined that SQL_TRACE cannot be set to TRUE from your application environment or from another session.

You can turn on trace for your current session by executing the following commands:

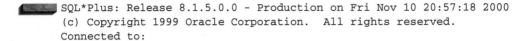

```
SQL*Plus: Release 8.1.5.0.0 - Production on Fri Nov 10 20:57:18 2000
(c) Copyright 1999 Oracle Corporation.  All rights reserved.
Connected to:
```

```
Oracle8i Enterprise Edition Release 8.1.5.0.0 - Production
With the Partitioning and Java options
PL/SQL Release 8.1.5.0.0 - Production
SQL> alter session set timed_statistics=true /* Optional - Only if
setting at the instance level permanently causes problems */;
Session altered.
SQL> alter session set sql_trace=true;
Session altered.
SQL> /* Execute your SQL statements */
SQL> alter session set timed_statistics=false /* Only if it were set
to true in the current session */;
Session altered.
SQL> alter session set sql_trace=false;
Session altered.
```

The problem with using this method prior to Oracle 7.2 was that you had to wait until all of your SQL statements had completed before you could turn SQL_TRACE off within that session. However, in Oracle 7.2 and up, a method has been provided to turn trace off from another session. The recommended method to turn off tracing is to set SQL_TRACE to FALSE, either within the session or from another session. Trace should not be turned off by just killing sessions. Turning trace off in that manner can cause the contents of trace files to be truncated and/or to contain invalid information.

The following method illustrates how to turn on SQL_TRACE on someone else's session. This is especially useful when you encounter a performance problem with an application, which may or may not support turning on SQL_TRACE from within. Further, this method also allows you to turn on and turn off SQL_TRACE at will, without having to wait for the job to run to completion. If needed, set TIMED_STATISTICS to TRUE. Here is how:

```
SQL*Plus: Release 8.1.5.0.0 - Production on Fri Nov 10 21:10:38 2000
(c) Copyright 1999 Oracle Corporation.  All rights reserved.
Connected to:
Oracle8i Enterprise Edition Release 8.1.5.0.0 - Production
With the Partitioning and Java options
PL/SQL Release 8.1.5.0.0 - Production
SQL> select Sid,Serial#
  2    from V$SESSION
  3    where Username = 'BENCHMARK' /* Determine the SID, SERIAL# of the
session that you are trying to trace from v$session /;

    SID       SERIAL#
---------- ----------
       11         54
SQL> execute dbms_system.set_sql_trace_in_session('11','54',TRUE);
PL/SQL procedure successfully completed.
```

```
SQL> /* Wait for SQL statements to execute for a certain period */
SQL> execute dbms_system.set_sql_trace_in_session('11','54',FALSE);
PL/SQL procedure successfully completed.
```

VIP

Since the core of this book is "wait-event based tuning," it should be noted that writing the wait events of a job to a trace file and then studying it is a very powerful troubleshooting tool. This method has been discussed in the section "Trapping Wait Events to a Trace File" in the chapter "The Method Behind the Madness."

Where Is My Trace File and How Do I Find It?

The trace file generated by one of the above methods can be found in the directory location pointed to by the Oracle initialization parameter USER_DUMP_DEST. If you are not sure where that destination is, you can execute the following query to determine the destination:

```
SQL*Plus: Release 8.1.5.0.0 - Production on Fri Nov 10 21:19:41 2000
(c) Copyright 1999 Oracle Corporation.  All rights reserved.
Connected to:
Oracle8i Enterprise Edition Release 8.1.5.0.0 - Production
With the Partitioning and Java options
PL/SQL Release 8.1.5.0.0 - Production
SQL> select Value
  2    from V$PARAMETER
  3    where Name = 'user_dump_dest' /* Determine the destination of
USER_DUMP_DEST */;
VALUE
-----------------------------------
/u01/app/oracle/admin/prod815/udump
```

The trace files are named using the <$ORACLE_SID>_ora_<process ID of the server process> format. The process ID mentioned here is the Spid column in V$SESSION. The following query will assist you in determining the process ID of the server connected by the user named ST001:

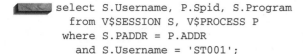

```
select S.Username, P.Spid, S.Program
  from V$SESSION S, V$PROCESS P
 where S.PADDR = P.ADDR
   and S.Username = 'ST001';
```

If you are unable to determine the server/session process ID using the above method (because there are multiple sessions including yours logged in using the same username), there is another way to determine your trace file, if you are running Oracle on UNIX. This method is not that elegant and is relevant only for applications (user processes) that are launched from the server machine where the Oracle database is running. Further, only applications that support the **host** command are relevant to this discussion. The following steps will facilitate in identifying your trace file. This method is not relevant for trace file identification on Windows NT.

```
SQL> ! /* Host out of SQL*Plus, Do not exit */

$ps      /* Determine the processes within your current shell. This is
to determine the process ID of your SQL*Plus session */
   1262 pts/2     0:00 tcsh
1279 pts/2     0:03 sqlplus
   1327 pts/2     0:00 ksh
$ps -ef | grep 1279 /* Now scan all the processes on the system and
filter out the ones with your SQL*Plus's process ID. This is to
determine the process ID of the server process that this SQL*Plus
session is attached to */
   oracle   1280   1279   0 21:41:00 ?         0:12 oracleprod815
(DESCRIPTION=(LOCAL=YES)(ADDRESS=(PROTOCOL=beq)))
 oracle   1279   1262   0 21:40:59 pts/2      0:03 sqlplus
 oracle   1327   1279   0 22:38:57 pts/2      0:00 /bin/ksh

$cd /u01/app/oracle/admin/prod815/udump /* Change directory to the
USER_DUMP_DEST directory */

$ls -lt | grep 1280
total 816
-rw-r-----   1 oracle  dba       408548 Nov 10 21:04 prod815_ora_1280.trc
```

Running tkprof on the Trace Files

The next step in the SQL tuning process is to run the utility *tkprof* that analyzes and dissects trace files to provide readable trace output that is meaningful to an Oracle DBA. To learn more about tkprof, you can execute the command without any arguments and it will list the syntax and all of the sort options for trace output display. Here is how:

```
C:\tkprof
Usage: tkprof tracefile outputfile [explain= ] [table= ]
             [print= ] [insert= ] [sys= ] [sort= ]
```

```
table=schema.tablename    Use 'schema.tablename' with 'explain=' option.
explain=user/password     Connect to ORACLE and issue EXPLAIN PLAIN.
print=integer     List only the first 'integer' SQL statements.
aggregate=yes|no
insert=filename   List SQL statements and data inside INSERT statements.
sys=no            TKPROF does not list SQL statements run as user SYS.
record=filename   Record non-recursive statements found in the trace file.
sort=option       Set of zero or more of the following sort options:
  prscnt  number of times parse was called
  prscpu  cpu time parsing
  prsela  elapsed time parsing
  prsdsk  number of disk reads during parse
  prsqry  number of buffers for consistent read during parse
  prscu   number of buffers for current read during parse
  prsmis  number of misses in library cache during parse
  execnt  number of execute was called
  execpu  cpu time spent executing
  exeela  elapsed time executing
  exedsk  number of disk reads during execute
  exeqry  number of buffers for consistent read during execute
  execu   number of buffers for current read during execute
  exerow  number of rows processed during execute
  exemis  number of library cache misses during execute
  fchcnt  number of times fetch was called
  fchcpu  cpu time spent fetching
  fchela  elapsed time fetching
  fchdsk  number of disk reads during fetch
  fchqry  number of buffers for consistent read during fetch
  fchcu   number of buffers for current read during fetch
  fchrow  number of rows fetched
  userid  userid of user that parsed the cursor
```

As you can see, there are plenty of options available for you to sort the trace output data, and it can be done by simply specifying the sort=<option> in the command-line syntax. The default sort option for the trace output from tkprof is *fchela*—elapsed time fetching. Needless to say, trace outputs are sorted in decreasing or descending order of values for a given option.

If you want to see the execution plan displayed as part of the trace output, you need to ensure that the userid that you specify to run the Explain Plan in tkprof owns the PLAN_TABLE under its schema. In the absence of the PLAN_TABLE in the user's schema, you will need to run the script *utlxplan.sql*, which is located under the $ORACLE_HOME/rdbms/admin directory as the user, before running tkprof.

Following is an example run of tkprof that interprets the trace data collected in the file named *prod815_ora_1280.trc*. It also creates a trace output file called *output.prf*, utilizes a user called *benchmark* with a password of *benchmark*, does not show output of SQL statements run as user SYS, and sorts the output in decreasing order of "*number of disk reads during the fetch phase.*"

```
$ tkprof  prod815_ora_1280.trc output.prf explain=benchmark/benchmark sys=no sort=fchdsk
```

Some of the more preferred sort options are *prsela*, *exeela*, and *fchela*, as elapsed time is the actual time that it takes to run a given phase of SQL statement processing. We personally have used *fchela* quite a bit, as the parse and execute phases of most SQL statements are not usually the problem areas. Most of the work for a *select* statement is done in the fetch phase, which is why *fchela* is more relevant for *select* statements. For SQL statements that modify data (INSERT, UPDATE, DELETE), *exeela* is a more viable option. If you need your statements ordered by total CPU utilization, use the sort option of sort=(prsela, exeela, fchela). Similar output can be acquired for total physical I/O (I/O operations that do not find the required Oracle blocks in the database buffer cache) by using sort=(prsdsk, exedsk, fchdsk).

Total logical I/O (I/O operations that find the required Oracle blocks in the database buffer cache) can be acquired by setting sort=(prsqry, prscu, exeqry, execu, fchqry, fchcu). It is important to understand here that sorting by logical I/O is a more consistent method, as physical I/O can change due to various reasons such as an increase in the size of the database buffer cache. The perspective on logical I/O provides a relative comparison of how much CPU time will be saved, given that logical I/O (buffer cache manipulation) consumes CPU cycles.

NOTE
Since you are the DBA, you should be able to log in as the oracle operating system user to run tkprof and get the required access to the trace files. But if tkprof needs to be run by some of your application developers (who obviously should not be logging in as oracle), you will need to set the init.ora parameter _TRACE_FILES_PUBLIC=TRUE to provide them with read access to the trace files.

Interpreting the Output from tkprof

Let us now look at a sample output from tkprof and understand the various components. The following output is formatted for readability:

```
select A.Id,A.Name,B.Name
  from AUTHOR A,  BOOK B
 where A.Author_Id = B.Book_Author_Id
   and A.Author_Id = 101
 order by B.Name;
```

call	count	cpu	elapsed	disk	query	current	rows
Parse	1	0.02	0.02	0	0	0	0
Execute	1	0.01	0.01	0	0	0	0
Fetch	27	0.24	0.36	1230	2342	0	399
------	-------	----	-------	----	----	-------	----
Totals	29	0.27	0.39	1230	2342	0	399

Now, let us understand the various columns in the tkprof trace output:

- **Call** A phase in SQL statement processing (the *define* and *bind* phases are also included in the Parse phase).

- **Count** The number of times (in seconds) a phase was called/executed.

- **CPU** Actual CPU time utilized in executing a phase.

- **Elapsed** CPU time (in seconds) plus any time spent by the operating system performing context switches, servicing interrupts, responding to signals, performing I/O, waiting on resources, and so on.

- **Disk** The number of Oracle blocks read from disk (physical I/O) for a given phase.

- **Query** The number of Oracle blocks read from memory in consistent mode.

- **Current** The number of Oracle blocks read from memory in current mode.

- **Rows** The number of rows processed in each phase. You should really see values for *select* statements in the Fetch phase and for *insert/update/* operations in the execute phase.

That was cool, except that you really could not make out the real difference between Query and Current. For all practical reasons, there is no real need to split up the logical I/O into these two buckets. In our experience, we usually sum up (Query plus Current) to arrive at the total logical I/O for the SQL statement.

As mentioned in the chapter "Application Tuning—Issues that Concern a DBA," the ultimate goal of any SQL statement is to return the data to the user with the least utilization of system resources and in a reasonable timeframe. This means that some operations may require more I/O versus others that may require more CPU. There is no magic number for the percentage of physical I/O to logical I/O, as this is subject to the nature and frequency of the operations (SQL) being tuned. The core goals to keep in mind in your application-tuning efforts are response time and system throughput. As mentioned before, you need to determine the *wait events* on your system and tune your applications and your system accordingly. Ultimately, you are the best judge as to the amount of resources a given SQL statement can and should consume, given its response time requirements, its run frequency, and the load that is placed on the system.

If some SQL statement performs 1,000,000 physical block I/Os to return 100 rows, you should definitely question that and determine the cause. Something does not add up here. On the same note, you should also question an inordinate number of logical I/Os in an operation. And just because the textbook definition of logical I/O defines the operation to be at least 1,000 times faster than physical I/O, that does not immediately imply that logical I/Os are always better than physical I/Os (from Oracle's perspective).

The key factor to consider here is the number of blocks your application is *visiting* to return the data to the user. Another factor is the "elapsed time" to return a set of rows to the user, and this also provides some basis for the impact of your tuning efforts. You need to determine whether the number makes sense. Also remember that it is not always beneficial to use an index. If you determine one or more anomalies in your SQL statement from the above trace output, you will need to rewrite your SQL statement to use more optimal methods and lesser resources.

Hey, Oracle—What Is Your Plan of Action (P.O.A.)?

By Oracle's P.O.A, we by no means are referring to Oracle Corporation's plan of action. We would like to clarify, for the record, that we are not privy to that kind of information. What we are referring to is the P.O.A of a SQL statement's execution. The Explain Plan of a SQL statement can be compared to a normal question that we ask one another in our daily lives, when we are not sure about the other person's plans or agenda: What is your P.O.A.? The same holds true for Oracle.

How to Get Oracle's P.O.A.?

One way to get it (and it is easy) is to specify the *explain=userid/password* option in the tkprof command-line syntax. By doing that, you are requesting the Explain Plan for the SQL statements that you trace, so that you can verify whether Oracle is executing the SQL statements in a manner that makes performance sense. The Explain Plan then shows up in the trace output for each SQL statement (except recursive SQL and DDL SQL, which cannot be explained). When requesting that, tkprof uses the PLAN_TABLE in the user's schema for storing and then reporting the execution plan.

Here is a sample Explain Plan:

```
select A.Id,A.Name,B.Name
   from AUTHOR A, BOOK B
 where A.Author_Id = B.Book_Author_Id
   and A.Author_Id = 101
 order by B.Name;
```

```
Query Plan
------------------------------------------------------------------
1.0 SELECT STATEMENT   Statement1 Cost = 148
     2.1 SORT ORDER BY (7th)
          3.1 FILTER (6th)
               4.1 NESTED LOOPS (5th)
                    5.1 TABLE ACCESS BY ROWID AUTHOR (2nd)
                         6.1 INDEX UNIQUE SCAN AUTHOR_ID UNIQUE (1st)
                    5.2 TABLE ACCESS BY ROWID BOOK (4th)
                         6.2 INDEX RANGE SCAN BOOK_AUTH_ID NON-UNIQUE (3rd)
```

Another method is to provide a SQL to an **Explain Plan** command. Here we go:

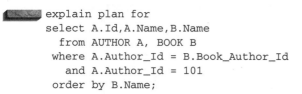

```
explain plan for
select A.Id,A.Name,B.Name
  from AUTHOR A, BOOK B
 where A.Author_Id = B.Book_Author_Id
   and A.Author_Id = 101
 order by B.Name;
```

You can then run the following command to retrieve the Explain Plan from the PLAN_TABLE:

```
select lpad(' ', 2*(Level -1))||Operation||' '||
       decode(Id, 0, 'Cost = '||position)  "Operation",
       Options, Object_Name
    from PLAN_TABLE
start with Id = 0
connect by prior Id = Parent_Id
order by Id;
```

NOTE
Remember to truncate your PLAN_TABLE frequently, to prevent it from consuming unnecessary space in your database (especially true for third-party tuning tools).

Now that I Have the Plan, Can Someone Help Me Read It?

The *explain plan* described in the previous section needs to be read in a tree-like format by recursively going to the deepest level and then walking back to the parent (first) level of the tree. In this case, the first occurrence of the deepest level we encounter is 6.1, which is a *unique scan* on the AUTHOR_ID index to look up data from the AUTHOR table. The results from step 6.1 are sent back to its parent, 5.1.

Now we check whether the level 5 has any other siblings and in this case there is one —5.2. The level 5.2 has a child 6.2, which is the second operation that is executed and is a RANGE SCAN on the BOOK_AUTH_ID index (mind you, this is a *non-unique* index) to look up data from the BOOK table. The results from 6.2 are sent back to its parent, 5.2.

There are no more siblings for level 5, so the combined results of 5.1 and 5.2 are sent back to its parent 4.1 (which performs the *nested loops* operation). The results of step 4.1 are sent to its parent 3.1, which is the *filter* (for the value 101). The results of 3.1 are then sent to its parent 2.1, which performs the ORDER BY operation, and the results of that are then sent to the highest-level parent 1.0, which then returns the data to the application. Now, wasn't that simple!

NOTE
Do not bet your life on the Cost=X number, as it may not make sense in certain cases. The Cost=X value is a measure of the amount of I/O the SQL statement is expected to perform. Although we can safely mention here that a Cost=1000000 is definitely a more expensive execution plan (and hence may take much more time to execute) than a Cost=4567, the same cannot be assumed for all cases. For example, we have observed SQL statements with, say, a Cost=4500 that are not necessarily faster than the one with a Cost=4567. There have been many occasions where we have observed higher cost for execution plans for SQL statements that ran the SQL much faster. You may also notice an increase in cost when you /*+ HINT*/ SQL statements, and that is not necessarily a bad thing.

What Is AUTOTRACE?

AUTOTRACE is quite possibly one of SQL*Plus's best kept secrets. This facility was made available in SQL*Plus 2.3, and it provides some great information at your fingertips without having to run SQL_TRACE, process the trace file through tkprof, clean up and manage the trace files, and perform other administrative overhead associated with those operations. It is very easy to set up the AUTOTRACE facility, and even easier to use it.

AUTOTRACE can be set up by running the *plustrce.sql* script, which is located under $ORACLE_HOME/sqlplus/admin. On releases of Oracle prior to 8.1.0 on the Windows NT platform, you will have to look into the *plusXX* directory for this script.

In some releases the *plustrce.sql* file has been found in the $ORACLE_HOME/dbs directory (to our surprise).

To set up a user for AUTOTRACE, just log in as SYS and run the aforementioned script. It creates among other objects a role called PLUSTRACE. When that script is done, all you have to do is to grant the PLUSTRACE role to the relevant users, and that gets them ready to use AUTOTRACE.

NOTE

Since AUTOTRACE automatically generates the Explain Plan for one or more SQL statements for a given user, the user's schema should already have the PLAN_TABLE created before attempting to use AUTOTRACE. If not, please run the utlxplan.sql script, which is located in the $ORACLE_HOME/ rdbms/admin directory, as the user running AUTOTRACE.

Although the default method to use AUTOTRACE is to **set autotrace on**, that may *not* always be feasible, especially if your query is returning hundreds of thousands of rows. The **traceonly** option allows you to just look at the statistics, without the data from the query.

TIP

*The **traceonly** option can also be used as a very quick method to get the Explain Plan for the SQL statement. This is true when AUTOTRACE is turned on from SQL*Plus's Windows version on a client machine, and as soon as the "Query is Executing" dialog box appears, you can click the Cancel button to just get the Explain Plan.*

The following is a sample run of AUTOTRACE:

```
SQL> set autotrace traceonly
SQL> select count(*) from TEST_OBJECTS;

Execution Plan
----------------------------------------------------------------

   0      SELECT STATEMENT Optimizer=CHOOSE (Cost=1 Card=1)
   1    0   SORT (AGGREGATE)
   2    1     TABLE ACCESS (FULL) OF 'TEST_OBJECTS' (Cost=1 Card=1)
```

```
Statistics
----------------------------------------------------------------
        28  recursive calls
        16  db block gets
         2  consistent gets
         0  physical reads
         0  redo size
      1083  bytes sent via SQL*Net to client
       669  bytes received via SQL*Net from client
         4  SQL*Net roundtrips to/from client
         1  sorts (memory)
         0  sorts (disk)
         1  rows processed
```

As you can observe from this output, AUTOTRACE provides a wealth of information, including the number of recursive calls, total logical I/O for the SQL statement, physical I/O, the amount of redo generated (if applicable), SQL*Net traffic information, sort statistics (memory versus disk), and the number of rows retrieved.

NOTE

As mentioned at the beginning of this chapter, you need to prioritize your tuning efforts based on the amount of resources consumed along with the execution frequency of SQL statements on your system. For example, in a 24-hour time period, if 100 SQL statements contributed to 2,000,000 logical I/Os, and if one query performed 1,000,000 logical I/Os during a single execution, you would need to focus on this query. Why? It comprised 1 percent of the workload yet consumed 50 percent of the resources, that's why. This information can be obtained by querying V$SQL for Buffer_Gets and Executions.

In a Nutshell

Hunting down bad SQL statements requires discipline and pushes you to be aware and adept in the various tools that Oracle provides to troubleshoot bad SQL statements. This is important because unless you get to the bottom of the performance problem with your SQL statements, you really can't tune your system. Allow us to say it one more time: 80 percent or more of your system's performance problems are caused due to bad SQL statements.

The core steps to tune your SQL statements are:

1. Ensure TIMED_STATISTICS is set to TRUE at the instance level (set it permanently in the init.ora or set it temporarily by executing an **alter system** command).

2. Ensure MAX_DUMP_FILE_SIZE is set high enough. This controls the size of your trace file.

3. Determine the location pointed to by USER_DUMP_DEST, and make sure there is plenty of free disk space. This is the home of your trace files.

4. Turn on SQL_TRACE for the session in question.

5. Run the application.

6. Locate the trace files.

7. Run *tkprof* (transient kernel profile) on the trace file that was located in step 4, to generate a trace output file.

8. Study the trace output file.

9. Tune the most expensive SQL statements.

10. Repeat steps 4 through 9 until required performance goals are achieved.

SQL_TRACE, **TKPROF**, **EXPLAIN PLAN**, and **AUTOTRACE** are some of the core tools that are shipped with the Oracle database software, and have been known to work consistently across multiple releases and operating system platforms. Understanding these tools is essential to your success in your application tuning efforts. Regardless of whom you choose as your third-party vendor for your Oracle database performance monitoring tools and SQL tuning tools, you absolutely have to understand and know your way around these core tools. Failing to do that may cause Mr. Murphy to play tricks with you. There just may be that one day on the horizon where you may not have access to your fancy GUI tools, but will need to determine the core cause of an application performance problem.

Not being able to use these core tools provided by Oracle can put you and your system in a wait mode (waiting to get to your GUI tools), which your system and your business may not be able to afford. It is not only a requirement for a DBA to know how to use these tools, but it also serves as an eye opener to understand what your fancy GUI tools are actually doing behind the scenes. Now, just go and track those bad SQL down, will you?

PART
III

Instance and
Database Tuning

CHAPTER
5

Instance Tuning—The Shared Pool Area

Myth & Folklore

Low statistics of less than 99 percent cache-hit ratios in the library or dictionary cache are evidence of a poorly performing system and can be corrected by increasing the size of the shared pool area.

Fact

Well, let's first ask the question: what makes you think the shared pool is the problem? Did you see any associated *wait events*? Simply increasing the size of the shared pool in an arbitrary fashion is unlikely to solve any shared pool–related performance problems. It should be noted that the positive effects of a larger shared pool (beyond a certain size) would only last for a short duration after the instance starts up. Plus, the more memory you allocate to the shared pool area, the higher the probability for increased CPU consumption in managing it and the longer processes hold some of the latches for these memory structures. The Oracle RDBMS has been effectively designed to deal with I/O not as an "in-memory" database. If, in fact, it were designed to be solely in-memory, it would take a whole different set of algorithms to optimize it. A trap some less experienced DBAs fall into is to constantly increase the size of the shared pool, thinking that just a little more memory will do the trick. As with almost all performance issues, just throwing more resources at Oracle (in this case, the shared pool area) does little more than push the problem out a few days or weeks. And in some cases, adding more memory may create other problems that you did not envision and thus hurt performance. You must understand that most challenges in dealing with the shared pool are related to the type of access to this memory structure, in addition to the lack of meaningful and proactive management of space within this structure. Among other things, the segregation of large and small packages and the identification of frequently used stored SQL (packages, procedures, functions) are important. Equally critical is the allocation of adequate space within the shared pool area for operations conducted by the Recovery Manager (RMAN), Parallel Query, Java, and the Oracle multithreaded server (MTS). Last but not least, the best use and reuse of SQL statements within this memory structure will go a long way in keeping contention down and performance up.

antastic! We get this feeling that not so far in the distant future we will be so specialized in tuning Oracle that we might call ourselves pool consultants or pool experts. Now, there is a catchy job title. And there may be some buzz in the industry—*Call the Pool Guys, they will take care of you.* Well, by the time we get done talking about the various pools in this chapter and the next one, you will be 100-percent convinced that we are in fact the Pool Guys. Think about it: shared pool, reserved area (area within the shared pool), large pool, java pool and default pool, keep pool and recycle pool. You will be up to your ears (but not drowning!) with our discussions about the various pools. Now we better get on with our business quickly, as we have been told that we may not have anything to tune in Oracle9i. This is because Oracle9i is supposed to be self-tuning, self-configuring, and really does not need our tuning services. Right!

Welcome to the shared pool area—our technically invigorating SPA. By the end of this chapter, you will feel as though you have spent a day having the following done on you: a detoxifying sulfur-rich mud wrap, herbal facial, blanket wrap, and a full body massage with foot reflexology, which lasts for two whole hours. Our point is, your database should be feeling that way. Peace and harmony!

We are now getting into the nuts and bolts of tuning Oracle. But before we go too far down this road, let's talk about what *you* can hope to accomplish here. Remember our basic premise: you, our esteemed customer, need to get the biggest bang for your tuning buck. This is not just from a pure dollar perspective, but also from a time perspective. We do not want you or anyone else to go on a wild goose chase or get tangled up with arcane and useless efforts.

This means tuning only those components that will improve overall system response times for the user community. In the next few chapters, we will share information about the configuration and tuning various aspects of the System Global Area (SGA). This includes the SPA as well as the other pools. The *reserved area* has been available since Oracle 7.3. The other pools have been available since Oracle8 and up. We will also talk to you about the database buffer cache and the redo log buffer as well as other constructs that require your attention.

Significant performance increases can be realized by focusing on these areas, but keep this in mind: they may be less dramatic than increases resulting from application tuning. Here you will learn how to optimize performance of the shared pool, but only if you have already resolved the application tuning issues. If not, now is the time to go back to the chapters "Application Tuning—Issues that concern a DBA" and "Application Tuning—Tracking down bad SQL." Since by this point in your tuning efforts you should have identified the components of your application that require work, the next steps are to ensure that your database and your instance are configured in an optimal fashion.

In order to make certain that everyone is on the same page (as authors, we like that phrase), we'll start with a review of the Oracle architecture and provide you with some details regarding processing of SQL statements. We will then follow that up with the details of tuning the shared pool area. We promise that this is not yet another endless lecture on the Oracle architecture. We will keep it short and sweet, but we want to make sure that we are all singing the same song, from the same page, of the same book.

Oracle Architecture

As with all things, understanding what you are dealing with is key to how successfully you can deal with it. Oracle is no different. By taking time to review the Oracle architecture, you will be more certain of the effects of any changes you make. Let's review the basic terms and concepts used here so we are all using the same language. Figure 5-1 illustrates the internals of an Oracle database from a high level.

The following table is a list of terms that you should already be familiar with.

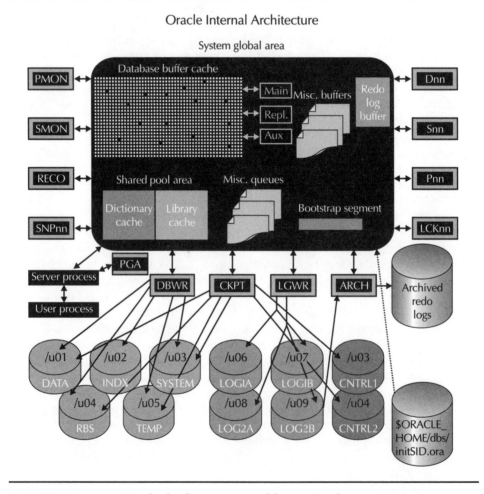

FIGURE 5-1. *An Oracle database supported by an Oracle instance*

Term	Description
Host	The machine on which Oracle runs. Sometimes called a server.
Instance	This is comprised of the System Global Area (SGA), its associated background processes, and related shared memory structures. This is transient and created on each instance startup.
Database	The data files, control files, and redo logs. These are the permanent structures of an Oracle server.
Background Process	Any process (such as the database writer process) that performs a defined task for Oracle—writes modified blocks from memory to disk.
Server Process	A process that does work on behalf of only one user. The exception to this rule is when the server process is *shared* and this is relevant when you configure Oracle in the MTS mode.
System Global Area	The System Global Area is the collection of all shared memory structures that belong to Oracle. This includes the shared pool area, the database buffer cache, the redo log buffer, and other miscellaneous buffers, queues, and structures that Oracle maintains. In simple terms, it is the area where data and SQL statements reside and work is accomplished.
Shared Pool Area	The portion of the SGA where SQL statements, stored procedures, and specific dictionary information are stored in memory.
Database Buffer Cache	The area where data blocks in use are kept and manipulated.
Reserved Area	Available in Oracle 7.3 and up. A reserved area to store large SQL objects (including packages, procedures, functions).
Large Pool	Available in Oracle8 and up. An area reserved for special operations used by RMAN, Parallel Query, and MTS. Facilitates better management of the shared pool.

Term	Description
Java Pool	Available in Oracle8i and up. This is memory structure reserved for Java and its many associated objects.
Redo Log Buffer	A usually small area of the SGA where change records or change journals are stored prior to being written to the redo log files on disk.

The System Global Area

The System Global Area (SGA) is the part of Oracle made up of shared memory segments supported by the operating system. It is Oracle's work area where pretty much everything gets done. The size of the SGA is determined by the sum of its components. This value is displayed at instance startup or by querying V$SGA:

```
SVRMGR> startup
ORACLE instance started.
Total System Global Area                122838416 bytes
Fixed Size                                  64912 bytes
Variable Size                            55484416 bytes
Database Buffers                         67108864 bytes
Redo Buffers                               180224 bytes
Database mounted.
Database opened.
SVRMGR> select sum(Value)
   2>    from V$SGA;
SUM(VALUE)
----------
 122838416
1 row selected.
SVRMGR>
```

The major components of the SGA are the SPA, the database buffer cache (DB cache), and the redo log buffer. In Oracle 7.3, the reserved area could be configured in the shared pool area. Additionally, in Oracle8 and up, the SGA includes the large pool and the java pool. Each of these areas of memory is configured by parameters in the initialization file (init.ora). The performance efficiency of these areas is affected by their respective parameter settings in the init.ora. The following sections describe all major areas of the SGA common to all versions of Oracle up to Oracle8i.

The Shared Pool Area (SPA)

The SPA is sized with the parameter SHARED_POOL_SIZE. At a very high level, the resources set aside for the SPA are automatically divided between the library cache (LC) and the data dictionary cache (DDC) and other internal components (the discussion of those is beyond the scope of this book). Unless you have an Oracle6 system you should not be concerned with how this happens. If you do have an Oracle6 system, it is high time you did an upgrade. The LC contains all the SQL and stored procedures and functions that are in use or have been used recently. The DDC contains *metadata* from the data dictionary about all the objects, their structures, security, and so on, referenced in the most recently used SQL statements. The DDC contains "data about data."

The Database Buffer Cache

The database buffer cache is composed of copies of Oracle blocks from the data files. These blocks could be one of the following types: data, index, temporary, rollback, or bootstrap/cached segment blocks. In fact, the database buffer cache often contains many versions of the most actively used blocks from the data files. The many versions of the data blocks are created for various transactions requiring read-consistent images of the data.

Oracle implements *multiversion read consistency* using the *before image* from the rollback segments (when applicable) to provide consistent reads across transactions. The basic concept here is that the rows retrieved and sent to you will always be committed data. The exception to this rule is if you are the initiator of a transaction, and you want to query your changes before deciding to commit or rollback the changes. By default, with Oracle you will never do *dirty reads* (changes made to data by others that are yet to be committed). This concept is discussed in greater detail in the chapter "Contention Tuning."

The size of the database buffer cache is determined by the initialization parameter DB_BLOCK_BUFFERS. The amount of memory utilized by this memory structure is a function of DB_BLOCK_SIZE multiplied by DB_BLOCK_BUFFERS. If you cache 10,000 blocks of 8K each, the memory allocation will be 81920000 bytes or about 78MB.

The Redo Log Buffer

The parameter LOG_BUFFER sets the amount of memory used to store redo information or change journals of the database. Sizing this memory structure correctly is critical on systems where a lot of DML occurs. Since this is the heart of Oracle's recovery mechanism, it is important to size this appropriately without going overboard. We will discuss this in greater detail in the chapter "Instance Tuning—The Redo Log Buffer and Miscellaneous Tuning."

The Reserved Area

With the advent of Oracle 7.3, there was better support for managing the issues posed by large stored SQL or PL/SQL (packages, procedures, and functions). This segregation of SQL was long overdue, as small SQL statements and large SQL statements (or stored SQL) often interfered with one another when stored in the same area and caused both aging of SQL and fragmentation of the shared pool. The SHARED_POOL_RESERVED_SIZE was thus introduced, and the whole purpose of this was to segregate small and large SQL in separate areas so they do not interfere with one another.

The Large Pool

With the advent of Oracle8, a new memory pool (outside the shared pool area) was introduced. The large pool was added to provide room specifically for parallel operations, for use by the MTS configuration and by RMAN. Setting the initialization parameter LARGE_POOL_SIZE configures this area.

The Java Pool

The Java pool is available in Oracle8i. It is configured by the parameter JAVA_ POOL_SIZE and is used by Java programs just like the shared pool area is used by SQL. Note that the installation of the Java component requires that this be configured, but the Oracle recommendation is far too small. It may need to be set above 100MB to get it to install properly.

NOTE
*Until 8.1.6, the memory allocated to the java pool was not accurately reported in the **show sga** command or V$SGASTAT.*

The Background Processes

The SGA associated with today's Oracle instances can be extremely large, but no matter how large or small, someone has to take care of the activities associated with the instance. A small army of operating system processes (UNIX) or threads (Windows NT) manages these tasks. It is important to distinguish between background processes and other processes. Background processes are independent of user connections. They perform operations on the instance and database on behalf of all users. They perform operations such as writing to data files, recovering the database, or resolving errors. Some of the processes also aid in increasing overall performance.

Figure 5-1 shows all the background processes. Some of them are required (Oracle cannot run without them) and we will point them out. All the others are used to support specialized options or provide performance boosts. They will be discussed in the appropriate sections. The following table defines the mandatory processes plus the two optional default processes.

Process	Description
SMON	The system monitor is responsible for many of the maintenance routines in the SGA and even in tablespaces, for example, coalescing free space. SMON also manages rollback segments (shrinks them to size when OPTIMAL is set) and performs recovery operations during startup (when required). It is a required process.
PMON	This process monitors the Oracle foreground processes (server processes). It is the first process that is started. It oversees tasks such as cleanup of memory, process space, and locks of terminated connections and lost connections. It is a required process.
DBWR or DBW#	The database writer process is usually the only process that actually writes data blocks to the data files in a database. The exception to this is when SQL*Loader is run (in direct mode) or when SORT_DIRECT_WRITES is set to TRUE. Of course, the CKPT process writes to the headers during a checkpoint. It is possible to have more than one. This process is involved in the management of writing modified blocks from the database buffer cache to disk. It is a required process.
LGWR	The log writer process manages the redo log buffer. It writes redo information from the redo log buffer to the redo log files. It is a required process.
RECO	The recovery process that is required for resolving *in doubt* distributed transactions. It resolves problems using the two-phase commit construct. This is required when any distributed constructs such as DBLINKS is used. It is automatically started when DISTRIBUTED_TRANSACTIONS is either derived or set to a non-zero value.
CKPT	A performance enhancer, the checkpoint process helps complete checkpoints reducing the workload on the LGWR process. From Oracle8 and up, this is a required background process.

Some additional notes about DBWR and LGWR are in order. These two processes are real workhorses and as such are subject to bottlenecks. Of course, since both of them are I/O-based processes, care needs to be taken to avoid and prevent contention between these processes. To see why, you will need to know a few more points about how they do their work.

DBWR writes copies of modified blocks of tables, indexes, rollback segments, and temporary segments (if SORT_DIRECT_WRITES is not set to TRUE) on four events. Here we go:

- Every three seconds.

- Whenever the list of dirty blocks reaches its threshold length (internally predetermined).

- Whenever another process searches the list of least recently used blocks (LRU list) and cannot locate a free buffer, after an internally set number of block searches.

- At checkpoints.

LGWR writes the redo buffers to the current log file based on five conditions:

- Every three seconds (independent of DBWR).

- On a commit. Remember that the write of the redo entry must physically be completed before control is returned to the program issuing the commit.

- Whenever redo information equal to one third of the size of the redo buffer has been written to the redo buffer. For example, if the redo buffer is 131072 bytes, when 43690 bytes of new information has been written to the redo buffer, log writer will copy the new redo information to disk. Starting from Oracle8, log writer will write to the redo logs when MIN (1 MB., LOG_BUFFER/3) is true.

- At checkpoints.

- When posted by the DBWR process (see the following note).

Notice where the two coincide? Yes, at checkpoints. Now you can see that there could be a flurry of activity when a checkpoint is occurring, and configuring data files and redo log files on the same physical device could result in I/O waits during checkpoints (if your device does not have adequate I/O processing capacity).

NOTE
*Even though DBWR wakes up every three seconds
to write, LGWR will be pinged every three seconds
and on every DBWR write to ensure that the redo
entries associated with the dirty blocks are in fact
written to the logs. This needs to happen to prevent
the database from becoming inconsistent in the event
of an instance failure. Redo entries for dirty blocks
need to be written to the redo logs before the dirty
blocks themselves can be written to the data files.*

One additional piece of information on the CKPT process: from Oracle8, it keeps
a heartbeat of the instance/database with the control files every three seconds. This is
to help determine the starting point of a recovery, if applicable and when needed.

One More Process: The Server Process

The last process to review is the server process. Some folks call it a shadow process.
This is because every application (user process) that connects to an Oracle database gets
one of these created on its behalf. When you start SQL*Plus and connect to a database,
one of these is started. It is one per user unless the Oracle MTS configuration is used.

When Oracle is configured in MTS mode, each user process communicates with
a dispatcher process (one dispatcher can communicate with multiple users) and
the dispatcher process stores SQL statements for processing in a *request queue*. The
shared server processes continuously monitor the request queue and process the
SQL statements (as explained later in this chapter) and store the results in the *response
queue*. The dispatcher processes continuously monitor the response queue, and as they
receive results, they forward them back to the user process that requested those results.

The server process (in the normal/dedicated mode of Oracle) is the one that
actually does the work for you. In a dedicated server environment, each connection
has one of these processes just waiting to carry out whatever orders (SQL statements)
are sent from the application. The server process reads blocks from the data files (if
not already in memory), manipulates data in the database blocks, and returns data as
requested. Ultimately, it is this process that needs your help, as it actually uses the
resources on the system.

Following is a sample output from a UNIX system running an Oracle database.
This output shows the background processes, one server process, and one
application process (SQL*Plus).

NOTE
The SQL*Plus process will not be listed if it is launched as an application from a client. The SQL*Plus process shown here is one from a terminal emulation session (telnet) on the host where the Oracle database resides.

```
oracle  15956     1 0 11:23 ?      00:00:01 ora_pmon_oradev
oracle  15958     1 0 11:23 ?      00:00:00 ora_dbw0_oradev
oracle  15960     1 0 11:23 ?      00:00:00 ora_lgwr_oradev
oracle  15962     1 0 11:23 ?      00:00:00 ora_ckpt_oradev
oracle  15964     1 0 11:23 ?      00:00:06 ora_smon_oradev
oracle  15966     1 0 11:23 ?      00:00:00 ora_reco_oradev
oracle  16032 15939 0 14:10 pts/1 00:00:01 sqlplus
oracle  16033 16032 1 14:10 ?      00:00:02 oracleoradev (DESCRIPTION=
```

After reviewing this architectural information, you can see how a change that you may make in one area might potentially affect performance in other areas. Additionally, it becomes clear that I/O bottlenecks experienced by major background processes can cascade across the entire system.

Imagine if DBWR is unable to write dirty buffers to disk fast enough to keep free buffers available to server processes. Consider what happens if LGWR is unable to flush the redo buffer fast enough. All of these create opportunities for performance degradation and thus for tuning. But proactively configuring an Oracle instance and utilizing the methodology discussed in the chapter "The Method Behind the Madness" will enable you to spend your time and your system resources in a more wise fashion. We don't want you to arbitrarily try to allocate memory to one or more structures in the Oracle SGA on a continual basis and feel frustrated about performance. We want you to identify the problem using the wait events method, plan a solution, implement the solution, and then monitor to determine whether the problem is fixed. You should desist the urge to just throw more memory at Oracle, even if that is what you have been taught to do in the past.

The Program Global Area (PGA)

For a minute, when you saw PGA in Figure 5-1, you may have thought it meant Professional Golfers Association. Well, your thought is noble, but unfortunately it is a bit of a *long drive* for Oracle. The PGA, or program global area, is private memory for the server process and it contains three sections: stack space, cursor state, and user session data. Yes, it says global, but it is really not quite global (unless you run Oracle MTS, then parts of the PGA become global).

The stack space contains values for variables, scalars, and constants used in the current session. The cursor state contains cursor information (open, closed, persistency, handle information, and so on). The user session data contains, among other things, the current session's information, the current transaction ID (if applicable), the current rollback segment number (if applicable), and space for performing memory sorts (when allocated). And that concludes tonight's program.

Parsing SQL: What Happens When the User Presses ENTER?

Whenever a user or a program makes a connection to an Oracle instance and issues SQL or PL/SQL commands, the server process goes to work on those commands. Processing SQL statements is broken into multiple phases (depending on whether the SQL is a *select* statement or not). These phases are Parse, Define, Bind, Execute, and Fetch. The Fetch phase is relevant only for *select* statements. All statements go through the first four phases mentioned in the following table, but only *select* statements have to fetch rows back to the user process. The following table provides a summary of what happens in each of the various phases.

SQL Statement Processing Phase	Description
Parse	In this phase, the server process checks the syntax of the SQL statement and also performs object resolution and security checks for SQL execution. Further, it builds the parse tree and develops the execution plan for the SQL statement.
Define	In this phase, among other things, the user and server processes exchange data type information about the various columns referenced in the SQL statements. SQL*Net or Net8/Net8i is involved here.
Bind	This is the phase where values for bind variables (:b1, :v1) that are referenced in the SQL statement are resolved.

SQL Statement Processing Phase	Description
Execute	During the Execute phase, the server process reads data blocks from file into memory (for *insert*, *update*, and *delete* statements only) as needed and manipulates the data in memory. It is in this phase that the execution plan is executed. It is important to note here that any "parallelization" of queries takes place before the Execute phase begins.
Fetch	For *select* statements, this phase signifies reading the relevant blocks into the database buffer cache and applying the execution plan and returning of rows to the initiating application (user process).

In the Parse phase, the server process hashes the statement based on the ASCII value of each character. The resulting value is translated to an address corresponding to a location in the library cache in the shared pool area. If the statement does not exist in the hash address, it performs checks on the statement for correct syntax, security privileges for the executing user, and object resolution of all objects referenced in the SQL.

On arriving at the hashed memory address, the server process looks to see if there is a statement already that matches the inbound statement. If it does not find one, it needs to perform a hard parse. Hmmm. That implies there might be something called a soft parse. Well, there is. And applications that do repetitive hard parses provide you with an opportunity to soften the blow. No pun intended. We will talk about it in the following section, "Hard versus Soft Parse."

If there is no SQL statement in the hash address, the process continues, executes more recursive SQL, and develops a parse tree and an execution plan. The parse tree is really the SQL statement reformatted and structured in the form of a tree. The execution plan is derived from this map, and it dictates the best method (most of the time) to retrieve the data.

The Define phase is when SQL*Net or Net8/Net8i is engaged to do data type resolution between the user and server processes. This is important as the client (user process) could be running Windows NT (whose native representation is in ASCII) and the server could be an IBM mainframe running Oracle on MVS (whose native representation is in EBCDIC). This means a long, a short, a word, a double, or any other data type needs to be mapped to the native environments on both sides. That is what the Define phase is all about.

The Bind phase is when the values to the bind variables are resolved. The use of bind variables in SQL statements go a long way in "reusing SQL" and also reducing the contention on the shared pool area. It is very important to reuse SQL and this can be achieved by the use of bind variables.

The Execute phase of SQL processing is the actual application of the execution plan or map to the data. If the SQL statement is an *insert*, *update*, or *delete* statement, it modifies data. For these statements the relevant redo entries (for instance and database recovery) and rollback entries (for transaction recovery) need to be generated and logged appropriately, before the data is modified in memory.

The Fetch phase is only applicable to *select* statements and is the process of actually reading the data into the database buffer cache, applying the execution plan, and returning the selected rows to the user process. This is the last step in SQL processing.

Hard versus Soft Parse

A soft parse occurs if the server process can find a matching SQL statement in the hash address that was generated by the SQL hashing algorithm. This means that the server process may be experiencing *déjà vu*. And that is good. Since that statement has already been executed at least once before, it will already have a parse tree and an execution plan associated with it, and hence there is no need to rebuild it. Well, most of the time.

If the underlying objects referenced by the SQL statement have undergone any structural changes (**alter, analyze**, and so on) between the last and current execution, the statement will be flagged as *INVALID*, so the current server process that executes that statement can rebuild the execution plan for that SQL statement. For example, in the case of an **analyze**, all SQL in the library cache that references the object that is analyzed will be invalidated. Why?

If your table originally contained 1,000,000 rows, and a batch job just infused an additional 5,000,000 rows, as a responsible DBA you will do your part and **analyze** your table after the data infusion is done. Well, don't you think the Oracle Optimizer has a right to know about the fact that you ran an **analyze** on your table? After all, it needs to use the most current statistics on the objects, doesn't it?

If the optimizer was not aware of new statistics, how can it even think of changing the execution plan for that SQL statement, even with such a significant increase in data in the table? Without the invalidation, it will be virtually impossible to know when execution plans for SQL in the library cache need rebuilding. Hence the invalidation of the SQL statement in the library cache is done for any DDL operations that modify the structure of any object or any collection of object statistics. Okay, let's get back to hard versus soft parse.

The server process then progresses to the Bind phase (described in the previous section) and then to the Execute and Fetch phases. Again, it goes to the Fetch phase only if the SQL statement is a *select*.

By skipping the step for building a parse tree and an execution plan, a significant amount of resources can be conserved—not to mention a considerable reduction in contention for the various internal resources needed to perform a hard parse. In the case of a soft parse, time and resources are spent on executing the statement instead of trying to figure out how to execute it. Four out of five dentists recommend soft parses over hard parses. Four out of four dentists recommend no parses over soft parses. Or was that toothbrushes?

NOTE
It is imperative that any aging of SQL statements from the shared pool area also causes hard parses of those SQL statements, as those SQL statements will not be present at the hash addresses in the shared pool area. But when these SQL statements are reparsed, they will map to the same hash address unless the statement has been modified in some fashion.

To Parse or Not to Parse...That Is the Question

How can a SQL statement be not parsed? Well, actually, it does get parsed the first time, but if your application reuses the same SQL statement over and over again, within the same session, then keeping the cursor open and persistent will even eliminate the need for a soft parse within the same session. Most database experts agree that reducing the number of hard parses also improves performance. Some of us go the next step and say that reducing the number of soft parses also improves performance. And it does so without the need to add more memory to the shared pool area. So to support optimally performing shared pool areas, you have to first reduce unnecessary parsing by sharing SQL and using bind variables. When possible, the cursors should be kept open for the duration of the session.

Initialization Parameters and the Shared Pool

The following table lists the initialization parameters of primary concern when tuning the shared pool. Not all of them affect the shared pool directly, but several provide support to overly taxed shared pools on systems using all the latest features, such as Java and RMAN. They also support shared pools that use Parallel Query and the MTS.

Oracle Initialization Parameter	Meaning/Relevance
SHARED_POOL_SIZE	Sets the total size of the shared pool in bytes.
SHARED_POOL_RESERVED_SIZE	Reserves part of the shared pool for large objects—the reserved area.
SHARED_POOL_RESERVED_MIN_ALLOC	Defines the threshold for large objects. Not relevant since Oracle 8.0.3.
LARGE_POOL_SIZE	Introduced in Oracle8 to better manage the space for the shared pool and support shared pool space management for the new features in a more proactive fashion. The cursor-state and user-session-data components of the PGA reside here when Oracle is configured in MTS. This is not part of the default shared pool area.
LARGE_POOL_MIN_ALLOC	Defines the threshold for allocation of objects in the large pool. Not relevant since Oracle 8.0.3.
PARALLEL_AUTOMATIC_TUNING	Causes parallel operations to use the large pool, by automatically setting the LARGE_POOL_SIZE to 15MB if not already set. Available from Oracle8i and up.
JAVA_POOL_SIZE	Reserves space for Java and its related components. This is not part of the shared pool area.
SESSION_CACHED_CURSORS	Although this parameter does not directly affect the shared pool, it does configure the number of cursors that can be kept in the session cursor cache to reduce the probability of soft parses and thus reduce the contention in the shared pool area. Set this parameter so a reasonable number of cursors can be cached. It does consume additional memory on a per session basis.

Configuring the Pools

With Oracle7 there was only one pool to consider, until version 7.3 came around. With Oracle 7.3, the reserved pool was introduced to effectively manage space within the shared pool and segregate large SQL objects from smaller SQL. With Oracle8, the large pool and, with Oracle8i, the Java pool (to support Java programs) was introduced. In spite of all of these new pools, the shared pool still remains the center of attention. With the library and data dictionary caches, as well as space set aside to support the Oracle MTS in Oracle7 systems, it is a critical area for performance. While everyone knows that I/O is expensive and we work hard to avoid it, many forget that as far as CPU time goes, hard parsing done in the shared pool is one of the more CPU-intensive operations. All of this makes configuring the shared pool and the other pools quite important. Fortunately, it is not that difficult.

Configuring the pools is nothing more than setting the parameter in the init.ora and starting or restarting the instance. As with all tuning in the workaday world, the trick is setting the values optimally, so as not to impede other systems or cause repeated changes to these parameters that cause bouncing of the database multiple times, yet provide the needed processing and throughput.

The Shared Pool

There are four parameters that directly affect the shared pool. The three important ones are SHARED_POOL_SIZE, SHARED_POOL_RESERVED_SIZE, and LARGE_POOL_SIZE. The SHARED_POOL_SIZE decides the size of the regular shared pool. The SHARED_POOL_RESERVED_SIZE specifies how much of the shared pool should be configured for the *reserved pool*. The reserved pool is used for large packages, procedures, functions, and such. The LARGE_POOL_SIZE is used for Oracle MTS, Parallel Query, and RMAN. This memory is in addition to the value configured for SHARED_POOL_SIZE. For example, if your SHARED_POOL_SIZE is 128MB and your LARGE_POOL_SIZE is 32MB, this 32MB of memory is in addition to the 128MB allocated for SHARED_POOL_SIZE.

The parameter (SHARED_POOL_RESERVED_MIN_ALLOC) is only valid if your database version is prior to 8.0.3. From 8.0.3 onward, this is an undocumented parameter as it begins with an underscore (_) and like any other undocumented parameter, should be used only on advice from Oracle support.

The Large Pool

The large pool can be configured by using the LARGE_POOL_SIZE parameter in the init.ora. It will take effect when your instance is restarted. Prior to Oracle 8.0.3, the value of LARGE_POOL_MIN_ALLOC indicated the minimum amount to allocate from the large pool for any operation. Since 8.0.3 it has been desupported and can only be used by entering _LARGE_POOL_MIN_ALLOC in the init.ora. There is really no need to do that.

The large pool is especially useful if Oracle is configured to use MTS or if RMAN is used to perform backup operations. When Oracle is configured in the MTS mode, the Cursor State and User Session Data sections of the PGA get moved into the shared pool area. This, of course, competes with the other uses of the shared pool and degrades performance. It is exactly for that reason that you should configure the large pool.

NOTE
Contrary to popular belief, the sort areas for sessions attaching to the Oracle database using the MTS configuration are allocated in the session's PGA instead of the shared pool area. This was last tested in Oracle 8.1.6.

RMAN also uses the regular shared pool, if the large pool is not configured. Parallel operations performed by parallel query slaves require workspace in the shared pool, and configuring the large pool prevents contention and fragmentation of the regular shared pool. In Oracle8i, setting PARALLEL_AUTOMATIC_TUNING to TRUE allows these operations to use the large pool instead of the shared pool, if LARGE_POOL_SIZE is not already set.

The large pool can be initially set to 15–20 percent of the size of the shared pool, depending on the frequency and type of usage. The preferred method to tune the large pool is to increase its size as long as the area named as "large pool memory in use" increases in V$SGASTAT. If the increase shows up as "large pool free memory," you have added more memory than is necessary for the large pool. By configuring the large pool, there is better management of the default shared pool area. Of course, the net effect is that the SGA grows, but by segregating the different functions, contention is reduced and you avoid any one pool becoming overly large. As the size of any pool grows, the cost to maintain it grows—sometimes, beyond the potential return.

The Java Pool

Configuring the Java pool is done with the parameter JAVA_POOL_SIZE. As mentioned earlier, the recommendations for setting this parameter as described in the documentation are too small. Who would have thought that? Several implementations of Oracle on various platforms indicate that a minimum of 100MB should be used for this parameter. Again, this is a separate area independent of the default shared pool area. The default value for JAVA_POOL_SIZE is OS dependent and can be reduced to about 1MB if Java is not used.

Tuning Your Exotic SPA

Before you jump right in and make changes to the init.ora, you will want to get a solid understanding of what is in your shared pool and what problems, if any, it is experiencing. There are a few measurements that can indicate a need to tune the shared pool. In legalese, the indicators that demonstrate a failure toward optimal shared pool performance include but are not limited to:

- High CPU utilization caused by excessive parsing

- ORA-4031 errors (indicating a failure to allocate memory)

- Use of Oracle's MTS

- Installation of Java

- Use of RMAN or parallel operations

And while simple statistics do not define poor performance, low cache-hit ratios in the library and dictionary cache may be symptoms of problems in the shared pool. The focus of the tuning effort here is to understand if the performance issues in the shared pool area are caused due to bad sizing or because the space within the shared pool is not properly managed.

CAUTION
It is very counterproductive to Oracle system performance to over-allocate memory to one or more components of your shared pool.
*Over-allocation of memory here can and will cause significant parsing delays (in some cases we have noticed ten-minute response times for a query such as – **select * from dual;**). Such extreme parsing delays also are accompanied by significant waits for the shared pool and library cache latches. Do not go overboard just to get your ratios in the upper 90s. One more thing: please don't schedule jobs to flush your shared pool every five minutes to get around a problem. Find out what is causing your parsing problems and cure the disease, instead of the symptoms.*

First, take a look at the utilization of the shared pool and other pools. Select the relevant pool from V$SGASTAT, to show the allocation to each pool and what is in each pool. Then query V$SGASTAT and look at the total bytes allocated to the shared pool compared to the amount still free.

```
SVRMGR> select Pool,sum(Bytes)
     2>    from V$SGASTAT
     3>  where pool = 'shared pool'
     4> group by pool;
POOL         SUM(BYTES)
----------- ----------
shared pool   55464348
1 row selected.

SVRMGR> select Pool,Bytes
     2>    from V$SGASTAT
     3>  where Name = 'free memory';
POOL         BYTES
----------- ----------
shared pool   23338928
large pool    14367854
2 rows selected.
```

NOTE
A low value for "free memory" does not necessarily indicate a problem. Realize that the shared pool area is a cache, and it is perfectly normal to use up all of the allocated space. If anything, if you see a very large value for "free memory" (as in the output just shown), it should indicate that you have oversized your shared pool area. A high value for free memory can also indicate a lot of aging that is occurring in your shared pool (if you were to query V$SGASTAT at the right time). The key here is to manage the space appropriately and make use of all the available pools in your version of Oracle. On the flip side, you should periodically query V$SHARED_POOL_RESERVED (if available in your version of Oracle) dynamic performance view and look for increasing values in the Request_Misses column, to indicate a shared pool that is too small.

Use this information along with information about the two major areas of the shared pool(namely the library and dictionary cache), to make an informed decision about changing the value of SHARED_POOL_SIZE. Alternatively, make other decisions such as using SHARED_POOL_RESERVED_SIZE, LARGE_POOL_SIZE, or JAVA_POOL_SIZE, to provide the required zoning of objects within the shared pool area.

The Library Cache

The library cache contains the SQL statements being processed and information about them. By delving into this area it is possible to determine the health of the shared pool. If the shared pool is in good shape, these ratios will be fairly high. But do not run your life purely on the ratios, as in data-warehouse and decision-support applications the ratios may be low yet not portray any significant performance problem.

NOTE

If the application does not use bind variables, looking at these statistics does nothing but generate heartburn. If you can't fix the application or set CURSOR_SHARING=FORCE (Oracle8i and up), just turn the other way, after you have done nominal sizing of the shared pool structure.

```
SVRMGR> select Namespace, Gethitratio, Pinhitratio
      2>    from V$LIBRARYCACHE;
NAMESPACE         GETHITRATIO PINHITRATIO
----------------- ----------- -----------
SQL AREA           .868686869  .916376307
TABLE/PROCEDURE    .784251969  .745541023
BODY                      .75         .75
TRIGGER                     1           1
INDEX                       0           0
CLUSTER            .963768116   .97382199
OBJECT                      1           1
PIPE                        1           1
8 rows selected.
SVRMGR>
```

What is the difference between GETS and PINS? This will help you understand the differences between the GETHITRATIO and the PINHITRATIO. The term GETS is defined to be the number of requests for one or more items in the library cache, and the term PINS is defined to be the number of executions of a given item.

If the GETHITRATIO for several namespaces is low or is declining, there may be room for improvement. If the "SQL AREA" namespace is very low, it indicates that Oracle is not finding very many cursors to share.

Cursors may not be shareable for two reasons. The first reason—quite common in too many applications—is the failure to use bind variables. This causes two statements that are essentially the same to have separate areas in the library cache. Bad! One way to see if this is the case is to query V$SQLAREA and filter the output with a *where clause* that looks for similar SQL statements and count the number of occurrences of each type.

With many off-the-shelf applications, you will find the same statement over and over using a literal instead of a bind variable. To put it mildly, this may very well be one of the costliest and most pervasive disasters in application coding. This results in additional hard parses and increased CPU utilization. The best way to avoid or fix this issue is to incorporate bind variables in the SQL.

If reuse of SQL is not possible, but the database is version 8.1.6 or higher, you can set CURSOR_SHARING to FORCE. This allows Oracle to substitute a system-generated bind variable and thus allow sharing in the future. Information on how many parses have occurred is available by querying V$SYSSTAT for the system or V$SESSTAT for a given session. Here is a sample query from an Oracle8i database (8.1.6.1):

```
SVRMGR> select A.Value total,
    2>          B.Value hard,
    3>          A.Value-B.Value soft,
    4>          round((B.Value/A.Value)*100,1) hardparseperc
    5>    from V$SYSSTAT A, V$SYSSTAT B, V$SYSSTAT C
    6>   where A.Statistic# = 171
    7>     and B.Statistic# = 172;
    TOTAL         HARD        SOFT   HARDPARSEPERC
---------- ---------- ---------- --------------
      536         149         387           27.8
1 row selected.
SVRMGR>
```

NOTE
This query is accurate for Oracle 8.1.6.1 and up, but you will need to query V$SYSSTAT by name to confirm the STATISTIC# for parse count (total) and parse count (hard) as these change from version to version.

NOTE
*Oracle7 does not provide a direct mechanism to determine the number of soft parses using the just-shown V$ views. However, if you want to look at hard versus soft parsing for a given session, you need to turn trace on for that session. You then can study the output of the trace file by processing it via **tkprof**. In the **tkprof** output, the line "Misses in library cache during parse" will provide you with the information you are looking for.*

A high percentage of hard parses indicates that there may be a lot of dynamic SQL or insufficient use of bind variables. Both are costly, since the server process must do a hard parse for each of those statements. The second reason that cursors are not available for sharing could be that the statements are getting aged out. An indicator of this is the ratio of RELOADS to PINS. High values here indicate that statements are aging out and perhaps the shared pool could be larger or better managed. But remember, if the application does not use bind variables, these numbers are meaningless, and resizing of the shared pool just to get the numbers within a certain percentage should be avoided at all costs. Reloads could result from too many objects or large objects (such as packages).

```
SVRMGR> select sum(Reloads)/sum(Pins)
    2>    from V$LIBRARYCACHE;
SUM(RELOADS)/SUM(PINS)
----------------------
         .001234873
```

The aging out of objects in the library cache is a natural function of doing business with limited memory. Values of less than 1 percent are not worth any additional effort. Any performance problems you have are not the result of having to reload a SQL or PL/SQL object.

If you do have a reload problem, but the application uses bind variables and does not have any problems with dynamic SQL, you may simply have too small a shared pool. Your regular shared pool is potentially competing with a few large objects for space. In this case, it would be beneficial to store these large SQL or PL/SQL objects in the reserved pool. If you suspect this is the case, configure the shared pool to have the reserved pool and set the minimum allocation low enough. The following query will help identify which large objects might be competing unfairly for space in the shared pool:

```
SVRMGR> select Name, Sharable_mem
    2>    from V$DB_OBJECT_CACHE
    3>   where type in ('PACKAGE','PACKAGE BODY','FUNCTION'
    4>                   ,'PROCEDURE');
NAME                                                       SHARABLE_MEM
---------------------------------------------------------- ------------
DBMS_APPLICATION_INFO                                             12873
DBMS_APPLICATION_INFO                                              2709
DBMS_STANDARD                                                     15809
STANDARD                                                         218332
DBMS_OUTPUT                                                       14155
DBMS_OUTPUT                                                        6419
6 rows selected.
SVRMGR>
```

The output from this query shows one sizeable package, *standard*. This is one package that should be moved to the reserved area. If there were others, it would definitely be a good idea to reserve some additional space from the shared pool for larger SQL objects by setting the value of SHARED_POOL_RESERVED_SIZE to a value of 15–20 percent of the total of the shared pool. Then set the value of SHARED_POOL_RESERVED_MIN_ALLOC to a value just less than the smallest package you would like to segregate.

NOTE
SHARED_POOL_RESERVED_MIN_ALLOC is a desupported parameter since Oracle 8.0.3, and it is now _SHARED_POOL_RESERVED_MIN_ALLOC. It is recommended that you do not change the value of this parameter unless advised by Oracle Support to do so.

Because these larger packages are now in their own space, they will not compete with smaller statements and packages. When possible, it is a good idea to create smaller packages of related procedures that are called with about the same frequency. One thing to note is that when a procedure from a package is called, the entire package is parsed and loaded in the shared pool. A similar query can be executed against V$SQLAREA to look at Sharable_Mem values for SQL statements. Use this information to find the big ones.

The Data Dictionary Cache

The data dictionary cache contains the rows that have been read from the data dictionary in response to recursive SQL. The data from the data dictionary tables are read into the database buffer cache (like any other table), and the relevant information is transferred into the dictionary cache. Recursive SQL is executed in response to regular SQL. As long as Oracle can resolve recursive SQL from the data dictionary cache, no need arises to reread from disk. This means reduced I/O. The following query can give you an idea of the hit rate and thus how often the system has to do extra work:

```
SVRMGR> select to_char(
  2>        round((1-sum(Getmisses)/sum(Gets))*100,
  3>        1))||'%' "Hit Ratio"
  4>   from V$ROWCACHE;
```

```
Hit Ratio
-----------------------------------------
89.8%
1 row selected.
SVRMGR>
```

In our experience, we have usually seen very high dictionary cache-hit ratios (upper 90s). On systems that don't reflect such high ratios, the typical problem was that the size of the shared pool was too small.

Keep 'em Home

Oracle provides a package that can help improve performance by not allowing selected objects to age out of the shared pool. The package is *DBMS_ SHARED_ POOL*. The procedure to call is **keep**. This process is called pinning or keeping an object. If the procedure execution outlined next generates an error, you might have to run the *dbmspool.sql* script located in the $ORACLE_HOME/rdbms/admin directory.

```
SQL> exec dbms_shared_pool.keep('STANDARD');
PL/SQL procedure successfully completed.
```

After executing this procedure, Oracle will keep this package in memory. Some folks like to use this on very large packages that aren't necessarily used frequently enough to keep them in memory, naturally. By pinning them, they ensure that the package is present in memory when needed, and that it will not encounter any runtime errors while trying to load. Use this judiciously as it can cause other objects to age out at a faster rate by not allowing memory to be freed for other objects. This can lead to errors in allocating space for new objects needing to be parsed. Once the package is no longer needed, it can be released by calling the **unkeep** procedure in the *DBMS_SHARED_POOL* package.

To see what has been pinned, look at the Kept column of V$DB_OBJECT_CACHE:

```
SVRMGR> select Owner, Name, Type, Sharable_mem, Kept
     2>    from V$DB_OBJECT_CACHE
     3>   where Type in ('FUNCTION','PACKAGE','PACKAGE BODY',
     4>                   'PROCEDURE')
     5>   order by Owner, Name;
OWNE NAME                            TYPE             SHARABLE_MEM KEP
---- ------------------------------- ---------------- ------------ ---
SYS  DBMS_APPLICATION_INFO           PACKAGE                 12873 NO
SYS  DBMS_APPLICATION_INFO           PACKAGE BODY             2865 NO
```

```
SYS  STANDARD                    PACKAGE           218604 YES
SYS  STANDARD                    PACKAGE BODY       28576 YES
4 rows selected.
SVRMGR>
```

It is also possible to pin unnamed objects such as cursors (handles to SQL statements). To keep a cursor, you must select the ADDRESS and the HASH_VALUE for that cursor from V$SQLAREA and then use their values as arguments to the *keep* procedure.

```
SQL> exec dbms_shared_pool.keep('21589568,4139960791','C');
PL/SQL procedure successfully completed.
```

For more information on the syntax of the DBMS_SHARED_POOL package, run the **desc** command providing the package name as an argument.

Many database administrators recommend pinning the key system packages as soon as the instance starts. This avoids problems for those packages, and it avoids having them step on smaller objects. It is also a good idea to identify any large application packages and pin them as well. The ones most often recommended for pinning are STANDARD, DBMS_DESCRIBE, DBMS_APPLICATION_INFO, DBMS_STANDARD, DBMS_OUTPUT, and DBMS_UTILITY. These can be pinned as SYS during startup, and no special privileges are needed to do just that.

NOTE

*When tested on Oracle 8.1.6 (may be relevant in other versions too), the flushing of the shared pool did not flush "pinned objects," that is, objects you have Kept. These objects get flushed when the instance is bounced (obviously) or if you were to specifically execute the **unkeep** commands.*

Shared Pool Fragmentation: Proactively Managing ORA-04031

Besides poor performance due to reloads and failure to reuse SQL, the most common complaint about the shared pool is fragmentation. The ORA-04031 is the single most powerful statement that Oracle is trying to communicate to you to proactively manage your shared pool and its related components. Looking it up in some of Oracle's information sources yields a wealth of meaningful information. Not really! What they have to say is next.

- **Cause**   More shared memory is needed than was allocated in the shared pool.

- **Action**   If the shared pool is out of memory, either use the DBMS_ SHARED_ POOL package to pin large packages, reduce your use of shared memory, or increase the amount of available shared memory by increasing the value of the init.ora parameters "SHARED_POOL_ RESERVED_ SIZE" and "SHARED_ POOL_SIZE". If the large pool is out of memory, increase the INIT.ORA parameter "LARGE_POOL_SIZE".

Well, now you know as much as before the error. The question is which of those options will fix the problem. To solve the issue, first understand the problem.

What Causes Fragmentation of the Shared Pool?

Many things control the rate and frequency of fragmentation in the shared pool area. Here are some perpetrators:

- Frequent object aging from the shared pool (may be a sizing problem)

- A high value for free memory in V$SGASTAT (if it is caused due to aging)

- Large objects are not KEPT in the shared pool

- Many SQL statements of the same kind that do not use bind variables

- Not using CURSOR_SHARING in Oracle 8.1.6, if the application cannot be modified to use bind variables

- Excessive parsing (partly as a result of large objects not being KEPT in the shared pool and also due to lack of caching cursors in the sessions (not using SESSION_CACHED_CURSORS)

- Many large anonymous PL/SQL blocks

- Not configuring and using the reserved pool (Oracle 7.3 and up) and the large pool (Oracle 8.0 and up)

Imagine that when the shared pool is allocated it is one contiguous chunk of memory. Now as the first packages and statements are parsed, they get memory allocated in nice contiguous chunks of exactly the size they need. No problem here. After the shared pool gets filled, Oracle has to make room for additional objects. This requires use of the least recently used (LRU) algorithm to manage the space within the shared pool.

Oracle pitches out the least recently used objects. Since the objects were loaded on a first come first served basis and not in order of their future use, the shared pool ends up looking a bit like Swiss cheese. Still okay. Assume that most new statements will fit in those holes, so they just plug right in. But now along comes a gargantuan package that will not fit in any of those holes. Oracle starts scrambling around to clear more objects out until there is enough room.

This is not an issue until one of those little packages is pinned (in use) and cannot be cleared. That little package is like the little old lady who won't sell her house to the shopping center developer even though all of her neighbors have. The shopping center developers still can't build a mall, because they can't get the old lady to clear out. Basically, the developers have to call the venture capitalists, and declare an ORA-04031. "unable to allocate %s bytes of shared memory."

The ORA-04031 Error in Oracle 7.3 and Up

The probability of ORA-04031 errors occurring has reduced a great deal in Oracle 7.3 and up, and this due to changes made to the shared pool space allocation algorithm. Prior to Oracle 7.3, when an object was %s bytes in size, then "%s contiguous bytes" were required to store it in the shared pool. Failing that an ORA-04031 was generated. Since Oracle 7.3, Oracle just needs to find %s bytes between the free memory and the objects that could be tossed out.

Prior to Oracle 8.0, apart from the normal usage of the shared pool for SQL statements, it was also the home for the stack space and the cursor state components of the PGA, when a user connection was made using the MTS. This further added to the fragmentation of the shared pool. In late versions of Oracle 7.3, Parallel Query provided more competition for space in the shared pool, and RMAN joined the fray in 8.0.

To alleviate this problem, in Oracle 8.0 the initialization parameter LARGE_POOL_SIZE was introduced. When this parameter is configured, MTS/Parallel Query/RMAN will utilize the space allocated for the large pool for its operations, rather than the default shared pool area. This further reduced the frequency of encounters with ORA-04031. Of course, none of these improvements deal with the issues of dynamic and ad hoc SQL or bad coding.

To avoid encountering this situation, you will need to make sure you have the right amount of acreage for your shopping center and you may want to do some zoning. This is where SHARED_POOL_RESERVED_SIZE comes into play along with SHARED_POOL_RESERVED_MIN_ALLOC, as well as setting LARGE_POOL_SIZE. These allow the database administrator to set limits on who gets into what part of the shared pool. Additionally, pinning (*dbms_shared_pool.keep*) large objects in memory prevents their space from being chewed up by the little guys. Set the size of the reserved pool based on the sum of the sizes of the objects you want to pin.

Wait Events that Affect the Shared Pool Area

Regardless of what the hit ratios are for the library and dictionary cache, you should make it a habit to determine the "wait events" that affect the shared pool area. These can be found by querying V$SESSION_WAIT and looking for events such as latch free if the latch is shared pool, library cache, library cache load lock, and so on.

```
Select SW.Sid, S.Username, substr(SW.Event, 1, 35), SW.Wait_time
   from V$SESSION S, V$SESSION_WAIT SW
 where SW.Event not like 'SQL*Net%'
   and SW.Sid = S.Sid
order by SW.Wait_time, SW.Event;
```

This query produces a list of events currently in a wait state. If wait events exist for shared pool resources, use this information to direct the problem solving. Most problems in the shared pool area can be addressed by either increasing its size (up to a certain limit) or more importantly by making better use of the various pools (large pool, reserved area, java pool). However it should be noted that reducing the need for those resources by reusing SQL and keeping parsing to a minimum will go a long way toward keeping this cache "contention free." The following are some common events that are related to the shared pool area. A complete list of wait events is available in the Oracle Reference manual.

latch free	Indicates latch contention for the latch# that is being waited on. If the problem persists, you should determine what is causing the contention for the latch and fix the underlying problem. Your goal should be to cure the disease not the symptom. A *latch free* event is a symptom of a bigger problem. For example, if the latch# derived from this is a library cache latch (assuming that the shared pool is configured appropriately), it may indicate a significant amount of hard parsing. This usually is a problem with applications that have *hard-coded* values in them. Either rewrite them with bind variables or upgrade to Oracle 8i and use CURSOR_SHARING=FORCE— or just look the other way.

library cache load lock	This is required to load objects into the library cache. This wait event can occur when a significant amount of reloads/loads are occurring (normally caused due to either lack of reuse of SQL statements or a improperly sized shared pool area).
library cache lock	Waits associated with concurrency of multiple processes accessing the library cache. Can indicate an improperly sized shared pool area, as this lock needs to be acquired to locate objects in the library cache.
library cache pin	This wait event is also associated with library cache concurrency and can occur when a given object needs to be modified or examined in the library cache.

In a Nutshell

Tuning the shared pool, like any other part of your Oracle system, requires understanding the interdependencies of all components. In this case, it means knowing the nature of the SQL being used. The relative sizes of packages, procedures, and functions affect the shared pool and the other related pools. It requires that the database administrator proactively manage the shared pool and large pool where applicable. Knowing which options the system is using determines the configuration of some of the pools. If RMAN is used as a part of the backup methodology, or if parallel operations or MTS is used, the large pool must be configured to support these tools. If Java is installed, Oracle will need a robust Java pool.

Don't let cache-hit ratios be the only driver of tuning decisions. Use wait events to direct your tuning efforts down the right path. If the system is experiencing a high number of reloads in the library cache, it may be starving for memory. Consider increasing SHARED_POOL_SIZE. But before doing that, also consider the benefits of SQL tuning or segregating large packages and procedures or utilizing open and persistent cursors.

Excessive aging may be caused due to one or more large objects called by one or more programs. These large objects should be pinned in the reserved shared pool area. Query V$SQLTEXT to confirm that the aging issue is not caused by the parsing of hundreds of essentially identical statements, with the only difference being the literal value in the *where clause*. If this is the case, more memory isn't going to help except for a short while. If the application can be rewritten to use bind variables, do so. If not, and if the system is based on Oracle 8.1.6 or higher, try setting CURSOR_SHARING to FORCE.

NOTE
There is a significant overhead during parsing for your Oracle system if CURSOR_SHARING is set to FORCE. Anecdotal evidence puts the overhead at approximately 25 percent. Test and verify this in your environment before implementing on production systems.

Avoid simply *flushing* the shared pool to clear everything out. You might get one package to run, but at a high cost in performance to all the other users on the system who are subject to hard parses where they would have used a soft parse.

If poor performance is traced back to recursive SQL having to constantly repopulate the data dictionary cache, definitely increase the shared pool. However, be careful that the ensuing increase in the SGA does not cause problems elsewhere that might be worse.

Pinning or keeping packages and other objects in the shared pool can provide excellent relief from aging issues as well as shared pool fragmentation, thus avoiding the ORA-04031 error. This is done with the package *DBMS_SHARED_POOL* using the *keep* procedure. Many database administrators find pinning key system and application packages at the startup of an instance helps dramatically. These steps are often added to the startup scripts.

The key point is to add memory when needed and reconfigure the memory for best use by reallocating it among the pools and reserved area as appropriate. And last but not least, as with all other tuning efforts, stop when the agreed-upon performance goals are met.

CHAPTER
6

Instance Tuning—The Database Buffer Cache

Myth & Folklore

A 60 percent database buffer cache-hit ratio indicates bad database performance.

Fact

Not true. As the nature of operations on the database changes, so should this value. During the day, a high cache-hit ratio (CHR) may be observed for OLTP operations as they access the same set of blocks. But at night, as batch jobs run and manipulate a wide range of data blocks, you should expect the CHR to fall. Keep in mind that blocks that were needed during the day are still there, but suddenly many new blocks are being requested. This will result in a lower CHR. If user processes are not *waiting* for blocks to be read from disk, *waiting* for free buffers, or complaining about bad performance, a 60 percent CHR is just fine. Tuning is about what users need to get their jobs done. It is not about achieving an arbitrary ratio.

Myth & Folklore

A cache-hit ratio in the database buffer cache of 99 percent or more means that the Oracle database is performing at its peak levels.

Fact

A very high cache-hit ratio in the database buffer cache can be misleading. Frequently executed SQL statements that perform full table scans of the same small table or correlated subqueries (that read the same set of blocks over and over) can elevate the CHR to artificially high levels. This can make you believe that Oracle is working at peak efficiency when trouble is brewing. From the users' perspective, if they are waiting for blocks to be read from disk, waiting for free buffers, or waiting on the LRU chain in the database buffer cache, it doesn't matter if the CHR is 99 percent —you should recognize that you have a performance problem on your hands. We will go so far as to say that on most "real systems" a high CHR (such as 99 percent) usually indicates extremely inefficient SQL in the applications. You need to troubleshoot and tune those offending SQL statements to get acceptable response times.

he myths we talk about in this chapter are some of our pet peeves in the world of Oracle Performance Management. And we have good reason to feel this way. Allow us to share with you a "war story" that will put things in the right perspective.

One of us was onsite at a customer that was experiencing a severe system performance problem with an Oracle database. The application was third-party supplied and performed the task of tracking the time of the corporation's temporary employees. After some initial measurements of system performance were done, it was determined that the system was experiencing severe CPU bottlenecks. Further investigation revealed six Oracle processes running batch reports that caused the CPU bottleneck. These reports needed to be repeatedly executed at various times during the course of a business day. Each Oracle process was consuming more than 99 percent of a single CPU (when there was really no need for that). The system was configured with six processors. You can see why there was a CPU bottleneck on this system, apart from the fact that there had to be some method of scheduling these jobs, say no more than four of these jobs could run concurrently.

The real culprit causing the CPU contention was unearthed when the Oracle processes were traced and the most expensive SQL was ascertained. Before this · exercise, the database CHR was 98 percent and the Oracle database administrator (DBA) was under the assumption that Oracle was performing optimally, when the reality was something totally opposite. The culprit SQL statements were all correlated subqueries and each ran for 45 minutes, utilizing all of the horsepower of a single CPU. Six such queries ran and literally crippled the system.

When the correlated subqueries were rewritten to queries with "inline views" (there is an example of how to do this in the chapter "Application Tuning—Issues that Concern a DBA" in the "How Not to Write SQL" section), the SQL statements ran for 45 seconds, utilizing only 65 percent of the horsepower of a single CPU. It was pretty obvious that we had achieved much better application scalability after the rewrite. Further, after the rewritten queries were deployed, the CHR dropped to 72 percent, but there was a lot more work getting done during a day. For the DBA, this was a whole new paradigm, as historically he was used to correlating high cache-hit ratios with optimal performance. Do you now see why it can be very dangerous to tune Oracle using cache-hit ratios instead of wait events?

In this chapter, we will discuss how the database buffer cache works, the newer components of the database buffer cache, important initialization parameters to consider when tuning this cache, and how to reduce the likelihood of a table aging out of the cache. Tuning the database buffer cache is a matter of understanding how it works and how to detect the symptoms of poor performance. As pointed out by the myths, the CHR can be high and the users may still complain about performance issues. Or the CHR may be low, and yet no one is complaining.

What Is the Five-Minute Caching Rule—or Is It Ten Now?

A cache in the context of a database management system is a segment of shared memory that is allocated for data retrieval and manipulation. The data cache of Oracle is called the *database buffer cache*. It should be emphasized here that any cache (including Oracle's) suffers from the law of diminishing returns after reaching a certain size. The exceptions to this rule are operating systems and hardware platforms that support *supercaches*. The concept of supercaching (relevant to certain hardware platforms) is based on the fact that the memory management unit (MMU) within the server is in charge of handling the translations of memory addresses. Some servers support very sophisticated MMU manipulations and thus are capable of managing very large chunks of memory in an efficient manner.

Although there are many advanced techniques within Oracle and the operating system to determine whether the database buffer cache is sized right, a common rule, called the "five-minute rule," can provide some high-level insight into this important aspect of Oracle. This rule was proposed by Gray and Reuter in their work *Transaction Processing: Techniques and Concepts* and is derived from the following equation:

Frequency = ((Memory Cost per Byte – Disk Cost per Byte) * Object Size)/Object Access per Second Cost

Using disk, memory, and I/O subsystem prices in 1997, it was determined that the point of diminishing returns for a cache was approximately around five minutes. Given current day prices of the aforementioned components, it is possible (based on your operating system platform) that the frequency is between 8–10 minutes, as prices have gone down since 1997. What this all means for Oracle is that any object (such as table, index, and so on) that is accessed at least once in the past 10 minutes should be a candidate for memory caching. In our world, memory caching is data in the database buffer cache. Data that is not accessed at least once in the past 10 minutes should really not be forced to stay in memory, as the performance of a cache does not increase in a significant manner after a certain size. In that case it is cheaper and more efficient to perform physical I/O.

Further, Oracle is very well designed to perform I/O and it does it very well. Also, there have been significant improvements in storage hardware that make large-sized Oracle caching not that attractive. The point we are trying to make here is that you should resist the urge to arbitrarily increase the size of your database buffer cache. Be aware of Sir Isaac Newton's third law of motion: for every action there is an equal and opposite reaction. Do not make dramatic changes to the database buffer cache size without understanding its implications.

How Does the Database Buffer Cache Work?

First, data is read into memory (if not already present) before it can be manipulated (read or write). Second, Oracle manages this data transfer from file to memory and back again by reading and writing database blocks, not individual rows. Therefore, when a row is requested, the server process reads the appropriate database block in memory. If the row is retrieved using an index scan, the necessary index blocks will also be read into memory. The requested blocks get read into the database buffer cache, which is segmented into blocks of memory equal to the size of a database block. Third, there is a finite amount of memory available to hold these blocks, so eventually some blocks need to be overwritten by more recently requested blocks.

Database Buffer Cache Management Prior to Oracle8i

In versions of Oracle prior to Oracle8i, it was easy to see that the database buffer cache in its most basic form is a type of inventory control system. It includes a place (the cache) to put the inventory (the database blocks). It also has a means of managing which blocks to get rid of to make room for new blocks by following a modified first-in-first-out (FIFO) management practice. The management method is called the least recently used (LRU) algorithm.

Let's think of an example that explains LRU management in the database buffer cache: your neighborhood supermarket. When you are waiting to check out, you are usually standing in a cramped space between shelves crammed with little things—a last-ditch effort to sell you things you usually don't need. Many of those items are available only on these shelves, and you may often see new things on these shelves. Some of the items tend to show up for a short period and then disappear. Some items in great demand are always there, such as *TV Guide* and chewing gum. The space occupied by some things is eventually taken over by other neat-looking little things. But items in great demand don't seem to leave this "real estate." Items that are not in demand or least bought (used) by the store's customers just sit on the shelf. Since this shelf space is expensive and precious, the store manager periodically replaces items that are not in demand with new items that customers may buy. A similar process occurs in the LRU list of the database buffer cache. Blocks that are not being used will eventually get replaced by new data blocks...you get the picture!

Oracle uses this modified FIFO management method based on the LRU algorithm and it is managed through a linked list of block addresses. The server processes accessing the blocks manages the LRU list by way of one or more LRU latches (structures that facilitate some important mutually exclusive tasks that are common for memory operations).

When a block is read into memory, the server process that reads it from disk copies it into an "available buffer" in the database buffer cache. It is important to note here that an available buffer may not necessarily have been empty (it could contain data from a previous read operation). It then adds the block's address to the most recently used (MRU) end of the LRU list. As each block is read into the database buffer cache, it is added to the most recently used end, thus pushing the previous block closer to the least recently used end. At some point, the blocks will have to be reused.

Besides the LRU list, there is another list associated with the database buffer cache. This is the dirty list—a list of buffers whose contents have been changed. Once the contents of a buffer has changed, Oracle will not allow the buffer to be overwritten until the contents have been written to disk. The database writer (DBWR) is responsible for keeping the dirty list to a manageable size. Unfortunately, since this operation involves physical I/O, it is subject to the performance limits of the I/O system. If the I/O system limits the database writer from fulfilling these responsibilities in a timely manner, more wait events may arise. As DBWR writes these blocks to disk, they (logically) get moved back to the LRU list (as they are no longer dirty). A given block can either be dirty or available for reuse (free).

The management of the LRU list for Oracle versions, including 7.3, can be explained using a simple example of a five-block database buffer cache. Imagine that the database buffer cache has five blocks, 1 through 5. Now imagine that a process starts reading blocks into memory. Five blocks of data (A–E) are read into the buffers (1–5) of the database buffer cache. Block A goes into buffer 1, B into 2, C into 3, D into 4, and E into 5. When block F (a new block) needs to be read, where will it go? Let's look at the LRU list from least to most recently used end before F gets into the picture. It is in the order 1, 2, 3, 4, and 5 as depicted by the following table:

1 = block A   2 = block B   3 = block C   4 = block D   5 = block E

Therefore the new block could go into buffer 1 since the block in buffer 1 was the first read and so seemingly the last used. And the data in buffer 1 (block A) can get overwritten (if the demand for buffers warrants that). If the data in buffer 1 (block A) was modified and not yet written to disk, then it is written to disk first before it is reused for another block. Thus the LRU list is modified as shown in the following table:

1 = block F   2 = block B   3 = block C   4 = block D   5 = block E

Additionally, it is important to know that all associated data, index, and rollback blocks must be read into the database buffer cache before the data itself can be retrieved or manipulated. Now stop and think about that for a minute. If a job requires that data be read and it uses indexes to find that data, there are now blocks from both tables and any indexes used in the database buffer cache. If the data is being updated, the process performing the update has to read rollback segment blocks (and rollback segment headers) into memory as well. This can cause the buffer cache to get quite crowded and some blocks to be aged out.

If some other processes need the data in the aged-out blocks at a later time, they will have to perform physical I/O and get those blocks back into memory. And now, to add insult to injury, we find that different operations and table attributes affect how the server process deals with updating the LRU list as it reads blocks. For example, when doing full table scans, Oracle puts the blocks for the table being scanned at the LRU end of the list, so that these blocks can be aged the fastest. But if the table's *cache* attribute is on, the server process puts those blocks on the MRU end of the list. When improperly used, this can cause contention and unnecessary physical I/O. The number of blocks it utilizes in the MRU end of the list when the cache attribute is on is subject to an internal Oracle kernel setting.

Database Buffer Cache Management in Oracle8i and Up

The algorithm that manages the database buffer cache in Oracle8i and up is a lot different than the old LRU algorithm. It is called the *touch-count algorithm*. The basic concept behind this new algorithm is to manage the buffers in the database buffer cache based on the number of accesses or "touches" to a block. This is more efficient than moving a block "chronologically" to the top of an LRU list every time it is used. This algorithm significantly eliminates the overhead associated with managing the LRU list. Further, it totally eliminates any need to constantly "latch" a buffer to move it on the list. A buffer is no longer moved from its current location on the list upon each access or "touch." When a buffer is accessed, its touch-count counter is *incremented*.

So how do blocks get aged? It is a pretty complicated process, but we will explain it in very simple terms. There is an internal threshold that is set to decide which buffers stay on the list and which ones are aged. When a block needs to be aged, its touch-count is checked against this threshold. If the touch-count is greater than the threshold, the block's touch-count is set to either a low value or half of its original value (internally defined and configurable). This is to give the block a second chance to stay in the cache, as it has been used in the near past.

If a block's touch-count is less than the threshold, it is selected for aging and is replaced with the new data that is brought into the database buffer cache. Unlike the LRU algorithm, where the new block is brought to the top of the LRU list, the touch-point algorithm inserts the block in the middle of the list after resetting the block's touch-count counter. The rationale behind this method is to make the block "earn" its way up to the top of a list.

There can only be a finite number of blocks above the midpoint, and subject to that limitation, all blocks with touch-counts above the threshold are moved to the top of the list (which for all practical reasons are blocks above the midpoint). The implementation of this new algorithm causes the database buffer cache to be supported by three lists: the main list, the auxiliary list, and the replacement list. The details of this are beyond the scope of this book, but we hope we have at least whetted your appetite.

NOTE
Even though there is enough documentation to suggest that this new algorithm is implemented in Oracle8, our investigation of the "internal parameters" that are required for this new algorithm suggest that the change occurred only in Oracle8i.

Configuring the Buffer Pools

The database buffer cache has been traditionally configured by setting only two initialization parameters, namely, DB_BLOCK_SIZE and DB_BLOCK_BUFFERS. DB_BLOCK_BUFFERS is set to the number of blocks that can be buffered. Typical values range from a few hundred to tens of thousands. Since the size of a block determines the size of each of the buffers, the value of DB_BLOCK_SIZE is important as well. The total size of the database buffer cache is determined by the number of buffers times the block size. Thus if DB_BLOCK_SIZE = 8192 and DB_BLOCK_BUFFERS = 10000, the database buffer cache is 81,920,000 bytes in size or about 80MB. This is still the most basic configuration required. The value for this cache can be seen immediately after starting an instance on the line for Database Buffers:

```
SVRMGR> startup
ORACLE instance started.
Total System Global Area          48572320 bytes
Fixed Size                           64912 bytes
Variable Size                     45137920 bytes
Database Buffers                   2048000 bytes
Redo Buffers                         73728 bytes
Database mounted.
Database opened.
```

Just as Oracle recognized how large-sized SQL and PL/SQL wreaked havoc with the shared pool area, Oracle also realized that differing access patterns for tables made quite a mess in the database buffer cache. With Oracle8 came subsets of the database buffer cache that allow the database administrator to segregate tables with differing cache needs in much the same way we segregate large PL/SQL from smaller packages. By adding the *keep* pool and the *recycle* pool, there are now three different areas to manage the database buffer cache. The third is, of course, the original, now known as the *default* pool. From Oracle 7.3 and up, it is also possible to configure multiple LRU latches to avoid contention in accessing the LRU list and finding useable buffers.

Start with the Default Pool

The default pool is actually the original database buffer cache. It is not specifically allocated. Setting the value of DB_BLOCK_BUFFERS to some number of buffers configures the total number of buffers available for all pools. For example:

```
DB_BLOCK_BUFFERS = 10000
```

Any object not specifically targeted at one of the other pools will be placed in the default pool. When configuring multiple pools, it is also necessary to configure multiple LRU latches. This is accomplished by setting the value of DB_BLOCK_LRU_LATCHES. Ideally, this value should be set to twice the number of CPUs available to the instance. This is to proactively configure the number of LRU latches to the allowed maximum, so that there is no contention caused due to lack of LRU latches. In our experience, we have observed no measurable overhead for setting it at the maximum value. Oracle defaults this parameter to the number of CPUs on the system:

```
DB_BLOCK_LRU_LATCHES = 16 /* This is for an 8-CPU machine */
```

The Keep Pool

The keep pool is designed to specifically address the needs of small tables that require very fast access. Lookup tables and other small (but often used) tables should be assigned to the keep pool. This facilitates avoiding the effort required to reread the data block from disk after it has been aged out. Objects placed in the keep pool will not compete with objects placed in the other two pools and will only get aged out as competition from other keep pool objects forces them out. The keep pool is established by setting the initialization parameter BUFFER_POOL_KEEP to a certain number of blocks (from the value of DB_BLOCK_BUFFERS). However, you must also set the number of LRU latches for this pool from the value of DB_BLOCK_LRU_LATCHES:

```
BUFFER_POOL_KEEP = (buffers:2000, lru_latches:2)
```

Also keep in mind that the sum of the default, keep, and recycle pool buffers cannot be more than was allocated to DB_BLOCK_BUFFERS. Nor can the sum of latches for the three pools be more than the number of latches specified by DB_BLOCK_LRU_LATCHES.

The Recycle Pool

The recycle pool is configured in a similar manner to the keep pool. The parameter BUFFER_POOL_RECYCLE is set to some number of buffers and some number of latches:

```
BUFFER_POOL_RECYCLE = (buffers:1000, lru_latches:1)
```

This allocates 1,000 of the 10,000 (per setting in DB_BLOCK_BUFFERS) available to the database buffer cache pools to the recycle pool, along with one LRU latch to manage those blocks. Assign large objects to this pool that are likely to be accessed with some frequency, but that may cause other objects to be aged out prematurely. Large objects are those that are accessed in a random fashion and that account for a sizeable percentage of the random reads. The definition of the term "sizeable" is specific to each application and database. It is recommended to assign those objects to the recycle pool where the number of block gets (logical reads) for that object is about the same as the number of physical reads. This near one-to-one relationship between logical and physical reads is a good indicator that this object does not benefit from caching and is likely to cause other important objects to age out of the default pool if they have to share the same pool. Identify these tables by executing queries against suspect tables with autotrace turned on, by using tkprof to look at the number of physical reads versus logical reads, or by viewing V$CACHE and V$BH.

NOTE
The instance will not start if the number of latches to be configured for the keep or recycle pool is not specified. Also note that the number of buffers in the default pool will be equal to (DB_BLOCK_BUFFERS–(BUFFER_POOL_KEEP+BUFFER_POOL_RECYCLE)). A similar calculation is done for the number of latches for the default pool as long as there are at least 50 buffers per latch. The V$BUFFER_POOL dynamic performance view provides information on how many buffers are allocated to each of the pools.

NOTE
For accurate information to be shown in V$CACHE and V$BH, the catparr.sql script, which is located under $ORACLE_HOME/rdbms/admin, needs to be executed every time an object is added or dropped from the database.

Assigning Objects to a Pool

Objects can be assigned to the pool of choice when they are created. For example:

```
create table EMP (Empid number,
                  Lname varchar2(30),
                  Fname varchar2(30),
                  Salary number(8,2))
tablespace EMP_DATA01
storage (buffer_pool keep);
```

This assigns the EMP table to the keep pool. When the *buffer_pool* parameter is not specified, the object is placed in the default pool. An object can also be altered by changing the value of the *buffer_pool* attribute in the storage clause in an alter statement.

Using the Cache Option

This is not the lottery—nothing about your instance should be a game of chance. The cache option is another attribute of a segment that will change the way Oracle manages that segment's presence in the database buffer cache. This is especially true for database versions prior to Oracle8. Specifically, this affects tables undergoing full table scans. By default, the cache option is turned off when an object is created unless otherwise specified. This results in the blocks for that segment being added to the least recently used end of the LRU list (recall that this has changed in Oracle8i) during a full table scan. That's good, because it means that you don't flush the cache out when doing a full table scan. But it is not so good if that segment is frequently used and always accessed by full table scans, as is often the case with smaller tables. This means that if the *cache* attribute is not used, the probability for a process to perform physical I/O to return data on that segment is high. Further, the probability of the blocks aging out of the cache is also high.

When creating or altering the segment, the *cache* attribute can be turned on. For example, **alter table EMP cache;** turns on caching for the EMP table. Now any time a full table scan is performed on the EMP table, the blocks will be added to the most recently used (MRU) end of the LRU list. This results in increasing the probability of the EMP table to stay in the database buffer cache. But it may also result in other table blocks aging out to make room for "the new blocks." Thus the EMP table with the cache attribute should now be considered for placement in the keep pool.

Analyzing the Database Buffer Cache

Analyzing the database buffer cache involves getting statistics on it, which include logical reads and physical reads, checking to see which segments currently have blocks in it, and identifying which resources related to the database buffer cache are in short supply. This information can be gleaned from the report.txt, STATSPACK reports, and V$SYSTEM_EVENT, V$SESSION_EVENT. Additionally, the database buffer cache provides information that can help in diagnosing I/O application-related problems. So let's start with the one we all know, the cache-hit ratio.

Understanding Cache-Hit Ratios

This sounds like a Las Vegas term for doing well at the slot machines. Though it is not as exciting as being in Las Vegas, it is more meaningful in terms of an Oracle instance. Besides, the Oracle CHR is likely to be significantly higher than any "Cash" hit ratio you're likely to achieve in Las Vegas.

This value is the ratio of how many times a block is requested and the breakdown of how many times the Oracle database buffer cache was able to supply it by way of a logical read versus a physical read. Logical reads occur when the server process finds the block in the database buffer cache. A physical read occurs if the server has to read the data file and copy the block into the cache. Physical reads are always followed by logical reads (the block is read from disk into the cache, then Oracle logically reads it from the cache), though not all logical reads are preceded by physical reads. Logical reads are the combination of *consistent gets* and *db block gets* from V$SYSSTAT or report.txt.

Following is a common formula to determine the CHR. It considers the ratio of physical to logical reads, and subtracts the physical reads that preceded the logical reads.

```
CHR = 100 * (1 - (physical reads / (consistent gets + db block gets
                                    - physical reads))
```

If V$SYSSTAT shows the following values:

```
consistent gets = 47229
db block gets = 2148
physical reads = 3923
```

we can calculate the CHR as

```
CHR = 100 * (1- (3923/(47229+2148-3923))) = 91.37%
```

When doing analysis of the CHR, be certain to correlate the value to the time of day. Compare readings from 2:00P.M. on one day to the same time on another day to determine if performance has degraded. When comparing performance between two different times, be sure you understand the differences in the load and types of operations being performed. For example, a comparison between 2:00P.M. at the height of OLTP activity to 2:00A.M. when massive updating by way of batch jobs is happening is not particularly valid. It is not unreasonable for performance to be different in a case like that.

NOTE
When comparing performance numbers even during the same time periods, you should know that the second day's numbers have the first day's numbers embedded in them. Performance numbers retrieved from almost all dynamic performance views (V$ views) are cumulative from the time the instance was last started. To factor the first day's numbers in the second day is a very important consideration during performance data collections.

If multiple pools have been implemented, it is possible to drill down further with cache-hit ratios and get the cache-hit ratio for the specific pool. The information of concern is in V$BUFFER_POOL_STATISTICS. This view is created by executing $ORACLE_HOME/rdbms/admin/catperf.sql (if you have not already done so). Use the same formula as was used for the generic CHR. The following is a sample query on V$BUFFER_POOL_STATISTICS:

```
select Physical_Reads, Db_Block_Gets, Consistent_Gets
   from V$BUFFER_POOL_STATISTICS
 where Name = 'KEEP';
```

This query can be used for the recycle pool as well by substituting the string KEEP with RECYCLE. With this information, you can resize the database buffer cache or just one of the pools as needed. To get meaningful results, run the query multiple times and get a trend.

With the keep pool, the goal will be a very high cache-hit ratio. This means that the tables most often sought are always in memory and therefore available immediately.

Again, caution is in order. A value of 100 percent may be an indicator that too many buffers have been allocated to the keep pool that might be better used elsewhere. On the other hand, the CHR for the recycle pool is likely to be dismal. The idea is to free those blocks up as quickly as possible for the next "recyclable" object. As with all tuning issues, it may take several iterations before a suitable value is found for each of the pools. Again, this discussion on CHRs should be kept in perspective of the "Five-Minute Caching Rule."

What's in the Database Buffer Cache?

For those of you with inquiring minds, it can be fun and useful to see which objects are using the largest part of the database buffer cache. The same objects are often the ones that when put in the appropriate pool can reduce physical I/O. The following query provides some insight:

```
select O.Owner, O.Object_Type, O.Object_Name, count(B.Objd)
   from V$BH B, DBA_OBJECTS O
 where B.Objd = O.Object_Id
 group by O.Owner, O.Object_Type, O.Object_Name
 having count(B.Objd) > (select to_number(Value*.05)
                    from V$PARAMETER
                    where Name = 'db_block_buffers');
```

This will return a list of all objects using more than 5 percent of the database buffer cache. These are the objects to consider first when assigning objects to pools. Here is an example using a 5 percent threshold:

OWNER	OBJECT_TYPE	OBJECT_NAME	COUNT(B.OBJD)
DSTG	INDEX	COMPANY_STATUS_PK	245
SYS	CLUSTER	C_OBJ#	440
SYS	INDEX	I_OBJAUTH1	206
SYS	TABLE	OBJAUTH$	185

Depending on the size of the database buffer cache, you can set the threshold value for this query appropriately.

Wait Events that Affect the Database Buffer Cache

Regardless of the CHR, you should make it a habit to periodically determine the "wait events" that affect the database buffer cache. These can be found by querying V$SESSION_WAIT and looking for events such as *buffer busy waits* or *free buffer waits*. The event *latch free* is also relevant if the latch is *cache buffers chains* or *cache buffers lru chain*. Remember, if your database is not experiencing I/O-related events, a low CHR is not a performance problem.

```
select SW.Sid, S.Username, substr(SW.Event, 1, 35), SW.Wait_Time
   from V$SESSION S, V$SESSION_WAIT SW
 where SW.Event not like 'SQL*Net%'
   and SW.Sid = S.Sid
 order by SW.Wait_Time, SW.Event;
```

This query produces a list of events for the connected sessions currently in a wait state. If wait events exist for database buffer cache resources, use this information to direct the problem-solving efforts. Most problems in the database buffer cache can be addressed by either increasing the number of buffers or by making better use of the resources. However, it should be noted that reducing the need for those resources by tuning the SQL and I/O needs of the application will go a long way toward keeping this cache contention free. The following are a common set of events related to the database buffer cache. Some relate to I/O issues, others to actual events in the database buffer cache. A complete list of wait events is available in the Oracle Reference manual.

buffer busy waits	Indicates wait for buffers in the database buffer cache. This indicates that a session is reading this buffer into the cache and/or modifying it. Can also be a symptom of lack of enough free lists, on tables that support concurrent *insert* operations. This is because multiple transactions are concurrently attempting to insert data into the first block of the freelist.
db file sequential read	Indicates among other things waits associated with an index scan. May indicate I/O contention or an excessive amount of I/O.

db file scattered read	Indicates waits associated with a full table scan. May indicate I/O contention or an excessive amount of I/O.
free buffer waits	Indicates lack of free buffers in the database buffer cache. This could mean either the database buffer cache is too small or the dirty list (list of modified blocks in the cache) is not getting written to disk fast enough. This event occurs when the *free buffer inspected* event does not find any free buffers.
latch free	Indicates latch contention for the latch# that is being waited on. Ensure that you already have tuned the number of latches to their allowed maximums by setting the relevant init.ora parameters. If the problem persists, you should determine what is causing the contention for the latch and fix the underlying problem. Your goal should be to cure the disease, not the symptom. A *latch free* event is a symptom of a bigger problem.

Fixing the Problem

Once you have identified the issue of concern with the database buffer cache, you can take appropriate corrective action. This may involve one or more of the following:

- Increase the size of the database buffer cache by increasing the number of blocks buffered. Changing the value of DB_BLOCK_BUFFERS will result in more memory being used, so make sure that the operating system can handle that additional shared memory without additional paging or swapping. However, be aware that if your database is already suffering from database buffer cache latch problems, increasing the number of DB_BLOCK_BUFFERS can exacerbate the problem.

- Increase the size of the database buffer cache by increasing the database block size. The only way to accomplish this is to create a new database with a more appropriate block size and importing the data from the old database. This is easier said than done, but it does improve data density by making room for more rows in any single block. Therefore, more data is in memory with the same number of buffers. Be aware that increased data density can mean increased contention for any given block. It becomes even more important to set the values for *initrans* and *freelists* since more users will be accessing the same block.

NOTE
Make sure to review the init.ora setting for DB_BLOCK_BUFFERS, as the amount of memory used for the database buffer cache will increase by the same factor as the block size did.

■ Segregate segments in the appropriate pool based on segment usage. If the segment is a small lookup table (or another segment that requires instant access and needs to be kept in memory), configure the keep pool and alter that segment to use the keep pool. For large segments that might flush smaller segments out of the default pool, configure the recycle pool and alter those segments to use it.

■ Configure the LRU latches to the platform-specific maximums to avoid latch contention that is caused by a "lack of enough latches" on the system. Again, in our experience, there is no measurable overhead in doing that.

■ Set the cache attribute for those segments for which you wish to reduce the probability of block aging.

Also, if you discover I/O problems, be sure to address those. The database buffer cache can suffer if I/O performance is poor. The positive side is that as the performance in the I/O subsystem increases, performance of the database buffer cache improves as well.

Initialization Parameters that Affect the Database Buffer Cache

In this chapter, we have discussed various initialization parameters. Following is a list of those parameters that affect performance in the database buffer cache, along with their definitions. As mentioned earlier, the database buffer cache is the first line of defense against unnecessary physical I/O. Therefore, you will find information about how these parameters relate to I/O. Also keep in mind that performing physical I/O is not always a bad thing.

DB_BLOCK_SIZE	This parameter is set at database creation. It determines the size of each block within the database and thus the size of each buffer allocated in the database buffer cache.

DB_BLOCK_BUFFERS	This parameter determines the number of blocks in the database buffer cache in the SGA. Since this is the area Oracle reads data from and writes data to, improper sizing can cause serious I/O-related performance problems. Oversizing this parameter can result in systemwide memory starvation and cause the OS to page excessively and potentially swap.
DB_BLOCK_LRU_LATCHES	This parameter defines the number of latches that are configured for the LRU lists of the database buffer cache. It can be set to its platform-specific maximums without any degradation in performance. Do keep in mind that the number of latches for all the pools configured for the database buffer cache cannot exceed this number.
BUFFER_POOL_KEEP	This parameter allocates some number of buffers and latches from DB_BLOCK_BUFFERS and DB_BLOCK_LRU_LATCHES to the keep pool. This provides separate space management for those segments assigned to the keep pool. It thus prevents these segments from aging out as a result of some wild dynamic query or other unforeseen action.
BUFFER_POOL_RECYCLE	By setting BUFFER_POOL_RECYCLE to a subset of DB_BLOCK_BUFFERS and DB_BLOCK_LRU_LATCHES, a third pool in the database buffer cache is established. This pool is best suited to segments that are involved in a large percentage of random I/O.

NOTE
There are many I/O-related parameters that affect the performance of the database buffer cache, and they will be discussed in detail in the chapter "I/O Tuning."

In a Nutshell

As with all tuning, begin with an open mind. Determine the cache-hit ratio and compare it to readings taken over time. Be sure to compare like times with like times to analyze I/O patterns. But don't run your life just on a CHR. It is just an indicator, not an all-inclusive method to determine whether your database is performing at optimal levels.

You should very seriously consider implementing multiple pools in the database buffer cache if you can identify segments that have differing access patterns or characteristics. Small segments that are frequently accessed by applications or segments that require very fast access should be placed in the keep pool. Segments that are observed to have as many physical reads as logical reads are good candidates for the recycle pool. Those that can't be categorized should be left in the default pool. When increasing the database buffer cache size, be certain that the larger size of the SGA will not cause additional paging or swapping.

Proactively avoid latch contention by setting DB_BLOCK_LRU_LATCHES to the platform-specific allowed maximums. There is no measurable overhead in doing that. Be cautious while implementing any unsupported parameters. Their behavior may change once they are de-supported.

Don't fall for "expert recommendations" with respect to cache-hit ratios. There are no optimal or magical numbers here. This is true even if your application supports e-commerce. We are fully aware of the sub-second response time requirement for Web applications. However, that in itself should not force you to store every block of your data in the database buffer cache. There are many other ways to achieve sub-second response times (optimal application and schema design, meaningful SQL, application-layer caching, multi-tier architectures, and so on).

In this day and age, caching all of your data is not even possible. If indeed you are caching all of your data, chances are that your database is very small. Oracle was designed and built to perform I/O very efficiently. With the significant advances in Oracle's kernel engine and storage hardware, doing a reasonable amount of physical I/O is normal and acceptable. The ideal CHR for one environment may make no sense for another. Okay, allow us to say it one last time. It is absolutely normal for your CHR to be even in the 60 percent range so long as your database is not plagued by I/O-related wait events. On the flip side, don't sit back and think everything is picture perfect just because your CHR is 99.999 percent. There could be I/O-related wait events in the database closet. Watch out!

CHAPTER
7

Instance Tuning—The
Redo Log Buffer and
Miscellaneous Tuning

Myth & Folklore

The bigger the redo log buffer, the better. If a 1MB redo log buffer is good, an 8MB redo log buffer must be even better.

Fact

Many times a database administrator gets alarmed by system statistic that reports not-so-attractive numbers for redo log space requests and some others related to redo activity. However, one must pay more attention to the *wait events* that are caused by such statistics. Excessive non-idle waits of any kind can adversely affect the performance of your database. True, there should not be a large number of waits for the redo log buffer, but a small non-zero value is not a problem. Particularly, if this memory structure is not the cause for wait events in the database, increasing the size of this memory structure should be avoided. Continuing to increase the value of LOG_BUFFER will eventually create a problem of its own. If this buffer is too large, it can cost more to manage the space than any potential benefits that can be gained. Bigger is not necessarily better in this case!

Myth & Folklore

Third-party packaged applications do not expose their SQL, hence there are no real tuning opportunities in those environments.

Fact

Although most third-party packaged application vendors bury their SQL at depths that are not reachable to most DBAs, there are some instance-level tuning opportunities that have surfaced in Oracle8, which make these applications a lot more tunable. Prior to Oracle8, the extent of tuning some of these applications was limited to creating, modifying (adding one or more columns or changing the type—from B*-*tree* to bitmapped indexes) and removing existing indexes, which provided a limited effect on the application's execution behavior. In Oracle8, the advent of some optimizer-specific initialization parameters allowed DBAs to control the behavior of the Oracle optimizer in a more flexible fashion. Needless to say, these parameters should be thoroughly tested in your environment before deploying on production systems.

In this chapter, we want to address areas of the instance that are important, but that don't carry the same weight as the shared pool area or the database buffer cache. Just the same, they can cause plenty of heartache and grief if not addressed adequately. These areas include the redo log buffer, background processes such as the database writer (DBWR), the log writer (LGWR), the archiver (ARCH), and checkpoints. We also want to look for tuning avenues in third-party packaged applications where the SQL is usually not reachable. This tuning effort is accomplished by tuning the Oracle optimizer. The task of tuning the Oracle optimizer should be undertaken only after all of the tuning methods outlined in the previous chapters have been exhausted.

Configuring the Redo Log Buffer

Before configuring the redo log buffer it is a good idea to understand what it is and how it works. The redo log buffer is the first step in recording changes to data in the database. This also includes any metadata changes in the database. The redo log buffer is usually the smallest of the caches in the SGA. It is a fixed-size buffer that is determined by the Oracle initialization parameter LOG_BUFFER. The redo log buffer is used by all server processes that modify the data or the structure of one or more tables. The server processes writes the before image, the after image of the changed rows, along with the transaction ID, into the redo log buffer.

The LGWR process reads the contents of the redo log buffer and writes those to the online redo log files on disk. Based on whether the database is in *archivelog* mode, the redo log files may or may not be copied by the ARCH process to archive log destination. The LGWR can be compared to a copy boy in a newspaper office. For those of you who have lived in some part of the past British Empire this should be very familiar to you. In the olden days when e-mail and electronic workflows were just things of one's imagination, it was the copy boy who got things done. (For our female readers, we want to explain that a copy boy could have been a girl too. It was the days when gender-bias was very prevalent and little attention was paid for "politically correct" speech or term usage. Please do not hold this against us, as this is not our doing.)

The main function of a copy boy was to collect the final copy of the news reports from the various reporters and editors and get it to the pressroom in a timely and ordered fashion. Even reporters who were prompt in finishing their work were still dependent on this little person to do his or her job on time and in a proper fashion. Why was this person little? It was because the job always attracted very young people. If the copy boy slacked off or was distracted with other matters or just did not do his job right, the entire paper copy printing could be held up. If the newspaper office had many news reporters, the copy boy could very easily become the bottleneck for the entire process of printing news. This is a very good example of a seemingly insignificant person (in the larger scheme of the newspaper office's pecking order) becoming crucial to the smooth flow of things.

Our goal here is to explain in simple terms how the redo log buffer and its support systems, LGWR and the redo logs, work. Hmmm, sounds like a great name for a band! When a user process issues a DML statement, the associated server process must guarantee that the change being made can be recovered in the event of an instance or media failure. This is accomplished with the redo log buffer, some redo-specific latches (internal structures within Oracle that provide mutually exclusive access to its memory structures), and that soon to be famous band, LGWR and the redo logs. The order of events is very important here. Let's review this process, as it changed significantly in Oracle 7.3:

1. A user process issues an insert, update, or delete statement. Let us assume that it is the start of a transaction and Oracle assigns a transaction identifier for this operation.

2. The server process associated with the user process reads the required data, index, and rollback blocks into memory and locks the relevant row(s) that require manipulation.

3. The server process then acquires what is called a redo copy latch first. Acquiring this redo copy latch is a prerequisite condition before the process can write to the redo log buffer. However, the write does not take place just yet. It is useful to note that there are as many redo copy latches as are defined by the Oracle initialization parameter LOG_SIMULTANEOUS_COPIES. This parameter is obsolete in Oracle8i (automatically set to two times the number of CPUs). But in prior releases, such as in Oracle 7.3.x, this parameter could be set to the allowed maximum of two times the number of CPUs. In Oracle8, this parameter could be set to up to eight times the number of CPUs. On some operating system platforms, the support for eight times the number of CPUs was back-ported to Oracle 7.3.4. There is no measurable overhead of setting this to the platform-specific maximums.

4. The server process then acquires the redo allocation latch to reserve space in the redo log buffer. The amount of space is dependent on the size of the redo entry to be written. As soon as the space is reserved, the redo allocation latch is released, as there is only one redo allocation latch per database and hogging this latch can cause significant performance problems.

5. The server process then writes the redo entry into the redo log buffer using the redo copy latch. (The redo entries when written to the redo log files are used to recover one or more components of Oracle in the event of instance or media failure.)

6. The server process then releases the redo copy latch.

7. Once the redo information is written into the redo log buffer, the server process writes the rollback information into the blocks of the rollback segment assigned to the transaction. This is used in the event the user process issues a rollback instead of a commit. Please note that rollback entries also generate a redo of their own and must also be logged in the redo log buffer.

8. Now that all the bases are covered to protect the transaction (including the data that is about to change) the server process can now update the row(s) in the data and the index blocks.

NOTE
Given that the redo log buffer is a circular buffer, simultaneous writes to this memory structure can and will happen. This is of course subject to how quickly the redo allocation latch is acquired and released. Also note that the processing of the redo information takes precedence over all other data changes or activity. From a tuning perspective this means that anything that holds up getting that information into the redo log buffer will hold up everything else. So keep this little guy in the SGA happy! Remember the copy boy story!

LGWR writes the redo log buffer to disk on one of the following events:

- Every three seconds (independent of DBWR). Yes, from Oracle8 and up, it has its own timer.

- On a commit. Remember that the write of the redo entry must physically be completed before control is returned to the program issuing the commit.

- Whenever redo information equal to one third of the size of the redo log buffer has been written to the redo log buffer. For example, if the size of the redo log buffer is 131072 bytes, when 43690 bytes of new information has been written to the redo log buffer, LGWR will copy the new redo information to disk. Starting from Oracle8, LGWR will write to the redo logs when MIN (1MB,LOG_BUFFER/3) is true. This is to support better performance when Oracle instances are configured with large redo log buffers. However, this fact should not be misunderstood as a recommendation to set larger redo log buffers. The point we are trying to make here is *not* that the redo log buffer will never get more than one-third full. What we are trying to communicate is that when it reaches the one-third full threshold, LGWR will write the contents of the redo log buffer. However, given the circular nature of the buffer, the remaining two-thirds of the buffer will be utilized for writes by other server processes that need to write to the redo log buffer. From Oracle8 and up, this one-third write will not exceed a size of 1MB (in the event the instance is configured with a redo log buffer larger than 3MB) per the above formula. Said another way, if you size your redo log buffer at 15MB, LGWR will initiate a write when 1MB worth of redo entries have been written to the redo log buffer. It should be noted here that in our tests we could not find any evidence to corroborate the "consistent working" of the one-third full event. The threshold at which LGWR was writing varied significantly from one-sixth full to two-thirds full. Don't count on this one.

■ At checkpoints.

■ When posted by the DBWR process. But you must always remember that modified data blocks in a database are always written *after* the corresponding redo entries for those blocks are written to disk.

The size of this buffer can be seen immediately after starting an instance on the line for "Redo log buffers" in the messages from the startup command:

```
SVRMGR> startup
ORACLE instance started.
Total System Global Area          48572320 bytes
Fixed Size                           64912 bytes
Variable Size                     45137920 bytes
Database Buffers                   2048000 bytes
Redo log buffers                    524288 bytes
Database mounted.
Database opened.
```

It can also be queried from V$PARAMETER:

```
select Name, Value
  from V$PARAMETER
 where Name = 'log_buffer';
NAME             VALUE
----------       ----------
log_buffer       524288
```

This is the value in bytes. The default for this parameter varies from version to version. In Oracle 8.0, the smallest size allocated for the redo log buffer is 73728 bytes (72K). In Oracle 8.1.5, the default value is 524288 bytes (512K).

It is recommended to start with a smaller value and increase the size as needed until this resource is no longer the point of contention. We have seen many database administrators start with LOG_BUFFER = 131072 (128K) for their environments. And that's a good size to start with. *Increase the size only if there are wait events associated with the redo log buffer* (this is discussed later in the "Wait Events that Affect the Redo Log Buffer" section). If your redo log buffer is, say, 32MB, chances are that it is oversized and you may be wasting memory. Check the wait events in your database for more information.

Initialization Parameters that Affect the Redo Log Buffer

This list of parameters includes those that directly affect the redo log buffer and its performance. Additional parameters are discussed later in the "Initialization Parameters for Miscellaneous Instance Tuning" section.

LOG_BUFFER	Set this to a byte value appropriate for the system. Start with 131072 and increase as wait events dictate.
LOG_SIMULTANEOUS_COPIES	Simply set this to the platform-allowed maximum. The default is the number of CPUs. This parameter is obsolete in Oracle8i (is now _LOG_SIMULTANEOUS_ COPIES), but defaults to two times the number of CPUs. Modify_LOG_SIMULTANEOUS_COPIES only after gathering evidence for redo copy latch contention.

Wait Events that Affect the Redo Log Buffer

The following wait events indicate that there are redo log buffer-related problems in your database. Be sure to evaluate all of them before taking action. Don't rush to increase the size of the redo log buffer until you have confirmed that to be the actual cause of your wait event. Increasing the size of the redo log buffer without a specific reason is not good practice.

log buffer space	Indicates a potential problem of LGWR not being able to keep up with the rate of writes into the redo log buffer by server processes. Usually indicates a log buffer size problem (too small) or slow device(s) or contention where the online redo logs are located.
log file parallel write	Waits associated with writing of redo records from the redo log buffer to disk. Usually indicates slow device(s) or contention where the online redo logs are located.
log file single write	Indicates writing to the header block of the log files. May indicate waits during checkpoints.

log file switch (archiving needed)	Waits indicate ARCH is not keeping up with LGWR. Could be because of online redo logs being too small, slow devices, or high contention on devices (usually caused by the log files placed on the devices where data files are located). As a corrective measure, you may want to investigate the possibility of using multiple ARCH processes or I/O slaves, or configure the archive buffer-related Oracle initialization parameters (where applicable).
log file switch (checkpoint incomplete)	Waits associated with improperly sized online redo log files (usually too small and/or too few redo log groups). This is caused when log switches occur too frequently, which results in too- frequent checkpointing. When checkpoints get queued up, they have to complete before the subsequent log switches can be processed.
log file sync	Waits associated with the flushing of redo log buffers on a user commit. If the waits are persistent, it may indicate device contention where the online redo log files are placed and/or slow devices.
latch free	Indicates latch contention for the latch# that is being waited on. Ensure that you already have tuned the number of latches to their allowed maximums by setting the relevant init.ora parameters. If the problem persists, you should determine what is causing the contention for the latch and fix the underlying problem. Your goal should be to cure the disease not the symptom. A latch free event is a symptom of a bigger problem. In the context of the redo log buffer, the redo copy latches are the only supported configurable parameter (LOG_SIMULTANEOUS_COPIES) and even that is obsolete in Oracle8i.

Solving Redo Log Buffer Issues

Problems directly affecting the redo log buffer are very simple. In fact, there can only be one of two things holding the process up. Either the server process can't get the necessary latch or the redo log buffer is full and there is no place to write the redo information. If the *log buffer space* event is frequent and accrues a significant amount of time, it is safe to assume there is a problem. If this event is accompanied by one or more *log file* events (listed in the previous section), it indicates that the problem is likely with the I/O system.

If you find *latch free* events along with the *log buffer space* events, you can be sure there is a latch or redo log sizing issue. By querying V$LATCH for the *redo copy latch* and *redo allocation latch* you can see the latch statistics. This will confirm that there is a latch problem when the ratio of misses to gets or immediate_misses to immediate_gets is greater than 1 percent. This can be corrected by setting the value of LOG_SIMULTANEOUS_COPIES to the platform allowed maximum (obsolete in Oracle8i). This increases the number of copy latches. In fact, you can avoid dealing with this at all by setting that maximum value at the outset. In Oracle8i, LOG_SIMULTANEOUS_COPIES is auto-configured to two times the number of CPUs on the system.

So if the latches are in good order, the problem has to be that the server process can't get space in the redo log buffer. It comes into play when we realize that the redo log buffer is not being flushed fast or often enough. Making the redo log buffer larger is not a big deal, but experience has shown that it is possible to reach a point of diminishing returns very quickly. You should not increase the size of your redo log buffer unless you have concrete evidence that warrants it in V$SESSION_WAIT.

 VIP

From a pure I/O perspective, the most common mistake is to put the redo logs with database files or other types of files. This creates competition for resources where it is least tolerated. Redo logs need to go on independent storage devices, and they need to be separated from all other files to perform optimally. Don't forget that redo log switches on archiving databases are also subject to the limitations of how fast the redo logs can be safely copied and made available to LGWR again. So check your redo logs and make sure they are on properly configured storage devices. Remember, you don't want to overload the copy boy and have her perform mailroom tasks and run errands for you. If you do, you run the risk of preventing her from doing her job right.

After correcting any storage device layout issues, it is safe to resize the redo log buffer (if needed). Change the value for LOG_BUFFER in the initialization file and restart the instance. You can start with a size of 128K or 256K and monitor the database for redo log buffer-related wait events. If it is already getting large—say, more than 1MB—something less dramatic might be in order. In fact, the database may be experiencing a point of diminishing returns with regard to sizing the redo log buffer.

The sure-fire method to calculate the optimal size for the redo log buffer (or any other memory structure, for that matter) should be based on wait events and wait events only.

Miscellaneous Instance Tuning

So far in this book, we have covered in good detail the main tuning avenues in the Oracle instance. In this section, we will look at the remaining components in the Oracle instance that affect performance and may need tuning or adjusting. From a purist's perspective, we are not only dealing with the *Oracle instance*, but also the *Oracle database*. It should be noted here that the improper configuration of these database components may have a profound negative effect on the performance of some of the background processes.

Checkpoints

No, these are not guardposts on the border! They are moments in time when Oracle makes sure that everything has been synchronized. They occur naturally every time a log switch occurs or any time a DBA issues an **alter system checkpoint** command. They create and record known synchronization points in the database so that recovery can be easily facilitated in the event of an instance or a media failure. Occasionally, it is useful to have them performed more often than nature dictates. To increase the frequency of checkpoints, you can use either the LOG_CHECKPOINT_INTERVAL or LOG_CHECKPOINT_TIMEOUT Oracle initialization parameter. The former parameter is I/O-based and is set to the number of OS blocks' worth of information that must be written to the redo log files before a checkpoint is initiated. The latter parameter is time-based and indirectly controls the maximum duration that dirty blocks can remain in the database buffer cache. The definition of LOG_CHECKPOINT_TIMEOUT has changed in Oracle8i.

Also it is useful to observe that checkpoints no longer occur *on* log switches. They actually occur *before* a log switch. Obviously both aforementioned parameters keep the previous checkpoint as a point of reference. Just remember that checkpoints take resources and can impact system performance when done very frequently.

In our production experience, we have configured LOG_CHECKPOINT_INTERVAL to a high number or 0 (the effect is the same), so that checkpoints occur only during log switches. It is okay to leave LOG_CHECKPOINTS_TIMEOUT to its default value of 0 (1800 in Oracle8i) so long as your system performs okay with checkpoints on log switches only. But if these parameters are configured in the aforementioned method, the redo log files need to be sized appropriately. Although it is difficult to generalize the optimal frequency of log switching as it is dependent on a variety of issues (such as whether you are running a standby database, what your service level agreement for instance recovery is, and so on), it is safe to say that the number of log switches in your system should not average more than one every twenty minutes. This is to prevent the database from experiencing performance bottlenecks or performance hiccups associated with frequent checkpoints.

It is possible to get help with checkpoints and improve their efficiency by setting CHECKPOINT_PROCESS =TRUE in 7.3 and lower. When this parameter is set, the CKPT process is launched and it performs certain operations associated with checkpoints and reduces the workload on LGWR. Note that CKPT only updates the headers of the data files, redo log files, and control files, but does not perform the act of checkpointing (flushing of dirty blocks is always done by DBWR). In Oracle8, CKPT is one of the required processes. But it doesn't mean you don't need to worry about checkpoint efficiency in Oracle8 and up. You should pay attention to how much time it takes to complete the checkpoint. This is especially true if your database has periodic heavy DML activity. The log files may switch more frequently and more checkpoints may take place. You can set the init.ora parameter LOG_CHECKPOINTS_TO_ALERT to TRUE to log checkpoint start and stop times in the database alert log. This information will tell you at what frequency the checkpoints are occurring and the duration of each checkpoint.

NOTE
From Oracle8 onward, the CKPT process maintains a "heartbeat" every three seconds with the control file. CKPT also writes a checkpoint's progress to the control file.

Oracle generates a warning message in the alert log when the checkpoint process runs into a problem. Many DBAs have seen the message "checkpoint not complete" in the alert log and have wondered what it means and how they go about fixing it. This warning is generated when Oracle is ready to overwrite a redo log, but the checkpoint process has not yet completed. This will cause the database to halt until the checkpoint process completes and Oracle is able to overwrite the log file. To correct this problem, you should provide more time for the checkpoint process to complete, either by adding more log file groups or by creating larger redo log files.

Redo Log Files

We know that LGWR writes the contents of the redo log buffer to redo log files on disk. These files maintain a permanent record of all data changes made in a database. The redo record contains both the old and new value of the data. Every database needs to have at least two redo log files (but may have more). Oracle uses these files to recover from an instance or a media failure. For this reason, it is important to protect them from any disk corruption or disk I/O problems. In general, it is good practice to have multiple copies of these redo log files on separate storage devices. Please refer to Oracle's

Administrator Guide for more information on how to configure multiple redo logs and redo log groups. Here we are concerned with their physical size and how this affects the performance of your database.

How to Size Your Redo Log Files

Let's begin by asking the question, "How does the size of the redo log files affect database performance?" Well, one thing is sure, it should not be smaller than LOG_BUFFER or else you will have quite a few problems to deal with. The redo log files are OS files and are written in OS blocks.

In general, a larger log file will take longer time to fill up, thus causing fewer checkpoints (more about this follows below) and causing less frequent archiving to be done (but it may take more time to complete). But instance recovery can potentially take a longer time if the redo log files are sized too large. In addition, if you are employing a standby database you may lose quite a bit of work if your primary database experiences a complete disaster.

On the other hand, smaller log files will cause more checkpoints and cause more performance hiccups due to checkpoint activity, and will keep ARCH pretty busy. But instance recovery could be a snap! So take your pick. Also related to this discussion is a new parameter in Oracle8i called FAST_START_IO_TARGET. This parameter provides control on the number of I/Os that should not be exceeded during instance recovery. When this parameter is set, you will cause DBWR to write out dirty blocks to disk in a more aggressive fashion.

So you need to identify what is more important to you. Sometimes you will have to compromise between performance and availability. And there can be more than one thing that is important to you. One size does not fit all! You may need to experiment with what size works best in your environment.

Apart from talking about how to size the redo log files, the other related issue is, "How many redo logs should be configured?" Oracle needs at least two groups to stay up and running. But sometimes the size is less of an issue than the number of redo logs configured for a database. This is especially true in environments that can afford to configure more storage devices for their redo log files. It is important to understand that all related db buffer cache entries related to an online redo log must be written by the DBWR to a data file before LGWR will begin overwriting the next associated online redo log. If LGWR must wait to write to the next redo log, for the above reason, a *checkpoint cannot complete* error message will result. Therefore, the fewer the number of redo logs, the more likely the occurrence of a *checkpoint cannot complete* error. For example, with two redo log groups, 50 percent of the total redo log space must be available on a log switch. With four redo log groups, 25 percent of the total redo log space must be available. Empirical evidence (thanks to

some experiments conducted by Craig Shallahammer of OraPub Inc.) suggests that the law of diminishing returns kicks in around ten redo log groups.
So for redo-heavy systems, you may consider configuring more online redo log groups than the minimum requirement of two groups.

Archiving

Once a database is put in *archivelog* mode, it is necessary to turn on the ARCH process for automatic archiving of redo logs when log switches occur. The ARCH process copies the redo logs to one or more destinations (depending on your Oracle version). Configuring this in a proper fashion ensures that the archive logs are written without any contention and, more importantly, are readily available when needed for recovery. Configuring it haphazardly can create contention on storage devices. Apart from using optimal storage devices and avoiding competition from other files, the archive process can be tuned by setting LOG_ARCHIVE_BUFFERS and LOG_ARCHIVE_BUFFER_SIZE. It must be noted that both of these parameters are de-supported in Oracle8i. Oracle recommends leaving this at the default, but if the archive system is having trouble keeping up, these parameters should be modified to improve things. When required we have set this to the platform-specific maximums and have had good archiving performance. But remember that creating multiple redo log groups with multiple members has a higher probability of better performance.

Using multiple log members in a redo log file group will also speed up the archiving process. All members in a group are used to perform the archiving process. Oracle will optimize the archiving process by reading portions of data at a time from all log members in a staggered round-robin fashion to distribute I/O. The benefit of defining multiple log members rather than mirroring them at the OS level may translate into some performance gains. Oracle does not see the multiple members created via OS mirroring, but will effectively use all log members within a group to optimize archiving process.

Initialization Parameters for Miscellaneous Instance Tuning

Following is a list of parameters that can impact redo log, checkpoint, and archiving performance.

LOG_ARCHIVE_START	TRUE turns automatic archiving on. Use this if the database is in *archivelog* mode.

LOG_ARCHIVE_FORMAT LOG_ARCHIVE_DEST	These parameters control where the archived redo logs are written. In Oracle8 and above there are additional parameters (such as LOG_ARCHIVE_DUPLEX_DEST) to facilitate writing of the archived redo logs to multiple destinations. Further parameters such as LOG_ARCHIVE_DEST_n can be set (n can range from 1 to 5) to achieve redundancy in the archived redo log files destination. Each additional copy of the archived redo log files can be made "required" for the archival process. Making a destination "required" further guarantees the recoverability of the database (because it provides the functionality of mirrored archived logs), but this may cause the system to hang if any of the relevant file systems run out of space.
LOG_ARCHIVE_ MIN_SUCCEED_DEST	This sets the number of destination copies of an archived log that must succeed when ARCH writes the archived log to multiple destinations. The default value is 1. This parameter controls the number of copies that are required to "proclaim" that a given archival operation has succeeded. The free space in the multiple archive destinations needs to be proactively managed, to reduce the likelihood of Oracle hanging during a log switch. But when implemented correctly it provides better recovery protection.
LOG_ARCHIVE_BUFFER_SIZE	Determines the size of the buffers used during the write operation of the ARCH process. This parameter is obsolete in Oracle8i.
LOG_ARCHIVE_BUFFERS	Determines the number of buffers to use during archiving. The default number of archive buffers is 1. This parameter is obsolete in Oracle8i.

LOG_CHECKPOINT_INTERVAL   This is set to the number of OS blocks to be written to redo between checkpoints. This can be set to a high value or to 0 to force checkpoints only during log switches. Default is 0.

LOG_CHECKPOINT_TIMEOUT   When set to a value of *n*, this parameter specifies that the incremental checkpoint is at the position where the last write occurred to the redo log file (also known as the "tail of the log") n seconds ago. This parameter also signifies that there will be no dirty buffers (in the database buffer cache) for more than n seconds. The value is specified in seconds. The default in Oracle 8.1.7 is 1800. Setting this parameter will cause checkpoint to happen at least as often as *n* seconds.

LOG_CHECKPOINTS_TO_ALERT   Causes Oracle to timestamp the start and stop time of checkpoints in the alert log. Useful to determine whether checkpoints are running into each other.

FAST_START_IO_TARGET   This parameter allows you to control the maximum amount of I/O that SMON can perform while performing recovery on instance startup caused due to an instance failure. This parameter also controls the aggressiveness with which DBWR will write dirty blocks to disk.

ARCH_IO_SLAVES
LGWR_IO_SLAVES   These parameters, supported in some versions of Oracle, allow you to take advantage of simulating multiple ARCH and LGWR I/O slaves. Both of these parameters are nonexistent in Oracle8i. The ARCH_IO_SLAVES is replaced by a new Oracle parameter called LOG_ARCHIVE_MAX_PROCESSES.

Tuning the Oracle Optimizer

When Oracle8 was released in early 1997, it generated a lot of excitement and was considered a stellar event in the RDBMS world, as it claimed the following four major benefits:

- It was the database for network computing.

- It was to support all of your users.

- It was to support all of your data.

- It was supposed to be faster.

And faster it was. With significant improvements in its kernel, added by support for database partitioning, faster connectivity, and a variety of other features, it truly was a major release. For some of us who had lived through the many bad hair days trying to migrate from Oracle6 to Oracle7, we thought it was time to live a little (we were definitely influenced by the marketing hype). We decided to dive into Oracle8 with our head hitting the water first. Thankfully the point of contact of the dive did not feel like a ton of bricks. We were pleasantly surprised at the relative ease when we compared it to the Oracle6 to Oracle7 migration. For starters, the migration utility actually worked. Now that was like a breath of fresh air, as some of the databases that we supported would have taken many hours to export and then many days to import.

It is hard to believe that Oracle8 is only four years old...it sure does seem longer than that. Is that a sign of our old age? The long feeling could be attributed to the fact that "One year in the Oracle IT industry really is equivalent to seven normal years." For those of you who have been around the block, you know exactly what we mean. The calculation, and the fact that we have been working with Oracle8 for four years, puts our combined experience at 56 years. Now, there is an explanation for that long and maybe even old feeling!

One of the major features that made a great positive impact was the optimizer's capability to perform partition-aware processing of large tables and indexes. This made a night and day difference in performance of the data warehouses of those days. Plus, the support for some specialized parameters that controlled its behavior further lent flexibility in configuring the Oracle optimizer.

Initialization Parameters that Tune the Optimizer's Behavior

The following list of parameters should *not* be modified from the default values until all documented performance-tuning techniques (outlined in the prior chapters of this book) have been exhausted. The working efficacy of these parameters should be tested thoroughly before implementing them in a production environment.

WARNING
We have successfully implemented all of the parameters discussed in this section at many large production sites to produce predictable results. However, it is your responsibility to test them in your environment before implementing them.

These parameters are most significant for third-party packaged applications where the code is usually inaccessible. They are also relevant for environments that require hash joins for batch processing, but need the control mechanisms to hold back the optimizer from being over-influenced by the hash join method for transactional processing. And, by the way, hash joins are not as bad as people make them out to be.

Most of these parameters are relevant from Oracle 8.0.5, but some of them may have been back-ported to prior releases. We thank Probal Shome of Oracle Corporation for sharing his expertise and insight with us during the Oracle Open World 1999 conference, with his paper "Using Stored Outlines in Oracle 8i for Plan Stability" and the long and lively discussion that ensued. Bottom line, this section is worth your time and effort if you are running any third-party packaged applications. So without too much ado, go ahead and check it out.

OPTIMIZER_MAX_PERMUTATIONS
This parameter restricts the number of permutations of the tables the optimizer will consider in queries with joins. Such a restriction ensures that the parse time for the query stays within acceptable limits. However, a slight risk exists that the optimizer will overlook a good plan it would otherwise have found. It also lets you limit the amount of work the optimizer expends on optimizing queries with large joins. The value of the integer is the number of permutations of the tables the optimizer will consider with large joins.

OPTIMIZER_MAX_PERMUTATIONS defaults to a value of 80,000. When set to a value below 80,000 (say, 79,000), it forces the optimizer to try up to eight different tables as the driving table for queries that involve joins. This usually results in the optimizer picking the least expensive of the 79,000 plans that it generates. Said in another way, this parameter provides more options to decide the order of joining tables for a given query. The default behavior (with the default value) is to build a plan usually with the smallest table as the driving table. This default behavior may not always generate the most suitable plan and the performance you expected, especially for the third-party packaged applications.

When this parameter is set, it does result in a nominal increase in the parse time of the SQL statements. But in the bigger scheme of things, this nominal increase in parse time is well worth the overhead when compared to the significant reduction in the execution time of SQL statements.

OPTIMIZER_INDEX_COST_ADJ
This parameter directly adjusts the cost of using an index. The default value of 100 makes the optimizer evaluate the cost of the index as normal, and a value of 50 makes the optimizer evaluate the cost to be half as expensive as normal. This parameter encourages the use of all indexes, regardless of their selectivity. It applies to index use in general. The range of values for this parameter is 1–10,000. When set to a low value (say, 1–10), the optimizer is encouraged to perform index scans over full table scans.

OPTIMIZER_SEARCH_LIMIT
This parameter defaults to a value of 5. When set to a value of 1, the optimizer is totally discouraged from considering *cartesian product* as the execution method. With its default value of 5, the optimizer can and will perform cartesian product (if applicable) for queries with five or fewer tables in the FROM clause. This behavior of performing cartesian products may be acceptable for small tables, but for obvious reasons is a no-no for large tables. Depending on the nature of the application, this parameter needs to be adjusted. If you are seeing cartesian product execution plans, you may want to set this parameter to 1.

NOTE
A cartesian product between two tables with 100 rows each will generate a result set of 10,000 rows. Hence as the size of a table increases the cost of performing a cartesian product increases proportionately. Watch out for this one!

OPTIMIZER_INDEX_CACHING
This parameter defaults to a value of 0. The range of values for this parameter is 0–100. When set to a high value (say, 99), the optimizer is encouraged to use the *nested loops* join method over other methods. This parameter is especially useful if the initialization parameter HASH_JOIN_ENABLED is set to TRUE and HASH_MULTIBLOCK_IO_COUNT is set to a non-default value (say, equal to DB_FILE_MULTIBLOCK_READ_COUNT). Setting this parameter to a high value of 99 provides the capability to have the cake and eat it too. This is because the default value for this parameter will put undue influence on the optimizer to consider hash joins over all other joins (when HASH_JOIN_ENABLED is set to TRUE).

Hash joins are suitable for applications, where a small table(s) joined to a very large table(s), and the *where* clause predicates cause processing of a significant portion of the large table(s). Hash joins are also suitable for applications that join two or more large tables. Both scenarios mentioned here are relevant for batch processing where the application usually processes a significant amount of data. Configuring this parameter to a value of 99 does not necessarily turn off hash joins, but does hold back the optimizer from going overboard with hash joins as the default join method.

NOTE

Please exercise due diligence in monitoring the performance of your batch reports after setting this parameter. In some very special scenarios, it is possible for some of your batch reports to require a USE_HASH hint.

In a Nutshell

Tuning the redo mechanism, including the redo log buffer, is one of the final things to tune as part of instance tuning. You can go ahead and always set the value of the Oracle initialization parameter LOG_SIMULTANEOUS_COPIES to the platform-specific maximum if your Oracle database version is prior to Oracle8i. This proactively avoids redo copy latch problems that occur due to lack of latches. Then set the size of the redo log buffer to a reasonable starting value by setting LOG_BUFFER = 131072 (128K). Some folks start with 256K as well. Be cautious, though, as getting too aggressive with this can create more problems than it fixes. Increase this value if you observe the *log buffer space* wait event. However, if you also observe wait events such as *log file switch*, *log file sync*, or *log file parallel write*, there may be an underlying I/O issue. If this is the case, ensure that the redo logs and the archive logs are on independent devices separated from the data files of the database.

The archiving system can be tuned by setting LOG_ARCHIVE_BUFFER_SIZE and LOG_ARCHIVE_BUFFERS. Additionally, tune checkpoints by ensuring that they occur only on log switches. Size the redo log files appropriately to control checkpoint frequency, and allow sufficient time for the checkpoint process to complete so you won't get those pesky "checkpoint not complete" messages. Also ensure that they are on independent storage devices, as they need their space (if you know what we mean). Though gains in this section of instance tuning are not as significant as the other areas, you need to proactively configure this. Every little bit (and byte) counts!

We are all aware that most third-party packaged application vendors, in their efforts to "encapsulate" the complexity of their application, bury their SQL many fathoms below sea level and make it unreachable to mortals such as us. We studied in good detail some instance-level tuning opportunities that are supported since Oracle8, which modify the behavior of the Oracle optimizer and thus make these packaged applications more amenable to our tuning efforts. And that ends the broadcast on this chapter!

CHAPTER

8

Database Tuning

Myth & Folklore

The optimum number of extents for every object is one.

Fact

There cannot be anything farther from the reality than this. We call this myth the father of all Oracle myths. Let there be no doubt, there is no magical number for the optimum number of extents for an Oracle object. The perpetrators of this myth do not understand the potential fragmentation and space management nightmare that this optimum number of extents myth creates. The nightmare is created because not all objects in a database contain the same amount of data. Therefore having objects that are supported by varying sizes of a single extent within a tablespace can and will cause space fragmentation problems and eventually present a space management nightmare. It is perfectly acceptable to have multiple extents for an object. However, if your object lives in the other end of the spectrum and is comprised of many thousands of extents, there are other issues you have to deal with. But having 1,000 extents for an object by itself does not pose any performance problems, so long as the extents are sized as a multiple of (DB_FILE_MULTIBLOCK_READ_COUNT * DB_BLOCK_SIZE).

This ensures that Oracle will issue the same number of read system calls regardless of whether the object consists of 1 extent or 1,000 extents. If the extents are not aligned with the aforementioned size, additional read system calls can cause unnecessary overhead on the I/O subsystem. In the bigger scheme of things, assuming worst-case scenario, it is one additional read system call per extent of the most heavily hit objects in your database. If you have a lot of objects with a lot of extents that are misaligned, you are posing more overhead on your I/O subsystem.

Myth & Folklore

Reorganizing a table (export, drop, recreate, import) that contains many hundreds of extents to one extent provides better performance.

Fact

This is definitely a corollary to the first myth. The export followed by the import eliminates block-level fragmentation, row-level fragmentation (if applicable), and resets the high-water mark of the table, which in turn provides better performance. So, it is the defragmentation operation (within a block and/or a row) and the reduction of the number of blocks that will be read during a full table scan that eventually provides better performance.

It must be noted that the effect of the entire table's data stored in one extent has nothing to do with the performance increase. Table reorganization eliminates block-level fragmentation because the import process refills each block up to the level of pctfree within the block. This provides for better block compaction and utilization, as each block is filled to the maximum allowable capacity.

Row-level fragmentation is eliminated when the erstwhile chained or migrated rows get fixed (because they get reinserted into brand new blocks). A chained row is when a row is stored in multiple blocks, because its length exceeds the free space size of one block. Said in another way, a chained row is a row that spans multiple blocks. A row is migrated when it cannot fit in its current block and thus is relocated to another block (where there is adequate space), keeping a pointer in the original block. The pointer in the original block is required, as index ROWID entries still point to that location. While chaining is usually a problem related to a row's length and the size of the Oracle database block, migration is usually related to the lack of adequate free space in a block to keep the row in the same block when an update operation increases its length. Needless to say, Oracle will always attempt to migrate a row before it decides to chain it.

Although, you can be guaranteed that all migrated rows will be fixed after a table gets reorganized, chaining may still pose a problem if the row length exceeds the available free space in a database block. If the table in question undergoes a significant amount of inserts followed by deletes, it is important to adjust *pctfree* (to reduce row-level fragmentation) and *pctused* (to reduce block-level fragmentation). It is equally important to adjust the *initial* and *next* storage parameters (if they are too small) to keep the table from reaching *maxextents*. Just because Oracle supports *unlimited maxextents,* you don't have to go out of your way to use it.

I n this chapter, we will discuss the issues you will need to consider for tuning various storage-related components in the database. We will talk about the things that need configuration and management that provides optimal performance. The primary goal in this chapter is much more than tuning. It is the proactive configuration and management of various components of the database to reduce the number of tuning issues that eventually become production problems. The Oracle RDBMS has undergone many improvements in the past five years. Now more than ever, there is a need to harness all of the available functionality for a given release of Oracle. It is easy to get stuck in the past, and it is important to keep abreast of the new features that Oracle supports.

Further, for the sake of completeness we also have provided some high-level coverage of some of the issues we have experienced while dealing with hybrid and data warehouse databases. This by no means is an exhaustive coverage of the topics and is mentioned here purely for the sake of completeness. Although the data warehousing topic by itself warrants so much attention that there are many books written just on that topic (one of our favorites is *Oracle8i Data Warehousing*, by Gary Dodge and Tim Gorman), we wanted to at least touch on some of the key issues and challenges in managing large Oracle databases.

Picking the Right Database Block Size

First things first! The optimal configuration of the Oracle database block size is one of the most critical and important tasks you will perform in the life of a database. This is because the block size of a database has a great performance impact on various issues and it needs to be configured right the first time, every time. Changing the database block size is an involved process and requires a complete rebuild of your database—a luxury you may not have time for once you are in production. So get it right the first time!

How Does Database Block Size Impact Performance?

The positive or negative impact on application and system performance imposed by the database block size is multifaceted. There are several factors to consider here, but optimal application design and meaningful SQL statements are paramount to everything else. Nothing will replace the power of an optimal SQL statement. However, the size of the Oracle database block size can and will impact the application. Here are some issues that require thought and planning:

- How much time does it takes to perform I/O of one database block?

- What is the size and usage of the database buffer cache?

- What is the impact of having a larger index block in your environment?

- What is the impact of having rows that exceed the size of the database block size?

- What is the impact of having less free space in a block due to the size of the block?

- How is query performance impacted when update operations increase the length of column values and the lack of free space chains the row across multiple blocks?

- How will row migration and/or row chaining affect I/O performance?

How to Optimally Size the Oracle Database Block Size

Most 32-bit versions of Oracle support a database block size up to 16K. This value can increase up to 64K or higher on the 64-bit implementations of Oracle on certain hardware platforms. The importance of configuring the Oracle database block size correctly the first time cannot be over-emphasized, as it cannot be changed during the life of a database (as of Oracle version 8.1.7). Oracle9i supports a flexible method to have different database block sizes for different tablespaces, giving you another chance to correct the problem after the database is created.

Optimal sizing of the Oracle database block can impact the efficacy of the application's I/O access patterns. This is because of the varying patterns portrayed by the different kinds of applications. Transactional or hybrid systems portray totally different I/O access patterns versus data warehouse or decision support systems.

VIP

With each doubling of the Oracle database block size, there are two things that double in size: the amount of data within a block and the contention for data within a block caused by more rows. If the contention aspect is not taken into consideration it can very easily fall through the cracks and come back to bite you later. At a very high level, the act of doubling the database block size should be followed by doubling of the block-level storage parameters that control the degree of concurrent data access within a block (such as initrans and freelists). Failure to do that will result in increased block-level contention. We will discuss this in more detail in the section "Changing the Database Block Size: Core Issues."

Guidelines to Pick the Right Size

It is normal practice to configure an Oracle database with a smaller block size for applications that are transactional in nature (OLTP). The primary focus here is to reduce the amount of block-level contention for transactional systems, as most transactional applications retrieve a few rows from a block, and thus should not have to deal with more data than what is required. This does not in any way imply that larger block sizes are bad for hybrid systems, as long as *initrans* and *freelists* are proactively configured for the relevant objects. This is because block-level contention needs to be consciously managed, and configuring large Oracle database block sizes should not cause block-level contention. Another factor to consider is that very few databases are truly transactional in nature. Most databases are hybrid in nature and support mixed I/O patterns in the form of writes (via transactions) and reads (via reports). Given that the read aspect is as important as the write aspect, configuring the Oracle database block size should be done keeping both aspects in mind. Applications that are read-intensive or report-intensive (such as data warehouses or decision support applications) should be configured with the largest available block size supported on the version of Oracle installed.

NOTE
It is possible that third-party packaged applications in the ERP world could be as read-intensive as a data warehouse application. Of course, this depends on the time of the day, week, or month.

VIP
Based on current default values for file system block sizes for advanced file systems (such as xfs, jfs, efs, vxfs), it is recommended that you do not create a database (regardless of its I/O pattern) with an Oracle block size of less than 8K. Most hybrid transactional systems perform well with 8K block sizes, but some systems may require larger block sizes, depending on the amount, nature, and frequency of their read access patterns.

The Sizing Formula

There are many issues that require serious consideration while sizing the Oracle database block size. We have used the following formula to configure many production systems:

DB_BLOCK_SIZE = Operating System (OS) block size >= OS page size

NOTE
If advanced file systems (such as xfs, jfs, efs, vxfs) are configured and implemented for Oracle data files, the OS block is overridden with the file system (FS) block size. In that case the formula changes to:
DB_BLOCK_SIZE = FS block size >= OS page size.

The Oracle database block size should always be equal to the value of the operating system (OS) block size. The OS block size can be determined by executing a platform- or filesystem-specific command on each operating system. In some cases you may have to check the documentation of your OS or your Volume Manager vendor. On Windows NT, check the system documentation for further information. This is to ensure that when Oracle requests to read one database block from disk, the operating system does not perform physical I/O greater or less than the size of the Oracle-block. That makes sense, doesn't it? Let us explain it further.

If you created an advanced file system with a block size of 8K and created an Oracle database with a block size of 4K, every request by Oracle to read one database block will result in the OS reading 8K worth of data (even though only 4K was requested). This is due to the fact that at the lowest level it is the file system block size that is utilized as a blocking factor to read/write data from a file. Configuring a 4K Oracle block size when the OS block size is 8K is guaranteed to put undue stress on the I/O subsystem, as every single-block request will generate twice the amount of I/O that is actually required. Put another way, in the above example configuration you have lost 50 percent of the built-in capacity of your I/O subsystem by configuring the database block size less than the OS block size or FS block size for single block read requests. If the converse were true (Oracle database block size was 8K and FS block size was 4K), then on some operating systems the I/O system may accidently trigger the read-ahead algorithm under a false assumption that the application is performing a sequential scan.

Well, that's fine, but what is the relationship of all this with the OS page size? That factor is usually relevant only for those systems where pinning or locking the Oracle SGA is not possible. (The act of pinning or locking the SGA in memory tells the OS's paging algorithm to ignore those shared memory segments allocated by Oracle for the SGA, until the system experiences extreme levels of memory starvation).

The page size is the unit of I/O utilized by the paging algorithm to page-in and page-out memory pages to and from main memory. When a page-out occurs, the contents of that memory page is written to the swapfiles of the OS. This again implies physical I/O. The frequency of paging is related to the amount of free memory available and the number and size of memory requests that need to be serviced for various processes on the system. Given that paging is a core function of the OS, and that the Oracle SGA is in memory (in DB_BLOCK_SIZE block boundaries), it is important to ensure that there is no additional overhead (similar to the relationship between DB_BLOCK_SIZE and OS block size or FS block size) while paging one or more pages of the Oracle SGA. The page size is normally system-specific, and the default values on most systems are adequate. On Solaris, the page size can be determind by the **pagesize** command. Similar commands may be available on other OS platforms.

Let's recap. And we will do it starting with the OS page size. The OS page size should be less than or equal to the OS block size (or FS block size). The OS (or FS) block size should, in turn, be less than or equal to DB_BLOCK_SIZE. From the above discussion, it is evident that it does not make any I/O sense to create a file system with a block size that is smaller than the OS's page size. It definitely does not make any I/O sense to create a database with a database block size that is different than the OS block size.

NOTE
The OS block size is closely related to the discussion of the Oracle database block size. On most UNIX systems, the default value of the OS block size is 512 bytes and this is usually relevant for ufs file systems. As mentioned earlier, on most systems that use advanced file systems, the default value for the file system block size is 8K. So for all practical reasons, the OS block size is 8K (as it gets overridden by the FS block size). If ufs file systems are used, the file system should be created with a block size of at least 8K. The default OS page size on most systems today is at least 4K, with 8K becoming a standard on the newer chip architectures.

Changing the Database Block Size: Core Issues

The only way to change the database block size is to take a full export of the database, shut down the database, delete all files associated with the database, and then recreate the database from scratch by using the desired block size in the init.ora (by configuring DB_BLOCK_SIZE). We hope that clarifies the earlier statement we made: "The database block size cannot be changed in the life of a database." The only method to change the Oracle database block size may not be feasible or even possible in most environments due to the following reasons:

- The time it would take to perform a full export of the database could be too long even if exports were done using the *direct* attribute.

- The sheer size of the database would make a full export a theoretical dream.

- Even if you got the export done, the slowest component of this method is the import.

- Even if your database is relatively small, you just may not have an available downtime window to do this.

So let's put things in perspective: you really have one shot at this and if you don't get it right the first time, your applications and your database will pay the price in performance loss for the life of the database. Houston, do you copy that? Of course, this changes in Oracle9i.

Small versus Large Block Size: An Interesting Perspective

Eyal Aronoff, in his paper titled "Oracle Database Block Size," compares the performance characteristics of an Oracle database with database block sizes of 2K and 8K. The performance numbers gathered by his experiments for single block reads are interesting. The following table is a synopsis of the performance numbers from that paper for single block reads.

Description	2K Block Size	8K Block Size
Number of rows in the table	150,000	150,000
Number of read requests	14,100	3,400
Time spent reading a block	19 ms.	20 ms.
Total time spent	268 sec.	68 sec.

By looking only at the numbers for a single block read, the difference is not that much (1 millisecond). Also note that the number of read requests for a database with an 8K Oracle database block size dropped by 75 percent. This is also very significant for iterative single block index scans, as more index entries will be stored in one Oracle block, thus reducing the size of an index and the number of read requests to read the index blocks.

The 75 percent reduction in read requests should be kept in mind along with the fact that the size of the Oracle database block size was increased four-fold (from 2K to 8K). However, if applications continually request single block reads from disk, the 1 millisecond difference will add up to a sizeable number in the long run. In that case, it is conceivable that the iterative pattern of reading single blocks from disk can place more load on the I/O subsystem than what is required. Basically, Oracle is issuing more I/O requests than it would if a larger block size were used.

NOTE

*Based on the performance numbers from Eyal Aronoff's paper and our combined personal experience, we have found that the size of the database block has less impact on the performance of multiblock reads (sequential reads), if the parameter DB_FILE_MULTIBLOCK_READ_COUNT is set such that (DB_BLOCK_SIZE * DB_FILE_ MULTIBLOCK_ READ_COUNT) = I/O chunk-size of the operating system. The I/O chunk-size of the operating system is configurable on many platforms and will be covered in more detail in the chapter "I/O Tuning."*

VIP
Please refrain from setting DB_FILE_ MULTIBLOCK_READ_COUNT to a very high values (normally 32 or higher), as this may send the message to the Oracle optimizer that full table scans are cheap. You definitely do not want the optimizer to go overboard on full table scans. It does not take much to confuse it.

Summary

It is important to configure the Oracle database block size appropriately, as it impacts the overall performance of your database. Again, you get one shot at getting it right. When in doubt, go with the larger block size, but make sure you follow it up by increasing any relevant block-level parameters to manage contention proactively. Viewed in another perspective, application I/O performance really boils down to the frequency and efficiency of block reads from disk and their impact on application performance. The efficiency of block reads is measured by the amount of data made available to the application by reading one block from an Oracle data file.

Configuring Block-Level Storage Parameters

The core block-level performance-related storage parameters that require proactive configuration are *pctused*, *pctfree*, *initrans*, *maxtrans*, and *freelists*. This section is dedicated to discussing the relevant configuration details of these parameters.

Configuring pctused

The best way to explain *pctused* is to think of a dining experience in a restaurant. In some restaurants, waiters and waitresses provide awesome service to enhance your dining experience. They always have an eye on the level of water in your glass. As the water level in your glass reduces (as you take sips of water), they promptly come around and fill your glass.

If you think of the blocks in your Oracle table like glasses of water, understanding *pctused* is very easy. The waiter (server process) fills up the glass (insert) with water and when it is full, the glass goes off the freelist (which means no more water can be poured into the glass). When you consume water (delete), the level (percent full) of your glass reduces. If the waiter fills your glass when the water level drops at approximately the exact same level, you can envision that level as *pctused*. *pctused* is the percent utilization level of a block when it goes back on the freelist for more insert operations. So, the better the restaurant, the higher the *pctused*.

As you sip water from your glass and its level falls below *pctused*, your glass makes it to the front of the freelist of blocks (blocks into which insert operations are done). When that occurs, the waiter fills the glass to its maximum possible level (up to *pctfree*). *pctfree* is relevant to this discussion here. This is because, if you are the kind who usually adds additional cubes of ice to your water, you need to reserve some free space in the glass to allow for the ice cubes to update your glass of water. This is to ensure that the additional ice cubes do not result in water overflowing from your glass. You never want water to overflow from your glass and wet the tablecloth, the same way you never will want data to overflow from an Oracle block.

In the event of a potential situation where the water might overflow, you ask the waiter for another empty glass to ensure that the overflow amount is stored in the second glass. This is exactly what happens in row chaining where some pieces of the row are stored in one block and the others are in another block, with pointers that connect them. Sorry, at this time we don't have a restaurant water drinking analogy to explain row migration. Whenever we think about row migration we think about the post office, which allows you to forward your mail when you move from one place to another, even though all of your mail is still sent to the original address.

pctused, Restaurant Quality, and Database Performance

You can basically gauge the quality of the restaurant by the promptness of the waiters in filling your glass of water. There are some restaurants where they fill your glass once and never come back. You will have to prompt them to fill your glass. You probably will not go back to those restaurants very often. Then there are others who don't even allow you to take a breather after taking a sip of water. They will fill your glass just as you put it down. When done enough times during a dining experience with your beloved one, that can get annoying. In Oracle's perspective, both situations need to be avoided.

In the first scenario, *pctused* is set too low, hence the block never gets on the freelist on time. This can cause block-level fragmentation, as the table may be comprised of many partially filled blocks. This results in wasted disk space and generates more I/O for range scans.

In the second scenario, *pctused* is set too high, and this results in the block bouncing on and off the freelist too many times. This results in unnecessary contention and overhead associated with managing the first block on the freelist(s). One thing is for sure, the next time you dine with your loved ones, you will think of *pctfree* and *pctused*. We thus take credit for permanently altering the "value proposition" of your future dining experiences.

Configuring pctfree

The parameter *pctfree* (set as a percentage) is used to reserve a certain percentage of space in each block for future update operations that increase the length of one or more column values. It is important to configure this parameter appropriately for update- intensive tables, as this parameter controls the amount and frequency of row migration and row chaining. The amount of row migration and row chaining on a table impacts application performance on that table. This is because row migration or row chaining causes more I/O to be performed to retrieve data.

The Oracle documentation has formulas to calculate the values for *pctfree*, *pctused*, and other block-level storage parameters. But the core need here is to reserve adequate space, based on the nature of data manipulation in the important tables of your application. If the length of the table's rows can potentially increase by 25 percent, you may want to consider setting *pctfree* to 25. On the flip side, setting a high *pctfree* for all tables globally will result in wasted disk space and force the application to perform more I/O than required. This is because not all tables require 25 percent of their allocated storage reserved for future update operations. The default value for *pctfree* is 10 percent, and any tables that need more (based on application write patterns on that table) need to be configured with a higher value. On the flip side, you should reduce the default value of *pctfree* for those tables that do not experience any updates that increase the length of rows. In practice, you need to determine the amount of fragmentation in the objects in your database and then make necessary adjustments.

Configuring initrans

Every Oracle data block has a header area which is used to store (among other structures) a table directory, a row directory, and transaction slots. *Transaction slots* are used by transactions to identify themselves within that block, before they attempt to modify one or more rows within the block. These slots play a major role in Oracle's methodology that is used to implement row-level locking and to provide read consistent views of data.

When a transaction needs to modify rows in a block, it first has to "sign in" to an available transaction slot in the header area of the block. Then, based on the slot-number that it utilized in the block, a lock byte is set for each row the transaction modifies to indicate it is currently modifying those rows in that block. So, if a transaction signs into transaction slot 2 in the block's header, the value 2 will be set for the lock byte for each row it modifies (within the scope of that transaction). This facilitates other queries or transactions that visit the same block to determine whether the block is currently undergoing any changes and/or whether the data the new transaction is trying to modify is currently locked by another transaction. Transaction slots and the row-level lock byte are core components that facilitate row-level locking and provide support for Oracle's multiversion read consistency model. We will discuss this in more detail in the chapter "Contention Tuning."

The block-level storage parameter *initrans* configures the initial number of transaction slots (and thus the slot numbers) that are allocated for each block, so transactions can avoid spending time and resources for dynamically allocating transaction slots in the block's header area at runtime. The default value for *initrans* is 1 for tables and 2 for indexes, which means that if a second transaction should attempt to modify data in the same block (via an insert, update, or delete operation), and if the first transaction slot is not currently available, it will borrow 24 bytes from *pctfree* to allocate the second transaction slot in the block's header area. If this occurs frequently, it can cause a couple of problems:

■ The dynamic allocation of transaction slots slows down the performance of the transactions, as it has to engage in block-level space management tasks, instead of just modifying data in the block.

■ If a large number of extra transaction slots are dynamically allocated for a table, any tailored calculations for *pctfree* for that table may eventually become invalid, as the 24 bytes per slot that are borrowed from *pctfree* are never returned when the transaction completes.

As mentioned before, proactively configuring *initrans* to avoid block-level contention whenever the Oracle database block size is increased is not only desired but also required.

Configuring maxtrans

The parameter *maxtrans* controls the maximum level of transactional concurrency within a block. This truly defines how many transactions can concurrently perform changes within a block at the same time. The default value for *maxtrans* is 255, but that does not mean that every block can support 255 transactions right away. The required transaction slots need to be allocated before multiple transactions can modify data within a block at the same time. The actual meaning of the default value is that every block can support up to 255 transactions.

If you do not wish to pay the penalty of runtime dynamic transaction slot allocation in your blocks and thus slow down your transaction, you may be better served to configure *initrans* to what you think is the projected maximum number of concurrent transactions within a block that your application will need. And to provide this discussion with a dose of reality, it is relevant for you to know that the probability of multiple transactions modifying data in a block is the highest on those tables that experience a high number of concurrent insert operations. These are your typical OLTP tables. For those tables, you should also be configuring multiple freelists for the table. And that leads us to the next section.

Configuring freelists

A *freelist* is a set of free blocks in a table into which data can be inserted. Freelists are maintained for tables by linking the block headers with pointers starting from the segment header of the table. A free block does not necessarily imply that it is empty. A free block indicates that there is room (space) in that block and it is available for insert operations.

When a block is full (contains data up to *pctfree*), it is taken off the freelist. Subsequent delete operations on that block may cause the block utilization to fall below *pctused*, and this causes the block to be put back at the head of the freelist. The default setting for the number of freelists on a table is 1. This can cause a bottleneck for those tables that need to support multiple concurrent insert operations from multiple transactions. All transactions will need to get access to the first block on the freelist (head of the freelist) to insert data into that block.

Although there is plenty of printed and electronic material out there that recommends configuring freelists to the number of concurrent transactions, a value of two times the number of CPUs has been observed to be adequate for most systems. On systems that are configured with a large number of CPUs, this number may be lower. By configuring multiple freelists, the free blocks on the freelists are segmented across the number of freelists configured. This facilitates access to different first blocks of the multiple freelists by multiple transactions. By configuring multiple freelists, you can ensure that no single block will become a point of contention for multiple concurrent insert operations.

If you go overboard on this, there is a potential for artificially increasing the high-water mark of the table. This is because Oracle inserts blocks into a freelist five blocks at a time for each freelist. For example, if you have 40 freelists configured on a table, an insertion process into the freelists causes 200 blocks to be added. This means in a worst case scenario, the server process will have to read an additional 160 blocks (that may not contain data) while performing a full table scan. Also, there is no guarantee that all of the data inserted by all of the users will be evenly spread across all of the freelists. This is caused by the formula used by Oracle to assign a specific freelist to a server process. Freelist contention needs to be dealt with in a proactive fashion, by setting it to an appropriate value for those tables that will experience multiple concurrent insert operations via multiple transactions.

NOTE
Although freelist contention is impossible to investigate and unearth using the V$WAITSTAT and V$SYSSTAT dynamic performance views, drilling down on the buffer busy waits Oracle wait event in V$SESSION_WAIT will provide you with insight into the nature and cause of the event. In our experience on many production systems, the buffer busy waits wait event has acted like a thermometer for freelist contention.

Designing, Configuring, and Tuning Tablespaces

Tablespaces, when designed and implemented correctly, facilitate easy administration and management. The added benefit is better application and data availability. There is not much to performance tuning with tablespaces, with one exception. In Oracle8i, tablespaces can be configured as *locally managed* tablespaces, eliminating data dictionary management calls for allocating and deallocating space for objects within that tablespace. This does eliminate a lot of recursive SQL during space allocation operations. Further, locally managed tablespaces are never coalesced by SMON.

Apart from locally managed tablespaces or if your database version is not Oracle8i, the tuning efforts for tablespaces should include separation of objects that are accessed concurrently into multiple tablespaces and the configuration of the data files for those tablespaces on separate storage devices. It is also equally important to set reasonable default storage parameters in your tablespaces.

The Four-Bucket Tablespace Configuration Method

The process of configuring the default storage clause for tablespaces revolves around proactively reducing tablespace-level fragmentation. Tablespace-level fragmentation occurs when objects within the tablespace are sized differently and thus cause fragmentation of free space within the tablespace. When the free space within a tablespace is fragmented, it causes space allocation problems when new extents are allocated. This is because an extent is a set of contiguous blocks, and even though there might be more than 128MB of free space in a tablespace, the extent allocation operation for 128MB fails with an ORA-1653 or ORA-1654, due to lack of contiguous space.

Thus by reducing or eliminating tablespace-level fragmentation, the frequency of object reorganization (to get back some wasted space) or addition of data files for a tablespace (in response to the ORA-1653 or ORA-1654 errors) is greatly reduced. As they say, the best way to cure fragmentation is to not have fragmentation. This is only possible if tablespaces are configured with appropriate and meaningful default storage clauses.

The four-bucket method is a process of physically grouping objects together, based on their current and predicted size. For this effort, four buckets—namely small, medium, large, and x-large—are used. So what do buckets have to do with tablespace storage? Actually a lot, more than you can imagine. The better job you perform defining the logical buckets for your objects, the less prone your database will become to fragmentation and reorganization. Let us explain with a real-life example.

Assume that you are moving from one continent to another (or maybe even within a country) and all of your belongings need to packed, shipped, and then delivered at your new residence. You decide to rent/lease a shipping container (one of those huge boxes that you see stacked up in a shipping yard) for the effort. The packers arrive with four sets of boxes: small, medium, big, and one for mirrors and other odd-shaped stuff. When they pack, you may wonder how it will all fit into the shipping container. But the even sizes of the boxes will help pack everything with room to spare. If the packers had used 20 different sizes of boxes, there would be a mess. Sometimes the space inside a box may be "wasted" (filled with wrapping paper). Remember, you paid for the whole shipping container and don't have to worry as long as the available space inside the shipping container is not exceeded.

The fundamental principle of the four-bucket method is that if all extents within a tablespace are of the same size, by definition there will be virtually no tablespace-level fragmentation. This is because all extents (free or used) will be of the same size and Oracle can acquire the needed space for an object within that tablespace without much ado. This principle also has an ancillary benefit of eliminating the need to periodically coalesce the free space in a tablespace.

What is tablespace coalescing? Consider a restaurant where six DBAs want to sit together during the lunch rush. These DBAs are not willing to sit at three other available tables with two chairs each in different areas of the restaurant. The waiter puts more tables from a nearby area together to accommodate them.

Also, we would rather wait for the next appearance of Haley's comet than wait for SMON to "automatically" coalesce the free space in a tablespace. Implementing the four-bucket method, which allows for equally sized extents, facilitates a low-maintenance, well-designed free space management scheme, without depending on SMON's services. In the bigger scheme of things, you would not want SMON to do the coalescing anyway.

Implementation Details of the Four-Bucket Tablespace Configuration Method

The four-bucket method outlined below is a field-tested object grouping and storage configuration method, deployed in early 1998 on a 700GB Oracle8 database. Another good source of information on preventing fragmentation is the paper "Stop Defragmenting and Start Living," by Bhaskar Himatsingka and Juan Loaiza. This is available at http://metalink.oracle.com/cgi-bin/cr/getfile_cr.cgi?239049.

Again, the core focus of the four-bucket method is to proactively manage space fragmentation. It is understandable that there might be some disk space wastage with this method, but it is not substantial and the benefits that this method brings make it worthwhile. The following are the main steps in the four-bucket method:

1. Create four logical buckets for your objects: small, medium, large, and x-large.

2. Group the objects in your database into these four buckets.

3. Define appropriate tablespace default storage parameters (*initial* and *next)* for each bucket. Ensure *initial* and *next* are set to the same value. Set the *pctincrease* tablespace default storage parameter to 0. Setting *pctincrease* to 0 is very important, as this facilitates equal-sized extents. Again, don't worry about SMON not coalescing free space if the tablespace-level default storage parameter *pctincrease* is set to 0, as you don't need that feature.

4. Create the necessary tablespaces with the default storage clauses defined in step 3.

5. Create the objects with the appropriate tablespace in the tablespace clause without the storage clause for the objects to force them to take the characteristics of the default storage clause of the tablespace where you create them.

6. Make exceptions for those objects that are accessed concurrently and/or are of significant size.

7. Repeat steps 1–6 for every distinct object type in your environment (such as table, index, cluster).

Steps 1–3 require further explanation and the following subsections elucidate the detail behind these steps.

Step 1: Create the Buckets   This is self-explanatory. Depending on your environment you will need to create the appropriate number of buckets that are meaningful. What is so special about the number four? Absolutely nothing. It was just the most common number in our implementations. If your environment needs five or more buckets, by all means go ahead and create the additional buckets. Depending on your data and its size, you may want to adjust the number of buckets.

Step 2: Group the Objects   This requires some analysis work, as you need to define the size limits for each bucket. This might seem arduous, but all you need to do is to collate your objects based on their current size and their projected growth rates. A very simple query grouping the objects by ranges using the blocks or bytes columns for a given *Segment_Type* in DBA_SEGMENTS will easily provide you with the required information. This step is important as it facilitates collating objects in the appropriate buckets. The following table is an example that defines the buckets and their size limits. Adjust these numbers appropriately for your environment.

Bucket	Size Limit
Small	Less than 64MB
Medium	Larger than small, but less than 256MB
Large	Larger than medium, but less than 1024MB
X-Large	Larger than 1024MB

Step 3: Defining the Tablespace's Default Storage Parameters: Initial and Next   After the buckets have been defined in step 2, we move to defining values for the tablespace default storage clause parameters *initial* and *next*. But before we do that, there are a few questions that need some environment-specific answers:

■ Is there a need to create multiple large/x-large tablespaces?

Answer: This is an important consideration, as you might have multiple x-large objects that are accessed concurrently by your applications. For example, your environment might have four 2GB tables that are accessed concurrently and therefore might need to be separated across multiple tablespaces to reduce or eliminate I/O contention.

■ How many extents can each object have, given that your intention is to store all objects of similar size in a tablespace?

Answer: This is not a trick question and we have already dealt with this in the Myth & Folklore section. However, realize that the following issues are relevant to objects that are comprised of many thousands of extents:

■ *Truncate table* or *drop table* operations on these objects may take many hours. This may have an impact on the duration of reorganization for this object or the availability of this object to the application.

■ The many thousands of extents create many thousands of entries in the object space management tables in the data dictionary (such as sys.uet$ and sys.fet$). This may impact the performance of recursive SQL (SQL statements that run in the background when normal SQL statements are executed) that perform object space management in your environment.

■ What is the growth potential for these objects and will the tablespace have adequate free space after all objects have been created? Which objects will grow more than others?

Answer: This is an important consideration as it helps you determine how to size your data files for your tablespaces. Although 2GB data files are standard, using 4GB data files should be considered if the database is large (several hundred gigabytes to terabytes) and if the operating system supports large files. You will have to explicitly enable large file support in your environment. Further, you need to know your data. If you are intimately familiar with your application and your database, you will have no problems in determining which objects will post more growth than others.

■ Can additional data files be created in the future for these tablespaces and spread across multiple independent physical devices?

Answer: Again, this goes back to the question of how you plan for your data growth. This will also help determine appropriate extent sizes for your tablespaces. This raises other questions such as, how much of the data will you have to retain, and how much can be purged or archived? If you initially configure your storage environment with adequate space and with logical volumes supported by multiple drives (striped and/or mirrored), data files can be added and they will support larger tablespaces.

The following table is an example that sizes the tablespace default storage clause parameters *initial* and *next*. Adjust these numbers appropriately for your environment.

Bucket	Size for *initial* and *next*
Small	256K
Medium	1MB
Large	4MB
X-Large	16MB

All right, it is time to put some numbers to the above example, to get a perspective on how much space wastage actually occurs. Let us assume that we are working in an environment with 20,000 objects. Further assume that 16,000 objects are assigned the small bucket, 2,500 objects are assigned the medium bucket, 1,000 objects are assigned the large bucket, and finally, 500 objects are assigned the x-large bucket. If you assume the worst case scenario that the last extent allocated to each object is almost empty and hence wasted, the breakdown of the amount of space wastage in your environment is next.

Bucket	Max. Wastage per Object	Number of Objects in the Bucket	Total Wastage per Bucket
Small	256K	16,000	4.00GB
Medium	1MB	2,500	2.44GB
Large	4MB	1,000	3.90GB
X-Large	16MB	500	7.81GB
Total			**18.15GB**

Okay, so with 20,000 objects the total worst case scenario disk wastage amounts to 18.15GB. Even at a price of $100 per gigabyte (average street prices for high-end disk storage for production systems), the total cost of the wastage is $1,815. If you are supporting a large environment with the above characteristics, we are really talking about small change here. In today's world, you will waste one 18GB drive. On the flip side, think about the benefit. It costs your organization $1,815 to have a database that by design possesses a very low probability of suffering from tablespace-level fragmentation. That in turn will translate into many more hours of uptime, as there will be fewer object reorganizations and more of your time free to do more important things in life. We are optimistic that any CIO or CTO who has been around the block will gladly give you the nod to waste 18GB for this effort.

NOTE
Although there have been no quantifiable results published on the optimum number of tablespaces or data files a database should have, fundamental knowledge about the Oracle architecture leads us to conclude that as the number of tablespaces increases, the amount of time it would take to complete a checkpoint will also increase, as a result of the many file headers that Oracle needs to update. This is true for environments that have thousands of data files supporting thousands of tablespaces. Also, bear in mind that object-level fragmentation in the form of partially filled blocks and row-level fragmentation in the form of chained or migrated rows will still require object reorganization, if DB_BLOCK_SIZE and object-level storage parameters are not proactively configured.

VIP
The benefits that the four-bucket tablespace configuration method provides are relative to the implementation. This means that when objects are created, they should not contain any storage clause, as it will undo all the good work done. However, in Oracle8i, locally managed tablespaces provide an additional layer of protection that prevents tablespace fragmentation.

It is extremely important that if you are to reorganize your objects after implementing the four-bucket tablespace configuration method, you do it without the compress=y attribute. This is because the goal of your reorganization is not to reduce the number of extents. It is to reduce or eliminate block-level and row-level fragmentation. If you reorganized your object with the compress attribute, you will eventually undo the benefits that this method provides, as you will start having objects with different sized extents.

Configuring Temporary Tablespaces

In Oracle 7.3, the concept of pure temporary tablespaces was introduced and the temporary clause was added to the **create tablespace** command. The introduction of pure temporary tablespaces was significant on a couple of points. First and foremost, it supported the ability to allow sorts, to directly write to disk. This was done by configuring an initialization parameter SORT_DIRECT_WRITES (this is obsolete in Oracle8i). When set to TRUE, every sort that was larger than SORT_AREA_SIZE was directly written to the temporary tablespace. This meant that the database buffer cache was *not* used for sort segments, but purely for data, index, cluster, and rollback segments.

The second aspect was the behavior change of the temporary tablespace and temporary segments in Oracle 7.3. This change alleviated the overhead and performance bottleneck for environments that generated a lot of activity in the temporary tablespace.

Prior to Oracle 7.3, the overhead was caused each time a server process required temporary space (for sorts during summary operations, *group by*, *order by*, joins, creation of indexes, and so on) larger than SORT_AREA_SIZE, as it allocated (created) a temp segment in the temporary tablespace (as defined when the user was created or altered later). When the sort operation completed, the temporary segment was deallocated (dropped). This obviously was wasted effort as the next process that required temporary space larger than SORT_AREA_SIZE had to allocate a temp segment again, only to deallocate at the end of the sorting operation. The core problem here was the lack of reuse of the temp segments across multiple sort operations.

In Oracle 7.3 with pure temporary tablespaces, the first process that required temporary space larger than SORT_AREA_SIZE after the instance is started allocated a temporary segment in the temporary tablespace and allocated as many extents to this temporary segment as required. When that first process completed its sorting operation, it left the temporary segment for use by another sort operation. Subsequent processes increased the size of this temp segment (whose storage characteristics were determined by the default storage clause in the **create tablespace** command that created the TEMP tablespace).

The space within this temporary segment was maintained using a sort extent pool algorithm (which still used the data dictionary). Thus there was one temporary segment per temporary tablespace at any given time. This temporary segment got deallocated by SMON on instance *shutdown* or *startup* (as the case may be, depending on the type of *shutdown—immediate* or *abort*). In Oracle8, a new dynamic performance view V$SORT_USAGE was added to provide information about the usage characteristics of the temporary tablespaces.

NOTE
Depending on the number of users on your system, you may want to consider creating multiple temporary tablespaces, so that one temporary tablespace does not become a single point of bottleneck.

Global Temporary Tables and Temporary Tablespaces

While we are still on the subject of temporary tablespaces, we wanted to bring to your attention the relationship between global temporary tables and temporary tablespaces. In Oracle8i, a brand new functionality called global temporary tables was introduced to hold data that is private to a session. Therefore, every session can view and change only its data. The data in the global temporary table can be configured to last for the duration of either a transaction or session (depending on the *on commit* attribute of the global temporary table).

This new feature is supported by the **create global temporary table** command, which creates the structure of a temporary table in a user's schema. Subsequent insert, update, and delete operations on that table by any other user sessions allow the data to be private to a user's session. The temporary table's structure is created once and the table (not the data) is globally available across multiple sessions. The table-level attribute *on commit* facilitates control over whether the data needs to be retained at the transaction level or the session level. One of the most incredible features of global temporary tables is that they do not generate redo logs entries for the data and index blocks during insert, update, and delete operations. But rollback entries for the data and redo logs for the rollback entries are always generated.

The important point that needs to be brought up here is that the data that is manipulated in the session exists in the PGA of the session within the session's *sort areas*. What this means is that if the amount of data that is manipulated exceeds the session's SORT_AREA_SIZE, the data is written to the user's temporary tablespace. It is important for you to take this into consideration for your temporary tablespace usage, especially if the amount of data manipulated by the global temporary table is large.

Configuring Locally Managed Tablespaces

Hmm, this sounds like the marketing slogan that some local restaurants use to advertise their food and their service. No discussion on tablespaces in Oracle8i would be complete without due mention of the new functionality of self-managing tablespaces. The concept of self-management stems from the fact that locally managed tablespaces do not involve the data dictionary for space management. This is very significant, as management of space using the data dictionary poses the overhead on the database in the form of recursive SQL calls that occur during space management operations such as extent allocation and deallocation.

Depending on the number of objects and the frequency of extent allocation or deallocation in the database, this can be a performance bottleneck. So, when you talk about "tuning tablespaces," Oracle8i provides yet another option for database administrators. You must absolutely consider using locally managed tablespace for your temporary tablespaces (if not other tablespaces), as it eliminates the use of the data dictionary for space management of the temporary segment.

Locally managed tablespaces use a bitmap within the data file of the tablespace to manage the used and free space within the tablespace. They also provide the additional layer of fragmentation prevention by overriding the storage clause on object creation. Here are some things about locally managed tablespaces that you should be aware of:

■ Extent allocation can be done either automatically or uniformly. You pick which one is appropriate for your environment. To avoid tablespace-level free space fragmentation in the long run, pick the uniform method. However, please note that you cannot create a locally managed temporary tablespace using the *extent management local autoallocate* clause, you must use *extent management local uniform size nnn* or just *extent management local*.

■ Automatic allocation implies that Oracle decides the extent sizes and the sizes could be different across objects, but they are usually reasonable multiples of the smallest extent. This is *not* relevant and cannot be used for rollback segments or temporary tablespaces. With the *extent management local autoallocate* clause in the **create tablespace** command, you tell Oracle to take care of extent allocation for you. Oracle then uses 64K, 1MB, 8MB, and 64MB to size extents, based on the current size and growth pattern of the object.

■ Uniform allocation implies the extent sizes for all objects will be the same. With the *extent management local uniform 8m* clause in the **create tablespace** command, you tell Oracle to allocate every extent for every object within that tablespace to 8MB, regardless of what is specified in the object's storage clause. However, the extent allocation is done in such a manner that Oracle provides you with at least as much space as you requested via the storage clause of the object (if you provided the storage clause on object creation).

■ When creating temporary tablespaces that are locally managed, the syntax to create them is not the same as regular tablespaces. In Oracle8i, the syntax to create a temporary tablespace of type *temporary* which is locally managed is outlined in the following code listing:

```
Create Temporary Tablespace TEMP
Tempfile '/u01/oradata/prod/temp01.dbf' size 1024m
Extent Management Local Uniform Size 8M;
```

NOTE
*The data file created in the above code example can be viewed by querying the DBA_TEMP_FILES data dictionary view instead of DBA_DATA_FILES. This tempfile is a temporary data file and is different from the data files that are created for tablespaces. Some of the core differences between normal data files and tempfiles is that tempfiles cannot be created in any manner other than the **create temporary tablespace** command, are ignored during media recovery, always have the nologging attribute set, cannot be set to read-only mode, and cannot be renamed. You can also view the dynamic performance view V$TEMPFILE for more information.*

Database Partitioning for Better Performance

The database partitioning functionality was first introduced in Oracle8 and the underlying principle is "Divide and conquer." This principle has served as the foundation for various software engineering disciplines for many years. In the database's perspective, partitioning allows decomposition of table data and index data. It facilitates (but does not guarantee) higher availability, performance, manageability, and scalability of the database. The ability to partition data into meaningful chunks is required for current databases. The databases of today typically have data storage requirements that range from many hundreds of gigabytes to multiple terabytes.

Functional Benefits of Partitioning

Partitioning has many benefits, especially in an Oracle database environment. The key benefits are

- Size-up and scale-up

- Partial data availability

- Increased performance

Size-Up Your Database and Scale-Up Your Performance

If partitioning is implemented in an optimal fashion, it will virtually guarantee performance *scale-up*, linear to a *size-up* of the database. This is extremely important, as an increase in database size cannot justify a decrease in performance.

Partial Data Availability

Partitioning in Oracle8 facilitates segmentation of the data at a lower level of granularity than was available in Oracle7. The key difference between an Oracle7 table and an Oracle8 partitioned table is that an Oracle7 table is supported by one data segment and an Oracle8 partitioned table is supported by as many data segments as the number of partitions in the table. This also allows you to easily spread the data over multiple storage devices in a controlled fashion, if you create the partitions in separate tablespaces and create the data files for the tablespaces on separate storage devices. The same correlation can be made between an Oracle7 index and an Oracle8 partitioned index. With each partition supported by an independent segment, there is support for partial data availability, even if some partitions of the table are unavailable due to media failures. This can be very easily achieved if the partitions are stored in multiple tablespaces, and the tablespaces themselves are supported by data files on independent storage devices.

Increased Performance

With the basic premise of "divide and conquer," decomposing tables and indexes into partitions can provide significant performance increases. This is primarily attributed to the size of the segments being much smaller. In Oracle8, the new ROWID assists in data elimination while processing a query by partition key, and this can result in excellent query performance. Partitioned indexes also allow faster scans, as the underlying B*-*tree* associated with a partition of an index is much smaller than that of an index that is not partitioned. This results in less I/O performed on the index segment, which in turn translates into better query performance.

The performance gains of partitioning can be summed up with three points:

- Partition-aware processing of tables and indexes by the cost-based optimizer (it is better to potentially process many small segments on an as-needed basis, rather than one large segment).

- Partition-level sorts for operations that require sorting (it is better to sort many smaller segments on an as-needed basis, rather than one large segment).

- The automatic "horizontal striping" achieved by partitioning supports better parallel processing of data.

Key Considerations for Database Partitioning

Partitioning tables and indexes in an optimal fashion results in many benefits. The following list of considerations will assist you in your effort to effectively partition tables. These considerations have been collected from various Oracle8 partitioning implementations. They should be used in addition to the recommendations in the Oracle Tuning Manual:

- Partition key columns of the table should ideally characterize data that is:

  - Time-bound or decomposable by some range.

  - Predominantly used in the *where clause* of queries on the partitioned table.

- While range partitioning will probably be the default choice for most partitioning efforts, consider hash partitioning, where data cannot be easily decomposed into ranges. Also, consider composite partitioning when both range and hash partitioning are required.

- When implementing partitioning, creating one tablespace per partition should be considered for better availability and management. This provides the capability to turn on and off your data. This is useful for those sites that need to hide their data after a certain period of time, and then bring it online on demand. If the data in a partition is no longer required, it can be turned off by issuing an **alter tablespace x offline** command. When the data in that partition is required at a later date, it can be turned on by issuing an **alter tablespace x online** command. Archiving and purging data by exporting it off to tape for future retrieval is no longer a feasible or acceptable method. This is due to the long duration of the import process. With current storage prices, data should be retained on disk using the method outlined here.

■ The tables and indexes that are partitioned need to be analyzed and the Oracle initialization parameter OPTIMIZER_MODE needs to be set to CHOOSE. This is to ensure that the optimizer can perform partition elimination (or pruning) while running queries. Partition data elimination is *only* supported with the cost-based optimizer, and generation of statistics on the said tables and indexes is a prerequisite.

■ The degree of parallelism on partitioned objects needs serious consideration while designing database partitioning. This is covered in greater detail in the chapter "Parallel Query Tuning."

■ Create at least one local prefixed partitioned index. This will ensure partition elimination, when the queries perform seeks using the partition key of the table. For example, if the SALES table has Month_No as its partition key, creating a local-prefixed partitioned index (leading column of the index is Month_No) will significantly assist in query performance. The optimizer will automatically perform partition elimination on queries that use the Month_No in the *where clause* of the query.

■ Create bitmapped local partitioned indexes on predominantly read-only tables. This has a two-faceted performance benefit. First, the size of the index will be significantly smaller (which will result in fewer index block reads). Next, for low-cardinality column data access, the bitmap-to-ROWID conversion process to access data will be significantly faster than the traditional method used for data access in regular indexes. Please use the necessary application and environment prudence when implementing bitmapped indexes. They need to be implemented only where appropriate, such as with low-cardinality columns that are not frequently updated. (This restriction is for Oracle 8.0 or lower, implying higher cardinality columns for bitmapped indexes are supported in Oracle8i).

■ Create local partitioned indexes whenever possible, regardless of whether they are prefixed or non-prefixed. This is to ensure equi-partitioning of values based on the partition key of the table. You may ask, what in the world is equi-partitioning? The answer is pretty simple—it is the process of equally dividing the data across the number of partitions in the table or index. Here are some reasons why you might want to consider using local partitioned indexes:

- A local index is partitioned on the partition key of the table (since the index partitions will be equi-partitioned with respect to table partitions).

- Equi-partitioning of indexes facilitates equitable distribution of the data values across multiple index partitions.

- Local indexes provide better availability, as only the relevant partitions of local indexes are made unusable on certain table partition-maintenance operations (such as dropping a partition, truncating a partition, and so on).

- In data warehouses, the use of nonprefixed indexes is preferred, even if the partition key of the table is not part of the index definition. This is because most queries are characterized by large range-scans, reading significant amounts of data from the table. In those cases, nonprefixed indexes will provide better throughput, especially when used with the parallel clause.

- Minimize the use of global indexes when ever possible. Global indexes are partitioned on the partition key of the said global index and do not guarantee equi-partitioning of the index values. Minimizing their use will ensure that certain table partition-maintenance operations will not affect the entire index. This factor is key for partial data/index availability. Further:

  - Global partitioned indexes are most useful in supporting unique constraints on non-partition-key columns.

  - If the *where clause* predicate of certain queries has columns other than the partition key, global indexes are essential, as they will prevent full table scans.

- Make indexes unusable prior to performing any bulk DML operations on a partitioned table. This has two benefits. First, it speeds up the time it takes to execute the bulk DML, and next, it speeds up subsequent index recreation (after the bulk DML). For obvious reasons (such as better performance and better availability of the index), it is better to use the **alter index index_ name rebuild** command for index rebuilds, rather than dropping indexes and then creating them from scratch.

Initialization Parameters to Configure

This chapter has primarily focused on database tuning and its related components. However, there were references to various Oracle initialization parameters in the preceding sections. The following table summarizes them and adds a few others that are relevant.

Oracle Initialization Parameter	Meaning/Relevance
DB_BLOCK_SIZE	This parameter defines the size of a block in the database. The Oracle database block size is the lowest granularity of storage in an Oracle environment.
DB_FILE_MULTIBLOCK_READ_COUNT	This parameter defines the I/O chunk-size used when Oracle issues a read system call at the OS. It is relevant for full table scans and index range scans.
OPTIMIZER_MODE	This parameter defines and controls the type of optimization that is applied to SQL statements.
SORT_AREA_SIZE	This parameter defines the amount of memory allocated to the sort phase of a sort.
SORT_AREA_RETAINED_SIZE	This parameter defines the amount of memory that is utilized during the fetch phase of a sort. Your PGA always consumes at least this much amount of memory.
SORT_DIRECT_WRITES	This parameter directs the server process to write any sort data that is larger than SORT_AREA_SIZE directly to the temporary tablespace. This parameter was introduced in Oracle 7.3 with a default value of TRUE and is obsolete in Oracle8i.

Oracle Initialization Parameter	Meaning/Relevance
SORT_MULTIBLOCK_READ_COUNT	This parameter was introduced in Oracle8i and replaces all past sort-related parameters. It is usually recommended to set this parameter to a value of either 1 or 2.

Tuning Issues on Hybrid Databases

A hybrid database (or system) is one that displays the characteristics and behaves like an online transaction processing (OLTP) system during certain times of the day and like a decision support system (DSS) during other times. To take stock of reality, there are very few OLTP systems in our world today when you look at it from a pure transactional perspective. And let's face it, the whole idea of getting data into a database is to query it and run reports that allow us to convert data into information. The online and batch queries do just that. The primary goal while tuning hybrid systems is to achieve a balance between the needs of the transactional and reporting aspects of the system. This can make configuration and tuning that much more challenging. This section is geared toward outlining some of the key issues and challenges in managing hybrid systems.

For example, earlier in the chapter we recommended that you pick the right Oracle database block size for your system by choosing relatively smaller block sizes for OLTP systems versus larger block sizes for DSS systems. When faced with a hybrid system, it is normal to find yourself in a dilemma. Which one do you pick, 8K or 16K? Remember another piece of advice from that section: "When in doubt, go with the larger block size."

The rationale behind that advice was based on the fact that you could always proactively configure your block-level storage parameters to avoid and manage contention that results from the larger size. A larger database block size increases the amount of data stored in a block, which causes fewer read requests by Oracle to the operating system. And larger database block sizes naturally shrink the size and height of the indexes in your system.

The OLTP aspect of the system provides its share of challenges. Some of the challenges are

- Optimal rollback segment configuration

- Effective management of block-level contention

- Management of locks

- Number of concurrent users on the database

- Number of concurrent connections on the database

- Service level agreements, including mean time to recover the database

- Frequency and management of backups

- Frequency of the job to analyze your tables and indexes

- High-availability requirements

- Data management, including data archiving and purging

The DSS aspect has its own set of unique issues. They include (among others):

- Manipulation and massaging of data

- Management of complex reporting requirements

- Indexing strategies

- Segregation of the read-only objects from the read/write objects

- Memory sorts and temporary tablespace configuration

The real challenge on your hands is to balance the needs of the two aspects, so that a configuration or tuning decision that helps one aspect does not hurt the other. Remember the importance of both aspects. They will need your attention in different ways, and you will have to constantly perform an impact analysis for both aspects before implementing any tuning solutions or configuration changes. Like a balancing scale, where putting weight on one side raises the other, you will need to monitor and maintain the weights (tuning efforts) for each of these aspects so that your database remains in balance and every user gets the best performance possible.

NOTE
There is one piece of friendly technical advice we would like to provide regarding managing hybrid systems. Even if your environment has independent windows for the DSS aspect and the OLTP aspect, and even if you know that these windows will never overlap one another, please assume at least for the sake of system-sizing (memory, CPU, and disk) that they will. We share this with you from the bottom of our hearts and our combined production experience. There is absolutely no room for the word "never" in the world you live in. As 007 once said, "Never say never again!"

Tuning Issues on Data Warehouse Databases

These days, there is a proliferation of data warehouses left and right in every business organization. The need to collect, analyze, dissect, and refine data is critical to an organization more than ever. But the single most challenging aspect of current data warehouses is the sheer size and volume of the data store. Gone are the days where a 100GB database was considered a *very large database* (VLDB). The VLDBs of today are sized at many hundreds of gigabytes to many terabytes. And contrary to popular belief, OLTP or hybrid systems can be VLDBs in their own right, just by virtue of their size. The following are a set of common performance issues that are faced when dealing with data warehouses:

- Process flow between various entities in the system

- Data model design and implementation

- Schema design and configuration

- I/O configuration (this will be covered in great detail in the chapter "I/O Tuning")

- Application design and deployment

- Data management with database partitioning for very large objects

- Extraction, transportation, and loading of data

- Analysis of data

- Management of summarized data

- Sampling of data

- Parallel execution of voluminous operations

- Support for data availability on partial failures

In a Nutshell

This chapter was about database tuning, and it dealt with proactively configuring and managing various storage-related components in the database. It focused on the changes that have occurred in various environments that affect Oracle database configuration. The configuration of the Oracle database block size is one of the most important steps that you as a DBA will perform. It needs to be done right the first time, every time. When in doubt, go with a bigger database block size, but proactively control block-level contention.

To manage block-level fragmentation and to better use the available space that you allocate to an object, block-level storage parameters such as *pctfree* and *pctused* need configuration. Block-level concurrency support for multiple transactions needs to be done by configuring *initrans* and *maxtrans* for the relevant tables that will have to support concurrent data manipulation. If a table is heavily inserted into, configuring adequate *freelists* is essential to manage contention. Every step needs to be taken to reduce and eliminate tablespace-level fragmentation. Fragmentation can be managed by implementing the "four-bucket tablespace configuration" method. It is perfectly okay to waste some disk space and keep all extent sizes in a tablespace uniform, rather than deal with free space fragmentation, which can become a production problem.

If your database version is Oracle8i, locally managed tablespaces need to be considered and implemented. This provides significant increases in performance and ease of maintenance. Partitioning is a key feature that was introduced in Oracle8, and it provides the capability to decompose an object into smaller segments, and thus provide better performance while dealing with these smaller segments.

We hope you will spend your precious days performing tasks that are of value to your system and your business, rather than trying to get every object in your environment to fit into one extent. It is time for us to put an end to the "one extent compulsion" and accept the fact that an object can have many hundred extents and still perform at peak levels, so long as it does not suffer from severe block-level or row-level fragmentation and the extent sizing is done keeping in mind DB_ FILE_ MULTIBLOCK_READ_COUNT and DB_BLOCK_SIZE. And we hope that we have convinced you that compressing an object into one extent in no way makes performance better. It just gives fragmentation a new lease on life, which will rear its ugly head when you least expect it.

The complexities of managing and tuning hybrid environments and current-day data warehouses are very demanding. Although justice cannot be done to these topics without writing volumes on it, our goal was to touch the high-level issues, which will at least get you to proactively think about these important issues.

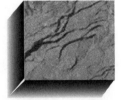

PART
IV

Specialized Tuning

CHAPTER
9

Parallel Query Tuning

Myth & Folklore
Using parallelism for SQL operations will always result in performance increases.

Fact
Using parallelism for queries or for DML statements (Oracle8 and above) will *not* always increase the performance. If it were that simple, we would all be using parallelism on everything in sight and all those high-paid Oracle performance-tuning experts and consultants would be looking for other careers. However, if parallelism is used judiciously in an environment that is conducive (you design it to be conducive), it can dramatically improve performance. Otherwise, it has potential to paralyze your system.

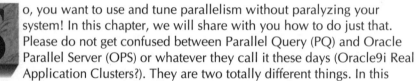 o, you want to use and tune parallelism without paralyzing your system! In this chapter, we will share with you how to do just that. Please do not get confused between Parallel Query (PQ) and Oracle Parallel Server (OPS) or whatever they call it these days (Oracle9i Real Application Clusters?). They are two totally different things. In this chapter, we deal with PQ. Even though PQ sounds like an extra charge option (which it was once upon a time), today it is part of the Enterprise Edition of Oracle and is installed when you install the Oracle RDBMS.

When Oracle executes a SQL statement that does not use parallelism, there is only a single process involved in completing the task. But when the same statement is executed with parallelism, Oracle divides the work and assigns it to multiple processes. By doing so, the work gets done faster, but only if the environment is conducive to parallelism. That is the theory behind parallelism. But optimal implementation of PQ is another story.

What Is Parallelism and How Does Oracle Do It?

Remember the old math problem from school: If one worker takes eight hours to do a particular job, how much time will two workers take when the job is done together? Was the answer four hours? Well, it may be in theory. In reality, however, that may not be the case. If those workers interrupted each other, talked about their weekend plans or last night's ball game while trying to get the job done, it may take more than eight hours for them to complete the job. But if their work was properly managed to keep such interruptions at bay, they could get the job done faster. The same is true for parallelism. It needs proper design, adequate resources, and built-in controls to improve overall performance. The primary goal behind Oracle's Parallel Query architecture is to have all parallel query slaves perform approximately the same amount of work, so that they will all complete their portion of the work at approximately the same time.

When to Use Parallel Query

The concept of parallel operations is based on dividing the work among multiple processes. It assumes that multiple jobs of small magnitude can be completed much faster than a single job with a somewhat larger magnitude, both producing the same result. For example, when a full table scan is performed by multiple processes, there is a possibility (depending on the design and nature of the environment) that it can return the data faster than even an indexed scan. However, this requires an environment that is conducive to parallelism.

Parallelism requires (among other things) that the table be spread over multiple storage devices to facilitate access by multiple processes without I/O contention. It also requires adequate capacity for CPU and memory, to handle the resource requirements of the parallel query slaves. Using PQ does not always require a multiple CPU system. Really?

Sure. If a single CPU system is underutilized, PQ can make better use of it. Why not? You have paid good money for your system, so there is nothing wrong in finding ways to make the most of it. But remember that the availability of required resources is the key when considering PQ, because lack of resources would definitely paralyze your system. Don't go overboard without determining whether you have enough resources. It may be important to design for parallelism keeping in mind the busiest period of processing, so that if need be, the parallel operations can peacefully coexist with the other jobs and sessions on the system.

Parallel execution of SQL statements is useful for operations where a large amount of data gets processed: full table scans, joining of large tables, large range-scans of indexes, insertion of massive amounts of data to a data warehouse, and so on. PQ rewrites the underlying SQL statement in such a way that the query can be divided into multiple tasks. Multiple processes running simultaneously to produce desired output can handle these multiple tasks. These processes are often called the *parallel query slaves* or *parallel query servers,* the operations of which are controlled and coordinated by the server process which takes on a new name: *parallel execution coordinator* or *parallel query coordinator (PQC).*

The key to proper use of PQ is to keep the parallel query slaves' processes from interfering with one another. For example, too many PQ slaves should not access the same storage devices at the same time, or wait on each other for CPU and other system resources. Going overboard with PQ by configuring and launching too many parallel query slave processes and/or enabling parallelism on every table on the system has the potential to cause systemwide contention, increase OS-level context switching, and degrade overall system performance. In addition, these processes will be counted against the total number of Oracle processes. If you reach the limit, new database connections will not be possible. So please handle and use PQ with care!

How to Use Parallelism

Now that you know what parallelism is, let's discuss how your SQL statement can use it. The number of parallel query slaves for a single task is called the *degree of parallelism*. Normally, PQ would attempt to use parallel query slave processes equal to the value of degree of parallelism. But if a sorting operation is involved, the number of processes required is doubled.

VIP
It is very important to note here that PQ will utilize twice the number of processes defined in the degree if the SQL statement requires a sort operation. This is a very crucial aspect of PQ and needs your undivided attention, as it has the potential to cripple performance system-wide.

As you will see shortly, there are other initialization parameters that actually control the number of such processes irrespective of the degree of parallelism. However, there are the following ways to set this degree of parallelism:

■ At the table or index level

■ At the SQL statement level with a *parallel* hint

■ As a default based on the number of CPUs or the number of storage devices that Oracle believes that you are using

The following example shows how to set the degree of parallelism when creating a new table. The "parallel (degree 4)" clause sets the table's degree of parallelism to 4.

```
SQL> create table MYTABLE
        (ColA number(2),
         ColB number(2)
        )
        parallel (degree 4);
Table created.
```

You can see the value of the degree of parallelism for the table in the USER_TABLES, ALL_TABLES, and DBA_TABLES views in a column titled Degree:

```
SQL> select Degree
       from USER_TABLES
      where Table_Name = 'MYTABLE';
DEGREE
----------
       4
```

You can change the degree of parallelism for a table using the **alter table** command. In the following example, the degree of parallelism is changed to 6:

```
SQL> alter table MYTABLE parallel(degree 6);
Table altered.
SQL> select Degree
       from USER_TABLES
       where Table_Name = 'MYTABLE';
DEGREE
----------
         6
```

The following code listing shows how to set the degree of parallelism on an index to 4 while creating the index. Depending on your Oracle version, the data dictionary views USER_INDEXES, DBA_INDEXES, and ALL_INDEXES will have a column titled Degree, which will contain the value of the degree of parallelism for the index.

```
SQL> create index MYINDEX
       on MYTABLE (ColA)
       storage (initial 1M  next 1M)
       parallel (degree 4);
Index created.
SQL> select Degree
       from USER_INDEXES
       where Index_Name = 'MYINDEX';
DEGREE
---------------------------------------
4
```

NOTE
Since all the parallel query slaves operate independent of each other, each will use the associated storage parameters as their own. In the preceding example, four query slaves will each use the initial extent's value of 1MB while building the index, thereby using 4MB at once during the index creation process. Also, these parallel query slaves will need their own space in temporary tablespace to perform the sort. Please keep in mind the impact on disk space when using parallelism for building indexes.

You can also use the **alter index** command to change the degree of parallelism for an index, as shown here:

```
SQL> alter index MYINDEX parallel(degree 6);
Index altered.
SQL> select Degree
       from USER_INDEXES
       where Index_Name = 'MYINDEX';
DEGREE
----------------------------------------
6
```

The following sample code shows how to set the degree of parallelism on a table to 6, via a PARALLEL hint in a SQL statement. Please also note that if you use a table alias, the alias needs to be referenced in the *hint*, as shown. Only the few last lines from the output are shown in the following example:

```
select /*+ PARALLEL (CM, 6) */ Customer_Id Custid, Last_Contract_Yr Lcy
    from CUSTOMER_MASTER CM
    order by Customer_Id;

CUSTID      LCY
----------  ------
................
................
 101119153  2000
 101119164  2000
 101119197  2000
5065192 rows selected.
```

Please note that since the previous example uses an "order by" clause to sort the result set, Oracle may attempt to allocate at least twelve parallel query slaves to this operation.

The following example sets the degree of parallelism on a table to a value of *default*. In Oracle 7.3 and 8.0, this *default* degree is determined by Oracle based on various factors, such as number of CPUs, or number of storage devices on which the table or index is stored.

```
SQL> alter table MYTABLE parallel;
Table altered.
SQL> select Degree
       from USER_TABLES
       where Table_Name='MYTABLE';
DEGREE
----------
    DEFAULT
```

In Oracle 8.1.6, a new initialization parameter, PARALLEL_THREADS_PER_CPU, defines the default degree of parallelism. Its default value is platform-specific and is adequate in most cases. Oracle suggests decreasing the value of this parameter if the system appears to be overloaded when parallel query is running. It is very easy to determine this if you look at V$SESSION_WAIT for wait events that relate to parallel query slaves. Of course, it's your job to figure out whether or not your system appears to be overloaded. The good news is that the value of this parameter can be changed dynamically.

If you set the degree of parallelism at table and/or index level, and also specify a different value via a hint in the SQL statement, which one would Oracle use? Well, Oracle always uses the following order of precedence:

1. SQL statement with the PARALLEL hint

2. Parallel degree set at the table or index

3. Default degree of parallelism

NOTE
Once the degree of parallelism is determined, it becomes the degree of parallelism for the entire operation.

All the aforementioned methods to set the degree of parallelism only determine the number of parallel query slaves the PQC will request for a given operation. In certain situations the PQC may not get what it asks for. This is because the actual number of parallel query slaves that are eventually assigned to an operation depends on the number of available processes in what is called the *parallel execution server pool.*

In very simple terms, this means that if there are not enough available parallel query slaves, the degree you specify (or expect) may not be the actual degree of parallelism with which the SQL statement is executed. We will talk about this in more detail in the coming sections. But this should be enough to draw your attention to the fact that using parallelism without understanding all these other things will cause you more headaches when you don't see the expected improvement in your query performance.

If you decide that no parallelism is required and would like to remove the degree of parallelism from the table or index definition, you can use the *noparallel* clause in the **alter** command as shown next. Also, to disable parallelism in a SQL statement that would otherwise use parallelism because of the definition of the degree of parallelism on the table, you can use the NOPARALLEL hint.

```
SQL> alter table MYTABLE noparallel;
Table altered.
SQL> select /*+ NOPARALLEL */ count (*)
        from CUSTOMER_MASTER;
COUNT(*)
----------
   5065192
```

SQL Statements that Benefit from Parallelism

As mentioned before, parallel execution of SQL statements can improve performance of SQL statements when they process or access large amounts of data. Not only can you use it in just plain old SQL statements to select data, you can use it for a number of DDL and DML operations as well.

As of Oracle 7.3, you can use parallelism for the following types of operations:

- Select statements

- Subqueries in update and delete statements

- Subqueries in insert and create table statements

- Create Table As Select (CTAS) statements

- Create index statements (parallel DDL)

In addition, from Oracle 8.0 and up, the following types of DDL operations can use parallelism:

- Rebuilding an index

- Rebuilding an index partition

- Splitting a partition

- Moving a partition

In addition to these DDL operations, Oracle8 introduced parallelism for insert, update, and delete statements. Oracle uses the term Parallel DML (PDML) to refer to these operations, although the ANSI definition of Data Manipulation Language (DML) generally includes query statements too. PDML can be used to speed up bulk DML operations against large tables. PDML can be of great benefit to many of the operations in decision support systems and data warehouse systems that typically handle large amounts of data. On systems such as these, performance and scalability of accessing such large amounts of data is very important. At the same time, PDML can also be helpful in certain OLTP operations.

PDML can also be used with non-partitioned tables. However, full benefit of PDML can be realized only when tables are partitioned. This is because only parallel insert operations can be performed on non-partitioned tables. But remember that the parallelism is spread across all the partitions and that there is no parallelism within a partition. This means you can have only one parallel query slave per partition. The major advantage of using PDML is performance and the elimination for the need to "hand hold" parallelism for DML operations. However, as mentioned before, the needed resources must be available.

Parallel DML can only be enabled or disabled within a session. Before a session can be enabled (using an **alter session** command) to use PDML, you need to either commit or rollback all work done previously in the session. Since a PDML session executes the SQL statements as an autonomous transaction, it cannot be part of the previous transaction. To enable or disable Parallel DML you can use the **alter session** command. Thankfully, there are no new Oracle initialization parameters to set and bounce the database. Once the session is enabled for PDML, Oracle executes subsequent statements in the session in parallel mode. You need to specify the degree of parallelism via a PARALLEL hint or the degree of parallelism will default to whatever is set on the table.

The following code example shows a sample PDML session. As you can see, an attempt to enable Parallel DML failed with ORA-12841 when a commit or rollback for the previous transaction was not issued. Also, note that a commit or rollback is needed to end the transaction that was executed in parallel, before disabling the Parallel DML session.

```
SQL> insert into MYTEST values (1);
1 row created.
SQL> alter session enable parallel dml;
ERROR:
ORA-12841: Cannot alter the session parallel DML state within a transaction
SQL> commit;
Commit complete.
SQL> alter session enable parallel dml;
Session altered.
SQL> update /*+ PARALLEL (MYTABLE, 3) */ MYTABLE set Num=Num+4;
4800000 rows updated.
SQL>alter session disable parallel dml;
ERROR:
ORA-12841: Cannot alter the session parallel DML state within a transaction
SQL> commit;
Commit complete.
SQL> alter session disable parallel dml;
Session altered.
```

Initialization Parameters that Affect Parallelism

The following table lists the initialization parameters that affect parallelism. Most of these have direct impact on how parallelism works in your system.

PARALLEL_MIN_SERVERS	Sets the minimum number of parallel query slave processes that are initiated when the instance is started. Default is 0.
PARALLEL_MAX_SERVERS	Sets the maximum number of parallel query slave processes or parallel recovery processes that Oracle starts based on the demand for such processes. Default is 5.
PARALLEL_MIN_PERCENT	Specifies the minimum percentage (of the value of requested degree of parallelism) of parallel query slave processes that must be available for parallel execution. Default is 0.
PARELLEL_SERVER_IDLE_TIME	Available from Oracle 7.1 and up to Oracle 8.0; obsolete in 8.1.3. It specifies idle time in minutes for parallel query slave process after which Oracle terminates the process. Default is 5 minutes.
PARALLEL_AUTOMATIC_TUNING	Available from Oracle 8.1, if set to TRUE, Oracle determines values for all other related parameters. However, the tables and indexes must be defined with degree of parallelism.
PARALLEL_ADAPTIVE_MULTI_USER	Available from Oracle 8.0, if set to TRUE, Oracle enables an adaptive algorithm that tries to improve performance of parallel executions in multiuser environment. Assumption is that you have tuned your system for optimum performance in a single user environment.

PARALLEL_EXECUTION_MESSAGE_SIZE	Available from Oracle 8.0, it specifies the size of messages for parallel execution. Defaults to a value of 2148 bytes on most platforms. According to Oracle, this may need to be changed to 16K or 32K for improving parallel query performance in Oracle 8.0.x. In Oracle8i it can be set to a maximum value of 16K, as the PQ messaging system uses UDP protocol instead of TCP.
PARALLEL_THREADS_PER_CPU	Available from Oracle 8.1, it specifies the default degree of parallelism for the instance. It is platform specific, but typically defaults to 2.
OPTIMIZER_PERCENT_PARALLEL	Specifies the amount of parallelism that the optimizer uses in cost functions. Usually does not need any modification from default value of 0.
LARGE_POOL_SIZE	Available from Oracle 8.0, it specifies the size of the large pool in SGA. As mentioned in the chapter "Instance Tuning—The Shared Pool Area" if PARALLEL_AUTOMATIC_TUNING is set to TRUE, the PARALLEL_ EXECUTION_MESSAGE_SIZE is allocated from the LARGE_POOL_ SIZE; if LARGE_POOL_SIZE is not defined in init.ora file, it will be created with a default size of 18MB.
SHARED_POOL_SIZE	Specifies the size for the shared pool in SGA. Memory for the PARALLEL_ EXECUTION_MESSAGE_SIZE is allocated from SHARED_ POOL_SIZE.
RECOVERY_PARALLELISM	Specifies the number of processes which run in parallel during instance or media recovery.

SORT_AREA_SIZE	Specifies maximum allocation of sort space per user for the "sort" phase of a sort. Each parallel query slave process will use this amount of sort space.
SORT_AREA_RETAINED_SIZE	Specifies the amount of sort space retained for the "fetch" phase of a sort. Each parallel query slave process will retain this amount of sort space.
SORT_DIRECT_WRITES	Obsolete in Oracle8i. In prior versions, when set to TRUE, allowed Oracle to bypass the buffer cache while writing sort data to temporary tablespace. We suggest you set this to TRUE in Oracle 8.0 and below, whether you use PQ or not.
SORT_MULTIBLOCK_READ_COUNT	This parameter specifies the number of database blocks to read each time a sort performs a read from a temporary segment. The default is either 1 or 2 depending on platform and should not be set greater than 2.

At minimum, we suggest you set up the following parameters in your initialization parameter file:

- PARALLEL_MIN_SERVERS
- PARALLEL_MAX_SERVERS
- PARALLEL_MIN_PERCENT

Interaction Between PARALLEL_MIN_SERVERS, PARALLEL_MAX_SERVERS, and PARALLEL_MIN_PERCENT

The parameter PARALLEL_MIN_SERVERS can be safely set to the number of CPUs in the machine. The upper limit for it is the value for PARALLEL_MAX_SERVERS, which in turn sets the maximum number of parallel query slave processes. Generally speaking, the parameter PARALLEL_MAX_SERVERS can be set to twice the number of CPUs, sometimes even higher, but the effectiveness is dependent on the I/O system characteristics and the amount of data striping across multiple volumes.

As the demand for the parallel query slave processes increases, Oracle will initiate additional such processes, but not to exceed the maximum set by the parameter PARALLEL_MAX_SERVERS. As these processes complete their assigned tasks and become idle, Oracle terminates them after a certain amount of idle time. This idle time can be set in minutes using the PARALLEL_SEVER_IDLE_TIME parameter. From Oracle 8.1.3, this parameter is obsolete and Oracle uses an internal timer. You no longer can control this using an initialization parameter. Terminating idle parallel query slave processes reduces the demand on system resources. However, the number of these processes will not fall below the minimum set in PARALLEL_MIN_SERVERS. The parameters PARALLEL_MIN_SERVERS and PARALLEL_MAX_SERVERS define the *parallel execution server pool* as mentioned earlier in the section "How to use Parallelism."

The parameter PARALLEL_MIN_PERCENT plays a very important role. It allows you to set the minimum degree of parallelism that is required to execute your query. If the system cannot support this minimum degree of parallelism (specified as a percentage of the actual degree of parallelism on the table or index), the query will fail. In that case, you can either choose not to run the operation or run it with a lesser number of parallel query slave processes. Consider the following example (for simplicity we have formatted the output), which shows the values set for PARALLEL_MAX_SERVERS, PARALLEL_MIN_SERVERS, and PARALLEL_MIN_PERCENT:

```
/* The output from the following command has been formatted */
SVRMGR> show parameter parallel
NAME                             TYPE       VALUE
--------------------------------  --------   -----
parallel_max_servers             integer    8
parallel_min_percent             integer    50
parallel_min_servers             integer    4
```

Let's suppose that six out of the maximum number of parallel query slave processes (eight) are busy. You just submitted a query requesting a degree of parallelism of, say, six. Oracle can only initiate two additional processes before reaching the limit of eight. But since PARALLEL_MIN_PERCENT is set to 50 percent (implying you need at least three parallel query slaves to run the query in parallel), and it is not possible to initiate three additional processes, Oracle will raise an error, ORA-12827, as shown in the following example:

```
SQL> select /*+ PARALLEL (CM, 6) */ count(*)
        from CUSTOMER_MASTER CM
      where Customer_Bill_Num is not null;
select /*+ PARALLEL(CM, 6) */ count(*)
*
ERROR at line 1:
ORA-12827: insufficient parallel query slaves available
```

If PARALLEL_MIN_PERCENT was left to its default value of 0, and if you reached the upper limit of parallel query slave processes as set by PARALLEL_MAX_SERVERS, any new query requesting parallelism would be run serially and hence very slowly (as though Parallel Query was *not* enabled). But you run the risk of the system getting hammered by bad performance as the operation is performed serially. So, suddenly a query that may have previously run much faster using parallelism may now run slower and take a longer time to complete. And you won't notice it until someone complains or you monitor the system when the query is running.

Do you really want this to happen? Would you rather run it in parallel or not at all? If you so desire, you can set PARALLEL_MIN_PERCENT to its maximum value of 100 to make sure your query runs with the requested degree of parallelism or doesn't run at all. However, your application requirements will dictate what is acceptable in such situations. We thought it is better if we inform you of all the available configuration options and how some of these work. In general, if this is for a production system, you don't want queries to fail at all, so we suggest that you set the value of this parameter to 0 or a very small number.

But there is another parameter you need to know about: OPTIMIZER_ PERCENT_PARALLEL. It affects the behavior of the cost-based optimizer in determining the execution path. Similar to PARALLEL_MIN_PERCENT, the value of this parameter tells the optimizer how much parallelism to consider in determining the cost of the execution plan for the query. Possible values for this parameter are 0 to 100. The default is 0. Lower values tend to favor a serial path via indexed access while higher values favor full table scans. Obviously, with full table scans, the benefits of parallelism is much more relevant and measurable.

Oracle8i introduces yet another new parameter, PARALLEL_AUTOMATIC_ TUNING. It can be set to either TRUE or FALSE. The default value is FALSE. If you set this parameter to TRUE, Oracle determines the values for other related parameters. It will also set PARALLEL_ADAPTIVE_MULTI_USER to TRUE, enabling Oracle to override user-given hints in favor of maintaining the load on the system within acceptable ranges. As a DBA, you just need to set the degree of parallelism at the table level. That's it! Sounds simple and wonderful, doesn't it? But when we set this parameter to TRUE without using the others, Oracle set PARALLEL_MIN_SERVERS and PARALLEL_MIN_PERCENT to 0 and the value for PARALLEL_MAX_SERVERS varied from 40 to a whopping 160 based on the hardware platform. Both of which were rather high for our environment. So use this parameter with caution and only after thorough testing.

Designing the Database for Parallelism

Now that we have covered what parallelism is and what its related initialization parameters are, let's talk about how to effectively design your database for parallelism to work in an optimal fashion.

First and foremost, you need to analyze, study, and learn about the storage device volume group configuration on your system. Implementing parallelism without regard to how the OS sees your disks can have disastrous results and you will paralyze your system without even knowing it.

Allow us to use an example to make this point more clear. Suppose you have 16 disk drives that are supported by two controllers. Your friendly neighborhood UNIX system administrator (or your dear disk array system vendor) decided that in the interest of "ease of management" there is a need to build only one logical volume group containing all these 16 drives. The OS will see this volume group as a single device.

Now, let's look at a second configuration. If four physical volume groups were built with four disk drives each, there will be four such "devices" that the OS would see. When PQ launches multiple processes to access data, the latter configuration would provide more throughput than the former and would assist in completing the query much faster. This is because the setup provides for more "independent" devices that each of the parallel query slaves can work on. In the first configuration, given that the OS treated the entire volume group as a single device, multiple processes hammering one device for reads can create I/O bottlenecks and breed contention.

You may now be tempted to suggest, if that is the case, why not build 16 volume groups with just one disk drive each to make it run even faster with more parallel query slave processes? Well, the speed is not achieved just by having more devices or more query slaves, but by the number of query slaves that can be effectively supported by the number of CPUs and available memory on the system. With 16 devices and query slaves, unless you have 16 or more processors (in addition to the number you need for your normal transactions), your system might experience CPU starvation and might result in the query taking more time to complete. So test what works best for your setup. To learn more on how to configure disk subsystems for maximum throughput, please refer to the chapter "I/O Tuning."

VIP

You, the Oracle DBA, are the best judge of the needs of your Oracle system. Although most hardware vendors understand how their products are suited to Oracle, it is finally your responsibility to determine what is good for your environment, because you know your environment the best. Creating one volume group with 16 drives is definitely not the same as creating four volume groups with four drives each. The degree of parallelism that can be supported is usually greater in the second configuration, other factors remaining constant. Another factor to keep in mind is the partitioning needs of your application and your database. If some core tables and indexes of your database need to be partitioned, separating the partitions of these tables and indexes is an important factor to consider while designing for parallelism. Partitioning will definitely have you rethink the one-volume, 16-drive configuration.

In addition to configuring the storage devices and volume groups in an optimal fashion, you also need to understand how to set the value for degree of parallelism. The manner in which the volume groups are configured has an impact on how a table or an index is stored. Remember to test it to finalize what value works best for you.

We recommend you set the minimum degree of parallelism on a table (or index) using the following formula:

Minimum degree of parallelism = Floor (two times the number of CPUs, number of partitions in the table, number of independent devices or drives on which the table or partitions reside)

For non-partitioned tables, ignore the number of partitions in the preceding formula. However, in most environments the maximum degree of parallelism is usually two times the number of CPUs. Obviously there are exceptions to this rule depending on the I/O system, and hardware characteristics. But there are plenty of other things you will also need to take into account to really have a good design for parallelism. These include tuning the initialization parameters, consideration for partitioning of tables and indexes, deciding on the upper limit of maximum number of parallel query slave processes, whether to use PARALLEL hints or set the degree of parallelism at table or index level, use of Parallel DML, and so on. These and many other issues are discussed in the Oracle Tuning Guide and Concepts Guide.

Parallel DML Considerations

Earlier, we introduced you to Parallel DML and showed how to use it. Very large databases are typically composed of large tables. PDML is indispensable for bulk DML operations on these. PDML complements PQ architecture, but it is fully supported on partitioned tables. However, parallel direct-load inserts on non-partitioned tables can be performed using the /*+ APPEND */ hint. With the /*+ APPEND */ hint, Oracle performs inserts above the high-water mark of the table, thus providing the capability of direct loads within the scope of your application.

PDML and Rollback Segment Configuration

As you know, the idea of parallelism is supported by multiple processes, and each process needs its own set of resources. When dealing with a DML operation in parallel, the "resources" take on additional meaning. It's not just the CPU or devices anymore. Large DML operations affect rollback segments usage, redo log writing and archiving, and maintenance of archived log directory. You get the point! When using PDML, the manner in which you address these issues is very important.

For instance, you should create large rollback segments for use by the bulk PDML operations. Also, consider creating these rollback segments in different tablespaces on different devices (preferably on different disk controllers). This will ensure reduction in I/O contention for accessing rollback segments as well as any rollback of the DML operation.

You should also consider creating as many large rollback segments as the degree of parallelism on the partitioned table. If the number of table partitions exceeds the degree of parallelism, make sure the rollback segments can hold the before images of the partitions manipulated by the PDML operation. For example, if the table has 36 partitions on six devices, and the server has six CPUs, the optimal degree of parallelism for the table is 12 (per the formula in the earlier section "Designing the Database for Parallelism"). Hence, 12 large rollback segments are needed for optimal performance. Nevertheless, care must be taken to ensure that these 12 large rollback segments can hold the before image of all 36 partitions, assuming that some of the PDML operations affect all 36 partitions.

PDML and Instance Recovery

If your system encounters an instance failure and a PDML operation gets aborted, upon instance startup a parallel query such as the following should be executed on the table that was manipulated by the PDML statement:

```
select /*+ FULL (tablename) PARALLEL (tablename, 6) */ count (*) from
tablename;
```

This will trigger a parallel rollback operation, as part of the instance recovery. This is required because the rollback operation is done serially in Oracle 8.0.x. Optionally, if the PDML operation is re-executed, the rollback will be done in parallel automatically by Oracle.

Further, if the initialization parameter RECOVERY_PARALLELISM is set to a value greater than 1 (for example, 8, since according to Oracle that is the threshold number where parallel recovery performs better than serial recovery), SMON will launch those many processes to perform the recovery in parallel. It must be noted that the number of independent storage devices on which Oracle data files are configured eventually determines the optimal number of recovery processes that need to be configured.

NOTE
If your version of Oracle is at least Oracle 8.1.3 and you have set the COMPATIBLE parameter to at least 8.1.3, two new features, fast start on-demand rollback and fast start parallel rollback, facilitate better availability of the database and thus your data. They allow your database to be back online faster. The fast start on-demand rollback allows on-demand recovery of aborted transactions, one block at a time. The fast start parallel rollback allows a set of transactions to be recovered using a group of server processes. This feature is configurable using the FAST_START_PARALLEL_ROLLBACK initialization parameter. The decision to recover a transaction in parallel or serial is made by SMON depending on the amount of work that needs to be done in the recovery process.

PDML Restrictions and Issues

There are certain restrictions on PDML operations. If those are violated, Oracle will perform the operation serially without telling you! In most cases, no warning or error message will be generated. There is no PDML support for triggers when certain data integrity constraints are enforced, or when tables contain LOB or object types, indexed organized tables, clustered tables, and so on. Please refer to the Oracle Concepts Guide for more information.

In addition, there are certain initialization parameters you may want to review before using PDML, as these parameters can potentially affect how PDML performs on your system. These include ENQUEUE_RESOURCES, DML_LOCKS, TRANSACTIONS, and LOG_BUFFER. Refer to the Oracle Tuning Guide for more information.

Parallel Query Monitoring

All right, so you have read the chapter so far, understood it, and have configured the system and the database and began using PQ. But how do you make sure the PQ operations are indeed taking place as designed and desired? Oracle offers a few of those dynamic performance V$ views that capture PQ operation statistics for you. These statistics are available at session or system level and are helpful in evaluating performance of parallel query slaves. The view V$PQ_SYSSTAT provides valuable information that can be used to determine the values for the initialization parameters PARALLEL_MIN_SERVERS and PARALLEL_MAX_SERVERS. The following is an example of the information from the V$PQ_SYSSTAT table:

```
SQL> select Statistic, Value
       from V$PQ_SYSSTAT;
STATISTIC                        VALUE
------------------------------   ----------
Servers Busy                          6
Servers Idle                          0
Servers Highwater                     6
Server Sessions                       8
Servers Started                       2
Servers Shutdown                      0
Servers Cleaned Up                    0
Queries Initiated                     2
DML Initiated                         0
DFO Trees                             2
Sessions Active                       2
Local Msgs Sent                       6
Distr Msgs Sent                       0
Local Msgs Recv'd                    12
Distr Msgs Recv'd                     0
15 rows selected.
SQL>
```

This view is the easiest way to find out if you need to adjust the values set for initialization parameters PARALLEL_MIN_SERVERS and PARALLEL_MAX_SERVERS. If you find that the *Servers Busy* statistic remains close to the value of PARALLEL_MAX_ SERVERS, you may need to increase the value of PARALLEL_MAX_SERVERS to make sure there will be enough available servers for any additional parallelism operations (if there is additional system capacity). On the other hand, if the *Servers Busy* statistic remains close to zero most of the time, there may not be a need for many PQ servers and you may want to reduce the value of PARALLEL_MAX_SERVERS.

If the *Servers Busy* statistic consistently exceeds the value set for PARALLEL_ MIN_SERVERS, you may want to increase the value of PARALLEL_MIN_SERVERS to match the value reported by the aforementioned statistic. This will ensure that the system has an optimal number of PQ servers available for use at all times.

The values shown in the *Servers Shutdown* and *Servers Started* statistics may indicate infrequent demand for additional PQ servers. Additional PQ servers, above the number set by PARALLEL_MIN_SERVERS, are started when requested, but those are shut down when they become idle over time. These statistics will also help you decide if the value for PARALLEL_MIN_SERVERS should be increased. The statistic *Servers Highwater*, on the other hand, indicates the maximum number of PQ servers that were ever launched.

You should frequently monitor the *Servers Busy*, *Servers Highwater*, *Servers Shutdown*, and *Servers Started* statistics, as these provide valuable information to gauge the processing load on the PQ servers.

The V$PQ_SESSTAT view reports summary statistics about the PQ operation conducted in a session. This information is valid only when queried from the same session. The following is an example of what it shows:

```
SQL> select Statistic, Last_Query, Session_Total
       from V$PQ_SESSTAT;
STATISTIC                        LAST_QUERY SESSION_TOTAL
-------------------------------- ---------- -------------
Queries Parallelized                      1             3
DML Parallelized                          0             0
DFO Trees                                 1             3
Server Threads                            4             0
Allocation Height                         4             0
Allocation Width                          1             0
Local Msgs Sent                         114           342
Distr Msgs Sent                           0             0
Local Msgs Recv'd                       114           342
Distr Msgs Recv'd                         0             0
10 rows selected.
SQL>
```

The preceding code listing shows that the query last run in the session was indeed run with parallelism as the statistic *Query Parallelized* is not zero. *Allocation Width* reports the number of instances the query was run against, *Allocation Height* reports the requested PQ servers per instance, and *Server Threads* reports the number of PQ servers used.

There is another view, V$PQ_SLAVE, that reports information about each PQ server. The information reported can be used to track each PQ server's current status, check if it is busy or idle and for how long, how much CPU time it has consumed, and so on.

In a Nutshell

Parallel Query was designed to squeeze every last drop of system resources out of your hardware and software investment. That's a good thing. However, using parallelism without paralyzing your system requires understanding of how parallelism really works, what affects it, and what it affects. It is very important to consider the side effects of using parallelism when there are not enough resources available and the environment is not conducive enough.

Parallelism involves dividing work among many processes, each performing its own allocated workload. The idea is to "divide and conquer." For starters, the table data should be spread over as many storage devices as possible so that multiple PQ server processes will not be hampered by I/O contention. You should also select a proper degree of parallelism for the operation, as it dictates how many PQ server processes will be utilized. The degree of parallelism can be set as part of a table or index definition, or by using the PARALLEL hint with a SQL statement.

There are some special initialization parameters to configure. Specifically, these include PARALLEL_MIN_SERVERS, PARALLEL_MAX_SERVERS, and PARALLEL_MIN_PERCENT. You should understand how these interact with each other and what important role PARALLEL_MIN_PERCENT plays. The new Oracle initialization parameter PARALLEL_AUTOMATIC_TUNING allows the DBA to set just one parameter for Parallel Query tuning and control the values of a variety of other parallel parameters. As fantastic as that sounds, please perform comprehensive tests in your environment before using this. Some other initialization parameters will also need to be understood in light of using parallelism, such as LARGE_POOL_SIZE, SORT_AREA_SIZE, and SORT_AREA_RETAINED_SIZE.

There are several SQL statements that can utilize PQ operations. From Oracle 8.0, many DDL operations can also utilize parallelism in addition to DML operations. Parallel DML can significantly improve the performance of bulk DML operations in large databases. However, there are some special issues you must be aware of when using PDML. PDML is fully supported with partitioned tables. When using PDML against such tables, make sure that adequately sized rollback segments are available. To improve I/O, spread these rollback segments over multiple tablespaces configured across multiple storage devices. In addition to the size of the rollback segments, there should be enough large rollback segments available, typically equal to the number of table partitions.

The dynamic performance view V$PQ_SYSSTAT provides information on how your system utilizes PQ servers. Monitoring it will enable you to determine adequate values at which to set initialization parameters PARALLEL_MIN_SERVERS and PARALLEL_MAX_SERVERS.

We hope we have convinced you why running your queries or DML statements using parallelism will not always result in performance increases. But we also hope you have adequate information to effectively utilize parallelism to improve performance of your queries and DML statements. C'mon, go ahead and parallelize your environment! Please just try not to paralyze it.

CHAPTER
10

Contention Tuning

Myth & Folklore

Tuning contention in the database provides huge performance benefits. Hence, let's tune the daylights out of the latches on the system.

Fact

Avoiding or eliminating contention is important, but seldom should this be the first thing you do in a managed performance tuning effort. Contention tuning should be a part of overall database tuning strategy. More importantly, as a DBA you need to know when and where to engage in such tuning efforts. However, tuning contention is not magic and rarely brings about orders of magnitude of performance increase like in application tuning. (One exception is I/O contention tuning, which is very important and is covered in great detail in the chapter "I/O Tuning.") As mentioned before, you need to follow a methodical approach to tuning Oracle, and we have covered this in detail in the chapter "The Method Behind the Madness."

Tuning contention definitely takes lower precedence over application tuning and instance tuning from the perspective of "What should I tune first?" Remember one thing: the best way to deal with contention is to not have it. This is because we want you to learn about the relevant issues, deal with them in a proactive manner, and spend time on other important things. Do not waste too much time pondering which latch needs tuning next! There is only so much latch tuning you can do. If your database experiences latch contention (and you have already configured all the relevant latches for your version of Oracle to its allowed maximum), you should investigate the cause of the contention. Latch contention is caused by serialization in one or more components of your application. Take all of the required and necessary steps to fix your application problems. As mentioned before many times, the goal in a performance tuning effort should be to treat the disease, not just the symptoms. Latch contention is a symptom of the bad application code (the disease).

So what is contention in an Oracle database? Simply put, it is the struggle between one or more processes to access the same resource at approximately the same time. Just like two or more kids fighting for the same toy to play with at the same time! If you had more than one identical toy, some kids will be happy to get another one, but there will be some kids who will want the exact same toy the other kid has. This is no different in an Oracle system. Sometimes Oracle will work fine if you have multiple copies of certain resource, but there may be situations where multiple processes will request the same resource, pretty much at the very same time. However, in Oracle there is a methodical approach to address and resolve such contention issues. With kids, that is a totally different matter and you are on your own! But before you embark on the journey to resolve contention, please note that there will always be some sort of contention or bottleneck. It is practically impossible to eliminate all of the contention and bottlenecks on your system all of the time. The bigger question is, "How bad is this contention and what effect does it have on the application performance?" This chapter is about understanding the common contention issues and dealing with them in a proactive fashion.

Monitoring Oracle for Contention

In a busy system, if all processes are waiting for resources, they may be waiting for the same resource more often than you think. This is what causes *contention*. As described in the chapter titled "The Method Behind the Madness," you must make V$SYSTEM_EVENT, V$SESSION_EVENT, and the V$SESSION_WAIT views your first line of offense when faced with an Oracle performance problem. The combined information that is provided in those views will provide you with information about the various types of contention related to latches, I/O, SGA structures, or database buffers (to name a few). Hand in hand with these views, you should track down the SQL statements causing the contention. In addition to all those V$ dynamic performance views we discussed in that chapter, you'll want to get familiar with the V$WAITSTAT view. This will be useful in checking the statistics for contention.

In the following sections, we will discuss contention as it applies to rollback segments, temporary segments, and latches. We have already discussed contention tuning as it relates to *freelists* in the chapter "Database Tuning." In this chapter, we will also discuss how some of the application system-related issues can give you a false impression of contention problems. These are the areas that a DBA can monitor and tune if needed. Rollback and temporary segments are comparatively easier to deal with. You need to get familiar with dynamic performance views such as V$ROLLSTAT, V$SORT_SEGMENT, and V$SORT_USAGE.

However, there are more than 50 different latches in Oracle 7.3.x and around 150 in Oracle8i. Only a very few of them can be changed or adjusted by you or even need to be changed. So get familiar with the ones you can change. Set them to their allowed maximum values, and move on. Refer to dynamic performance view V$LATCHNAME for the list of all latches on your system and take a look at V$LATCH_CHILDREN to determine how many latches are configured for each type.

Rollback Segments: Why, How, and How Much?

For an optimally performing Oracle database, proper configuration of rollback segments is very crucial. Sometimes a novice DBA may ponder about how Oracle actually uses rollback segments. He or she may also wonder why a database requires both rollback segments and redo log files. Good questions. Redo logs are used to recover the database from an instance or media failure. However, redo logs are not used when an application attempts to rollback (or undo) a transaction. In such cases, Oracle will restore the old information from rollback segments. In addition to this role as a custodian of the old data, rollback segments also facilitate one of Oracle's strongest features: *multi-version read consistency*.

What Is Multi-Version Read Consistency?

Read consistency is the act of providing all users with a consistent view of the data that was asked for. The multi-version aspect provides that consistent view across multiple user sessions. In very simplistic terms, it is a scenario where each user sees his or her own copy of the data. You may ask the relevance of creating a copy per user session. The answer is plain and simple: by default Oracle will always provide data that was committed at the time a query was started. Any changes made to the data while the query is executing will not be visible to you until you requery the data. Why? If the data is not confirmed or committed, it cannot be trusted for its accuracy or relevance. In industry lingo, Oracle will not perform "dirty reads." Some other relational databases allow and support dirty reads across user sessions. However, please note that a user who makes changes to his or her data can view the changes before committing (within the same session).

Dirty reads are exactly what you think—dirty data, data that is not committed. Just imagine the havoc that dirty reads can wreak to some financial or healthcare application. In Oracle, even if the changes are committed after your query started, you will see the data as it existed at the start of your query. However, if rollback segments are not configured properly and the query runs for a long time while changes to the data are committed, you may encounter the error "Snapshot too old." This error has nothing to do with the Oracle object snapshots. We will tackle this error very shortly. But first, let us review how rollback segments are used and how read-consistent views of the data are created.

How Does Multi-Version Read Consistency Work?

Oracle maintains information in its kernel to help generate a number (which sort of acts like a sequence number) within the database called the system commit number (SCN) to represent the state (incarnation) of the database at any given time. This number advances on database changes caused by structural changes to the database objects or committed DML operations. As discussed in the section "Configuring *initrans*" in the chapter "Database Tuning," each data block contains a header area that stores transaction slots for transactions to identify themselves within a block as they are modifying data. These slots are also called interested transaction lists (ITL).

The ITL contains three important structures: the transaction ID (TID), the undo block address (UBA) pointing to where the before image is stored, and the SCN if the transaction has been committed. Each transaction that modifies data in the data block inserts its transaction ID in a transaction slot. The server process (servicing the transaction), copies the before image of the columns that are to be changed (if applicable) to the assigned rollback segment for that transaction. Once the data has been modified, the transaction slot is *not* cleaned immediately, as that job is left for the next process that reads from that block. This is called *delayed block cleanout.*

The header area of a block also contains a system change number (not to be confused with the *system commit number,* even though they may be referenced in some documents with the same acronym) and a sequence number used to determine the version of the block. When you start to make changes, you get a new system change number and start with sequence 1. This increases by one for each row updated until you commit or reach sequence number 254, after which you must get the SCN again. Similar to the transaction slots of the data block, each rollback segment stores a transaction table in the first block (the header block), which contains information about the transactions utilizing that rollback segment. It also includes the data block address (DBA) of the last undo block used for that transaction. The header block of a rollback segment is also known as the undo header block ("undo" is another term used to describe rollback).

When a query is initiated, the server process derives the current system-wide SCN of the database from the Oracle kernel to get a point of reference. As a server process reads a block of data, it checks the system change number in the ITL to verify whether the image of the block is read consistent. If the block's ITL contains a higher number, it knows that a change has occurred in that block and was committed after the query was initiated. It now has to recreate the before image of the block using the current version of the block and the before image of the data (from the undo block in the rollback segment), as of the SCN that it started with. This is to provide the read-consistent image of that block. It does this by getting the list of transaction IDs from the block's ITL and goes after the before image from one or more rollback segments (if multiple transaction IDs exist in the block's ITL). It is important to note here that a transaction ID never really gets removed from the ITL.

Another scenario is that the number in the ITL is less than the current systemwide SCN. This implies that data was committed before the query started. In this case, you read the block as-is, in its current state.

The last scenario is when there is no number in the block's ITL. The server process reads the rollback segment header to find out if all of the transactions are committed. If that is the case, the current SCN is stored in the transaction table located in the rollback segment header. Oracle then copies the SCN from the rollback segment's transaction table to the ITL within the data block. In this case again, you read the block as is. If not, Oracle will build a read-consistent version of the data block using the current version of the block and the data stored in the rollback segment undo block.

The data for that block is rebuilt using the before image stored in one of the rollback segments. The transaction ID(s) stored in the block's ITL is then searched in the transaction table stored in each rollback segment's header block. If for some reason the server process cannot reconstruct this read-consistent image (the before image is not present in the rollback segment), the query fails with the error "ORA- 01555 – Snapshot too old." If you have not seen it in your environment, you either have configured your rollback segments appropriately or you are just plain lucky. Later in the chapter, we will discuss some methods to avoid the "Snapshot too old" problem.

NOTE
When multiple transactions read and write the same data block at the same time, there will be multiple versions of the same data block in the buffer cache. In such cases, Oracle may have to rebuild the before image of the data block several times. This is known as block cloning. Given that the blocks in the database buffer cache are accessed using a hash table, multiple clones of the same block will resolve to the same hash address (the block's physical address does not change regardless of the number of clones. Excessive block cloning can cause severe contention for the cache buffers chains latch.

Defining and Debunking the Wrap Myth

Printed documentation from many reliable Oracle sources may suggest that a *wrap* occurs when a transaction writes back to the first extent of the rollback segment. This is not the case. Each transaction writes to the allocated extents of the rollback segment in an ordered and cyclical fashion. Allocated extents (initially) are those that are assigned to the rollback segment during its creation using the *minextents* parameter. The minimum number of extents with which a rollback segment can be created is two.

When an extent is filled with undo entries, Oracle continues to write to the next available extent. The count of such writing of the before image across extent boundaries by the same transaction is called a wrap and is reported under the column *wraps* in the V$ROLLSTAT view. In short, *wraps* indicates the number of times transactions crossed extents while writing the before image to the rollback segment. Further, it is useful to note that the column *extends* refers to the number of times the rollback segment had to be extended by allocating one or more extents above *minextents* since the last instance startup.

The following code listings and outputs captured from a test we performed corroborate our definition of *wraps* and *extends* in the previous paragraph. We started out with one online rollback segment *rbs02* (other than the system rollback segment), and it was configured with a *minextents* of 2. The *rbs02* rollback segment is identified by the value 2 under the *usn* column in V$ROLLSTAT. We then chose a table that had a million rows in it. We began deleting rows in multiple stages all within the same transaction.

After a few deletes, the *wraps* column increased to 1, indicating that the server process had advanced to the second extent of the rollback segment. The column *extends* remained at 0 and the number of *extents* in the segment was 2 (please note the difference between *extends* and *extents*). As more deletes were performed, the *writes* column kept increasing. The final set of deletes allocated a third extent for the rollback segment and increased the number of *extents* to 3, *wraps* to 2, and incremented *extends* to 1. The moral of the story: *wraps* are incremented every time a transaction starts writing across extent boundaries. Here is the proof:

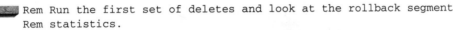

```
Rem Run the first set of deletes and look at the rollback segment
Rem statistics.
SVRMGR> select Usn, Extents, Wraps, Extends, Writes
    2>   from V$ROLLSTAT;
   USN      EXTENTS       WRAPS      EXTENDS      WRITES
 -------  ----------  ----------  ----------  ----------
     0          8           0           0        1976
     2          2           0           0       81605
2 rows selected.

Rem Run the second set of deletes and look at the rollback segment
Rem statistics.
SVRMGR> select Usn, Extents, Wraps, Extends, Writes
    2>   from V$ROLLSTAT;
   USN      EXTENTS       WRAPS      EXTENDS      WRITES
 -------  ----------  ----------  ----------  ----------
     0          8           0           0        1976
     2          2           1           0      204173
2 rows selected.
Rem If you go by various documentation that defines what a wrap is,
Rem we should not wrap until we rewrite over the first extent.
Rem That is impossible in the above scenario as there is only 1
Rem transaction in our database and we are the only one using this
Rem rollback segment. We have just started writing to the second
Rem extent of the rollback segment and wraps rose to 1.

Rem Run the third set of deletes and look at the rollback segment
Rem statistics.
SVRMGR> select Usn, Extents, Wraps, Extends, Writes
    2>   from V$ROLLSTAT;
```

```
     USN    EXTENTS      WRAPS    EXTENDS      WRITES
   ------- ---------- ---------- ---------- ----------
       0          8          0          0        1976
       2          2          1          0      665350
2 rows selected.

Rem No extends or wraps this time, as all of the undo entries
Rem fit into the current extent. However, the number of writes
Rem has increased showing that we are still writing undo entries.

Rem Run the last set of deletes and look at the rollback segment
Rem statistics.
SVRMGR> select Usn, Extents, Wraps, Extends, Writes
    2>    from V$ROLLSTAT;
     USN    EXTENTS      WRAPS    EXTENDS      WRITES
   ------- ---------- ---------- ---------- ----------
       0          8          0          0        1976
       2          3          2          1      716940
2 rows selected.
Rem Bingo, now you see the number of extents at 3 and the number
Rem of extends at 1.
```

The bottom line is, when there are no extents available to write more undo information, Oracle will allocate (add) a new extent based on the *next_extent* size to the rollback segment. This is reported in the V$ROLLSTAT view under the column *extends*. Oracle extends the allocated size of the rollback segment. It is exactly the same thing that occurs when tables or indexes allocate new extents dynamically as they run out of free space with the current extents. More than one transaction can write to the same extent; however, each rollback segment block contains information from only one transaction at a given time.

When a transaction commits, if there is at least 400 bytes available in an undo block, it is put it into the free pool and another transaction can write to the space that is available in that block (this is true since Oracle 7.3) This can continue until free space within that block falls below 400 bytes. Now that we have reviewed what a rollback segment is, why it is used, and how it is used by Oracle, it is time to find out if there is contention for rollback segment information in your database.

Detecting Rollback Segment Contention

If the application system is DML intensive (for example, many updates and deletes), the rollback activity will influence the buffer cache-hit ratio. Note that in the case of insert operations, the previous ITL information (as of the start of the DML operation) and information required to remove the row are stored in the rollback segment. So, there is technically no before image for an insert operation.

However, if you need to roll back your insert operation, Oracle removes the inserted row from the data block.

Write operations to rollback segments require usage of blocks in the database buffer cache, as rollback segment blocks need to be read into memory first, before they can be manipulated. Currently there is no support for directly writing to rollback segments on disk. May we suggest an enhancement request and a name for a new Oracle initialization parameter—UNDO_DIRECT_WRITES. Just kidding!

It is useful to know that rollback segment blocks will use some of the buffers in the buffer cache that would otherwise be used for actual data or index blocks. You need to factor that into your database buffer cache sizing and also when looking at your cache-hit ratios (which by now should be a thing of the past). Queries that need to build a read-consistent view of data will perform slower, as they need to access both data and rollback segment blocks to rebuild the image of the data blocks to the SCN value when the query was started.

As we just discussed, each rollback segment contains a transaction table in the header of the rollback segment. This header is one block in size. It contains information on all the transactions currently active in the rollback segment, and it is frequently accessed and modified. Therefore, this rollback segment header block will remain in the buffer cache for a long time. Frequent accesses to this header block will contribute to an increase in the database buffer cache-hit ratio, although it is not related to table or index data blocks. This can and will inflate your database buffer cache-hit ratios, but as mentioned before (many times), a high cache-hit ratio does not in any way suggest that your database is running fine. At the same time, if there are multiple processes updating data, demand for rollback segment header block increases and that can cause some contention problems. Think of it as a case of more kids wanting the same toy!

So how do you find out if there is any rollback segment contention in your database? Let us put into use what we have been saying throughout this book. Start with the dynamic performance view, V$SYSTEM_EVENT. Since rollback segment blocks come from the database buffer cache, you can check for any *buffer busy waits* from this view. These waits would include waits for rollback segment blocks among other data block waits. We will use the following example to illustrate this:

```
SQL> select Event, Total_Waits, Time_Waited
  2    from V$SYSTEM_EVENT
  3   where Event = 'buffer busy waits';

EVENT                                        TOTAL_WAITS TIME_WAITED
-------------------------------------------- ----------- -----------
buffer busy waits                                 106021       46654
SQL>
```

Remember that the numbers in V$SYSTEM_EVENT are cumulative since the last instance startup. Query V$SYSTEM_EVENT a few times to get the system-level *baseline* and a *delta*. You can then drill down to V$SESSION_EVENT and run the preceding query a few of times to get the session-level *baseline* and *delta*. Armed with that information, query V$SESSION_WAIT looking for the *buffer busy waits* event(s) for the active sessions in the database. Jot down the values of P1 and P2. P1 is the file number and P2 is the block number where the buffer busy waits are occurring (these numbers may change rapidly, but you will at least be on the right file to determine the source of your bottleneck). Use the file number to join with the DBA_DATA_FILES view and use the block number to join with the DBA_EXTENTS or UET$ views to determine the segment name that is experiencing the contention. Now check the V$WAITSTAT view and check for any rollback (or undo) block waits:

```
SQL> select *
  2    from V$WAITSTAT
  3    where Class in ('undo header','undo block');
CLASS                     COUNT       TIME
------------------  ----------  ----------
undo header               43931        1922
undo block                34743        1121
2 rows selected.
SQL>
```

Again, run this query a few times to get the undo block-related *baseline* and a *delta*. If the *delta* is non-zero for the COUNT and TIME columns, this indicates some contention for both the rollback segment header and rollback segment blocks. Remember that these numbers are cumulative since the last instance startup.

Now that you have this information, how do you go about correcting the contention? Well, our answer to this question is: it depends. You can either add more rollback segments or find how the application is using the rollback segments. Adding more rollback segments is the quick and easy answer, but is it the final answer? There are many situations when that is not the final answer.

Rollback Segment Contention War Story

Let us share with you our experience with a production system where we noticed intermittent slow performance and contention for rollback segment blocks. The application otherwise ran with acceptable performance with no contention for rollback segments. We used the *statspack* tool to take snapshots at multiple intervals. We also asked the application programmer to take a snapshot before and after a suspect process. This process typically ran for about 10–15 minutes and updated a couple of tables based on a data file that was uploaded to the server. Many times there was more than one such file uploaded. The statspack snapshots included user comments to identify the before process and after process snapshot. We expected a series of before and after snapshot combinations for these processes.

The application did not have any scheduling mechanism and fired away multiple processes that updated that same set of tables for multiple input files. Sometimes there were more than a couple of dozen processes, all executing around the same time. It was evident when comparing the series of before process snapshots with the corresponding after process snapshots, that these processes would be the source of the contention and slow response. When we questioned the need for such concurrent processing of the files, there was none. Those could have been processed in sequence and all the processing would have fit in the batch window. So, by merely changing the way the application processed these files, the problem of slow response time and rollback segment contention was eliminated.

If we reacted by increasing the rollback segments, we are sure the contention problem would have come back to haunt us again, when the application processed even more numbers of files or more data in the same number of files. Besides, the slow response time would still be a problem, because Oracle would have to reconstruct the read-consistent view of the data by reading more information from the rollback segments.

However, this solution may not be applicable in all cases. Therefore, it is worth an exercise to review if there are enough rollback segments in your database that are sized appropriately to support required application processing.

Understanding Rollback Segment Usage

The V$ROLLSTAT view provides statistics pertaining to how rollback segments are used in the database. By joining this view with V$ROLLNAME you can get all the required information, as shown in the following example:

```
SQL> select N.Name,S.Xacts,S.Gets,S.Waits,
  2         S.Extents,S.Wraps,S.Extends,S.Hwmsize
  3    from V$ROLLNAME N, V$ROLLSTAT S
  4   where N.Usn = S.Usn;
```

NAME	XACTS	GETS	WAITS	EXTENTS	WRAPS	EXTENDS	HWMSIZE
SYSTEM	0	6925	0	13	0	0	794624
RBS01	2	56337	1877	11	1247	48	2146304
RBS02	3	162501	2298	11	1363	85	2043904

```
3 rows selected.
```

In this example, the column *gets* show the number of times the transactions were successful to access the undo header, while the column *waits* shows the number of times they had to wait to access it. Ideally, there should not be any waits for accessing the undo header.

Looking at this example, we also see a large number of *extends*. The *xacts* column shows that there are five transactions currently active. The column *hwmsize* shows the high-water mark or the upper limit, in terms of bytes, reached by the rollback segment, while column *extends* shows the number of times the segment had to dynamically allocate more extents.

The rather high numbers in these columns certainly indicate that the rollback segments are not appropriately configured for the number of transactions the database must support. A look at the storage parameters for these rollback segments confirms that they are not sized correctly, causing so many *extends*. Here is what we found out from view DBA_ROLLBACK_SEGS:

```
SQL> select Segment_Name Name, Initial_Extent,
  2         Next_Extent, Min_Extents
  3    from DBA_ROLLBACK_SEGS;

NAME             INITIAL_EXTENT NEXT_EXTENT MIN_EXTENTS
---------------- -------------- ----------- -----------
SYSTEM                    53248       53248           2
RBS01                    102400      102400          10
RBS02                    102400      102400          10
3 rows selected.
SQL>
```

As you can see, the rollback segments were initially created with about 1MB space allocated to each of them. However, from the earlier example, we see that these segments reached almost twice the initial size, reported under *hwmsize*.

So how do you size a rollback segment? In addition, how do you determine how many rollback segments you should have in the database? That is precisely what we discuss in the next section.

How to Configure Rollback Segments

Before we get into the rollback sizing discussion, keep in mind that a transaction (in its lifetime) can only use one rollback segment to save the before image of the data. However, a rollback segment can have multiple transactions write their data into its single extent. When a wrap occurs, and the server process cannot write to an extent that already has data from one or more active transactions, it will need to extend the rollback segment. The wrapping and extending are functions of time and the amount of undo information generated. If the transaction takes too long to commit its change, it may cause too much extending of the rollback segment. The wrapping without extending (a sign of a small rollback segment) will cause overwriting of committed changes and may cause the "ORA-01555 – Snapshot too old" error for long-running queries.

However, the size and number of the rollback segments should depend on the transaction activity in the database. The needs of an OLTP system will be far different than those of a data warehouse or a DSS system. OLTP systems tend to have a large number of short transactions, whereas in a data warehouse system the transactions will tend to be fewer in number but of longer duration. Most systems fall in a hybrid category with some OLTP and some data warehouse type activity. Managing rollback segments and their contention can be very tricky in such cases.

How Large Should I Size My Rollback Segments?

First let us address the situation with regular rollback segments, the ones typically used by not-so-large transactions. You can find out the size of a rollback or undo information from the transactions in your database. You can take the maximum size of such undo information to calculate the size of the rollback segments.

Here is how it is done:

1. The Oracle-supplied view V$TRANSACTION reports in its column *used_ublk* the number of data blocks used by the transaction for its undo information before committing its changes. The following simple query reports the maximum size of such blocks from all the current transactions. If you were to take multiple readings at regular intervals when the database is processing its peak transaction volume, you will get an idea of the maximum amount of undo information generated by those transactions.

```
SQL> select Max(Used_Ublk)
  2      from V$TRANSACTION;
MAX(USED_UBLK)
--------------
           250
SQL>
```

2. Once you have taken multiple readings and have established this value, multiply it by the database block size to get information in bytes.

3. Round up the bytes to the next multiple of *power of 2*, ensuring that it rounds up to the next multiple of your database block size.

4. This will give you the value for the *initial* and *next* extents for your rollback segment.

Suppose from this example that the maximum value of Max(Used_Ublk) is 250. If the database block size is 8192 bytes, the maximum amount of undo information generated by each transaction is 2048000 bytes (250×8192). Rounding this number to the next multiple of power of 2 gives us 2097152 or 2MB. Thus, the *initial* and *next* extent size of your rollback segment should be 2MB. If the size of your existing rollback segments is nowhere near what you have just calculated, you may want to consider recreating those with the proper size. Each rollback segment requires a minimum of two extents (*minextents*) allocated to it when created. Certain simulations and tests conducted at Oracle's internal labs in the past have shown that when *minextents* was set to 20 (with *initial* and *next* extent sized as just shown), the probability of the "Snapshot too old" error was reduced. Your mileage may vary, but the goals here are to avoid dynamic extension of rollback segments and to avoid contention when possible.

The downside of creating *minextents* of 20 for every rollback segment is usually a nominal wastage of disk space. Although dynamic extension of a single extent may not be as costly, for rollback segments it can add up rather fast, if it constantly allocates and de-allocates (with use of the *optimal* parameter) extents. This can adversely affect performance. So go ahead and set *minextents* to 20 (in some cases it may be more, in others it can be less). It is very easy to estimate the amount of rollback that you generate on a typical business day. You can sum up the *writes* column in V$ROLLSTAT for each rollback segment. Another method is to look at the number of extends for each rollback segment on a daily basis.

For long-running updates in a data warehouse environment or for batch jobs that perform quite a bit of DML activity, sizing the rollback segment needs some work. You need to find out the amount of undo generation for a typical job that updates or deletes rows. The view V$ROLLSTAT reports, under the column *writes*, the number of bytes written to the rollback segment. Select a typical job for your test, and then keep only one rollback segment online that the job will use. Note down the current value of *writes*. Run the job and check the value of *writes* again. The difference between these two values is the amount of rollback information generated by the job. Most likely, this will be a somewhat large number. You can then decide on *initial*, *next*, and *minextents* values to assign to this rollback segment, keeping in mind that the rollback segment would not extend. Rebuild the rollback segment with these sizes, and run the test again to confirm that the sizing is acceptable.

To make sure this larger rollback segment is used by intended batch jobs, use the command **set transaction use rollback segment** *rbs01*, where *rbs01* is the rollback segment. You can also use the PL/SQL package **dbms_transaction.use_ rollback_ segment** to set a specific rollback segment within a PL/SQL block of code. However, such a setting is in effect only for the duration of one transaction—that is, the first commit or rollback. Also, realize that pointing your transaction to a specific rollback segment should be done as the first statement of your transaction, immediately following a commit or rollback of the previous transaction.

How Many Rollback Segments Do I Need?

After sizing the rollback segments, obviously the next question is, how many? Again, the answer depends on the type of transactions the database is supporting. For OLTP or not-so-large-transactions, you can derive the number of rollback segments by the following formula: *number of concurrent transactions / 4.*

However, you can only bring online as many rollback segments up to the value set in the Oracle initialization parameter MAX_ROLLBACK_SEGMENTS. It typically defaults to 30 and you may have to increase it. Further, for large batch jobs and data warehouse environments, you should create one large rollback segment for each concurrent job.

In the V$ROLLSTAT view, there are two other columns that need to be mentioned here rather briefly. Those are *optsize* and *shrinks* (no, this is not about the number of psychiatric professionals). In addition to *initial, next,* and *minextents,* a rollback segment can optionally be defined with an *optimal* size. In the event the rollback segment extends beyond the *optimal* size, Oracle can automatically (sure!) de-allocate or shrink extents to bring its size back to the *optimal* setting. Thus, Oracle will try to keep the segment's size at the *optimal* level at all times! The column *shrinks* reports the number of such downsizing efforts on the rollback segments. However, the de-allocation of these extents does not happen instantaneously after the transaction has committed. It is useful to note here that the transaction that extended a rollback segment beyond *optimal* does not shrink it back to size. It is the next transaction that visits this rollback segment that does the shrinking.

NOTE
Be aware that if rollback segment ever reaches the maxextents, Oracle will not shrink it automatically.

Setting *optimal* to control the size of the rollback segments may be a good idea, however, the allocation and de-allocation of extents to comply with *optimal* settings will degrade the performance, particularly when *optimal* is set low. Secondly, the rollback segment could shrink at any time and thus increase the likelihood of the ORA-01555 error. So beware of the downside of using the *optimal* setting for your rollback segments. Instead, consider shrinking of rollback segments manually when required.

NOTE
We have made it a habit of not setting the optimal *clause for the rollback segments, as it causes a lot of overhead on the system. This is because of the constant allocation and de-allocation of extents in the rollback segments that have this attribute turned on. As mentioned before, the worst-case scenario of not using the* optimal *clause is a nominal wastage of disk storage. The other bane that* optimal *inflicts is a potential increase in the ORA-01555 errors. We avoid it for that very reason. Also, there is no performance difference while using public versus private rollback segments (the keyword public is used while creating the rollback segment). It is our recommendation that you create private rollback segments for better manageability, as public rollback segments have a life of their own and they are brought online based on the formula: TRANSACTIONS/TRANSACTIONS_ PER_ ROLLBACK_SEGMENT. The TRANSACTIONS_ PER_ ROLLBACK_SEGMENT parameter is not what you think. The number of transactions that a given rollback segment can support is not dependent on this parameter, but is dependent on the size of the database block. Use private rollback segments as you can control them via the ROLLBACK_ SEGMENTS initialization parameter. You can't do the same with public rollback segments.*

How to Avoid the "ORA-01555 – Snapshot Too Old" Error

We have talked about the ORA-01555 error a few times in previous sections, but not all the possible solutions were presented. So here we go again. The basic reason for this error is the failure to reconstruct the read-consistent image or snapshot of the data from rollback segments. Following are some recommendations to avoid this problem.

Increase the Size of the Rollback Segments and/or Add More Rollback Segments

The most common reason ORA-01555 occurs is due to fewer and/or smaller rollback segments. When rollback segments are not sized appropriately, the undo information will be overwritten as rollback segments reuse their existing extents to write new undo information. If your database processes many transactions that frequently modify and commit data, any long-running queries will not be able to reconstruct the read-consistent snapshot of the data and will receive this error. In this case, you have two choices to avoid this error. First, follow the methodology presented earlier in this chapter to size the rollback segments appropriately. Second, reschedule long-running queries to run when there is less DML activity in the database. Easier said than done!

Modify Application Code that Commits Across Fetches in a Cursor

The second most common cause of this error is the application code itself. Boy, here is your chance to pick on your friendly developers. But really, it is Oracle that is allowing them to code nonstandard SQL. Per ANSI standards, a cursor becomes invalid on a commit and must be reopened. But Oracle allows applications to fetch rows from the cursor across commits, which increases the likelihood of this error.

Although the application code is to blame here, you will get the wake-up call! In this case, Oracle marks the SCN at the time when the cursor is opened to present the read-consistent view of data. Subsequent processing takes place in a loop where data gets committed. Thus, the SCN for fetched and processed blocks is incremented. Any subsequent fetch operation against the committed blocks requires rebuilding of the block with a read-consistent view per the marked SCN. If Oracle can find the undo information pertaining to the marked SCN, there is no problem, but at times it cannot and issues this error.

Typically, such code works fine with small volumes of data, but as the table grows, so does the likelihood of this error. To solve this problem, consider committing less frequently, at the cost of larger rollback segments to keep undo information in them a little longer. Better yet, take a six-pack to the developer, explain to him or her the benefits of complying with ANSI standards, and suggest that he or she should consider closing the cursor after each commit. That would surely stop the wake-up calls. It may add some overhead to how the code is written, but it will avoid the cleanup by Oracle (rollback of failed transaction) and the need for the developer to deal with data inconsistency issues. However, such code modification may not be possible in all cases, since some time-sensitive applications cannot be changed very easily to access the same set of rows when closing and opening the cursor. Committing less often and configuring larger rollback segments may be the only choice in that case.

Perform Full Table Scans on All Modified Tables Before Changing a Tablespace to READ ONLY Mode

Before we discuss this solution, let us first understand what is meant by a *delayed block cleanout*. As transactions commit data, Oracle performs what is known as a *fast commit.* This updates the rollback segment header to mark that the transaction as committed, but it does not visit the changed data or index block to update (or clean) its header. It leaves that task to the next transaction that reads that block, however, it needs to access the rollback segment to confirm the commit. This is called *delayed block cleanout.* It is also relevant to note that the DBWR process will clean out the ITL if the block is still in memory after you commit.

Under very peculiar conditions, the query may fail to find the confirmation of the commits in the rollback segment header to clean the data block, and Oracle may issue the ORA-01555 error. In normal operation of the database, it is very rare to get ORA-01555 due to the delayed block cleanout issue. Generally, having appropriately sized rollback segments should solve this problem as well. However, you may encounter it when least suspected. We came across it at one of our clients' site. After performing a rather large update job, the tablespace was changed to read-only mode. No data was accessed from the updated tables before changing its mode.

Subsequent transactions in the database had recycled the rollback segments and the transaction ID associated with the large update was long gone. When queries were issued against the updated tables in the read-only tablespace, it encountered ORA-01555 errors. Data blocks in those tables were not clean—the SCNs in the ITLs were not cleaned out. Normally, queries to data in those blocks would have cleaned up the block headers, but since the tablespace was immediately put into read-only mode, no modifications to the data blocks were possible. The solution to prevent such errors from occurring is to perform a full table scan on all modified tables before changing the tablespace to read-only mode. This causes the blocks in those tables to be cleaned out and thus any subsequent queries do not need to visit the rollback segments.

Proactively Managing Contention on Temporary Segments

Temporary segments are created by Oracle primarily during a sort operation. In addition, from Oracle8i, global temporary tables are created as temporary segments. We will first discuss the ones created during the sort operation. Oracle performs a sort operation in a number of cases, such as when building indexes, using the order by, group by, distinct, union, intersect, or minus operations in a SQL statement. A sort-merge join will also trigger a sort, as well as the **analyze** command and so on. The actual sorting takes place in the memory. However, we all know that the data will always be larger than any available memory, at least for most of us. So how does Oracle go about sorting large volumes of data? When the allocated sort memory gets full, Oracle writes the sorted data to temporary segments to free up some space in the memory to get more data to sort. It creates these temporary segments as needed, in the TEMP tablespace assigned to the user. Once the sorting is completed, Oracle reads all these temporary segments (fetch operation) and presents the sorted data to the application. The temporary segments are then dropped. You may ask, how do these segments create contention problems if those are just used in sort and then dropped?

Understanding Temporary Segment Contention

Remember the case of some kids wanting the same exact toy the other one has? Well, a similar thing happens when a sort operation creates a temporary segment and drops it when the sort operation is complete. For creating and dropping any segment in the database, the process needs to acquire a *space management transaction (ST) enqueue*. It is required to serialize the operation as it updates data dictionary tables. An enqueue is a mechanism within Oracle to lock shared resources, such as data dictionary tables. This is the one toy all kids must have! There is only one such ST enqueue resource in the database. Every space management routine, such as allocating extents, deallocating extents, or coalescing of free space (by background process SMON or manually by you) must acquire and retain the ST enqueue until the activity is complete. The demand for this single resource increases when the sorting operation uses temporary segments. Sometimes when such a wait is too long, Oracle will issue the "ORA-01575 – Timeout waiting for space management resource" error. Needless to say, it is a good policy to conserve this resource as much as possible by finding ways to minimize space management events.

You can start by checking if your database is using disk space while performing sorts. The following example shows how to do it:

```
SQL> select Name, Value
  2    from V$SYSSTAT
  3    where Name like '%sort%';
NAME                          VALUE
--------------- ---------------
sorts (memory)                77027
sorts (disk)                   8471
sorts (rows)              138003699
3 rows selected.
SQL>
```

This example shows how many sorts took place in the memory and how many had to use disk (again remember this number is cumulative since the last instance startup). It also shows the total number of rows sorted. As you can see, there are quite a number of sorts using disk. Although it may not be possible to eliminate disk sorts completely, adjusting the init.ora parameters SORT_ AREA_SIZE and SORT_AREA_ RETAINED_SIZE can minimize them considerably. It is advisable to set a higher value for SORT_ AREA_ SIZE in a session by using the **alter session set sort_area_size=<bytes>;** command before a batch job that involves large sort operations or before building large indexes. This will be in effect for that particular session and will not be applicable to any other sessions performing sorts. Using a higher value for SORT_AREA_SIZE will improve the sort performance while reducing the contention for ST enqueue resource.

To further reduce the dynamic allocation of temporary segment extents, you can configure tablespaces of type temporary and size the *initial* and *next* extents for those tablespaces appropriately. This is available since Oracle 7.3. Please refer to the section "Configuring Temporary Tablespaces" in the chapter "Database Tuning" for more information on this feature and its role in sort operations in particular.

Recall that when pure temporary tablespaces are used, there is only one temporary segment for the entire tablespace and Oracle manages it using a *sort-extent pool algorithm*. Oracle will always write SORT_AREA_SIZE worth of data to the temporary segment. You can use the following formula to arrive at the *initial* and *next* extent size:

(SORT_AREA_SIZE in bytes)×(an arbitrary number, say 1–4)

NOTE
There are many sources of documentation that suggest adding a database block for sizing the default initial and next for the temporary tablespace. Although that may be relevant for temporary segments that are created in permanent tablespaces, such recommendations are invalid when using pure temporary tablespaces. Every file is going to be off by one block (due to the file header), so if you are worried about losing that last extent in your datafile to wasted free space, you might want to add one block to the size of the datafile, rather than adding one block to each extent of the temporary segment.

Keep *initial* and *next* extent sizes the same and set *pctincrease* to 0. Remember, you want equal-sized extents in all of your tablespaces. The arbitrary number is geared toward arriving at an extent size large enough for multiples of SORT_AREA_SIZE. As each sort has two phases—the sort phase and the fetch phase—it is useful to note that SORT_AREA_SIZE will be used during the sort phase and SORT_AREA_RETAINED_SIZE will be used by the fetch phase of the sort.

Monitoring Temporary Segment Tablespace Usage

You can query V$SORT_USAGE (available from Oracle 8.0) to view the space used by the current sort operation. Once the sort operation completes, this view will not show any information. The following example shows that two sessions are sorting data using the temporary segment in TEMP tablespace. The *segblk#* shows the block number of the initial extent for each of these sorts and *blocks* shows the number of blocks used by each of them at the time the query was run.

```
SQL> select User, Session_Addr Saddr, Session_Num SerNbr,
  2               Extents, Blocks, Segblk#
  3   from V$SORT_USAGE;

USER        SADDR SERNBR TABLESPACE   EXTENTS   BLOCKS   SEGBLK#
-------  --------- ------ ------------ -------- --------- ---------
ACME     95BCA778  7733  TEMP              34     4420     12480
APPS     95BCAFB8  1550  TEMP              35     4550     65650
2 rows selected.
SQL>
```

If you are using true temporary tablespaces for sort operations, Oracle creates one sort segment for each temporary tablespace as soon as the first disk sort takes place after the instance is started. The view V$SORT_SEGMENT provides ample information to you about all space usage for sort operations in your database. The following example shows some of the information when the sort operation was in progress:

```
SQL> select Tablespace_Name TSNAME, Current_Users USERS, Total_Extents TOTEXT,
  2          Total_Blocks TOTBLKS, Used_Extents USEDEXT, Used_Blocks USEDBLKS
  3   from V$SORT_SEGMENT;

TSNAME        USERS   TOTEXT   TOTBLKS   USEDEXT   USEDBLKS
------------ ------ --------- --------- --------- ----------
TEMP              2     211     27430      211      27430
1 row selected.
```

However, after a given sort operation is complete, the preceding query reported the following, summarizing the total number of blocks and extents ever created by all the sort operations:

```
TSNAME        USERS   TOTEXT   TOTBLKS   USEDEXT   USEDBLKS
------------ ------ --------- --------- --------- ----------
TEMP              0     220     28600        0         0
1 row selected.
```

Tracking space usage by all the sorts in your database by querying V$SORT_ SEGMENT view will help you size the temporary tablespace appropriately. The following query shows additional information from the view that would be useful to do just that. It reports the maximum space ever used by all the sort operations in the database:

```
SQL > select Tablespace_Name TSNAME, Max_Blocks,
  2         Max_Used_Blocks, Max_Sort_Size, Max_Sort_Blocks
  3     from V$SORT_SEGMENT;

TSNAME           MAX_BLOCKS MAX_USED_BLOCKS MAX_SORT_SIZE MAX_SORT_BLOCKS
---------------- ---------- --------------- ------------- ---------------
TEMP                  28600           28600           111           14430
1 row selected.
SQL>
```

You can refer to the Oracle8i Reference Guide for more information on the V$SORT_USAGE and V$SORT_SEGMENT views.

At the beginning of this section, we briefly mentioned the global temporary tables. These were introduced in Oracle8i. Global temporary tables are created as temporary segments in user's temporary tablespace. The chapter "Database Tuning" discusses these tables in the section "Global Temporary Tables and Temporary Tablespaces." You can refer to that chapter for more information. We just wanted to make it clear to you that if you are using global temporary tables and the user performs sorts, use of temporary segments will increase. It is advisable to use different temporary tablespaces for global temporary tables for groups of users who run applications that use these global temporary tables. This will surely help minimize contention and improve performance of sort operations as well as the use of global temporary tables.

To virtually eliminate contention for the ST enqueue resource during disk sort operations in Oracle8I, we would like to suggest that you use locally managed temporary tablespaces. Please refer to the section "Configuring Locally Managed Tablespaces" in the chapter "Database Tuning" for more information. As we said earlier, with Oracle you can manage contention, even for a single resource. However, you are on your own to manage those kids fighting for the same toy!

Latches

Latches are nothing but a specialized locking mechanism employed by Oracle to serialize access to shared data structures in the SGA. There are a number of data structures in the SGA that are concurrently accessed by many processes. Oracle uses latches to prevent more than one process from modifying or accessing such shared structures. Latches differ from locks in the sense that locks can be held for a long time and can be shared among processes. Most latches cannot be shared (from Oracle 7.3 and up, redo copy latches can be shared on some platforms). If a process acquires a particular latch, all other processes requiring that latch to perform identical operations must wait until the previous process releases the latch. As you can imagine, there are several latches, each protecting a set of data structures within the SGA.

You can get a complete list of all latches by querying the V$LATCHNAME view. From Oracle 7.3 to Oracle8i, the number of latches increased from around 50 to around 150. So, let's get busy: we have plenty of tuning to do!

Well, let us make your job very easy. Out of all these latches there are only a few that you can actually tune. The majority of them are just not accessible, so don't spend your time and energy to track them down and wonder what to do next. As we have said before, if you have tuned the applications, the I/O, and the various components of the database, there will be no need to worry about latch contention. Almost every time, latch contention problems are symptoms of bigger problems— unoptimized applications. Go get those problems resolved first!

However, as a DBA you should know a few of these latches and what to do to tune them before they become a problem later. Following this principle will relieve you from worrying about latch contention problems for the most part, so you can address the real cause of performance degradation in your database.

The latches you should be concerned with are *cache buffers lru chain*, *redo copy*, and *cache buffers chains*. The following Oracle initialization parameters can be set proactively to alleviate any contention problems with these latches.

Initialization Parameter	Meaning or Relevance
DB_BLOCK_LRU_LATCHES	This parameter defines the number of latches that are configured for the LRU list(s) of the database buffer cache. It can be set to its maximum value of between 2–12 times the number of CPUs, depending on your version of Oracle. This can be done without any measurable degradation in performance. Once set, you can quit worrying about *cache buffers lru chain* latch contention caused due to *lack of latches*. You still need to track down your application that is causing the problem. (SQL statements performing excessive logical I/O).

Initialization Parameter	Meaning or Relevance
LOG_SIMULTANEOUS_COPIES	This parameter defines the number of redo copy latches used for copying redo entries into the redo log buffer. It can be safely set to its maximum value of 2–8 times the number of CPUs, depending on your version of Oracle without any measurable degradation in performance. Once set, you can quit worrying about *redo copy* latch contention caused due to *lack of latches*. You still need to track down your application that is causing the problem. However, this parameter is obsolete in Oracle8i, and Oracle defaults to the maximum number as 2 times the number of CPUs. Surprised? On some platforms, with Oracle 7.3.4, you can set this parameter to an even higher number value of 8 times the number of CPUs.
_DB_BLOCK_HASH_BUCKETS	Yes, this is an undocumented parameter, which implies exactly that—don't use it unless advised otherwise. This parameter generally does not need to be modified from its default value, unless you notice contention for the *cache buffers chains* latch. This parameter defines the number of hash buckets that are available for faciliating access to the database buffer cache. This has a direct impact on the length of a chain that a server process has to traverse to identify and read a given data block in the database buffer cache. The default value for this parameter is the next prime number above DB_BLOCK_BUFFERS/4. You still need to track down the application that is causing the problem (SQL statements performing excessive logical I/Os and excessive block cloning).

A few other latches that will get your attention from time to time are the *library cache/load/lock/pin* latches. However, realize that library cache latch contention is an indication of a lack of reused SQL in the shared pool area, too much parsing, or in some cases a sizing problem with the shared pool area memory structure. For more information on this, please refer the "Parsing SQL" section in the chapter "Instance Tuning—The Shared Pool Area."

If you still want to find out what other latches may be experiencing contention problems in your database, you can follow the methodology presented in the chapter "The Method Behind the Madness." The views V$SYSTEM_EVENT and V$SESSION_EVENT will provide the wait times for the *latch free* event. The view V$SESSION_WAIT can provide you the *latch number* experiencing the contention problem in a session (column *P2*). You should then use this number to query the V$LATCH view to get more information on that specific latch statistics. Just in case!

In a Nutshell

It is our sincere hope that you are content with the level of contention tuning that you can engage. For some strange reason, contention tuning gets a lot more attention than it really deserves. What we attempted to show you in this chapter is how to proactively avoid or minimize contention, and not make it a part of your job that needs constant attention.

Every database will have bottlenecks and contention issues to deal with. There will be more processes competing for limited resources. The key to your success lies in how well you allocate and manage these resources to minimize such bottlenecks and contention.

Configuring appropriate rollback segments is important to a well-performing database in any environment, DSS or OLTP. If there are not enough properly sized rollback segments, performance of all DML activities will suffer. Application programmers and database administrators have seen the ORA-01555 error quite a few times. It is just not the database administrator's fault that there is not enough larger rollback segments to avoid these errors. But many times it is the way the code is written that causes this error to surface. Addressing it only from the database standpoint will have its limitations as well. Sometimes the code does require change.

All applications will perform sorts in addition to database maintenance tasks. This should be expected with a relational database like Oracle. Configuring appropriate temporary tablespaces to carry on sort operations is also very important. At the same time, care must be taken to find ways to avoid resource contention. When sorts are taking place on disk, the extent allocation and de-allocation will cause contention for space management transaction enqueue (ST enqueue) resources in a busy database. Proper values selected for the init.ora parameters SORT_AREA_SIZE and SORT_AREA_RETAINED_SIZE will minimize the need to use the disk for sorts. When disk sorts cannot be avoided, it is important that the storage for the temporary segments is properly sized. With the introduction of true temporary tablespaces, sort processes do not have to deal with multiple allocation and de-allocation of extents for temporary segments. With true temporary tablespaces, one large segment is used by all sorting operations. When possible, consider using multiple temporary tablespaces with data files on different disks to reduce contention for I/O. In addition to using true temporary tablespaces, consider using locally managed tablespaces for temporary segments. This combination will ensure that you will have minimum requirement for using ST enqueue resources.

Lastly, there is no magic to managing or tuning latch contention. Neither is it the most important thing to worry about. However, it gets a lot of attention, just like a squeaky wheel. People drive themselves crazy trying to tune their latches without really digging deep into what is causing the contention. If you track the trend that Oracle is following, many of the latches are slowly but surely becoming undocumented parameters, which implies that you do not touch it unless advised otherwise. A DBA can tune just a few latches. Fortunately, there are corresponding Oracle initialization parameters. So set those appropriately and forget about latch contention (at least from a parameter configuration perspective). Besides, almost all the time, latch contention is a symptom of a serious application problem: *too much serialization*. Stick to the tuning methodology and you will be content with not finding any latch contention! There are other fun things that need your attention. Like grabbing that toy the other kid has had for a long time!

PART V

Environment Tuning

CHAPTER
11

I/O Tuning

Myth & Folklore

We are ABC Corporation and we are the "gods of disks." Don't worry about separating the various files of your Oracle database, just create one huge logical volume with all the disk drives available and store all of the files there. It makes I/O management very simple and reduces hotspots in your database.

Fact

Okay, folks, we have heard this claim with uncanny frequency, but realize that real-life applications perform quite differently from the recommendation of some storage vendors. It should be noted that no two implementations of the same application would be the same. This is due to the great need to customize the application to suit the business's requirements. This phenomenon is especially true for third-party packaged applications that are comprised of many thousands of tables and indexes. Practical experience suggests that only in very exceptional cases does this method of making one logical volume with all your disks really work. The reason it is not optimal stems from how most applications perform I/O. If your applications constantly perform operations that involve significant index scans on one or more large tables in your database, the method mentioned above can cause significant I/O performance problems.

The core issue that needs understanding here is how index scans operate. When a SQL statement uses an index to execute a query, it reads one or more blocks of the index into the database buffer cache, based on the value of the indexed column referenced in the *where* clause of the SQL statement. The *rowid(s)* that match the value that is searched (in the index) are then used to read the data from specific blocks of the table in question. When significant index scans are performed, the index blocks and the data blocks of the table need to be constantly read in single-block reads. The real problem here is the need for your I/O system to seek to different locations in your logical volume while servicing I/O requests for index and data blocks. This is because of the physical location of the data and index blocks in different parts of the disks. Given that the three components I/O request are seek, latency, and transfer of data and also given that the seek is the most expensive component of servicing an I/O request, the ultimate goal here should be to reduce the number of seeks in your I/O system. Although I/O systems have made great advances in the past ten years, the seek component is still approximately 40–60 percent of the total time it takes to service an I/O request. Balancing the number of seeks on a system (where different blocks of data from multiple tables and indexes are accessed concurrently) should be paramount in efforts that attempt to eliminate I/O bottlenecks.

So, if the data files for the INDX and DATA tablespaces are located in the same set of physical drives (which will be the case when one huge logical volume is created from all of your disks), this will greatly increase the contention on seeks, and that can and will cause severe I/O bottlenecks.

AID, the final frontier…these are the voyages of an Oracle DBA, who boldly dealt with mass storage vendors and their claims, and achieved optimal I/O performance by application of common sense. Many misconceptions surround RAID technology. This chapter will define what RAID is and what it is not. It will also explain how RAID works, including the differences between each RAID level. Further, it will provide you with implementation recommendations for each of the RAID types, by sharing real-life examples that illustrate input/output (I/O) optimization on Oracle's very large databases (VLDBs).

The primary goal here is to successfully solve I/O problems in a consistent fashion with the appropriate RAID configurations. Even though the information provided is not intended to make you a RAID Expert, it will provide you with enough information to have an intelligent dialog with your system/storage administrator. It is our intention to dispel the myths surrounding the marriage of Oracle and RAID.

What Is RAID?

Besides being a leading brand insecticide, RAID is the technology for scaling (when applicable) the capacity and performance of the I/O system and providing the capability for data redundancy. This increases both I/O system performance and availability. Depending on whom you ask, it stands for redundant array of *inexpensive* disks or redundant array of *independent* disks. But since you are asking us, we are going with *inexpensive,* because that makes our friends in the finance department feel better when we ask for more disks. And we will!

Conceptually, RAID is the use of two or more physical disks to create one logical disk, where the physical disks operate in tandem or independently to provide greater size and more bandwidth. RAID has become an indispensable part of the I/O fabric of any system today and is the foundation for storage technologies supported by many mass storage vendors. The use of RAID technology has redefined the design methods used for building storage systems that support Oracle databases.

What RAID Is Not

RAID is *not* the cure to all I/O issues. It is not a panacea for all of your I/O problems. One myth about RAID is that it can eliminate the need for the database or system administrator to concern themselves with I/O issues. Like us, you have probably been in at least one sales presentation where the salesperson promised that if you bought their brand of disk arrays and ran their "easy to use" configuration program, you could just walk away and never have to consider any I/O issues again. And you never see them again! Another myth is that one does not have to make database backups if RAID is implemented. This is particularly the case with proprietary RAID-based systems.

True, the benefits of tuning the application cannot be compared to tuning anything else. However, you will be rudely awakened to the fact that some of the systemwide issues performance issues you are trying to solve got worse because of the blind faith you placed on storage vendors. Remember, they are mortals like us, and they definitely do not possess magical powers over their own disk drives. A disk cannot spin faster than its design specification, cannot service data transfers that exceed its I/O bandwidth, and cannot support a zillion concurrent I/O operations. This is true regardless of your storage vendor.

One such example of falling prey to blind faith is the story that storage vendors tell you that "you do not have to worry about where you physically place your tables and indexes" and that it could be in the same set of drives. They will further claim that their storage system and RAID will take care of all of your administrative pains and relieve you of tablespace placement headaches. Wrong! In our experience—and we have had the opportunity to prove this time and again to many of our esteemed customers—physical independence of tables and indexes is required for applications that utilize the tables and indexes in tandem. There are no two ways about it.

Batch environments are typical of such use where the application performs index range scans on large tables followed by corresponding table lookups. In this case, physically storing tables and indexes on the same set of disks will significantly hurt performance. This is true, even if the disk architecture supports storing the entire track's data in its track buffer cache to alleviate the cost of expensive seeks. RAID can and will provide excellent I/O performance when implemented with the same care that database administrators have historically taken in designing simple disk solutions—that is, separating tables from their corresponding indexes, if they are accessed in tandem.

On the other hand, it can wreak havoc when implemented in a haphazard fashion. Some things in life do not change and this is one of them. It must also be noted here that RAID does not possess the magic to protect your system from failures related to disk bus, host adapter, interface, disk controller, cooling system, power system, host, application, and human beings. Thought you should know!

Why You Should Care About RAID

Though one often sees database or system administrators choosing RAID to be technically in vogue or to impress their bosses, let's focus on the two main technical reasons for making the jump to RAID. These are *scalability* and *high availability* in the context of I/O and system performance. As discussed earlier, scalability and availability are the secrets to job security in our positions as database administrators or consultants.

No database administrator was ever fired (we hope) because the database was always up or because the system continued to provide fast responses regardless of the load. Over the past few years, the size of Oracle databases has grown dramatically. In fact, Oracle now supports databases in the petabyte range. With this growth has arrived increased complexity, and with this increase in size and complexity have come the challenges of managing the I/O required by these mammoth systems. If we were to ignore all other factors in tuning, the size alone requires new techniques to scale I/O performance to the growing demands of applications.

The following table illustrates the point driven in the aforementioned paragraph, by comparing the size ceilings between two major releases of Oracle and why RAID is becoming indispensable in an Oracle system:

Item	Oracle7	Oracle8 and Above
Database Size	32 terabytes	65533 files* (size of the largest file supported on your operating system platform)
Tablespaces	1022	65536
Data files per database	1022	65533
Columns per table	254	1000
Columns per index	16	32
Extents per table	Unlimited**	Unlimited
LOB columns per table	1 LONG/ LONGRAW	1000 LOBS
Maximum LOB size	2 gigabytes	4 gigabytes
CHAR column	255 bytes	2000 bytes
VARCHAR2 column	2000 bytes	4000 bytes

* Operating System dependent
** Available in Oracle 7.3 and above

Add to the increased size and complexity, terms such as *mission critical, e-business,* and *24x7xforever* make implementing RAID more beneficial. Corporate system availability needs have increased to all-time highs with more data being incorporated into the enterprise data stores and more users accessing that data.

With the growth in data and expansion of business use of that data, enterprises have become very dependent on their applications and databases. An availability requirement of 99.999 percent (the infamous five nines) or higher for mission-critical systems is not unusual.

These requirements mean that disk failures cannot become showstoppers. Failures at the disk level resulting in database or application downtime translate into revenue losses and ill will. Because of intense market competition and regulatory issues, many businesses may not be able to sustain these failures, even for a short time. The point made here is very simple: storage systems need to scale I/O performance commensurate to the increase in data volume without any loss of availability. RAID offers exactly that.

The Three Main Concepts in RAID

When you talk RAID, three terms are important and relevant: *striping, mirroring,* and *parity*.

What Is Striping?

Striping is the process of breaking data into pieces and distributing it across multiple disks that support a logical volume—"divide, conquer, and rule." This often results in a logical volume that is larger and has greater I/O bandwidth than a single disk. It is purely based on the linear power of incrementally adding disks to a volume to increase the size and I/O bandwidth of the logical volume. The increase in bandwidth is a result of how read/write operations are done on a striped volume.

Imagine that you are in a grocery store. With you are about 200 of your closest friends and neighbors all shopping for the week's groceries. Now consider what it's like when you get to the checkout area and find that only one checkout line is open. That poor clerk can only deal with a limited number of customers per hour. The line starts to grow progressively. The same is true of your I/O subsystem. A given disk can process a specific number of I/O operations per second. Anything more than that and the requests start to queue up. Now stop and think about how great it feels when you get to the front of the store and find that all 20 lines are open. You find your way to the shortest line and you're headed out the door in no time.

Striping has a similar effect on your I/O system. By creating a single volume from pieces of data on several disks, you can increase the capacity to handle I/O requests in a linear fashion by combining each disk's I/O bandwidth. Now when I/O requests for a file on a striped volume are processed, those (based on the size of the requests) can be serviced by multiple drives in the volume if the requests are subdivided across several disks. This way all drives in the striped volume can engage and service multiple I/O requests in a more efficient manner. This cohesive functioning of all drives in a logical volume is relevant for both read/write operations. It must be noted that striping by itself does not reduce response time for servicing I/O requests. However, it does provide predictable response times and facilitates the notion of better performance by balancing I/O requests across multiple drives in the striped volume. This is because of the reduction in the number of I/O requests waiting in the *run queue* and the *wait queue* of a given storage device.

Table 11-1 depicts a four-way striped volume (v1) with four disks (1–4). A given stripe of data (Data1) in a file on v1 will be split/striped across the four disks into four pieces (Data11–Data14). Similarly Data2 will be split/striped across the four disks into four pieces (Data21–Data24).

What Is Mirroring?

Mirroring is the process of writing the same data to another "member" of the same volume simultaneously. Mirroring provides protection for data by writing exactly the same information to every member in the volume. Additionally, mirroring can provide enhanced read operations because the read requests can be serviced from any member of the volume. If you have ever made a photocopy of a document before mailing the original, you have mirrored data. One of the common myths with mirroring is that it takes twice as long to write. But in many performance measurements and benchmarks, the overhead of mirroring has been observed to be around 15 to 20 percent. The number of read requests that can be serviced by a storage device doubles when it is mirrored.

Table 11-2 illustrates a four-way striped mirrored volume (v1) with eight disks (1–8). A given stripe of data (Data1) in a file on v1 will be split/striped across the disks 1–4 and then mirrored across disks 5–8. Disks 1–4 and 5–8 are called *mirror members* of the volume v1.

What Is Parity?

Parity is the term for error checking. Some levels of RAID perform calculations when reading and writing data. The calculations are primarily done on write

disk1	disk2	disk3	disk4
Data11	Data12	Data13	Data14
Data21	Data22	Data23	Data24

TABLE 11-1. *Examples of Striped RAID Volume*

disk1	disk2	disk3	disk4	disk5	disk6	disk7	disk8
Data11	Data12	Data13	Data14	Data11	Data12	Data13	Data14
Data21	Data22	Data23	Data24	Data21	Data22	Data23	Data24

TABLE 11-2. *Example of a Mirrored (and Striped) RAID Volume*

operations. However, if one or more disks in a volume are unavailable, then depending on the level of RAID, even read operations would require parity operations to rebuild the pieces on the failed disks. Parity is used to determine the write location and validity of each stripe that is written in a striped volume. Parity is implemented on those levels of RAID that do not support mirroring.

Parity algorithms contain *error correction code* (ECC) capabilities, which calculate parity for a given stripe or chunk of data within a RAID volume. The size of a chunk is operating system (OS) and hardware specific. The codes generated by the parity algorithm are used to recreate data in the event of disk failure. Because the algorithm can reverse this parity calculation, it can rebuild data lost as a result of disk failures. It's just like solving a math problem when you know the answer (checksum) and one part of the question—for example, if $2+x=5$, *what is x*? Of course, $x=3$.

Table 11-3 depicts a four-way striped RAID 3 volume with parity—v1 with five disks (1–5). A given stripe of data (Data1) in a file on v1 will be split/striped across disks 1–4 and the parity for Data1 will be stored on disk 5. There are other levels of RAID that store parity differently, and those will be covered in the following sections.

Putting It All Together

Striping yields better I/O performance, mirroring provides protection, and parity (when applicable) is a way to check the work. With these three aspects of RAID, you can achieve scalable, protected, highly available I/O performance.

disk1	disk2	disk3	disk4	disk5
Data11	Data12	Data13	Data14	Parity1
Data21	Data22	Data23	Data24	Parity2

TABLE 11-3. *Example of a RAID Volume with Parity*

The Types of RAID

RAID can be implemented as software-based, where the control software is usually either bundled with the OS or in the form of an add-on, such as a "volume manager" provided by Veritas, Sun, or HP. This type of RAID is also known as host-based RAID. This implementation does impose a small overhead, as it consumes memory, I/O bandwidth, and CPU resources on the host where it is implemented. Normally, this overhead is something that is not alarming, but it should be factored into the resource capacity plans of the host.

When implemented by hardware, the functionality of RAID is present in the microcode in the dedicated disk controller modules that connect to the host. These controllers are internal to the host where RAID is implemented. This type of RAID is also known as embedded controller-based RAID.

Further, RAID can also be implemented using controllers that are external to the host where it is implemented. These implementation are bridge-based and are not preferred, as they incur longer service times for I/O requests. This is due to the longer I/O paths from the disks to the host. This type of implementation is usually typical of I/O subsystems that are half fiber and half SCSI. It is also common to see this implementation on storage systems that support multiple hosts running multiple operating systems. The bridges also have a tendency to become saturated when the system is busy with I/O requests. Hardware-based RAID is always preferred over software-based or host-based RAID, which is preferable over bridge-based RAID.

The Levels of RAID

Initially, RAID was a very simple method of logically combining two or more disks, but like all things in our industry more choices were needed to meet different requirements. Today, RAID levels usually range from 0 to 7, and because of the peculiar way that we count in our world, it gives us more than eight choices. The differences between the various levels are based on varying I/O patterns across the disks. These I/O patterns by their inherent nature offer different levels and types of protection and performance characteristics.

RAID 0

This level of RAID is a normal file system with striping in which data loss is inherent with any disk failure. Simply put, it is data striped across a bunch of disks. This level provides good read/write performance, but no recoverability. Table 11-1 was an example configuration of RAID 0.

RAID 1

In very simple terms, this level of RAID provides mirroring and thus full data redundancy. This is often called a *mirrored disk*. In most cases, the storage device that the operating system sees is made up of two or more physical disks. However, this is presented to an application or a database as a single disk. As the system writes to this disk, it writes an exact copy of the data to all members of the storage device. This level of RAID requires twice the amount of disk storage as compared to RAID 0. Additionally, some performance gains can be reaped from parallel reading of the two mirror members. There are no parity calculations involved in this level of RAID. Table 11-2 was an example configuration of RAID 1.

RAID 0+1

"Stripe first, then mirror what you just striped." This level of RAID combines levels 0 and 1 (striping and mirroring). It also provides good write and read performance and redundancy without the overhead of parity calculations. In the event of disk failure, no reconstruction of data is required, as the data is read from the surviving mirror. This level of RAID is the most common implementation for write-intensive applications and is very widely used. The most common complaint is the cost, since it requires twice as much space. To justify this cost, you will have to spend some time understanding the performance requirements and availability needs of your systems. Table 11-2 was an example configuration of striping first, then mirroring what you just striped. Notice, however, that if one of the pieces (say, Data11 on disk 1) becomes unavailable due to a disk failure on disk 1, the entire mirror member (located on disks 1–4) becomes unavailable. This is a very important consideration as the loss of an entire mirror member reduces the I/O servicing capacity of the storage device by 50 percent.

RAID 1+0

"Mirror first, then stripe over what you just mirrored." This level of RAID has the same functionality as RAID 0+1, but is better suited for high availability. This is because on the loss of one disk in a mirror member, the entire member of a mirrored volume does not become unavailable. It must be noted here that the loss of one disk of a mirrored member does not reduce the I/O servicing capacity of the volume by 50 percent. This should be the preferred method for configurations that combine striping and mirroring, subject to hardware limitations.

Table 11-4 illustrates the concept of RAID 1+0. Notice here that if one of the pieces (say, Data11 on disk 1) becomes unavailable due to a disk failure on disk 1, the other disks in the member (disk 2–4) do not become unavailable. Only disk 1 is unavailable and disks 2–4 are still available to service I/O requests. It must be noted

disk1	disk2	disk3	disk4	disk5	disk6	disk7	disk8
Data11	Data11	Data12	Data12	Data13	Data13	Data14	Data14
Data21	Data21	Data22	Data22	Data23	Data23	Data24	Data24

TABLE 11-4. *Example Configuration of a RAID 1+0 Volume*

here that RAID 10 is a derivative of RAID 1+0 with similar performance and availability characteristics, but with some implementation differences.

RAID 2

This level of RAID incorporates striping, and the redundancy/protection is provided through parity. This method requires less disk space compared to RAID 1, but the need to calculate and write parity will make writes slower. This level of RAID was one of the early implementations of striping with parity using the famous hamming code technique, but was later replaced by RAID 3, 5, and 7. This level of RAID is very rarely implemented.

RAID 3

In this level of RAID, the ECC algorithm calculates parity to provide data redundancy as in RAID 2, but all of the parity is stored on one disk. The parity for this level of RAID is stored at the bit/byte level as opposed to the block/chunk level. RAID 3 is slowly gaining popularity, but is still not very widely used. It is best suited for data mart/data warehouse applications that support a few users, but require sequential bulk I/O performance (data-transfer intensive). When full table scans and/or index range scans are the norm for a given application and the user population is small, RAID 3 may be just the ticket. Table 11-3 illustrated the physical layout and characteristics of a RAID 3 volume.

RAID 4

This level of RAID is the same as RAID 3, but with block-level parity, and it is very rarely implemented. One of the few vendors who have successfully implemented this level of RAID is Network Appliance with their NetApp Filers line of storage arrays.

RAID 5

This is by far one of the most common RAID implementations today. In this level of RAID, data redundancy is provided via parity calculations as in RAID 2, 3, 4, and 7, but the parity is stored along with the data. Hence, the parity is distributed across the number of drives configured in the storage device. RAID 5 is very attractive for many environments, because it results in minimal loss of disk space to parity values, provides good performance on random read operations and light write operations, and saves the cost of mirroring. RAID 5 caters better to input/output per second (IOPS) with its support for concurrently servicing many I/O requests. It should *not* be implemented for write-intensive applications, since the continuous process of reading a stripe, calculating the new parity and writing the stripe back to disk (with the new parity) will make writes significantly slower.

An exception to this rule that requires consideration is when the I/O subsystem has significant amounts of write cache and the additional overhead imposed by the ECC algorithms is measured and confirmed by analysis to be minimal. The definition of "significant" is left to the discretion of the reader, but in general a write cache sized in many gigabytes can be considered significant.

On many systems, however, the performance penalty for write operations can be expensive even with a significant write cache, depending on the number of writes and the size of each write. RAID 5 is best suited to read-only applications. Like RAID 3, it is also best suited for data mart/data warehouse applications, but it can support many application users performing random I/O instead of sequential I/O.

Table 11-5 depicts a four-way striped RAID 5 volume where data and parity are distributed. It illustrates the physical placement of stripes (Data1–Data4) with their corresponding parities distributed across the five disks in the volume.

RAID 6

In this level of RAID, parity is calculated using a more complex algorithm, and redundancy is provided using an advanced multidimensional parity method. RAID 6 stores two sets of parity for each block of data and thus makes writes even slower

disk1	disk2	disk3	disk4	disk5
Data11	Data12	Data13	Data14	Parity1
Data21	Data22	Data23	Parity2	Data24
Data31	Data32	Parity3	Data33	Data34
Data41	Parity4	Data42	Data43	Data44

TABLE 11-5. *Example Configuration of a RAID 5 Volume*

than RAID 5. However, on disk failures, RAID 6 facilitates quicker availability of the drives in the storage device (after a disk failure), without incurring the negative performance impact of resyncing the drives in the storage device. This level of RAID is very rarely implemented.

RAID 7

This is a better implementation of RAID 3. Since read and write operations on RAID 3 are performed in a synchronous fashion, the parity disk can bottleneck during writes (not always true!). RAID 7 allows asynchronous reads and writes, which inherently improves overall I/O performance. RAID 7 has the same characteristics as RAID 3, where all of the parity is stored on a dedicated drive. RAID 7 is relatively new in the market and has potential to be a great candidate for implementations that historically have chosen RAID 3. With RAID 7, you can have your cake and eat it too: you can reap the data-transfer benefits of RAID 3 and not lose the transactional I/O features that RAID 7 offers.

RAID-S

If you are using EMC storage arrays, this is your version of RAID 3/5. It is well suited to data mart/data warehouse applications. This level of RAID should be avoided for write-intensive or high-volume transactional applications for the same reasons as any RAID 5 implementation. EMC storage solutions are usually configured with large write caches, but generally speaking, these write caches are not large enough to overcome the additional overhead of the parity calculations during writes.

Auto RAID

With Auto RAID (implemented by HP), the controller along with the intelligence built within the I/O subsystem dynamically modifies the level of RAID on a given disk block to either RAID 0+1 or RAID 5, depending on the recent history of the I/O requests on that block. The recent history of I/O patterns on the disk block is maintained using a "working set" (which is a set of disk blocks). For obvious reasons, there is one working set each for reads and writes, and blocks keep migrating back and forth between the two sets, based on the type activity. A disk block in this context is 64K in size.

Said in a different way, a RAID 5 block can be dynamically converted into a RAID 0+1 block, if the intelligence determines and predicts that the block will be primarily accessed for writes. The controller can also perform the converse of the previous operation, namely converting a RAID 0+1 block into a RAID 5 block, if it determines and predicts that the block will be primarily accessed for reads. To support this configuration, all the drives in the array are used for all RAID volumes that are configured on that array. This means that physical drive-independence across volumes cannot be achieved.

While this implementation of RAID relieves a significant amount of work and maintenance for the system administrator and the Oracle database administrator, care should be exercised while implementing this on hybrid Oracle systems, which can be read/write–intensive at the same time.

If your system becomes suddenly and seriously write intensive after a period of read-intensive activity, the conversion process may not occur immediately and your blocks may get stuck in RAID 5 (from the read phase) even though you are in the write phase. This can happen when the system load is high, and the conversion process defers to a quieter period. This behavior may be prevalent on busy hybrid Oracle systems.

If you implement this RAID technology on heavy-duty Oracle systems, be prepared for unpredictable changes in I/O performance, unless your system is normally write intensive or normally read intensive with occasional changes like those nightly batch jobs. So, when implementing Auto RAID, every effort should be taken to segregate write-intensive and read-intensive components on separate arrays. The following table is a summary of the various levels of RAID.

Level of RAID	Functionality
RAID 0	Provides striping and no recoverability. Your application requires read/write performance without recoverability (rare).
RAID 1	Provides mirroring and recoverability. Your application primarily requires write performance.
RAID 0+1/1+0	Provides the combination of 0 and 1 and recoverability. Your application requires read and write performance. This is very widely used (note that 1+0 is better than 0+1 for availability).
RAID 2	This was one of the early implementations of striping with parity, and it uses the hamming code technique for parity calculations. It was replaced by RAID 3, RAID 5, and RAID 7 and is very rarely implemented.
RAID 3	Provides striping with bit/byte-level parity and is supported by a dedicated parity disk. This also provides recoverability. Your application requires read performance for bulk sequential reads and requires better data-transfer rates for sequential reads over IOPS. It is not widely used, but is slowly gaining popularity.

Level of RAID	Functionality
RAID 4	Provides striping with block-level parity and is supported by a dedicated parity disk. It also provides recoverability, but is very rarely supported by hardware vendors.
RAID 5	Provides striping with block-level parity. The parity is distributed across the number of disks in the volume. It also provides recoverability. Your application requires read performance for random reads that are small in nature, and requires better IOPS over data-transfer rates. It is very widely used.
RAID 6	Provides striping with block-level multidimensional parity. Supports recoverability, but suffers from slower writes when compared to RAID 5. It is very rarely implemented.
RAID 7	Same functionality as in RAID 3, but with better asynchronous capability for reads and writes. This is significantly better overall I/O performance when compared to RAID 3, but it is also much more expensive than RAID 3.
RAID-S	This is EMC's implementation of RAID 3/5.
Auto RAID	This is HP's automatic RAID technology that autoconfigures the I/O system based on the nature and type of I/O performed on the disk blocks within the RAID array.

Oracle and RAID

Because RAID is either implemented as host-based (software-based) or hardware-based (which is best), it is transparent to the Oracle RDBMS. All RAID-specific operations are handled "under the covers" by the hardware, the OS, or the volume management control software. The manner in which I/O operations are performed and managed contributes tremendously to how well Oracle performs. Each component of an Oracle database is best suited to a specific RAID implementation. This means that a "one size fits all" concept will definitely not work. In fact, it also means that the RAID level you start with may not be appropriate at a later date, depending on the changing nature of data access patterns.

RAID 1

This level of RAID is best suited for both online and archived redo logs, as they are accessed in a sequential fashion and performance is enhanced by having the write head of the disk near the location of the last write. One important point to keep in mind is that as LGWR is writing to one redo log, ARCH may be reading from the previous log to create the archived log. This means that more than one RAID 1 volume may be required for optimal performance and elimination of contention between LGWR and ARCH. If you are strapped for disks, consider one volume each for the even and odd numbered redo-log groups, along with a separate volume for the archived logs.

RAID 0+1 or RAID 1+0

As a rule of thumb, write-intensive applications should be implemented using RAID 0+1/1+0, and read-intensive applications should be implemented using RAID 3/5. This works best because RAID 0+1/1+0 does not pose the performance penalty on the I/O subsystem during writes in the form of pesky parity calculations. Parity calculations are incurred on RAID 3, 5, or 7, but the access patterns on those volumes should mostly be reads. However, to optimally configure a RAID 0+1/1+0 volume, you require more disks when compared to a RAID 3/5/7 volume. As noted before, RAID 1+0 is preferred as it provides better availability when compared to RAID 0+1.

RAID 3 Versus RAID 5

So how do you choose between RAID 3 and RAID 5? The answer goes back to the DBA mantra, "Know your application." If the application performs sequential I/O (full or range table/index scan), the degree of striping has a direct impact on I/O performance. RAID 3 implementations should be preferred in read-intensive application environments where the read patterns are sequential and bulky in nature. This is because the spindles in a RAID 3 volume work in a synchronized fashion. All the disks in a given volume will service an I/O request from the same disk location (track, cylinder, sector).

On the other hand, RAID 5 implementations should be preferred where the read patterns are random and not very bulky in nature. This is because the spindles in a RAID 5 volume work in an independent fashion. All the disks in a given volume can potentially service multiple I/O requests from different disk locations.

Thus the architecture of RAID 3 is best suited for decision support systems (DSS) and data warehousing (DW) applications with small user populations and sustained bulk read patterns, as it better caters to data transfer and hence should be preferred. In contrast, the underlying architecture of RAID 5 better caters to IOPS and hence is preferable for DSS/DW applications with large user populations and small random read patterns.

So which do you have? You can get a good idea by determining the number of long and short table scans on your system. This information is available in the dynamic performance views and in the report.txt generated by utlbstat/utlestat. If you find that your application environment is characterized by many large table/index scans and you have a relatively small user population, RAID 3 should be your choice. One production system benchmark on RAID 3 showed a data-transfer rate of approximately 13 MB/s, compared to a similar RAID 5 volume, which showed 9 MB/s, for the same type of activity. Additionally please note that contrary to popular belief, the dedicated parity drive on a RAID 3 device does not create a write bottleneck, if the controller supporting the volume is not overloaded and the size of the writes equals the size of the stripe width on the volume This is definitely true with full fiber-channel storage systems.

RAID 7

If your system requires the data-transfer capacity of RAID 3, without hindering smaller transaction-based I/O requests, RAID 7 is your answer. But you'd better rework your storage system budget, as RAID7 will cost you a significant chunk of change.

VIP

The RAID 3 versus RAID 5 discussion on data-transfer bandwidth versus IOPS is done solely in the context of read-intensive applications. It is preferred and recommended that write-intensive applications always be configured using RAID 0+1/1+0 volumes. If you have made the decision to use RAID 3, based on your application and user population's characteristics, you may want to investigate the support of RAID 7 on your storage system.

NOTE

If RAID 7 is supported (and you can afford it), comparable tests should be done to validate its cost-benefit analysis performance against RAID 3. The ability to perform asynchronous reads and writes will increase the overall throughput of the storage system, and your tests should corroborate the cost and the selection of RAID 7 over RAID 3. One test is definitely worth a thousand speculations.

Auto RAID

As mentioned in the previous section, configuring and using Hewlett Packard's Auto RAID requires care, as the automatic disk block conversion process constantly converts disk blocks from RAID 0+1 segments to RAID 5 and vice versa, based on its determination and prediction of I/O on those blocks. The key exposure areas for Oracle are the rollback segment (RBS) and temporary (TEMP) tablespaces, which can be adversely affected by the conversion process.

Since the I/O patterns for these tablespaces often alternate between extensive reads and writes, performance may vary dramatically. The alternation between intense writes followed by intense reads can cause serious system performance degradation because the RAID controller may attempt to compensate for this by changing the RAID type frequently but not in a timely fashion. It has been observed that the conversion often doesn't get done in time to support the future nature of the operations requested.

The problem mentioned here can occur even on all other components of the database, if there are periods of lull followed by varying operations (reads followed by writes or vice versa) that cause the disk blocks to be converted back and forth. Further, as mentioned before, the lack of control over drive allocation for various volumes can cause serious disk contention problems if the application performs significant index-range scans followed by table lookups.

In a benchmark, it was observed that if the RBS tablespace was not written to for a period of time, but was read from (as part of building a read-consistent image for a long running query), the disk blocks housing the rollback segments of the database were converted to RAID 5. Then when a slew of write activity was launched at the database, the disk blocks remained as RAID 5. This degraded write performance significantly as parity had to be calculated and written for those blocks. Later when the I/O subsystem got a breather, these blocks were reconverted to RAID 0+1. A similar phenomenon was also noticed on the TEMP tablespace.

The following table outlines the usage of different RAID levels and the components of an Oracle database:

Level of RAID	When and Where to Use It
RAID 0	Not suitable for any critical component of an Oracle database. May be considered for development databases where recoverability is determined to be a non-issue. This is suitable when you can simply restore a copy of a production database and reapply any DDL differences to recreate a development environment.

Level of RAID	When and Where to Use It
RAID 1	Ideal for online and archived redo logs. Leaves the write-head at the location of the last write. On most systems, you will need three volumes for the online redo logs (for three groups) and one volume for the archived redo logs.
RAID 0+1 or 1+0	Ideally suited for data files that require read/write performance especially for online transaction processing (OLTP) or hybrid systems, where read/write performance is important. Pick 1+0 over 0+1 when possible.
RAID 3	Ideal for data mart/data warehouse applications with few users that require mostly range/full scans on its tables and indexes. Everything else remaining constant, RAID 3 provides better data transfer than RAID 5.
RAID 5	Ideal for data mart/data warehouse applications with many users that require mostly unique scans on its tables and indexes. RAID 5 provides better IOPS than RAID 3.
RAID 7	Ideal for data mart/data warehouse applications with support for more users than RAID 3. The application requires mostly range/full scans on its tables and indexes. If your application requires RAID 3 and better support for IOPS and you can afford it, RAID 7 is your key.

Fundamentals of Configuring Disk Arrays

So much for theory; now let's get down to actually figuring out how to configure your RAID disk arrays. Configuring RAID disk arrays must be done in a systematic and methodical fashion. The manner in which the disk arrays are configured is largely dependent on the number of drives, partial data availability requirements, and support for parallelism. The number of drives is primarily dependent on the required data-transfer rates or IOPS (as the case may be) and the amount of data that needs to be stored.

What? Well, obviously you have to have enough space, but the more important point is having enough disks to support the I/O access patterns of your application and your users. Remember, with RAID you can get additive overall throughput by grouping disks into volumes. This is a natural outgrowth of the tried and true approach that shows you can get more out of many smaller disks than just a few big disks. Something to think about!

Here are some of the core issues that require consideration:

- Determine the suitable level of RAID for the application, based on known/projected access patterns.

- When available, hardware-level RAID should be used over software-level RAID.

- Configure the disk controller's cache using a 60:40 ratio for writes:reads for hybrid applications that have both reads and writes. Configure a higher ratio for reads if the application is more read intensive.

- When possible, disable the write cache on volumes that support the online redo logs of the database, unless you have tested the workings of the battery backup for the cache and have verified it to be foolproof. The integrity of your database is at stake if Oracle expects redo entries to be on disk and does not find it at a later time.

- Procure the smallest drive money can buy, keeping in mind scalability, limits of the host machine, the disk array, and growth projections for the database. This is a tough one these days, with 18GB drives considered to be small drives.

- Bigger and faster drives are not always better than smaller slower drives, as the seek times for larger and faster drives with larger form factors may be more than their smaller and slower counterparts. This is not that big an issue if your drives support a built-in track buffer cache for storing an entire track's worth of data from read requests.

- Do not overload the controllers.

- Assume that all drives supported by the controller will engage at the same time.

- Do not daisy-chain disks or disk arrays.

- Determine the I/O bandwidth of the controller.

- Determine the I/O bandwidth of each disk.

- Spread your volumes across as many controllers on your storage system as possible to get better distribution of I/O request servicing and better availability. (A controller should not become a single point of failure in your system.)

■ Ensure that the number of drives per controller is configured per the following formula:

Disks per controller = (I/O bandwidth of controller)/(I/O bandwidth of one disk)

NOTE
In any disk array configuration, the bandwidth of the disk controller and the speed of each individual disk need to be in focus during its configuration. For example, if the controller supports a bandwidth of 100 MB/s and each disk supports a transfer rate of 10 MB/s, no more than ten drives should be configured on one controller. This factor should be considered keeping in mind the read activity on the database, the type and frequency of the reports that are generated, and the number of users requesting such reports.

Fundamentals of Disk Striping

There is a popular saying that the three rules for success in the real estate business are "Location, location, location." Well, it turns out that the three rules for success in optimal RAID implementations are "Striping, striping, striping." There cannot be enough importance given to disk striping, as it is an integral part of the art of configuring optimal RAID volumes.

Disk striping employs the simple concept of breaking up data into pieces and disbursing them across multiple drives of a given RAID volume to create stripes. This concept, albeit simple, is very powerful and is one of the most crucial elements in I/O performance scalability. In simple terms, employing many drives to service multiple I/O requests is better than a single drive doing all the work. In addition to providing scalable I/O performance, disk striping also offers better manageability (fewer file systems to create, mount, and maintain).

Given that each drive's I/O bandwidth ceiling is fixed, it is very evident that the degree of striping is what provides scalable I/O performance, when compared to no striping at all. While it may be argued (and it's a weak argument) that performing manual Oracle striping of the various tablespaces across multiple drives will achieve similar I/O performance boosts, this does add a significant amount of administrative overhead in database storage babysitting. This is something that most sites cannot afford. I sincerely hope you have better things to do with your precious time! It is much more desirable to let the OS and the hardware do the job of striping than manually doing it.

Also, Oracle DBA 101 (Database Administration Fundamentals) warrants application of common sense in ensuring the independence of the various components of the database to reduce the amount of interference. Magic will not happen if the DATA, INDX, RBS, TEMP, and SYSTEM tablespaces all are physically located on the same set of disks. It is apparent here that the system should be optimal flexible architecture (OFA) compliant to the extent possible.

NOTE
Whenever possible, striping should supercede physical separation of some database components such as SYSTEM, RBS, and TEMP. Configuring RBS and TEMP in the same set of physical drives is okay, so long as a high percentage of the sorts are performed in memory (you will need to optimally configure SORT_AREA_SIZE) and it has been verified that there is no evidence of sustained concurrent writes to rollback and temporary segments. For most environments, even sharing the SYSTEM tablespace with RBS and TEMP will be okay. The I/O on the SYSTEM tablespace should be at a minimum if the data dictionary cache has adequate memory to store the dictionary-related data (configured with the Oracle initialization parameter SHARED_POOL_SIZE).

Steps on Creating Striped Volumes, Part I

Following are some steps you need to be aware of while creating striped volumes:

1. Keep the degree of striping as a power of 2, namely 2, 4, 8, 16, and so on. This is because DB_BLOCK_SIZE is always a power of 2 (8k, 16k, 32k, and so on), and DB_FILE_MULTIBLOCK_READ_COUNT is normally set to a power of 2. It is important to note here that when using RAID levels 3, 5, and 7, the number of disks required for a volume with a degree of striping of n is $n+1$.

2. Determine the degree of striping for the DATA volumes (normally 4 or 8, sometimes 16 or higher). This decides the number of drives that will participate in a given DATA RAID volume.

3. Determine the degree of striping for the INDX volumes (normally 2 or 4, sometimes 8 or higher). This decides the number of drives that will

participate in a given INDX RAID volume. INDX requires a lower degree than DATA, as indexes by their inherent nature are smaller than tables and hence require a lower degree of striping.

4. The degree of striping in the DATA and INDX volumes should also consider factors such as data/index partitioning, availability requirements, and support for parallel operations. Please note that 16 data files placed on 16 individual drives can support a 16-way parallel operation (if you have memory and CPU to support it and your controller is not out of capacity because all 16 drives engaged at the same time). The same cannot be concluded with 16 data files placed on a 16-way RAID volume with 16 drives. The degree of parallelism that you deploy on a 16-way volume will be significantly less when compared to the former configuration of 16 individual drives. This factor should be factored when making degree of striping decisions, which in turn control the number of volumes on your system.

5. Determine and configure the maximum I/O chunk-size of the OS. The I/O chunk-size controls the amount of data that is read per read request, while performing full table scans or index range scans. On Solaris, the /etc/system kernel parameter that needs to be configured is *maxphys*. This parameter is set in bytes, defaults to 128K, and is appropriate for most systems where the I/O requests are transactional in nature. But for systems that are hybrid in nature and need to support large data-intensive transfers, it is recommended to set this at 1MB or even 4MB. For environments that utilize Veritas file systems, the *vxio:vol_maxio* parameter needs to be configured. This parameter is set in 512-byte units, and it is recommended to set this at 2048 (which translates to 1MB) or 8192 (which translates to 4MB).

6. Determine and configure the read-ahead cluster size for file systems by using a rule of thumb of no more than 200 I/O operations per second on the storage device. Setting this parameter is relevant for volumes that will service large data-intensive transfers. For example, if a storage array can deliver 200 MB/s, with 200 I/O operations per threshold, the cluster size for the file systems on that storage array should be set to at least 1MB (sometimes even 4MB). On Solaris, this can be achieved by setting the *maxcontig* parameter in the **mkfs** command. For existing file systems, the **fstyp –v <device name>** command can be executed to determine the cluster size. The *maxcontig* parameter is set in file system blocks, and the **fstyp** command will provide you with the block-size (*bsize*) on the device. The read-ahead cluster size is calculated as (*maxcontig* × *bsize*). The cluster size for existing file systems can be modified using the **tunefs** or **vxtunefs** commands. This step of determining and configuring the read-ahead cluster size is not relevant if the OS is configured to support direct I/O, as in that case all read-ahead algorithms are disabled.

7. The results from steps 1–6 will facilitate in calculating the stripe width that is optimal for the volume. Given the recommendations in the previous steps, it is obvious that stripe width = (*n* times cluster size, where *n* is the number of drives configured on a device), for volumes that service data-intensive transfers. On volumes that are transactional in nature, the stripe width can be configured with the value cluster size. However, if the I/O size (maxphys) is modified to 1MB, stripe width should be set at least at 1MB to utilize and benefit from this increased ceiling.

Stripe Width Configuration

The stripe width configuration for RAID devices should be done keeping in mind two important conditions:

■ Ensure that all drives configured in a given volume are engaged during sequential I/O operations that are bulk in nature (full table scans of large tables). However, note that you should do this keeping in mind that the degree of concurrency of your sequential scans, which will be affected by the number of I/O requests that can be serviced by the volume at any given time. Thought should also be given for concurrency of single-block I/O requests. Single-block I/O requests should be serviced by a single drive, without all drives engaging in the I/O operation.

■ Ensure that the stripe width of a given RAID volume is a multiple of the maximum I/O size (Step 5 in "Steps on Creating Striped Volumes, Part 1") of the hardware and/or the I/O drivers. Care needs to be taken with this condition that it does not negate the previous stripe width condition. Remember, the key in reaping the benefits of striping is to ensure a high degree of concurrency for I/O requests on a given volume. This is true in the case of breaking up one very large I/O request into many smaller ones and also for the support of many concurrent small I/O requests.

For example, in a given implementation if the maximum I/O size is 1MB and the number of drives in the RAID array is eight, the stripe width should be set at 8MB and the stripe unit size/interlace size at 1MB. Across many implementations on many different operating systems, it has been observed that a stripe width of 1MB is usually a good starting value. More recent versions of many an OS (such as Solaris 2.6/2.7) support a much higher I/O size (via maxphys), and this should be put to use in an appropriate manner. Stripe width should always be dependent on the maximum I/O size of the OS where the RAID volume is implemented.

WARNING
*Keep in mind the dependency between stripe width
and the Oracle initialization parameter DB_FILE_
MULTIBLOCK_READ_COUNT. This Oracle
parameter is set based on the value of the stripe width.
A wider stripe width can support a higher value for t
his parameter, and the effect of that will be improved
performance for full table or index fast full scans.*

Even though configuring volumes with large stripe widths provide better batch
processing performance, care needs to be taken, not to set DB_FILE_ MULTIBLOCK_
READ_COUNT at the instance level to a value that will cause the Oracle optimizer to
choose full table scans as the preferred method of executing a query.

From Oracle 7.3 and up, this issue can be easily solved by setting this parameter
conservatively at the instance level and then modifying it to a higher value at the
session level (if required).

Steps on Creating Striped Volumes, Part 2

Following are additional steps you need to be aware of while creating
striped volumes:

1. Configure the necessary logical volumes.

2. Create and mount file systems on the logical volumes (one file system per
   logical volume).

3. Slicing and dicing the logical volumes and creating multiple file systems
   under a single RAID volume does not provide any gain in performance.
   In fact, it may add some administrative overhead.

4. Create the file systems with their *minfree* parameters set to 0, as data files in
   Oracle are usually preallocated and usually do not benefit from this feature.
   The benefit of setting the file system storage parameter *minfree* to 0 is to
   reclaim 10 percent of disk storage which otherwise is potentially wasted.

5. For most hybrid or data warehouse systems, configure the file system block
   size as follows:

6. DB_BLOCK_SIZE = File system block size = OS page size

7. Most file systems today default to a block size of 8K. Care needs to be taken so the Oracle database is not created with a DB_BLOCK_SIZE of less than 8K. This topic has been discussed in great detail in the chapter "Database Tuning."

8. Test the I/O data-transfer rate on all volumes and visually examine the storage array to ensure that all drives in the volume are engaged in large parallel sequential read operations. You should see your storage array light up like a Christmas tree. This will provide evidence that the volume is functioning optimally and the stripe width configuration is working. This test can be done by copying a data file from a volume to /dev/null. The following is an example of how data-transfer rates can be calculated: timex dd if=/u08/oradata/acme/data01.dbf of=/dev/null bs or bsize=stripe-width.

9. The command in Step 8 will provide the necessary numbers to calculate the data-transfer rates using this formula: (# of records processed × bs)/ time elapsed).

Operating System Configuration

While most operating systems do not require any special kernel configuration parameters to implement RAID volumes, this section outlines some of the core issues that require consideration.

- In some operating systems, the kernel needs to be modified to set the "write behind" parameters to support fewer bulk writes, instead of many small writes. On most modern file systems, it is a parameter that can be tuned, such as *write_pref_io* on Veritas, and this needs to be set to the same value as the read-ahead cluster size.

- The OS and Oracle need to support large files so that files larger than 2048MB can be configured and utilized for VLDBs.

- It is also noteworthy here that the upper boundary for the file system buffer cache (which is usually configured by a kernel parameter) should be limited to 10–15 percent of total RAM, as failure to configure this parameter on some flavors of UNIX (for example, HP-UX) can cause significant degradation in performance. This degradation is noticed in the form of intensive paging, process inactivation, and swapping. This is because in some cases, default kernel parameters allow up to 50 percent of total RAM for the file system buffer cache.

- It is also important that while writing to RAID volumes that require parity calculations, the write penalty is at a minimum. This can be achieved if the size of the writes is equal to the value of the stripe width on those volumes. This is possible when the stripe width is set to the same value as the read-ahead cluster size. But if the writing of data begins halfway in a stripe, partially writing two stripes will be much more expensive than writing one full stripe. This is due to the increased overhead in reading the data, recomputing the parity, writing the new parity, and then writing the modified data back to disk. For this purpose, it is important to configure write alignment, which is supported on some file systems. On Veritas file systems, write alignment can be achieved by aligning the clustered writes with the stripe on a preset boundary. This can be done by creating the file system with the align option and setting this to a value of 512 bytes.

The Raw Devices Versus File Systems Religious Debate

When possible, advanced file systems such as xfs, jfs, or vxfs should be preferred over ufs file systems. This is to utilize the improved journal and performance features (such as elimination of double buffering) that advanced file systems offer over ufs. It must be noted that if you configure your system using ufs file systems, the necessary file system level parameters need to be configured and tuned, as the default values will not provide optimal performance.

When using Veritas vxfs file systems, Quick I/O can provide raw device comparable performance without losing the benefits of a file system. This is because the Quick I/O driver intercepts all DBWR writes (when enabled) thus bypassing the file system buffer cache. This provides raw device comparable performance, as the classic problems of double buffering and wasted CPU cycles in managing the file system buffer cache are avoided. When using other types of advanced file systems, direct I/O can be preferred if supported by the OS, as it too provides raw device comparable performance. The use of raw devices does not add any significant value when compared to advanced file systems with Quick/Direct I/O drivers (wherever applicable).

Raw devices do add a level of operational complexity without justifiable performance benefits, when compared to advanced file systems configured with Veritas Quick I/O or Direct I/O (supported by the OS). They also do not lend themselves to the placement of multiple files on a device. In these cases, the configuration and use of raw devices should be reserved for Oracle Parallel Server implementations.

Asynchronous I/O

Oracle configured with asynchronous I/O has been found to work effectively only on raw devices across most flavors of UNIX. Asynchronous I/O on regular file systems is supported on some operating systems such as Solaris and AIX. Depending on your I/O system configuration, you may observe that Direct I/O or Quick I/O can offer comparable performance when using specialized file systems such as Veritas (vxfs). You may also have the option of configuring the relevant Oracle instance parameters for multiple database writer support. But normally you either enable asynchronous I/O or multiple database writers, not both. Please refer to the chapter "OS Tuning" for details regarding asynchronous I/O for Solaris, HP-UX, and AIX.

Configuring Your Database for Optimal Placement

There are certain steps that can be taken to optimize placement of the various components of the Oracle database. The I/O-related aspects have been covered in good detail in this chapter. However, there are certain issues that need to be mentioned as hardware and storage advancements have made database placement and configuration just a little bit different.

Separation of Concurrently Accessed Objects

Even today, the issue of not storing multiple objects that are concurrently accessed in the same storage device is relevant. The primary focus here is to eliminate I/O bottlenecks and hotspots in the database. Although the core of this issue has really not changed from a few years ago, significant advancements in storage hardware have alleviated much of the pain that was previously experienced. This is because of the increase in speed in storage devices, configuration of I/O subsystem cache, and other related features.

Separate Data from its Associated indexes

Regardless of the storage vendor and their claims, common sense must prevail on issues such as separation of the DATA and INDX tablespaces. As mentioned in previous sections, for query-intensive applications that heavily utilize indexes, the DATA and INDX tablespaces should be separated. There are no two ways about it.

Coexistence of the Rollback and Temporary Tablespaces

Historically, we have always separated the rollback and temporary tablespaces on separate storage devices. However, with the significant advancements in storage technology and improvement in certain features in Oracle, that may no longer be a "must do." The key factor to determine is whether the rollback and temporary tablespaces contend with one another (for this and other discussions, a temporary tablespace is one whose contents are of type *temporary*). If they don't contend with one another, it is okay for them to coexist on the same physical devices, if the following two points are kept in mind:

■ There is no simultaneous generation of rollback entries and temporary sort data in your database. This is characteristic of current-day data warehouses, where data is loaded on a periodic basis using methods that do not generate rollback and in most cases can be configured not to even generate any redo (using the *nologging* attribute with SQL*Loader or the *nologging* attribute set at the table level combined with a /*+ APPEND */ hint in an insert statement).

■ A high percentage of sorts are done in memory, reducing both the usage and probability of contention of the temporary tablespace. This can be easily achieved by configuring SORT_AREA_SIZE appropriately at the instance level or at the session level. From Oracle 7.3, the SORT_AREA_SIZE initialization parameter can be configured at the session level and the use of the temporary tablespace can be reserved for extremely sort-intensive operations, such as creation of indexes or queries on large tables. This assumes that there is enough memory available to be allocated to the session for an increased SORT_ AREA_SIZE.

For applications that are write intensive, the DATA, INDX, and RBS tablespaces should be separated. The various groups of the online redo logs should be separated on different disks/volumes when possible. Further, the location where archived redo logs are written by the ARCH process should be different from the location of the online redo logs. It may be justifiable to put the RBS and TEMP tablespaces in the same volumes, if SORT_AREA_SIZE is configured optimally and there is no evidence of sustained simultaneous generation of "sorts on disk" and "undo entries for rollback."

Separation of Hot Objects Within a Tablespace

In some applications, you may find that a few tables or indexes are hotter than most of the other tables and indexes. Separating these tables or indexes from the others by moving them to new tablespaces placed on new or different RAID volumes remains a best practice. Time spent rebalancing I/O by moving data files is time well spent. However, the frequency of rebalancing will be far and few between if you configure your volumes keeping in mind the issues discussed in the previous sections.

How Should You Stripe Your Data?

A scientific comparison needs to be made to determine whether it is better to create fewer volumes with "thin-wide stripes" or more volumes with relatively "thick-narrow" stripes. This is dependent on issues such as data/index partitioning, required support parallelism for core operations and any service-level agreements on high or partial availability. While thin-wide stripes may be an attractive solution from the ease-of-administration point of view, the constraining factors of include reduced parallelism, reduced availability, and less-than-ideal support for data/index partitioning make it not that appealing. Our goal is to meet somewhere halfway between thin-wide stripes and thick-narrow stripes.

One too many database administrators find themselves cheating with their redo and archive logs. If your database is in NOARCHIVELOG mode, you probably can get away with a single RAID 1 volume for your redo logs. However, for databases in ARCHIVELOG mode you will need to further separate your redo log groups from each other and from your archive logs. An effective arrangement uses three RAID 1 volumes. Nothing else should be put on any of these volumes. This is where some administrators start to get uncomfortable. If your system is like most, it consists of 9GB or 18GB drives. Now, two of those went into each volume, but because they are mirrored you still only have the capacity of one. Therefore you just used up six 9GB drives to make three 9GB volumes. One of those is for the archived logs so you can now keep quite a few logs online. But those other two volumes have only a few redo logs on each one. And since your redo logs may be quite small—say, 250MB to 1GB—that leaves a lot of disk space barren. *Leave it alone.* Putting other active components of an Oracle database on the same volumes will only hamper performance. You may, however, make use of that space for storing export files and/or any other administrative items that will not interfere with the Oracle database.

The SYSTEM tablespace can be physically located on any volume and in most cases can share the same physical volume as the TEMP and RBS tablespaces. This is because contention among these components of the database is usually very minimal. The optimal configuration of the SHARED_POOL_SIZE and DB_BLOCK_BUFFERS initialization parameters is essential to reduce I/O on the SYSTEM tablespace.

Initialization Parameters that Affect I/O Performance

Following are the key Oracle initialization parameters that require configuring when deploying RAID on Oracle systems. The Oracle initialization parameter settings in the following table are for a database with four independent logical volumes, a database block-size of 8K, and an I/O size of 128K.

Parameter Name	Example Setting	Description
_DB_BLOCK_CHECKPOINT_BATCH	16	Write chunk size for DBWR during checkpoint writes, set it to stripe width.
DB_FILE_MULTIBLOCK_READ_COUNT	16	Read chunk size used when performing full-table scans and index fast full scans, set it to stripe width.
DB_WRITER_PROCESSES	8	Number of DBWR processes attached to the instance. Configure this to no more than two times the number of physically independent volumes. If you are using DBWR_IO_SLAVES, only one DB_WRITER_PROCESS will be used.
DBWR_IO_SLAVES	N	Where N equals the number of I/O slaves required for optimal configuration.
DISK_ASYNCH_IO	False	Turns off asynchronous I/O, supported on most flavors of UNIX only on raw devices. Check your version of the operating system and verify whether Oracle supports asynchronous I/O for file systems and, if so, set this parameter to TRUE.
HASH_MULTIBLOCK_IO_COUNT	16	I/O chunk-size used when performing hash joins.
USE_DIRECT_IO	True	Performs Direct I/O bypassing the file system buffer cache. Configure this when available on your operating system platform.

RAID and Oracle Databases: Core Issues

While most issues related to RAID are common across most applications and databases, there are some that affect VLDBs more than others. The following need consideration:

- Depending on whether the system is a hybrid system or OLTP, core initialization parameters such as DB_BLOCK_SIZE (which cannot be modified without database recreation) need special consideration. When in doubt, go with the bigger block size. This provides you with better I/O subsystem performance (fewer system calls for servicing your I/O requests) and reduces the number of blocks in your tables and indexes. In the case of indexes, this does have a positive effect on the height of the index.

- Depending on the nature of the application (transaction-heavy or reporting-heavy), the level of RAID needs to be carefully considered and configured. Further, the nature of the application should also be researched to determine whether the I/O patterns are sequential or random. Redoing this after the fact may be impossible.

- The ratio of used database size versus total database size is very relevant to the selection process of the appropriate level of RAID and all the relevant I/O parameters. Pareto's principle is probably working in your environment: 80 percent of your I/O is generated from 20 percent of your data. It is to your benefit to determine which objects comprise that 20 percent.

- The ability to segregate read-only tablespaces from read/write tablespaces will further influence the use of different levels of RAID that either read-friendly or write-friendly, as the case may be.

- The number of users that access the application and hence the number of concurrent sessions supported by the database also determines many configuration issues in the I/O system.

- Any service-level agreements that relate to availability need to be factored into the final equation when determining the balance between cost and availability. This issue determines the allowable mean time to recover (MTTR) and thus affects the frequency of backups. This issue also has a direct correlation to the degree of striping decisions you need to make.

- The level and complexity of data replication required for the application for protection against failure and disaster recovery will have long-reaching effects on the RAID configuration decisions that are made with respect to a given system. How much and how frequently does your data change?

■ The options to perform software-based replication versus hardware-based replication need to be determined.

Sample RAID Configurations

The following are sample RAID configurations that are currently supporting live production databases. These configurations have all been designed for optimal I/O performance. While cost is an important factor when designing optimal RAID configurations, the primary focus for all the following configurations were I/O scalability, predictable performance, availability, data and index partitioning, and parallelism of operations. The following table is the volume legend:

Legend	Degree of Striping	Mirroring	Parity
■	None	Yes	No
■	2	Yes	No
■	4	Yes	No
■	4	No	Yes
□	8	No	Yes

Figure 11-1 is a sample RAID 0+1 configuration consisting of 84 18GB disks, each capable of transfer rates of 5-7 MB/s and six controllers (three per cabinet), each capable of an I/O bandwidth of 100 MB/s.

Figure 11-2 sheds light on the internals of a RAID 0+1 volume.

Figure 11-3 is a sample RAID 3 configuration consisting of 180 9GB disks, each capable of transfer rates of 10 MB/s and nine controllers (three per rack), each capable of an I/O bandwidth of 100 MB/s.

Figure 11-4 illustrates the internals of a RAID 3 volume.

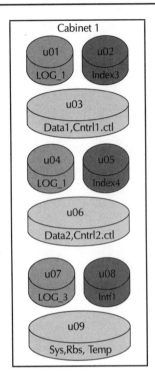
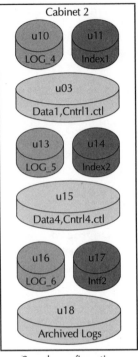

Sample configuration

FIGURE 11-1. *Sample configuration of a RAID 0+1 volume*

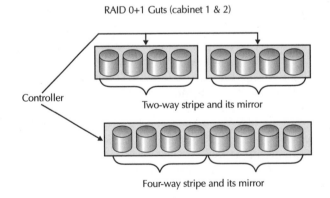

FIGURE 11-2. *Internals of a RAID 0+1 volume*

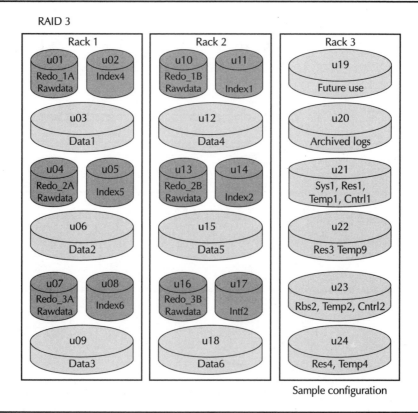

FIGURE 11-3. *Sample configuration of a RAID 3 volume*

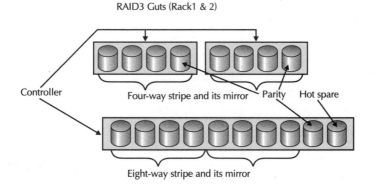

FIGURE 11-4. *Internals of a RAID 3 volume*

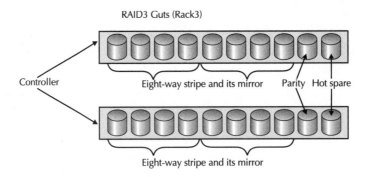

FIGURE 11-5. *More internals of a RAID 3 volume*

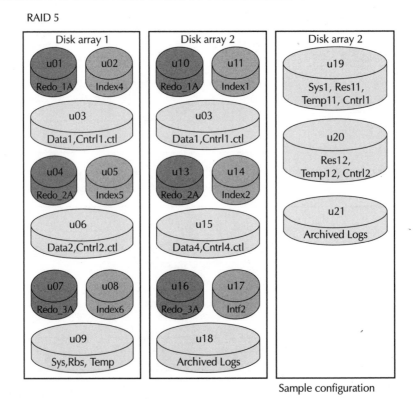

FIGURE 11-6. *Sample configuration of a RAID 5 volume*

Figure 11-5 graphically portrays the internals of a RAID 3 volume.

Figure 11-6 is a sample RAID 5 configuration consisting of 150 18GB disks, each capable of transfer rates of 5–7 MB/s and eight controllers (three in Disk Arrays 1 and 2 and two in Disk Array 3), each capable of an I/O bandwidth of 100 MB/s.

Figure 11-7 displays the internals of a RAID 5 volume.

Figure 11-8 shows more of the internals of a RAID 5 volume.

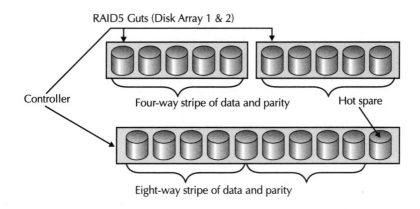

FIGURE 11-7.   *Internals of a RAID 5 volume*

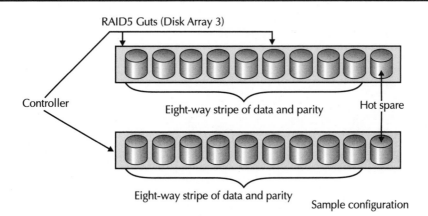

FIGURE 11-8.   *More internals of a RAID 5 volume*

In a Nutshell

There is more to RAID than being a bug spray. RAID provides the technology to scale I/O and system performance of applications and provide high availability. Proactive design, architecture, and deployment of optimal RAID configurations are quintessential to gaining scalable I/O performance. It is important to understand the RAID solutions offered by each hardware vendor before any implementation is done. A solid understanding of the application to be supported plays a large part in RAID selection. Researching the application and the details of your vendor's RAID offerings must be the starting point of any I/O subsystem design.

As always, DBA 101 common sense needs to be applied on a continuous basis. Some things never change: DATA tablespaces needs to be separated from INDX tablespaces. The three rules for successful optimal RAID configurations are, "Striping, striping, and striping." Oh, one last thing, regardless of what their claims may be, mass storage vendors are definitely not the gods of disks.

CHAPTER
12

Operating System
Tuning

Myth & Folklore

Your SGA should always be configured in one shared memory segment to attain maximum database performance. Configuring the OS parameters to accommodate the entire SGA in one shared memory segment always results in improved database performance.

Fact

Many DBAs in a UNIX environment go to great lengths in their efforts to keep the entire SGA in one shared memory segment in hopes of gaining performance. However, in most other environments there is no measurable performance degradation even if the SGA is comprised of multiple shared memory segments. Oracle processes access various components of your SGA with almost identical memory seek times that cost a few nanoseconds. We have done performance tests on many flavors of UNIX just to debunk this myth. The same components of the application were run before and after the UNIX kernel was modified, and there was absolutely no measurable increase or decrease in performance. Bottom line, on most UNIX platforms, it really does not matter if your SGA uses one or more shared memory segments.

Having said that, we do need to caution you about a couple of exceptions. On some hardware platforms that support non-uniform memory access (NUMA) configurations across multiple nodes, the communication between the system nodes occurs via an "interconnect" or a switch. If your SGA is configured as multiple shared memory segments, there is a possibility that those segments could be created across multiple nodes, resulting in Oracle having to constantly use the interconnect to read different parts of your SGA. This can create some performance problems if the bandwidth of this interconnect is limited, thus creating a communication bottleneck between the nodes. Also, if you intend to use the Intimate Shared Memory (ISM) feature in a Sun Solaris environment, configuring SHMMAX so that the entire SGA is allocated in one shared memory segment is a requirement. ISM will be discussed later in the chapter.

o how much tuning do you need to do at the level of the operating system (OS)? The OS itself can be considered a resource manager that coordinates the functions of the processors, disk subsystems, and memory of various processes or applications on a given system. All these components interact with one another. The manner in which each component carries out its functions has effects on the other components.

There are two aspects to tuning at the OS leve: first, you configure the OS to ensure that enough resources are available for Oracle database, second, tune the OS to improve performance of Oracle processes. In a UNIX environment, it mainly involves adjusting certain OS kernel parameters. In recent years, the Oracle Installation and Configuration Guide (ICG) has provided good guidelines for setting these parameters, but in certain environments some parameters may need further adjustment. Most OS kernel parameters can be left unchanged to use default values. We will address the relevant parameters in the following sections.

In a Windows NT environment, there are a few things you can adjust to improve its performance. Fortunately, there is no kernel rebuilding—just click the right buttons and off you go. Rebooting may be required after some of the configuration changes. We have included a section dedicated to Windows NT system configuration to quench the thirst for OS configuration knowledge of our Windows NT readers.

Tuning the OS: Generic Issues

Your job as a DBA does not stop at configuring and installing databases. Working with the system administrators to modify OS kernel parameters to support those databases and monitoring them from the Oracle side of things are integral parts of your job description. You must also learn a few required commands or tools/utilities to monitor the performance of OS. This will assist you in determining whether any OS component requires tuning.

Specifically, you should know how to check memory utilization, CPU utilization, and any I/O bottlenecks. Most UNIX flavors support **sar** and **vmstat** commands. Those can be used to monitor CPU utilization, I/O rates, and memory utilization. There are other tools available on most implementations of UNIX to do the same.

On Sun Solaris you can use Adrian's Tool for performance management. This is called the SymbEL (SE) tool set. It was developed by Adrian Cockcroft of Sun Microsystems and Rich Pettit of Foglight Software. In the world of Solaris performance monitoring and tuning, Adrian Cockcroft is considered a pioneer and expert. This tool set is not a Sun Microsystems product, however. On HP, you can use GlancePlus, and on AIX you can use the System Performance Toolbox (PTX). GlancePlus is also ported to other UNIX platforms. Further, on almost all flavors of UNIX, you have the option of using **top** as well. You can use one or more of these utilities to determine the health of your system and to determine resource utilization issues.

On Windows NT, you can use the Performance Monitor to get the same information. You can refer to the chapter "The Method Behind the Madness" to learn more about these and other commands.

Tuning the OS requires some homework up front. You will need to understand what parameters are available and how they interact with one another. Adjusting these parameters will have an impact on the system as a whole, not just your Oracle database. Besides, there are many flavors of UNIX, each having its own set of peculiarities and idiosyncrasies. However, the net result is usually the same. Some of these parameters get their values based on predefined formula and/or values assigned to other related parameters. Therefore, if you adjust one parameter it can and will affect others.

Fortunately, in most situations, no changes are needed. We suggest that you verify the default values and adjust them only when required, according to the instructions in the Oracle ICG for your OS version. If these parameters are changed, some versions of UNIX will require a kernel rebuild and rebooting of the server to take effect. So be friendly with your UNIX system administrator, since you will need help from him or her to get the job done (we've found a steady supply of chocolate helps). If your OS is Windows NT, you may have fewer things to configure and modify. The following sections discuss some of the generic issues that relate to almost all OS flavors.

Configuring Adequate RAM for Your System

We begin this section assuming that you already have configured adequate amount of processing power on your system. If you are contemplating a CPU upgrade (faster CPUs), don't do that until you have read and understood "The CPU Upgrade Myth" in the paper "Performance Management: Myths & Facts" by Cary Millsap, available at http://www.hotsos.com/. The source for this paper is a book by Neil Gunther, *The Practical Performance Analyst*, published by McGraw-Hill in 1998.

Also, if you are thinking about adding more CPUs and want to do it in a manner that is more scientific than just pulling a number from thin air, you should study the paper "The Ratio Modeling Technique" by Craig Shallahammer, et al., available at http://www.orapub.com/. Needless to say, either effort should not be attempted unless the CPU is determined to be the actual bottleneck.

The total available memory on your system should be configured in such a manner that all components of the system have adequate amounts of memory and they function at optimum levels. Having said that, one of the primary prerequisites for optimally functioning systems is to have a balanced system in the first place. Before allocating memory to various system components, you should determine whether there is enough memory configured on your system. While most hardware vendors have configuration tools that create balanced systems, it is useful for you to know some of the basics of optimal memory configuration.

First of all, configuring an insufficient amount of memory on your system is analogous to buying an eight-cylinder automobile and shutting off some of the cylinders. Systems configured with multiple CPUs should have the required memory to support these CPUs. Failure to configure enough memory will result in your system "not firing on all cylinders." This is because the kernel has built-in checks and balances to keep things reasonable.

Here is a war story we want to share with you. We once dealt with a systemwide performance problem at a customer site on a system with 16 CPUs, but with just 1GB. Apparently the customer ran out of hardware budget. The problem was that CPU utilization capped out at 12.5 percent and no matter what we did, it did not budge any higher than that. With 16 CPUs and 1GB of memory, it meant that each processor had a measly 64MB of memory. So, no matter how much they increased the workload, they could not get the overall CPU utilization to exceed 12.5 percent. When you do the math, it works out to be 2 CPUs on the 16-CPU system. So for all practical reasons, a 16-CPU machine was running like a 2-CPU machine.

Recommendations from many hardware vendors and real-life tests performed in our past experience suggest the need to allocate at least 512MB of memory per CPU, if the clock speed of the processor is less than 500 MHz. For clock speeds of 500 MHz (especially in the gigahertz range), you may need to allocate at least 1GB of memory per CPU. Please check with your hardware vendor for specific recommendations and any benchmark information related to CPU and memory configuration.

A Reasonable Method to Memory Allocation

Assuming that your system has adequate memory configured, the following table illustrates a rule-of-thumb breakdown for memory allocation to various components in a system running as an Oracle database server. Consider this a good starting point.

System Component	Percent Memory Allocation
Oracle SGA components (all instances combined)	~ 50
Operating system and related components	~ 15
User memory components (all instances combined)	~ 35

The related components of the operating system may include the file system buffer cache among other structures. The user memory is the memory pool from which PGA areas for the server processes will be allocated.

Configuring the 50 Percent for Oracle

The following table outlines the rule of thumb for breakdown of the ~50 percent memory that is allocated to the Oracle SGA. These are good starting numbers. They may need adjusting according to the nature and access patterns of the application system.

Oracle SGA Component	Percent Memory Allocation
Database buffer cache	~ 80
Shared pool area	~ 12
Fixed area and miscellaneous	~ 1
Redo log buffer	~ 0.1

The following table is an example that illustrates the aforementioned guidelines. If the system is configured with 2GB of physical memory and needs to support 100 concurrent user sessions at any given time, with each user session consuming 6MB of memory, here is how it all fits together.

System Component	Allocated Memory (MB)
Oracle SGA components	~ 1024
Operating system and related components	~ 306
User memory	~ 694

In the preceding example, approximately 694MB of memory would be available for PGA of the Oracle server processes. With 100 concurrent sessions for this configuration, the average memory consumption for a given PGA cannot exceed ~7MB. Please note that SORT_AREA_SIZE would be part of this PGA, so adjust it accordingly.

The following table outlines the memory allocation for the Oracle SGA.

Oracle SGA Component	Allocated Memory (MB)
Database buffer cache	~ 800
Shared pool area	~ 128–188
Fixed size and miscellaneous	~ 8
Redo log buffer	~ 1

NOTE
The final configuration after multiple iterations of tuning efforts may look different than the guidelines. Keep in mind that these numbers are a good start and may not be the final answer. Frequent monitoring of memory usage will determine the final numbers for the components.

Tuning the File System Buffer Cache

Some operating systems allocate a somewhat large amount of memory to their file system buffer cache to hold data read from files or to be written to files. This memory allocation is usually configured by a kernel parameter. You should normally limit this allocation to 10–15 percent of the total memory. Failure to do so on some flavors of UNIX can cause significant performance degradation. This degradation can be noticed in the form of intense level of paging, process inactivation, and swapping. This is due to the fact that the default kernel parameter may allocate up to 50 percent of the total memory for the file system buffer cache.

Tuning the Swap Space on Your System

Almost all operating systems today follow the Virtual Memory model. Additional areas of disk space supplement the actual physical memory. These areas are called *swap space* or *paging space*. General belief is that this swap area should be two to four times the installed physical memory in the system. However, if your system is configured with adequate memory to begin with, and the various components have been allocated optimal amounts of memory, the need for swap space should be minimal.

In many implementations, it has been observed that with an optimum memory configuration, the amount of swap space required is usually equal to the amount of physical memory. This becomes much more relevant if the SGA is pinned or locked in the shared memory using the initialization parameters (in some cases, you may need to adjust OS kernel parameters to support this). Ideally, if all of the server- side memory components are sized properly, there should be very low levels of paging, let alone swapping. However, if your system still pages out portions of the SGA, there is a solution to avoid it. The next section discusses the technique of reducing paging by locking the SGA.

Locking the Oracle SGA in Memory

On most OS platforms, Oracle supports the LOCK_SGA or MLOCK_SGA Oracle initialization parameters or some variation of it (on Sun Solaris, it is USE_ISM or _USE_ISM). Setting it to TRUE will keep the SGA in the memory. By setting MLOCK_ SGA or LOCK_SGA, the probability that the OS will page out one or more parts of the SGA is significantly reduced. However, it should be noted here that in extreme conditions, when system memory requirements are very high and the available pool of memory is low, one or more components of a locked SGA can be swapped. Obviously, this is not a situation you want your system to get into in the first place. Check to see if this feature is available for your platform and use it only if you already have done your homework concerning the memory requirements for your system.

Tuning the UNIX Kernel

The two important UNIX kernel resources that may need tuning to support Oracle databases and all related user processes are the shared memory segments and semaphores. Oracle uses shared memory segments and semaphores for interprocess communication. As the name suggests, shared memory contains data structures that are shared by various processes. Some just want to read what is in there, while others may want to change it. In addition, there could be multiple processes wanting to access the same exact piece of information. To synchronize such concurrent processes accessing the shared area, UNIX incorporates *semaphores*. The origin of the word semaphore can be traced to the Greek words *sema*, meaning mark or sign, and *phore*, meaning carrying.

So semaphores can be thought of a method to send messages using signs or signals. These signals can be turned on or off, indicating to other processes whether a particular resource is available to them. It can also signal when a process should wait and when it should continue processing. It is analogous to a flagman in the construction zone on a road, where the traffic in either direction has to use one common lane.

The flagman controls the open lane (shared resource) and signals who should stop and who should go. Semaphores are the flagmen (or women) in the UNIX world that coordinate access to shared resources that need to be accessed in a mutually exclusive fashion. Oracle uses semaphores to provide mutually exclusive access to certain structures that it uses in its own kernel and the operating system.

Every Oracle process uses a semaphore because it accesses a shared resource— namely, the SGA. However, the implementation of this facility is operating system dependent. Some operating systems support more than one type of semaphore. However, most UNIX systems use System V semaphores. These are implemented as a kernel resource using data structures so they can reside in the kernel's memory. However, in the case of IBM's AIX the functionality of mutually exclusive access is implemented using a pseudo device driver called a post-wait driver, and the semaphore data structures are not directly controllable.

Depending on the hardware architecture, such implementation may be more scalable as it inherently reduces the amount of context switching required to implement this facility among various processes. A context switch is the method of assigning or deassigning a resource from a process. Context switches occur when processes require a resource that is held by other processes (such as waiting for I/O). If Oracle supports a post-wait driver on your OS platform, check your platform-specific documentation to determine how to configure and use it.

The following table lists the shared memory and semaphores–related kernel parameters. The values suggested by Oracle in the ICG may not always be appropriate for your environment. (Support for some Enterprise Resource Planning [ERP] applications may require higher values.) Some of these may need to be increased if you support multiple instances on the same server or if other processes use interprocess communication, shared memory segments, and semaphores.

Type	Parameter	Description
Shared memory	SHMMAX	Sets the maximum size, in bytes, of a single shared memory segment. Oracle first tries to acquire shared memory segment large enough to fit the SGA in it. If not, it acquires multiple shared memory segments to allocate components of the SGA, however, it must find a contiguous shared memory segment large enough to fit the largest shared pool.
	SHMMIN	Sets the minimum size, in bytes, of one shared memory segment. Can be ignored.
	SHMMNI	Sets the systemwide maximum for the number of shared memory segments. The default is generally acceptable.
	SHMSEG	Sets the systemwide maximum for the number of shared memory segments a process can attach to.
Semaphore	SEMMNS	Sets the systemwide limit for the maximum number of semaphores. Configure this to support the maximum number of processes that will attach to the SGA of all Oracle instances on the server. If the database needs to support 1,000 users, Oracle will need 1,000 semaphores just to support those users, not to mention the required background processes. This parameter can be configured to two times the number of processes on the system to ensure there are enough semaphores available. Oracle will obtain semaphores equal to the sum of the number of processes defined for all instances on the server, whether those many processes will ever attach to respective SGA or not.
	SEMMNI	Sets the systemwide maximum for the number of semaphore sets. UNIX allocates semaphores in sets. The number ranges from one to the value set by the SEMMSL parameter.
	SEMMSL	Sets the systemwide maximum for the number of semaphores in a semaphore set.

In addition to the these kernel parameters, there are a few other ones that affect how the OS resources are configured. You may need to review and adjust some of these. The following table lists these other parameters. Please note that the various UNIX flavors out there may use slightly different names for these parameters, but the functionality should remain the same. In some flavors of UNIX, changing one can affect the value of others, as it may use a formula to derive other parameters.

Parameter	Description
maxusers	Maximum number of user sessions at the OS level. It will affect other parameters, such as *nproc*, *nfile*, and *maxuprc*. If the default value is not appropriate, you may have to increase the value of this parameter. Even if users do not log on to the server at UNIX level, you may need to increase this parameter to increase the value of other parameters.
nproc	Systemwide maximum for the number of processes that can be supported by the kernel. These include the user processes and Oracle background processes. If this number is reached no new processes can be launched. This parameter should be set higher than the SEMMNS kernel parameter.
nfile	Systemwide maximum for the number of open files that can be supported by the kernel. This sets the upper limit to the number of files that are open at the same time. Internally it sets the number of slots in the file descriptor table. You can be generous in setting this to a high value, as the memory required is very minimal.
maxuprc	Maximum number of processes per user. This sets the upper limit to the number of processes a single user can initiate. In most cases, all Oracle-related processes, background processes, and shadow processes are initiated by user *oracle*. If you have a number of instances with quite a few dedicated user processes, you may need to adjust the value of this parameter.

Now that we have dealt with some generic UNIX issues, we will now discuss some OS-specific tuning. Folks, this will be getting into some detailed and serious tuning efforts. You will learn some neat tricks to impress your system administrators and fellow DBAs. We will share with you the OS tuning efforts of those systems we have worked with. We will discuss tuning as it applies to Sun Solaris, IBM AIX, HP-UX, and Windows NT operating systems. Some of the concepts and ideas presented here will apply to other operating systems as well. Their implementation will differ, that's all. So, if you are ready, let us begin.

Tuning Solaris

Sun Solaris is probably the most commonly used operating system for servers on the Internet. At the time of writing, Oracle uses it to develop its database software. Among all the operating systems we've worked on, we like Solaris for its ease of use, its rich command set, and available tools. Generally all new releases of Oracle software become available first on the Sun Solaris platform. Newly found bugs and glitches require patches, and they are incorporated on Solaris first (if applicable). Other operating systems usually get the patched-up version of the Oracle software, which is then ported and generally tends to report fewer problems because the main problems have already been fixed.

On Solaris you should get familiar with the commands **vmstat**, **sar**, **iostat**, **swap**, and **mpstat**. Acquaint yourself with their respective switches and the output they produce by reading the manual pages. The chapter "The Method Behind the Madness" discusses **vmstat** and **sar** in the section "Identity the Current OS Bottlenecks." The command **swap** will report the current paging activity, and **mpstat** will report per-processor statistics. These commands can help you monitor your system performance and identify OS tuning opportunities. We would like to mention one additional command, **truss**, to trace system calls (internal commands of the OS for a user command). This is a very powerful command to resolve what the OS does when servicing user-requested commands or operations, such as an I/O request or any of these commands. We mention this command because it is currently not available with other operating systems in the same easy-to-use format. Comparable commands may exist, but as a non-root user, you will be limited to what you can see. As a DBA, you may need to use this command to figure out a few operations that do not have an easy explanation for their behavior. In addition, the command **sysdef** will show you the current values of all the kernel parameters, and **dmesg** will allow you to view some of the hardware characteristics, such as number of CPUs, clock speed, amount of memory configured, and so on. The following sections elaborate some of the core configuration and tuning avenues on Solaris.

Asynchronous I/O

Asynchronous I/O, as the name suggests, is the method to perform I/O in an "unblocked fashion," so that processes are not waiting for the I/O to complete (especially relevant for writes). The OS, eventually returns to the application (in our case, Oracle) an "I/O complete" status or flag on successful completion of, say, a write operation. The advantage here is that Oracle does not have to wait for the write to complete on the storage device.

On Solaris, asynchronous I/O is implemented in two ways: using user libraries (a thread-based approach) or within the kernel. This is true from Solaris 2.3 and above. On Solaris 2.4 and above, support for the kernel asynchronous I/O (KAIO) directly in the kernel was made available. It should be noted here that KAIO on Solaris is supported only for raw devices and for Veritas Quick I/O files. KAIO is not supported for normal file systems. However, asynchronous I/O using user libraries (threads) is supported for file systems. Asynchronous I/O can be enabled by setting the DISK_ASYNCH_IO Oracle initialization parameter to the value of TRUE. It is normal practice to use either asynchronous I/O or multiple database writers, implying that the number of database writer processes should normally be set to 1 while using asynchronous I/O.

NOTE

You will notice KAIO errors when using asynchronous I/O on normal file systems, and it might seem as though asynchronous I/O calls are failing. But behind the scenes, the API for the user libraries will allocate and use a pool of threads to perform the I/O in an asynchronous fashion anyway. A failed KAIO call signals a condition variable which is checked by one of the threads, which then executes the I/O system call to perform asynchronous I/O. This at best may be termed a "mock asynchronous I/O" for normal file systems. According to sources at Sun Microsystems, this is a feature, not a bug, as it potentially eliminates a system call when the device does support KAIO. However, we still believe that the implementation has room for improvement.

Locking the SGA in Memory

It sounds kind of cute, but intimate sharable memory (ISM) is one of the most effective techniques that Solaris uses to optimize the effectiveness and usage of shared memory segments. This technique allows for sharing the page table on the system by multiple processes, thus creating an intimate shared memory environment. One of the effects of ISM is that it effectively locks the shared memory pages in the physical memory to prevent them from paging out. However, it is a somewhat more involved process than just locking SGA in memory. Although it is not necessary to go into the details behind ISM, it is useful to note here that locking the Oracle SGA in memory can achieve performance gains on heavily loaded systems. The paging algorithm is indirectly slowed down by ISM because fewer pages need to be managed on a regular basis, making the paging daemon (algorithm) less active.

Sun introduced the ISM technique in Solaris version 2.2. However, until recently there had been some problems with it on certain Sun servers and their configuration. If you are using Sun Enterprise 10000 (E1000) server running Solaris version 2.6, there could still be some issues with ISM. So please make sure there are no known issues with your Sun server and the use of ISM for your environment. You need to start making it a habit of checking Oracle Metalink before you implement anything of significance on your production databases.

For Oracle versions 8.0.x and lower, the initialization parameter USE_ISM is set to TRUE by default, and thus ISM is turned on without you having to do anything. It is a hidden parameter (_USE_ISM) from Oracle version 8.1.3. Nonetheless, its value still defaults to TRUE. Unless there is a problem in using ISM, do not change this parameter. ISM is enabled by default in Solaris. If you need to disable ISM (for any special reason) you will have to add the following lines to your /etc/system file and reboot the server:

```
shmsys:ism_off=1
shsmsys:share_page_table=1
```

If there are no such lines in your /etc/system file, ISM is available and Oracle will use it. However, if Oracle does not find a shared memory segment large enough to accommodate the entire SGA, it will not use ISM. No errors or warnings are issued with respect to this.

NOTE
Keep in mind when using ISM IS that the entire SGA should be in one shared memory segment. If that is not the case, the OS will use non-ISM routines to manage the pages in the SGA and thus potentially increase the level of paging on your system, as the pages of the SGA are not locked in memory. Although on the surface this note seems to negate the myth for this chapter, this is a Solaris-specific requirement and does not apply for other flavors of UNIX.

Tuning the Paging Daemon

Prior to Solaris 2.8, the *priority paging algorithm* should always be enabled to achieve optimal performance for the system's virtual memory management. This is because the default paging daemon does not support the complex needs of today's systems and has the tendency of being overactive. Secondly, an improperly configured paging daemon or a paging daemon that is not an optimal fit to your environment can cause unnecessary paging on your system, leading to performance degradation. The priority paging algorithm (which is disabled by default) can be enabled by setting the following kernel parameters:

```
set fastscan=131072
set maxpgio=65536
set priority_paging=1
```

These settings are especially tailored for heavy-duty OLTP systems like the common ERP systems, such as SAP, Baan, PeopleSoft, Oracle Applications, and so on. For more information, please refer to various articles on this topic at SunWorld Online and the Sun Blueprints repository. It is also useful to note here that this priority paging algorithm has a new and improved successor in Solaris 2.8. The discussion of the details of that paging is beyond the scope of this book, and we refer you to a wealth of online information on Sun's Web site (http://www.sun.com/).

The following table lists some of the useful commands on Sun Solaris. You can use the man pages to obtain detail information for these commands.

Command Name	Fully Qualified Name	Description
dmesg	/usr/sbin/dmesg	Although this command lists messages, it can be used to check number of CPUs, memory, and other hardware information.
prtconf	/usr/sbin/prtconf	Lists system configuration in detail.
prtdiag	/Usr/platform/ <platform_name>/ sbin/prtdiag	Displays system diagnostic information. The platform_name is the hardware implementation name, found using the **uname -i** command.
psrinfo	/usr/sbin/psrinfo	Displays information about the processors.
mpstat	/bin/mpstat	Displays per-processor statistics in a tabular form.
sysdef	/usr/sbin/sysdef	Displays current system definition, listing all the devices and kernel tunable parameters.
swap	/usr/sbin/swap	With the **-l** option, this command will list the status of all the swap areas.

Tuning AIX

This is a unique flavor of UNIX invented by IBM. No kernel building and rebooting are required in most cases when you change some of the OS-related parameters. This is a dynamic kernel. There are no shared memory segments and semaphores to worry about. It is all internally configured and managed. The maximum value for shared memory segment (SHMMAX) is fixed. There were problems with some versions of AIX that limited SGA sizes to less than 2GB. However, Oracle provided software patches to correct the problem. Contact Oracle Support to make sure that your version of Oracle on your version of AIX allows larger sizes for SGA.

Oracle uses its own post-wait drivers and eliminates the need to configure semaphore-related parameters or to be concerned with their hard-coded limits.

So, what is there to tune? Read on.

Asynchronous I/O

AIX supports asynchronous I/O for raw devices as well as for journalized file systems. Unfortunately, not many installations are aware of this or use this impressive solution for performance gains.

For using this feature with Oracle 7.3.x, set initialization parameter USE_ASYNCH_IO to TRUE and DB_WRITERS to 1. You should usually not set multiple DB_WRITERS when using asynchronous I/O; just set it to 1.

For Oracle8 and up, the initialization parameter has been renamed to DISK_ASYNCH_IO and it will default to TRUE. Set DB_WRITER_PROCESSES to 1 and do not use DBWR_IO_SLAVES.

AIX handles asynchronous I/O requests via a separate process called the *aioserver*. It is a kernel process with the name *kproc*. One process can service just one request at a time. However, the number of such aioservers is configurable. The minimum number of aioservers configured when the asynchronous I/O is enabled is *one*. This can be changed using the *minservers* parameter in the asynchronous I/O configuration. There is also a maximum number for the aioservers that is configured using *maxservers* parameter. It defaults to 10. On system startup, a *minservers*' *worth* of aioservers will be initiated. As the number of asynchronous I/O requests increase, more aioservers will be activated, up to the number limited by *maxservers*. However, these aioservers will not be terminated when the demand drops. The *minservers* and *maxservers* parameters can be set using the **smit** command (smitty aio) or using the **chdev** command as follows:

```
# chdev -l aio0 -a maxservers = '20'
```

You can use the **pstat** command to see how many aioservers were used since the last reboot, as shown here:

```
# pstat -a | grep aios | wc -l
```

You can also use the **ps -k** command to see the aioserver as a kernel process kproc. But it will also show other kernel processes, if any. You need to have root privileges to run the **chdev** and **pstat** commands.

IBM recommends using ten aioservers per independent storage device that will be accessed simultaneously in an asynchronous fashion. However, the maximum value for this should not exceed ten times the number of processors in the machine. Set *minservers* to *maxservers*/2. You can then monitor how many additional aioservers are initiated and decide if any adjusting needs to be done.

For example, if you have a server with 20 *independent* storage devices accessed asynchronously, set *maxservers* to 200 and *minservers* to 100. However, if you had only four CPUs, setting *maxservers* to 40 and *minservers* to 20 would be sufficient. Using higher numbers for *minservers* and *maxservers* will not adversely affect performance. They will just add more processes to the system and not get used.

You can use the **lsattr -E -l aio0** command to view the configuration of aioservers. Here is an example of the output from this command:

```
oracle ibmrs601 [DBPR]: lsattr -E -l aio0
minservers  25         MINIMUM number of servers                    True
maxservers  100        MAXIMUM number of servers                    True
maxreqs     4096       Maximum number of REQUESTS                    True
kprocprio   39         Server PRIORITY                               True
autoconfig  available  STATE to be configured at system restart True
fastpath    enable     State of fast path                           True
oracle ibmrs601 [DBPR]:
```

The *maxreqs* parameter limits the number of concurrent asynchronous I/O requests. The value displayed is the default. IBM recommends to at least double this value when using asynchronous I/O with Oracle8i and JFS file systems. The *kprocprio* parameter sets the default priority for the kernel processes for asynchronous I/O. If the volume of asynchronous I/O requests is high, you may increase the priority for these processes.

At the time of writing this chapter, AIX did not provide any facility to gauge the volume of such asynchronous I/O requests. However, IBM Support can supply you with an unsupported command program, **aiostat**, that can show you the number of such asynchronous I/O requests. This command, when run with a sampling interval in seconds (just like **iostat**), will keep displaying the request count until you terminate it. The following is an output from **aiostat** when we monitored the asynchronous I/O requests for deleting rows from a table. The samples were taken every second.

```
# aiostat 1
AIO requestcount: 0
AIO requestcount: 0
AIO requestcount: 22
AIO requestcount: 61
AIO requestcount: 52
AIO requestcount: 80
AIO requestcount: 64
AIO requestcount: 5
AIO requestcount: 0
```

If you are using or planning to use asynchronous I/O on AIX, we recommend that you acquire **aiostat** from IBM Support. It is a helpful tool to monitor asynchronous I/O on your system. However, you will need root privileges to run it. We have already mentioned several times that you need to work closely with your system administrator when it comes to OS tuning and monitoring. Now you know why!

Using asynchronous I/O will boost performance if configured optimally. Given that the risk associated with this is very low, you can use it for your databases running on AIX. You will be glad you did!

Locking the SGA in Memory

In AIX version 4.3.3 and up, pages in shared memory can be pinned by the Virtual Memory Manager (VMM). To support that, the *v_pinshm* parameter must be set to 1, and applications must request shared memory segments with a "pin" flag turned on. From Oracle 8.1.5, specifying LOCK_SGA = TRUE in the init.ora file will turn on the "pin" flag while acquiring shared memory segments for the SGA. Locking SGA in shared memory will cause the paging algorithm to ignore the SGA during its normal paging process. This will help improve performance of the database as well as reduce overhead at the system level to manage paging. However, it will reduce available memory for other processes. It is likely that performance of those processes will suffer if they need more memory than what is available in the free pool.

To set the *v_pinshm* parameter, use the following command:

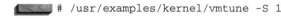

```
# /usr/examples/kernel/vmtune -S 1
```

You will need to run the preceding command during the machine startup process and before starting the database, since values set by **vmtune** get reset during a reboot.

NOTE
*AIX versions 4.3.2 and below do not support the v_pinshm (-S) option with the **vmtune** command, so locking SGA in physical memory is not available.*

Tuning the Paging Daemon

Paging is the process of recycling through the least recently used end of the list of memory pages to facilitate optimal use of those memory pages. Excessive paging is usually an indication of memory starvation on a system and is normally caused by tuning efforts that *over-allocate* memory to various components of Oracle. On a database server, excessive paging or swapping is bad news. Performance degrades significantly when there is excessive paging. When the paging increases to alarming levels, AIX may even begin swapping as well. You can use the AIX command **lsps** to list current paging information. The following is an example showing this command with two options: **-s** to get a summarized output; and **-a** to list detail information about paging space, allocated and used space, and so on.

```
oracle ibmrs601 [DBPR]: lsps -s
Total Paging Space    Percent Used
    3024MB                 1%


oracle ibmrs601 [DBPR]: lsps -a
Page Space  Physical Volume   Volume Group   Size   %Used  Active  Auto  Type
paging00    hdisk35           mdsvg          1000MB    1     yes    yes   lv
paging02    hdisk3            oemvg          1000MB    1     yes    yes   lv
hd6         hdisk48           rootvg         1024MB    1     yes    yes   lv
```

AIX uses real memory to save file pages that were recently read or written to. If requests are made for those pages before the pages are reassigned, it minimizes physical I/O required to fetch that information from disk. The real memory also has computational pages (program text, buffers, or processes). AIX uses an internal algorithm to determine which type of pages to page out. It is controlled by two parameters, *minperm* and *maxperm*. The supplied utility **vmtune** can limit the amount of real memory AIX uses for file pages by manipulating *minperm* (**-p**) and *maxperm* (**-P**). The *maxperm* default value is 80 percent, and the *minperm* default value is 20 percent of real memory.

Oracle keeps the data in its buffer cache in the SGA once it is read from the data file. There is no need to rely on the file pages (or cache) for this data for subsequent access, thus, reducing the amount of memory used for the file cache. The following example shows the use of the **vmtune** command to change *minperm* (**-p**) and *maxperm* (**-P**):

```
# /usr/examples/kernel/vmtune -p 15 -P 50
```

This will affect the paging algorithm and reduce paging. It is safe to reduce *maxperm* value for most AIX systems running Oracle database servers. One more thing to remember: changes to the values of these parameters using **vmtune** remain in effect until the next machine reboot. Following the reboot, the parameters will assume their default values until changed again. For this reason, it is advisable to include the preceding command in the scripts that run at reboot time. It can be made part of the /etc/inittab file.

The **vmtune** utility is installed in the directory /usr/examples/kernel. It is a licensed program product.

Running the **vmtune** command without any options shows the following display:

```
# /usr/examples/kernel/vmtune
vmtune:   current values:
   -p        -P        -r         -R         -f       -F       -N
minperm   maxperm  minpgahead maxpgahead minfree maxfree pd_npages
 183293    458746       2          8         120      128     524288

   -W         -M        -w        -k        -c        -b        -B
maxrandwrt maxpin  npswarn   npskill   numclust numfsbufs hd_pbuf_cnt
    0        733995   24192     6048        1        93         993

   -u          -l        -d         -s                  -n
lvm_bufcnt lrubucket defps  -hsync_release_ilock nokilluid
    9        131072      1          0                   0

   -S         -L         -g          -
v_pinshm lgpg_regions lgpg_size strict_maxperm
    0          0           0           0
number of valid memory pages = 917493   maxperm=50.0% of real memory
maximum pinable=80.0% of real memory   minperm=20.0% of real memory
number of file memory pages = 700018   numperm=76.3% of real memory
```

In this example (the output is formatted), the *minperm* and *maxperm* are set to 20 and 50 percent, respectively. Other lines show the various options, parameter names, and their values. Please refer to the **man** pages of AIX for this. Note the option **-S** with *v_pinshm* as the parameter name with value 0. Can you guess what this does for you? We'll discuss it in the next section.

The next table lists some of the useful commands on AIX. You can use the **man** pages to obtain detail information for these commands, as most of these need various options or flags to run.

Command Name	Fully Qualified Name	Description
chdev	/usr/sbin/chdev	Changes device characteristics. Needs root privileges to run it.
lsattr	/usr/sbin/lsattr	Displays information about the attributes of a given device or a type of device.
lsdev	/usr/sbin/lsdev	Displays information about the devices.
lsps	/usr/sbin/lsps	Displays information about the paging spaces.
lslpp	/bin/lslpp	Displays information about installed software and patches.
pstat	/usr/sbin/pstat	Displays information from various system tables. With the **-a** flag, it shows information from the processes table. Useful to list kernel processes such as the asynchronous I/O servers. Needs root privileges to run.
vmtune	/usr/samples/kern el/vmtune	Modifies VMM parameters to control the behavior of the memory-management subsystem. Needs root privileges to run.

Tuning HP-UX

On HP-UX, there are more kernel parameters to tune than on other operating systems. In almost all cases, kernel rebuilding and rebooting of the server is required. Further, some patches are required for the OS to conform to the requirements of Oracle. We would like to mention that, as a DBA for databases running under HP-UX, you should be aware of the OS patches that your SA installs. It is your responsibility to keep a close tab on which patches get installed and whether they violate any requirements of the version of Oracle on your system. Sometimes these patches may need additional patchwork to keep Oracle running without any problems. We have experienced this on a few occasions, so be cognizant of all patches applied to the OS. You will be the one called upon when things fail, even if the database is not at fault.

On HP-UX, you will need to check and tune the kernel parameters for shared memory and semaphores. To make changes to kernel parameters, the HP-provided menu-driven tool could be used. It is called **sam** (System Administration Manager). You need root privileges to use **sam**. If you are not the SA (in addition to being a DBA, that is), it is best to let the SA deal with this. However, you can use other OS commands to check values for all kernel parameters without root access to make sure you are getting the kernel configured the way you want. The command **sysdef** displays all relevant system information. You can redirect the output to a file and then search for an interested kernel parameter to check its value.

On version 11.0, you can use a niftier command, **kmtune** (does not require root **privilege** to query and list kernel parameters). You may have to specify the full path, **/usr/sbin/kmtune**, if /usr/sbin is not in your PATH environment variable. It can also be used to modify values of kernel parameters (as root), so use the necessary caution. With the **kmtune** command you can list the value for a particular kernel parameter rather than listing all of them as **sysdef** does, so it can come in very handy. You may want to read the manual pages for these commands for more information. The following example shows how to query the value for *semmns* in a short form and in long form using the **kmtune** command. The **-q** option is to query and the **-l** option is for the long listing. We like the long format, as it displays the default, current, and minimum values for the kernel parameter.

```
prodhp[oracle]% /usr/sbin/kmtune -q semmns
Parameter          Value
==================================================================
semmns             2048
prodhp[oracle]% /usr/sbin/kmtune -l -q semmns
Parameter:    semmns
Value:        2048
Default:      128
Minimum:      -
Module:       -
```

There are a few very specific kernel parameters to tune to improve performance of the HP-UX system. We will discuss those in the following sections.

Asynchronous I/O

HP-UX supports asynchronous I/O only with raw devices. If you are using raw devices for your database files, you may want to consider using asynchronous I/O. You will have to configure the asynchronous I/O driver into the kernel of HP-UX operating system using the **sam** utility.

The Oracle8i Administrator's Reference Guide for HP-UX lists all the steps that you can follow to implement asynchronous I/O for HP-UX systems. Please refer to this guide for further details.

Locking the SGA in Memory

HP-UX supports locking or pinning shared memory segments in the physical memory. A process requests such locking via a shared memory control operation with a specific option. A special privilege, MLOCK, must be granted to the *group* of the owner of the process requesting such operation. For Oracle, the database startup process, (usually owned by user *oracle* with group *dba)* would request such an operation. To achieve this, you need to add an entry to the file /etc/privgroup:

```
dba MLOCK
```

If the file /etc/privgroup does not exist, you will need to create it. Next, execute the command **setprivgrp -f /etc/privgroup** to grant listed privileges to the groups in the /etc/privgroup file. These privileges are reassigned to the listed groups during the boot process. The OS runs a script, /sbin/init.d/set_priv, during its startup process. This script executes the same command. All you need to do now is to set the initialization parameter LOCK_SGA to TRUE, which should complete the setup for using this feature. Upon restarting the database, the SGA will be locked in memory and will not be considered by the paging daemon for normal paging operations.

However, while this technique improves performance of your database, it will limit the available memory to other processes. So it is your responsibility to ensure that performance of other processes is not affected. You should do your homework by asking questions such as how much memory is configured on the system, how much is allocated for Oracle, how much is needed for the user processes, and so on.

Tuning the File System Buffer Cache

On HP-UX 10.x and above, the OS can and will use up to 50 percent of the real memory for its file system buffer cache (default setting). This cache holds blocks of data while it is transferred from disk to memory and from memory to disk. In the older versions of HP-UX (9.x and 10.x) the kernel parameter *bufpages* specified how many 4096-byte memory pages were allocated for the file system buffer cache. This set the upper limit for that cache. It was a static cache.

However, in HP-UX 10.x, it was recommended by Hewlett-Packard to set *bufpages* to 0, thus enabling a dynamic buffer cache. The dynamic nature allowed HP-UX to acquire up to 50 percent of the memory for the buffer cache. Two new kernel parameters, *dbc_max_pct* and *dbc_min_pct*, control the amount of real memory allocated to the buffer cache. *dbc_max_pct* sets the upper limit to which the buffer cache is allowed to grow. It defaults to 50 percent of the real memory. *dbc_min_pct* defaults to 5 percent of the real memory.

When the system load (in this case, demand for block I/O) reaches high levels, the OS will blissfully continue to increase the file system buffer cache to the maximum size allowed by *dbc_max_pct*. However (in theory), when there is demand for process space memory, the OS is supposed to shrink the buffer cache and allocate buffer cache memory pages to the process memory.

But if the demand for block I/O stays high, it will try to do the opposite, deallocating memory pages from process memory to allocate to buffer cache. This will create performance problems and it will most likely be reported as *page outs* (po) by the **vmstat** command and as %sys by the **sar** command as the activity on the system increases. If the memory requirements on the system further increase, the OS will start what is called "process deactivation," which in OS layperson terms means swapping. Intensive paging and/or swapping can and will add more overhead on your system, and overall system performance will degrade.

To solve this problem, you should consider tuning the file system buffer cache to a lower value. The idea is to have a value for *dbc_max_pct* low enough to have some buffer cache, leaving enough for process memory. We suggest you start with a value of 15 for *dbc_max_pct* and a value of 2 for *dbc_min_pct*. Oracle recommends adjusting *dbc_max_pct* to have less than or equal to 128MB for the buffer cache. After changing these parameters to the suggested values, it is prudent to monitor the system for paging and I/O bottlenecks and tune these parameters as required. Realize that if your Oracle database is supported by raw devices or is configured to use direct I/O, you should make all effort to shrink down your file system buffer cache, as it is no longer used by Oracle.

If you use the HP OnlineJFS product for your journalized file systems (VxFS), you can avoid the use of the file system buffer cache. You can use the option *mincache=direct* while mounting a particular file system. Data that is read from or written to journalized file systems will bypass the file system buffer cache. Also investigate the use of the *convosync* mount option in conjuction with *mincache*. So get friendly with your system administrator and experiment with your test databases first to find out what works for you. Remember, we said experiment with your test databases first!

Tuning Process Management

HP-UX allocates each process a certain amount of process space in the memory called virtual address space. Each address space is further divided into four segments: text, data, stack, and shared memory. The test segment contains the instructions for the process. The size of this segment is configurable by the kernel parameter maxtsiz. The data segment contains the process's data, data structures, the heap, user stack, and so on. The process can dynamically grow its heap size. The kernel parameter *maxdsiz* controls the amount of heap size per process. The stack segment is used for local variables, among others. The stack space is controlled by the kernel parameter *maxssiz.*

NOTE
That the kernel parameter names we are using in this section refer to a 32-bit processor. For a 64-bit processor, the parameter names are maxtsiz_64bit, maxdsiz_64bit, *and* maxssiz_64bit. *Use appropriate parameter names when configuring the kernel. In addition, the default and maximum values of these parameters for a 32-bit processor and 64-bit processor will differ. Refer to the HP-UX documentation for additional information.*

The default value for the data segment size, *maxdsiz*, is 64MB, which can be too small for many applications. If a process exceeds *maxdsiz*, it will terminate with a memory fault error producing a core dump. HP and Oracle recommend that *maxdsiz* should be set to its maximum value of 1.9GB.

The default value for the stack segment, *maxssiz*, is 8MB. HP recommends that this value be set to 79MB.

The default value for the text segment, *maxtsiz*, is 4MB. HP recommends that this value be set to 1024MB.

The following table lists some of the useful commands on HP-UX 11.0. You can use the **man** pages to obtain detail information for these commands.

Command Name	Fully Qualified Name	Description
getprivgrp	/usr/bin/getprivgrp	Lists the special attributes set for groups using the **setprivgrp** command.
glance	/opt/perf/bin/glance	Starts GlancePlus, the online performance monitor. The path name can change depending on your installation. It is a licensed product. Motif version of the performance monitor can be started with the **gpm** command.
kmtune	/usr/sbin/kmtune	With no options or flags, displays all system parameters including tunable kernel parameters.
setprivgrp	/usr/bin/setprivgrp	Sets special attributes for groups, such as MLOCK, to enable the dba group to lock SGA in the memory.
swapinfo	/usr/sbin/swapinfo	Displays information about file system paging space. Needs root privileges to run.
sysdef	/usr/sbin/sysdef	Displays system definition, including tunable kernel parameters.
top	/usr/bin/top	Displays and updates in real time, information about the top processes in the system. Uses the raw CPU percentage to rank the processes.

That concludes our trip in the UNIX world. Windows NT, here we come.

Tuning Windows NT

The Oracle architecture on Windows NT differs from the one on UNIX. On UNIX, you can see all the individual background processes related to an Oracle instance with its own process ID number. All these processes attach to the shared memory where the SGA resides. Each process is responsible for its own assigned task. The Windows NT architecture provides multithreading capability to a single process to perform many different tasks essentially at the same time. This thread-based architecture allows Oracle to run as a single executable program, while each background process runs as a *thread* within the single Oracle executable. All new user connections create a new thread within the single Oracle process. All the threads share the same code, memory space, and other data structures. This makes Oracle implementation rather simple. It also has a low overhead in managing the SGA, as there are no shared memory segments to acquire or release. In addition, it is faster to create threads for user connections than creating dedicated processes for them.

However, there are some drawbacks to this approach. The problem is that it is somewhat difficult to identify each thread that is running in the Oracle process. Thus, it is not very easy to identify a process to cancel it or find out what OS resource it is using. Secondly, since all the threads use the same memory space, available free memory can become an issue. This is particularly true during sort operations.

Tuning Windows NT involves making more resources available to applications by removing unused components and not running any unnecessary programs on the database server. Generally, a Windows NT server that is used as an Oracle database server should not act as a file or a print server, a router, a remote access server (RAS), or a domain name server/controller. These services take up resources such as network bandwidth, memory, and CPU, which can be better utilized for database activities. The following sections illustrate the tuning opportunities for Oracle running on Windows NT.

Increasing Windows NT's Usable Memory

Windows NT is a 32-bit operating system and so the maximum addressable memory in this environment is 4GB. Earlier versions of Windows NT (before Windows NT 4.0) reserved 2GB of memory for its own use and allowed only 2GB for applications. Windows NT 4.0 Enterprise Edition has a feature called 4GB RAM Tuning (4GT). This feature makes it possible for applications to use up to 3GB of memory space. This increase in available memory space will allow larger SGA sizes or more connections to the database. To enable this feature, you will have to add the "/3GB" switch to the operating system startup line in the boot.ini file. However, this procedure is available only for Windows NT running on Intel processors. shown next is an example of how to do this.

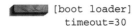

```
[boot loader]
   timeout=30
   default=multi(0)disk(0)rdisk(0)partition(2)\WINNT
   [operating systems] multi(0)disk(0)rdisk(0)partition(2)\WINNT="Windows NT
Server Version 4.00"/3GB
   multi(0)disk(0)rdisk(0)partition(2)\WINNT="Windows NT Server Version 4.00
[VGA mode]" /basevideo /sos
```

Reducing the Priority of Foreground Applications

The Oracle process on Windows NT runs as a *service*, not as a *program*. This allows Oracle databases to start upon machine reboot without any user intervention. All Windows NT services are background processes. By default, the Windows NT server provides more boost or higher priority to foreground processes. Since the Oracle process is not a foreground process, you should change the default setting to provide more boost to background processes. Here are the steps to achieve this:

1. Double-click the System icon from Control Panel under the Settings menu.

2. Click the Performance tab.

3. In the Application Performance box, move the slider to None.

4. Click OK.

5. Close Control Panel.

Removing Unused Network Protocols and Resetting the Bind Order

Windows NT supports more than one type of network protocol, and it is definitely possible that there is more than one installed on your system. Oracle normally uses TCP/IP on Windows NT. If other protocols are installed and are not used by the Windows NT server, there is no need to keep them. You can safely remove them to save processing time for required protocols. The steps to remove unused network protocols are as follows:

1. Select Settings | Control Panel.

2. Double-click the Network icon.

3. Click the Protocols tab.

4. Click the first unused protocol in the Network Protocol display window.

5. Click Remove.

6. Click Yes to confirm your action.

7. Repeat steps 3 through 5 for each unused network protocol.

8. Click OK to exit.

9. Close Control Panel.

If you do need to have more than one protocol, you can adjust the bind order so that the protocol used by Oracle is given highest priority. If the server is configured with multiple network interface cards, make sure the one used for Oracle processes is at the top of the list for each protocol. Here are the steps to do this:

1. Select Settings | Control Panel.

2. Double-click the Network icon.

3. Click the Bindings tab.

4. Select all services from the Show Bindings For window.

5. Double-click the Server to list current protocols.

6. Click the protocol used by Oracle if it is not at the top of the list already.

7. Click the Move Up button until the selected protocol is at the top of the list.

8. Double click on the protocol to expand it.

9. Move the network card that is used mostly by Oracle to the top of the list for each of the protocols.

10. Click OK to exit.

11. Close Control Panel.

Configuring Windows NT as a Database Server

By default, the Windows NT server is set up to act as a file and print server. Therefore, the file cache is allocated more memory as compared to the system kernel and other services. However, when you want to use this server as a database server with an Oracle database running on it, there is really no need to have such a large file cache, as Oracle caches its data in the SGA. You can reduce the file cache and make more memory available to the Oracle database process. Follow these steps to change the default behavior of the Windows NT server:

1. Select Settings | Control Panel.

2. Double-click the Network icon.

3. Click the Services tab.

4. Double-click on Server in the Network Services window.

5. Select Maximize Throughput For Network Applications in the Server dialog box.

6. Click OK in the Server dialog box.

7. Click OK in the Network dialog box.

8. Close Control Panel.

9. Reboot the server.

Configuring "No Windows Dressing"

Say what? Refrain yourself from setting up fancy graphics-laden wallpapers and nifty-looking screensavers. There is no need for these eye-catching distractions for a database server terminal. These things can consume a significant amount of memory and CPU resources. If a screensaver is a requirement, choose a blank screen. Otherwise, you can either lock the workstation or turn off the terminal when it is not needed. Saved resources can be used by various components of your Oracle database.

What Is Startup Starting?

You may also want to check the startup folder, as it may contain foreground applications that are not required to operate the server as a database server. We suggest you remove all such applications from this folder. The memory these applications use can be made available to the Oracle database to improve its performance.

Tuning Virtual Memory and the Paging File

Windows NT uses virtual memory just like many other operating systems. The management of virtual memory is done using equal-sized memory pages. The paged-out data is written to a file called pagefile.sys. It usually resides on the system partition, typically the infamous C drive. To avoid I/O contention, do not use this disk drive to store any database files. Also make sure you have an adequate amount of paging space allocated to the page file. In general, keep the size to at least the amount of RAM you have configured for your system. Follow these steps to review the default values for the page file size and to make changes to the minimum and maximum size:

1. Select Settings | Control Panel.

2. Double-click the System icon.

3. Click the Performance tab.

4. In the Virtual Memory dialog box, click Change.

5. In the Virtual Memory dialog box, change the Initial Size and Maximum Size under the Paging File Size for Selected Drive area (you can go ahead and set both values to be the same).

6. Click Set.

7. Click OK to close the Virtual Memory dialog box.

8. Click OK to close the System Properties dialog box.

9. Close Control Panel.

Microsoft Corporation periodically releases service packs that contain patches to known bugs and some product enhancements. In the past, applying the service packs to the database server was not always a positive experience for many DBAs and Windows NT administrators. Please check with Oracle Support to make sure the new service pack is certified for your hardware platform and works with your version of Oracle. If it is approved and certified, applying it may help improve your server's performance and may provide some new functions that can be of some help to you.

In a Nutshell

Instead of concentrating on tuning OS to accommodate the entire SGA in the shared memory— with a couple of exceptions, as noted at the beginning of this chapter—we feel you should pay more attention to other areas. These include activities such as making sure your system has adequate memory for the number of CPUs, the databases do not consume inordinate amount of available physical memory to cause paging and swapping, the kernel parameters for the OS are set at proper values, and so on. Addressing these areas in an effective manner will bring about the performance improvement you are looking for. You will need to understand what features Oracle supports on your OS platforms. It is your job to test those and make sure they work as advertised. You should know how to use certain OS commands and available tools to monitor CPU, memory utilization, and I/O throughput.

On UNIX, you need to know how Oracle uses shared memory and semaphores to manage interprocess communications and all the related kernel parameters. Implementation of these resources is OS specific. In addition, there are very specific areas with various operating systems that you can explore to improve the performance of your database. Some support asynchronous I/O with file systems, while others make it easy to lock the entire SGA in the memory. Some allow you to control the paging algorithm, while others allow you to modify process management. On Windows NT, there are a number of areas to address to improve the performance of not only the database, but also of the Windows NT server as such. The more you know about the OS and how Oracle uses its resources, there is no doubt in our minds that you will be the most popular DBA around when it comes to performance tuning at OS level! Oh, one more thing: if you haven't already done so, please sign up for one or more beginner system administrator classes on your OS platform where you run Oracle so that you get more in-depth knowledge about your OS. In the long run, it will make you a better DBA. Trust us, we have done exactly that.

CHAPTER
13

Wrapping It Up

Oracle Performance Management: A Summary

There is an old adage that reminds people that "All good things come to an end." The same holds for this book. Now that we have invested a significant portion of the last six months of our lives writing about Oracle Performance Management and its related components, it is time to bring the curtain down, wrap things up, and move on to other pursuits. Life is an endless journey of new challenges, and it continues to be fun when you learn from each challenge and grow with experience. Writing this book sure was a great experience for us in many aspects.

Any good presentation is required to have three components: an introduction, the text, and a summary. The introduction is supposed to introduce you to the topic (tell you what we will talk about), the text is supposed to provide you with all relevant details (talk about the things that we intended to), and the summary is supposed to capture the gist of everything that was said in the text (tell you what we just told you). To keep literary tradition and the norm intact, we are conforming to the same. So here we go, on the last lap of this great experience, summarizing every chapter.

What Is Oracle Performance Management?

Oracle Performance Management is a step-by-step process of iteratively investigating, determining, and implementing tuning solutions using a proven methodology. While tuning a system, it is important to know when to tune, what to tune, how much tuning it requires, and when the tuning efforts should stop. Specific goals need to be set and all tuning efforts need to cease when those goals are attained.

The Method Behind the Madness

Every Oracle Performance Management effort is potentially tri-faceted: tune, schedule, or buy. Ultimately, don't bet your professional life on performance tuning Oracle systems based on cache-hit ratios. By following the process of setting attainable goals, measuring current performance, making deliberate and well-considered changes, and reevaluating and reiterating the process, you can be assured of making positive progress in your tuning effort. Taking the two-pronged approach to monitoring the operating system for resource bottlenecks and using session wait statistics within Oracle to determine the exact nature of the performance bottlenecks allows for a very productive performance management effort. The key to this method is drilling down to the heart of the problem. Here is how:

1. Start with V$SYSTEM_EVENT and determine what resource is in highest demand, such as db file sequential read.

2. Drill down further to V$SESSION_EVENT and see which and how many sessions are involved for any given wait event.

3. Next, look at V$SESSION_WAIT to find the details of the resource contention, for example, which files, tables, latches, and so on.

4. Check the values for P1–P3 to find the relationships to other views.

5. Consider the time waited for these and other events. Work on the top five events.

6. Continue this process until all bottlenecks are unearthed.

7. At the same time, determine which SQL statements are contributing to these bottlenecks.

8. In a parallel effort, collect and analyze the OS statistics. Do this keeping the Oracle environment in mind. That means you should understand the OS statistics as they relate to Oracle.

9. Once you have determined the problem area, decide on a solution, test it, and implement it.

10. Deploy adequate change-control mechanisms so you can track what changes you have made and what effect they have had on the system.

11. After the solution is implemented, reevaluate to see if you have met your goals.

So for the last time, if the database buffer cache-hit ratio is low and you are beginning to get alarmed, stop and look at the wait events for the sessions. If there are no I/O-related wait events, your suspicion of a performance problem is unfounded. On the other side, if your cache-hit ratios are in the upper 90s, don't just sit back thinking that everything is fine, because in reality it may not be. All you have to do is to check for the wait events. Don't assume that a 99.999 percent cache-hit ratio implies that your Oracle database is performing at its peak efficiency, because even with that kind of cache-hit ratio, something nasty could be brewing. The behavior change that we have tried to bring about with this book is to get you to tune your Oracle systems based on wait events, not ratios.

Application Tuning: There Is No Substitute

Eighty percent of your Oracle system performance problems are due to bad SQL. Designing and developing optimal SQL is quintessential to scalable system performance and consistent response times. As a DBA, you need to be aware of the type of optimization methodology you are using, the method and frequency of calculating statistics, optimal indexing strategies, and selecting the right join methodology for a given SQL statement. Remember, it is not always beneficial to use an index. Care needs to be taken to identify this on a case-by-case basis.

You have the power to dramatically transform systemwide performance by just adding an index, changing the join methodology of a SQL statement, or providing a /*+ HINT */ to a SQL statement. Trust us, we are talking about many orders of magnitude in potential performance increase here.

Hunting down bad SQL statements requires discipline and makes you aware and adept in the various tools that Oracle provides to troubleshoot bad SQL statements. This is important because unless you get to the bottom of the performance problem with your SQL statements, you really can't tune your system performance problem. Okay, let's drive home that point one more time: 80 percent or more of your system's performance problems are caused due to bad SQL statements.

Here are some core steps to tune your SQL statements:

1. Ensure TIMED_STATISTICS is set to TRUE at the instance level (set it permanently in the init.ora or set it temporarily by executing an **alter system** command).

2. Ensure MAX_DUMP_FILE_SIZE is set high enough. This controls the size of your trace files.

3. Determine the location pointed to by USER_DUMP_DEST and ensure enough free disk space. This is where your trace files will live.

4. Turn on SQL_TRACE for the session in question while the application is running.

5. Run the application.

6. Locate the trace files.

7. Run **tkprof** (transient kernel profile) on the trace file that was located in step 4 to generate a trace output file.

8. Study the trace output file.

9. Tune the most expensive SQL statements.

10. Repeat steps 4–9 until required performance goals are achieved.

SQL_TRACE, **TKPROF**, **EXPLAIN PLAN**, and **AUTOTRACE** are some of the core tools that are shipped with the Oracle database software. They have been known to work consistently across multiple releases and operating system platforms. Understanding these tools is essential to your success in your application tuning efforts. Regardless of whom you choose as your third-party vendor for your Oracle database performance monitoring tools and SQL tuning tools, you absolutely have to understand and know your way around these core tools.

Shared Pool Area Tuning

Tuning the shared pool, like any other part of your Oracle system, requires understanding the interdependencies of all components. In this case, it means knowing the nature of the SQL being used. The relative sizes of packages, procedures, and functions affect the shared pool and the other related pools. It requires that the database administrator proactively manage the shared pool and large pool when applicable. Knowing which options the system is using determines the configuration of some of the pools. If RMAN is used as a part of the backup methodology, or if parallel operations or MTS is used, the large pool must be configured to support these tools. If Java is installed, Oracle will need a robust Java pool.

Don't let cache-hit ratios be the driver of tuning decisions. Use wait events to direct your tuning efforts down the right path. If the system is experiencing a high number of reloads in the library cache, it may be starving for memory. Consider increasing SHARED_POOL_SIZE. But before doing that, also consider the benefits of SQL tuning or segregating large packages and procedures or utilizing open and persistent cursors. Remember, soft parses are better than hard parses, and open cursors are better than soft parses. Investigate the use of SESSION_ CACHED_ CURSORS in your version of the Oracle database.

Avoid simply flushing the shared pool to clear everything out. You might get one package to run, but at a high cost in performance to all the other users on the system who are subject to hard parses where they would have used a soft parse.

If poor performance is traced back to recursive SQL having to constantly repopulate the data dictionary cache, definitely increase the shared pool. However, be careful that the ensuing increase in the SGA does not cause problems elsewhere that might be worse.

Pinning or keeping packages and other objects in the shared pool can provide excellent relief from aging issues as well as shared pool fragmentation, thus avoiding the ORA-04031 error. This is done with the package *dbms_shared_pool* using the keep procedure. Many database administrators find pinning key system and application packages at the startup of an instance helps in proactively managing the shared pool size. These steps are often added to the startup scripts.

Database Buffer Cache Tuning

You can analyze the I/O patterns in your system by querying the relevant parameters in V$SYSSTAT. Determine the cache-hit ratio and compare it to readings taken over time to understand physical I/O trends. Be sure to compare like times with like times keeping in mind that all instance-specific statistics are cumulative since the last startup.

You should very seriously consider implementing multiple pools in the database buffer cache if you can identify segments that have differing access patterns or characteristics. Small segments that are frequently accessed by applications or segments that require very fast access should be placed in the keep pool. Segments that are observed to have as many physical reads as logical reads are good candidates for the recycle pool. Those that can't be categorized should be left in the default pool. When increasing the database buffer cache size, be certain that the larger size of the SGA will not cause additional paging or swapping.

Proactively avoid latch contention by setting DB_BLOCK_LRU_LATCHES to the platform-specific allowed maximums. There is no measurable overhead in doing that. Be cautious while implementing any unsupported parameters. Their behavior may change once they are de-supported.

Don't fall for "expert recommendations" with respect to cache-hit ratios. There are no optimal or magical numbers here. This is true even if your application supports applications on the Web. We are fully aware of the sub-second response time requirement for these applications. However, that in itself should not force you to store every block of your data in the database buffer cache. There are many other ways to achieve sub-second response times (optimal application and schema design, meaningful SQL, application-layer caching, multi-tier architectures, and so on).

In today's world, caching all of your data is not even possible. If indeed you are caching all of your data, chances are that your database is very small. Oracle was designed and built to perform I/O very efficiently. With the significant advances in Oracle's kernel engine and storage hardware, doing a reasonable amount of physical I/O is normal and acceptable. The ideal cache hit ratio for one environment may make no sense for another.

Redo Log Buffer and Miscellaneous Tuning

Tuning the redo mechanism—including the redo log buffer—is one of the last components to tune as part of instance tuning. You can go ahead and always set the value of the Oracle initialization parameter LOG_SIMULTANEOUS_COPIES to the platform-specific maximum if your Oracle database version is prior to Oracle8i. This proactively avoids redo copy latch problems that occur due to lack of latches. Then set the size of the redo log buffer to a reasonable starting value by setting

LOG_BUFFER = 131072 (128K). Some folks start with 256K as well. Be cautious, though, as getting too aggressive with this can create more problems than it fixes. Increase this value if you observe the *log buffer space* wait event. However, if you also observe wait events such as *log file switch*, *log file sync*, or *log file parallel write*, there may be an underlying I/O issue on your storage devices. If this is the case, ensure that the redo logs and the archive logs are on independent devices separated from the data files of the database.

The archiving system can be tuned by setting LOG_ARCHIVE_BUFFER_SIZE and LOG_ARCHIVE_BUFFERS (these parameters don't exist in Oracle8i). Additionally, tune checkpoints by ensuring that they occur only on log switches. Size the redo log files appropriately to control checkpoint frequency and also allow sufficient time for the checkpoint process to complete so you won't get those "checkpoint not complete" messages. Also ensure that they are on independent storage devices, as they need their space (if you know what we mean).

We are all aware that most third-party packaged application vendors in their efforts to "encapsulate" the complexity of their application bury their SQL many fathoms below sea level and make it unreachable to mortals such as us. We studied in good detail some instance-level tuning opportunities that are supported since Oracle8, which modifies the behavior of the Oracle optimizer and thus makes these packaged applications more amenable to our tuning efforts.

Database Tuning

Database tuning deals with proactively configuring and managing various storage-related components in the database. The configuration of the Oracle database block size is one of the most important steps that you as a DBA will perform. It needs to be done right the first time, every time. When in doubt, go with a bigger database block size.

To manage block-level fragmentation and to better use the available space that you allocate to an object, block-level storage parameters such as *pctfree* and *pctused* need configuration. Block-level concurrency support for multiple transactions needs to be done by configuring *initrans* and *maxtrans* for the relevant tables that will have to support concurrent data manipulation. If a table is heavily inserted into, configuring adequate *freelists* is essential to manage contention. Every step needs to be taken to reduce and eliminate tablespace-level fragmentation. Fragmentation can be managed by implementing the "Four-Bucket Tablespace Configuration" method. It is perfectly okay to waste some disk space and keep all extents in a tablespace uniform, rather than deal with free space fragmentation.

Consider locally managed tablespaces in Oracle8i. This provides significant increases in performance and ease of maintenance. Partitioning is a key feature that was introduced in Oracle8. It provides the capability to decompose an object into smaller segments, and thus provide better performance while dealing with these smaller segments.

We hope you will spend your precious days performing tasks that are of value to your system and your business, rather than trying to get every object in your environment to fit into one extent. It is time for us to put an end to the one extent compulsion and accept the fact that an object can have many hundred extents and still perform at peak levels, so long as it does not suffer from severe block-level or row-level fragmentation and the extent sizing is done keeping in mind DB_ FILE_ MULTIBLOCK_READ_COUNT and DB_BLOCK_SIZE. Compressing an object's extents into one extent in no way makes performance better. It just gives fragmentation a new lease on life.

Parallel Query Tuning

Parallel Query was designed to squeeze every last drop of system resources out of your hardware and software investment. Now, that's a good thing, to get your money's worth. However, using parallelism without paralyzing your system requires understanding of how parallelism really works, what affects it, and what it affects. It is very important to consider the side effects of using parallelism when there are not enough resources available and the environment is not conducive enough.

Parallelism involves dividing work among many processes, each performing its own allocated workload. The idea is to "divide and conquer." For starters, the table data should be spread over as many storage devices as possible so that multiple PQ server processes will not be hampered by I/O contention. You should also select a proper degree of parallelism for the operation, as it dictates how many PQ server processes will be utilized. The degree of parallelism can be set as part of a table or index definition, or by using the PARALLEL hint with a SQL statement.

There are some special initialization parameters to configure. Specifically, these include PARALLEL_MIN_SERVERS, PARALLEL_MAX_SERVERS, and PARALLEL_ MIN_PERCENT. You should understand how these interact with each other and what important role PARALLEL_MIN_PERCENT plays. The new Oracle initialization parameter PARALLEL_AUTOMATIC_TUNING allows the DBA to set just one parameter for Parallel Query tuning and control the values of a variety of other parallel parameters. As fantastic as that sounds, please perform comprehensive tests in your environment before using this. Some other initialization parameters will also need to be understood in light of using parallelism, such as LARGE_POOL_SIZE, SORT_AREA_SIZE, and SORT_AREA_RETAINED_SIZE.

There are several SQL statements that can utilize PQ operations. From Oracle8, many DDL operations can also utilize parallelism in addition to DML operations. Parallel DML can significantly improve the performance of bulk DML operations in large databases. However, there are some special issues you must be aware of when using PDML. PDML is fully supported with partitioned tables. When using PDML against such tables, make sure that adequately sized rollback segments are available. To improve I/O, spread these rollback segments over multiple disk devices. In addition to the size of the rollback segments, there should be enough rollback segments available, typically equal to the number of table partitions, but not to exceed twice the number of CPUs in the server.

The dynamic performance view V$PQ_SYSSTAT provides information on how your system utilizes PQ servers. Monitoring it will enable you to determine adequate values to set initialization parameters PARALLEL_MIN_SERVERS and PARALLEL_MAX_SERVERS.

Contention Tuning

Every database will have bottlenecks and contention issues to deal with. There will be more processes competing for limited resources. The key to your success lies in how well you allocate and manage these resources to minimize such bottlenecks and contention.

Configuring appropriate rollback segments is important to a well-performing database in any environment, DSS or OLTP. If there are not enough correctly sized rollback segments, performance of all DML activities will suffer. Application programmers and database administrators have seen the ORA-01555 error quite a few times. It is not the database administrator's fault that there are not enough larger rollback segment to avoid this errors. But many times the way the code is written causes this error to surface. Addressing it only from the database standpoint will have its limitations as well. Sometimes the code does require change.

All applications will perform sorts in addition to database maintenance tasks. This should be expected with a relational database like Oracle. Configuring appropriate temporary tablespaces to carry on sort operations is also very important. At the same time, care must be taken to find ways to avoid resource contention. When sorts are taking place on disk, the extent allocation and de-allocation will cause contention for the space management transaction enqueue (ST enqueue) resource in a busy database. Proper values selected for the init.ora parameters SORT_AREA_SIZE and SORT_AREA_RETAINED_SIZE will minimize the need to use the disk for sorts. When disk sorts cannot be avoided, it is important that the storage for the temporary segments is properly sized. With the introduction of true temporary tablespaces, sort processes do not have to deal with multiple allocation and de-allocation of extents for temporary segments. With true temporary tablespaces, one large segment is used by all sorting operations. When possible, consider using multiple temporary tablespaces for multiple user groups with data files on different storage devices to reduce contention for I/O. In addition to using true temporary tablespaces, consider using locally managed tablespace for temporary segments. This combination will ensure that you will have minimum requirement for using the ST enqueue resource.

There is no magic to managing or tuning latch contention. Neither is it the most important thing to worry about. However, it gets a lot of attention. Just like a squeaky wheel! People drive themselves crazy trying to tune their latches without really digging deep into what is causing the contention. If you track the trend Oracle is following, many of the latches are slowly but surely becoming undocumented parameters, which implies that you do not touch it unless advised otherwise. A DBA can tune just a few latches. Fortunately, there are corresponding Oracle initialization parameters, so set those appropriately and forget about latch contention (at least from a number of latches perspective). Besides, almost all the time, latch contention is a symptom of a serious application problem—too much serialization. Stick to the tuning methodology and you will be content with not finding any latch contention! There are other fun things that need your attention.

I/O Tuning

I/O tuning (of which RAID is an important component) is essential to achieve scalable system performance when the database grows in size. RAID provides the technology to scale I/O and system performance of applications and provide high availability. Proactive design, architecture, and deployment of optimal RAID configurations are quintessential to gaining scalable I/O performance. It is important to understand the RAID solutions offered by each hardware vendor before any implementation is done. A solid understanding of the application to be supported plays a large part in RAID selection. Researching the application and the details of your vendor's RAID offerings must be the starting point of any I/O subsystem design. The following table summarizes the various levels of RAID:

Level of RAID	Functionality
RAID 0	Provides striping but no recoverability. Your application requires read/write performance without recoverability (rare).
RAID 1	Provides mirroring and recoverability. Your application primarily requires write performance.
RAID 0+1/1+0	Provides the combination of 0 and 1 and recoverability. Your application requires read and write performance. This is very widely used (note that 1+0 is better than 0+1 for availability).

Level of RAID	Functionality
RAID 2	This was one of the early implementations of striping with parity, and it uses the hamming code technique for parity calculations. It was replaced by RAID 3, RAID 5, and RAID 7 and is very rarely implemented.
RAID 3	Provides striping with bit/byte-level parity and is supported by a dedicated parity disk. This also provides recoverability. Your application requires read performance for bulk sequential reads and requires better data-transfer rates for sequential reads over IOPS. It is not widely used, but is slowly gaining popularity.
RAID 4	Provides striping with block-level parity and is supported by a dedicated parity disk. It also provides recoverability, but is very rarely supported by hardware vendors.
RAID 5	Provides striping with block-level parity. The parity is distributed across the number of disks in the volume. It also provides recoverability. Your application requires read performance for random reads that are small in nature, and requires better IOPS over data-transfer rates. It is very widely used.
RAID 6	Provides striping with block-level multidimensional parity. Supports recoverability, but suffers from slower writes when compared to RAID 5. It is very rarely implemented.
RAID 7	Same functionality as in RAID 3, but with better asynchronous capability for reads and writes. This is significantly better overall I/O performance when compared to RAID 3, but it is also much more expensive than RAID 3.
RAID-S	This is EMC's implementation of RAID 3/5.
Auto RAID	This is HP's automatic RAID technology that autoconfigures the I/O system based on the nature and type of I/O performed on the disk blocks within the RAID array.

Oracle and RAID have an interesting marriage; adequate thought and care needs to be put into them. A good design can go a long way in an optimal and scalable implementation. The following table summarizes the interaction between Oracle and RAID:

Level of RAID	When and Where to Use It
RAID 0	Not suitable for any critical component of an Oracle database. May be considered for development databases where recoverability is determined to be a non-issue. This is suitable when you can simply restore a copy of a production database and reapply any DDL differences to re-create a development environment.
RAID 1	Ideal for online and archived redo logs. Leaves the write-head at the location of the last write. On most systems, you will need three volumes for the online redo logs (for three groups) and one volume for the archived redo logs.
RAID 0+1 or 1+0	Ideally suited for data files that require read/write performance especially for online transaction processing (OLTP) or hybrid systems, where read/write performance is important. Pick 1+0 over 0+1 when possible.
RAID 3	Ideal for data mart/data warehouse applications with few users that require mostly range/full scans on its tables and indexes. Everything else remaining constant, RAID 3 provides better data transfer than RAID 5.
RAID 5	Ideal for data mart/data warehouse applications with many users that require mostly unique scans on its tables and indexes. RAID 5 provides better IOPS than RAID 3.
RAID 7	Ideal for data mart/data warehouse applications with support for more users than RAID 3. The application requires mostly range/full scans on its tables and indexes. If your application requires RAID 3 and better support for IOPS and you can afford it, RAID 7 is your key.

As always, DBA 101 common sense needs to be applied on a continuous basis. Some things never change: DATA tablespaces need to be separated from INDX tablespaces, regardless of anyone advising you to the contrary. The three rules for successful optimal RAID configurations are, "Striping, striping, and striping."

Operating System Tuning

Tuning the OS includes activities such as making sure your system has adequate memory for the number of CPUs, ensuring that the databases do not consume an inordinate amount of available physical memory to cause paging and swapping, verifying that the kernel parameters for the OS are set at proper values, and so on. Addressing these areas in an effective manner will bring about performance improvement you are looking for. You will need to understand what features Oracle supports on your OS platforms. It is your job to test those and make sure they work as desired. You should know how to use certain OS commands and available tools to monitor CPU, memory utilization, and I/O throughput.

On UNIX, you need to know how Oracle uses shared memory and semaphores to manage interprocess communications and all the related kernel parameters. Implementation of these resources is OS specific. In addition, there are very specific areas with various operating systems that you can explore to improve the performance of your database. Some support asynchronous I/O with file systems, while others make it easy to lock the entire SGA in memory. Some allow you to control the paging algorithm, while others allow you to modify process management. On Windows NT, there are a number of areas to address to improve the performance of not only the database, but also of the Windows NT server as such. The more you know about the OS and how Oracle uses its resources, there is no doubt in our minds that you will be the most popular DBA around when it comes to performance tuning at the OS level!

This Book...In a Nutshell

So go ahead, enjoy life, go out and get some fresh air every now and then, and have fun during your Oracle system tuning efforts. Please make it a priority to spend quality time with your family and loved ones. In the bigger scheme of things, they are ultimate in importance. By using the information in this book, we guarantee that you will engage in methodical and organized tuning efforts. You will embark on tuning efforts only when you detect bottlenecks. When you make that behavior change, you will actually find the time to spend with your family and loved ones. Good luck with your Oracle Performance Management efforts. May the force bestow you with intellect, health, peace, love, and prosperity! So long....

PART
VI

Appendixes

APPENDIX

A

Glossary

resented here is a set of brief definitions of most of the terms you will encounter in this book. Every attempt has been made to ensure that all of the important terms have been included.

- **AIX**   Advanced Interactive Executive, a flavor of UNIX from IBM Corporation.

- **Analyze**   A DDL command that collects or drops statistics on tables, indexes, or clusters in a database. Also used to validate structures.

- **Archive Log**   A copy of the redo log file created by the archiver process. An archive log is used to recover the database from a previous backup.

- **ARCHIVELOG Mode**   A database can be run in either ARCHIVELOG mode or NOARCHIVELOG mode. In ARCHIVELOG mode, the database uses an additional background process (ARCH) to create a copy of filled redo log file at one or more pre-determined archive destination(s).

- **Archiver Process (ARCH, or ARCn)**   Oracle background process responsible for managing archival of the redo log files. This process reads the filled redo log file and copies it to one or more archive destinations.

- **Asynchronous I/O**   A specialized form of I/O that improves throughput. Synchronous I/O takes place when processes wait for the operation to complete. Asynchronous I/O operations run in background and processes requesting it not to wait for its completion. Oracle takes full advantage of asynchronous I/O on some platforms with certain types of data storage implementations. Asynchronous I/O is also known as non-blocking I/O.

- **Auto RAID**   See **RAID, Auto**.

- **Autotrace**   SQL*Plus command that can be used to automatically obtain the execution plan and statistics for the SQL statement upon its execution.

- **Background Processes**   Processes performing specialized tasks on behalf of all sessions. For example, the Database Writer (DBWR or DBWn) is responsible for writing changed blocks from the buffer cache to the database files. The log writer (LGWR) is responsible for writing blocks from the redo log buffers to the redo log files. The archiver process (ARCH or ARCn) copies completed redo logs to one or more predetermined location(s). With Oracle8 and up, a checkpoint process (CKPT) performs the checkpoints, reducing the workload of the LGWR process. Other processes (such as SMON and PMON) perform specific housekeeping functions such as recovery operations, clean up of terminated sessions, and so on. Assorted background processes are enabled only if certain Oracle options are enabled.

■ **Bind**   As applicable to the SQL statement execution, during the *bind* phase, the values for any bind variables used in the statement, are resolved. See also **Parse, Define, Execute, Fetch**.

■ **Bit Mapped Index**   See **Index, Bit Mapped**.

■ **Blocks**   The smallest unit of storage in an Oracle environment, ranging from 2K–32K. Most systems use 8K block size for transactional systems and 16K block size or higher for data warehousing/decision-support systems. Larger block sizes may be available with the 64-bit implementation of Oracle.

■ **Buffer**   A generic term that represents memory areas to hold information. Such memory areas are defined in the initialization parameter file for the database.

■ **Buffer Pools**   Term used to define various memory areas, in the database buffer cache. These are keep pool, recycle pool, and default pool. The former two are defined using initialization parameters and are available in Oracle8 and up.

■ **Cache**   An attribute on a table that puts the blocks in the MRU end of the LRU list for the buffer cache.

■ **Cache, Database Buffer**   A portion of the system global area in the memory that contains copies of data blocks, index blocks, rollback segment blocks, and so on, from database files. It is configured primarily to reduce device I/O by allowing multiple sessions to access frequently or recently accessed data in memory.

■ **Cache, Dictionary**   A portion of the shared pool area within the system global area that contains the information from the data dictionary. This information is primarily used by recursive SQL.

■ **Cache Hit Ratio**   Percentage about accesses to the buffered information in Oracle memory structures. We don't believe in it for gauging the performance of the database.

■ **Cache, Library**   A portion of the shared pool area within the system global area that contains SQL statements and information about them. Oracle searches this area to determine whether an identical SQL statement already exists. If so, it will avoid hard parsing of the SQL statement.

■ **Checkpoint**   A procedure when the checkpoint process (CKPT) or the log writer (LGWR) process writes synchronization information to all the file headers.

■ **Checkpoint Process (CKPT)**   From Oracle8 and up, this background process helps complete the checkpoint procedure reducing the workload on the log writer process (LGWR). From Oracle8i, the CKPT process also keeps a heartbeat of the instance/database with the control file every three seconds. This helps determine the starting point of a recovery, if applicable and when needed.

- **Contention** A struggle between one or more processes to access the same resource at approximately the same time.

- **Correlated Sub-Query** See **Sub-Query**.

- **Cost Based Optimizer** See **Optimizer, Cost Based**.

- **CTD** Compulsive tuning disorder—a state of mind and body that refuses to stop tuning and cannot overcome the urge to "tweak just a little bit more."

- **Cursor** An identifier that allows naming a SQL statement, access information in the private SQL area of the statement, and, to some extent, controls its processing. A cursor is said to be open when the SQL statement is executed and the result is stored in the private SQL area.

- **Database** See **Oracle Database**.

- **Database Block** See **Blocks**.

- **Database Buffer Cache** See **Cache, Database Buffer**.

- **Database Files** Files that contain the data, index, rollback, and temporary segments that comprise an Oracle database.

- **Database Writer (DBWR, DBWn)** Oracle background process responsible for managing the database buffer cache and the dictionary cache. This process writes the dirty, or changed, blocks from the buffer cache to the data files.

- **Default Pool** Actually, it is the database buffer cache and not a specifically allocated area. With the introduction of other pools in the database buffer cache, from Oracle8, the term *default pool* is used to denote no special pool assignments for a given segment.

- **Define** As applicable to the SQL statement execution, during the *define* phase, the user and server processes exchange data type information about involved columns. See also **Parse, Bind, Execute, Fetch**.

- **Enqueue** A mechanism to track processes waiting to acquire lock that is held by other processes. It also keeps track of the order in which processes request the lock.

- **Event** See **Wait Event**.

■ **Execute**   As applicable to the SQL statement execution, during the *execute* phase, the server process reads data blocks from the data files into the memory (for **update**, **delete**, and **insert** operations) as needed. The data is manipulated in this phase, as execution plan is put to work. See also **Parse, Define, Bind, Fetch**.

■ **Extent**   A set of contiguous blocks within a datafile assigned to a specific segment within that tablespace.

■ **Fetch**   For **select** statements, during the SQL statement execution, this phase signifies reading the relevant data blocks into the database buffer cache and applying the execution plan. Results are returned to the user process. See also **Parse, Define, Bind, Execute**.

■ **Filesystem**   A block storage device that is mounted and used to stored Oracle files.

■ **Fragmentation**   The breaking up of contiguous space within data files and memory structures into smaller pieces. Also applies to unutilized space within a database block, and to migrated or chained rows.

■ **Function Based Indexes**   See **Index, Function Based**.

■ **Hash Join**   See **Join Methods**.

■ **Hint**   User-chosen directive for the cost-based optimizer to follow certain access paths while executing the SQL statement. The notation for a hint is /*+ HINT */.

■ **Histogram**   A bar graph that shows the frequency of the data values. Oracle supports constructing histograms for data values to aid the optimizer in building optimal execution plans.

■ **I/O**   Input from or output to one or more storage device.

■ **Index**   An object that supports faster retrieval of data from a table, it contains the information on which the index is created and pointers (ROWIDs) to the data in the table. An index is stored in a B*-*tree* data structure.

■ **Index, Bitmapped**   Unlike a regular index where each data value in an index has a corresponding ROWID that points to it, a bitmapped index contains data values with a corresponding bitmap for a range of ROWIDs to indicate which data value occurs in which row.

■ **Index, Function Based**   Introduced in Oracle8i, these indexes are built on columns with one or more functions, such as *upper, lower, round,* and so on. This allows the query to use this index rather than performing a full table scan due the presence of a function on the said indexed columns.

- **Init.ora**   Generic name for the Oracle initialization file that contains various parameters with user-defined values.

- **Instance**   See **Oracle Instance**.

- **ISM**   Intimate sharable memory. Only on Sun Solaris platform, a specialized method used to lock shared memory structures to improve their performance.

- **Java Pool**   Available in Oracle8i and up, this memory structure in the system global area is reserved for Java and its associated objects.

- **Join**   The process of combining data from two or more tables (or views) to produce the desired output.

- **Join Methods**   A generic term for different algorithms the optimizer builds to combine data from multiple tables or views. There are the following types of join methods:

  - **Nested Loop**   A row operation that sends processed rows from one step to the next step before completing processing of all rows in the first step.

  - **Sort Merge**   A set operation that completes each step before rows are sent to the next step.

  - **Hash Joins**   Usually involves full table scans. Oracle constructs a hash table in the memory for the smaller table and probes it with rows from the larger table.

- **Keep Pool**   Available from Oracle8, it can be defined to contain data from smaller tables or indexes. Data in this pool remain in memory, eliminating the time (and I/O) required to re-read often-used data blocks from disk.

- **Latch**   A mechanism to protect a memory structure from concurrent access by multiple processes. It is a specialized form of serializing access to shared memory structures used by Oracle.

- **Large Pool**   Available in Oracle8 and up, this memory structure in system global area is reserved for special operations used by RMAN, parallel query, and multi-threaded server implementations. It facilitates better management and reduction of fragmentation of the shared pool area.

■ **Library Cache**   See **Cache, Library**.

■ **Locally Managed Tablespace**   Available in Oracle8i and up, a tablespace can be configured to *self-manage* the available space within it—hence, "locally managed." The space management tasks do not access the data dictionary and the extents are all of the same size.

■ **Lock**   A mechanism used by Oracle to protect resources that a particular process needs for a certain period. Other processes requiring the same resource wait in line to acquire the lock on the resource, if the resource is currently locked by some other process. Oracle uses various types of locks and locking methods.

■ **Log Writer (LGWR)**   This Oracle background process responsible for managing the redo log buffer reads blocks from the redo log buffers and writes to the redo log files.

■ **LRU**   Least recently used.

■ **Metalink**   Name for the online support services available on the Internet from Oracle; the URL for the Web site is **http://metalink.oracle.com**. You must have support agreement with Oracle and your CSI number to register to access this Web site.

■ **Mirroring**   A process of writing the same data to two members of the same storage volume simultaneously, it provides protection for the data in the event one of the members of the storage device becomes unavailable.

■ **MRU**   Most recently used.

■ **Multiversion Read Consistency**   Read consistency is the act of providing all users with a consistent view of the data that was asked for. The multiversion aspect provides that consistent view across multiple user sessions. In very simplistic terms, it is a scenario where each user sees his or her own copy of the data.

■ **Nested Loops**   See **Join Methods**.

■ **Offline**   A tablespace or database file that is unavailable for access.

■ **Online**   A tablespace or database file that is available for access.

■ **Open Cursor**   See **Cursors**.

■ **Optimizer**   An optimization procedure that usually chooses the most efficient way to execute a SQL statement.

- **Optimizer, Cost-Based** A process to choose the most efficient way to execute a SQL statement based on various statistical information available on the objects. The optimizer computes the cost of each possible access path and chooses the one with the smallest cost.

- **Optimizer, Rule-Based** A process to choose the most efficient way to execute a SQL statement based on a set of pre-defined rules and ranks of available access paths.

- **Oracle Database** A set of files—data files, redo log files, and control files.

- **Oracle Instance** A set of shared memory segments and background processes that attach to it.

- **Oracle Performance Management (OPM)** Step-by-step process of iteratively investigating, determining, and implementing tuning solutions using a proven methodology.

- **OTN** Oracle Technology Network. This is another online resource on the Internet from Oracle and is free to use; the URL for the web site is **http://technet.oracle.com**. You will find online documentation and various Oracle software to download.

- **Paging** An operating system process that writes memory pages to predefined swap areas based on usage and demand for such memory areas in physical memory. See also **Swap Space**.

- **Parallel Query** A query that is divided into multiple tasks, performed by two more parallel query slaves.

- **Parallel Query Slaves** Processes that perform work on behalf of a server process.

- **Parse** The step in the execution of a SQL statement where the server process checks the syntax of the statement, performs object resolution, and checks security. Upon successful completion of this procedure a parse tree and an execution plan for the SQL statement is built. See also **Define, Bind, Execute, Fetch**.

- **Parse, Hard** When Oracle builds the parse tree and an execution plan for the SQL statement for the first time. However, there are other situations when it will need to rebuild it, causing additional and undesired hard parses.

- **Parse, Soft** When, Oracle finds a matching SQL statement in the memory with its already built parse tree and execution plan.

- **Partitioning** The process of dividing data into multiple smaller chunks for ease of management, availability, performance, and security.

- **PDML**   Parallel data manipulation language.

- **RAID**   Stands for *redundant array of independent* or *inexpensive disks*, depending on who you ask. However, it is the technology for expanding the capacity of the I/O system and providing the capability or data redundancy. There are various types of RAID configuration to choose from each offering differing capabilities.

- **RAID, Auto (Auto RAID)**   Hewlett Packard's automatic RAID technology that configures the I/O system based on the nature and type of the I/O performed on the disk blocks within the RAID array.

- **RAID 0**   A very simple type of RAID providing good read/write performance, it provides striping but no recoverability.

- **RAID 1**   Provides mirroring and full data redundancy. It is most often called "mirrored disk" and requires twice the amount of disk storage as compared to RAID 0.

- **RAID 0+1**   "Stripe first, then mirror what is striped." This RAID level combines RAID 0 and RAID 1, and also provides good write and read performance with data redundancy without the parity calculation overhead.

- **RAID 1+0**   "Mirror first, then stripe what is mirrored." This level of RAID has the same functionality as RAID 0+1, but is better suited for high availability requirements.

- **RAID 2**   This level of RAID incorporates striping. The redundancy and data protection is provided through parity, and the parity overhead will affect write performance. This is very rarely used, as other RAID levels have since replaced it.

- **RAID 3**   Similar to RAID 2, it uses parity; however, the parity is stored on just one dedicated disk. It is best suited for data mart or data warehouse applications that support a few users but require sequential bulk I/O access patterns.

- **RAID 4**   Slight variation of RAID 3, in which parity calculations differ. It is rarely used.

- **RAID 5**   The data redundancy is provided via parity calculation but the parity is stored along with the data. Thus, the parity information is distributed across the number of disk drives in a storage device. It offers good performance for read operations; however, write intensive applications will encounter slow performance due to parity calculation and distribution.

- **RAID 6**   A very rarely used level of RAID, the parity calculation uses a much more complex algorithm. It also stores two sets of parity for each block of data and thus makes writes even slower than RAID 5; however, it facilitates quicker recoverability in case of disk failures.

- **RAID 7** A better implementation of RAID 3, and it offers better asynchronous capability for reads and writes.

- **RAID S** EMC Corporation's implementation of RAID 5/3.

- **Raw Devices** A character storage device that is an unmounted file system but can store Oracle files.

- **Recycle Pool** Available from Oracle8, it can be defined to contain data from larger objects. When not assigned to the recycle pool, these objects may cause other objects to be aged out prematurely from the default pool, thus causing additional physical I/O.

- **Redo Log Buffer** Buffer containing database changes that have not yet been written to the redo log files. The contents of the redo log buffer are periodically flushed to the online redo log files. They are always flushed before completion of a commit, a checkpoint, or before a set of dirty data blocks need to be written to disk.

- **Redo Log Files** Files that contain transaction journals that assist in the recovery of a database in an event of a system, media, or database failure.

- **Reserved Area** An area in the shared pool, reserved to store large SQL objects, including PL/SQL packages, procedures, function, and so on.

- **RMAN** Available from Oracle8 and up, the Recovery Manager (RMAN) is a free tool set from Oracle to manage database backup and recovery tasks.

- **Rollback Segment** Segments that store original (or before-image) copies of database blocks that have been changed by transactions. Rollback segments contain the information that is utilized to undo a transaction, when you issue a ROLLBACK command. These before-images in rollback segments will be overwritten, as transactions reuse the space within a rollback segment.

- **Rule Based Optimizer** See **Optimizer, Rule Based**.

- **SCN** System Commit Number. Oracle uses this to represent the state (incarnation) of the database at any given time. This number increments on database changes caused by structural modifications to the database objects or committed DML operations. See also **System Change Number**.

- **SCSI** Small computer serial interface.

■ **Segment**   An object in an Oracle database comprised of one or more extents. Examples are tables, partitions, indexes, rollback segments, temporary segments, and clusters.

■ **Semaphores**   A signaling mechanism used to send messages to other processes. Oracle uses *semaphores* on UNIX platforms to synchronize concurrent processes that need access to shared resources.

■ **Server Process**   "Shadow" processes that act as arbitrators by processing SQL on behalf of user sessions, a server process can perform processing for a single session only (known as a dedicated server) or for multiple sessions (in the multi-threaded server configuration where the server processes are shared).

■ **Shared Memory**   A memory structure that multiple processes can use to interchange data and other information. Oracle processes access shared memory segments and use inter-process communication (IPC) to exchange information with one another.

■ **Shared Pool Area**   A portion of the system global area (SGA) that contains library cache, dictionary cache, control structures, and, sometimes, private session information (if multi-threaded servers are enabled).

■ **Sort**   A process to arrange data in a specific order.

■ **Sort-Merge**   See **Join Methods**.

■ **STATSPACK**   Available at no additional cost with Oracle8i, the STATSPACK tool set offers a better facility than utlbstat/utlestat scripts to gather performance related statistical information. This tool set makes it easy to create and save performance information for future use and to perform historical trend analysis.

■ **Striping**   A process of dividing data into pieces and distributing it across multiple disks, these disks support a single logical volume. This process facilitates increase in I/O bandwidth, improving read and write operations.

■ **Sub-Query**   A select statement (child) contained within another select statement (parent). A sub-query is called a correlated sub-query when the child statement is executed each time for every row returned by the parent statement.

■ **Swap Space**   A special area on a storage device that is reserved for the OS to write all the memory pages of an entire process when the system experiences memory starvation. See also **Paging**.

- **System Change Number**   Used with the sequence number (stored in the block header), it determines the version of the data block to apply changes to, for either a roll forward or rollback operation. See also **SCN**.

- **System Global Area (SGA)**   A collection of shared memory areas that can be accessed by multiple user sessions. The main components of an Oracle SGA are shared pool area, database buffer cache, and redo log buffers.

- **Table**   A collection of one or more rows and columns containing data.

- **Table, Temporary**   See **Temporary Table**.

- **Tablespace**   A logical structure that houses segments in a database, it is usually configured to store segments of one type. A tablespace can consist of one or more database files, but any given database file can belong to only one tablespace.

- **Tablespace, Locally Managed**   See **Locally Managed Tablespace**.

- **Tablespace, Temporary Type**   See **Temporary Type Tablespace**.

- **Temporary Segments**   These segments store sort data generated by joins, group by, order by, summary functions, or **create index** commands.

- **Temporary Table**   Available from Oracle8i, it is a global temporary table that can be used simultaneously by multiple sessions as scratch space. The rows in the table are visible to only to the session that inserted it, and can be retained either until the end of the transaction or the end of the session. There is no redo generated for any modifications to the data in the temporary tables. Remember that this table will be created in the temporary tablespace assigned to the user.

- **Temporary Type Tablespace**   From Oracle 7.3, a tablespace can be configured as purely temporary in nature. It improves the performance of sort operations. Instead of creating temporary segments to be dropped after the completion of sort a process, a temporary type tablespace keeps the temporary segment for reuse by subsequent sort operations. This minimizes space management operations during disk sorts, thus improving sort performance.

- **Tkprof**   *Transient kernel profile*. A free tool from Oracle, it analyzes trace files to provide readable output that is meaningful to the DBA. There are various options available to control what information is displayed and the order in which it is displayed.

■ **Two-Pronged Approach** A method to determine the current bottlenecks in your system, which utilizes OS monitoring techniques and the Oracle wait interface.

■ **Wait Event** As of Oracle8i, there are about 200 wait events. A named section of the Oracle kernel code, this concept was introduced in Oracle 7.0.12 and enhanced in each Oracle release thereafter. It is used to define certain events or steps during processing that can be categorized as *idle* or *non-idle* waits. Non-idle waits are when Oracle processes are waiting for resources to perform assigned work, while idle waits are when Oracle is waiting for more work.

■ **Wait Interface** A collection of wait event information from V$SYSTEM_EVENT, V$SESSION_EVENT, V$SESSION_WAIT, and trace files generated by the 10046 event number.

APPENDIX

B

More Tips & Resources

his appendix is a collection of tips on how to improve performance of some of the tasks that a DBA performs on a regular basis. We cover tuning tips for the Oracle utilities—*exp, imp,* and *SQL*Loader.* We also created a sample Oracle initialization file (init.ora) by collating the relevant tuning parameters in this book into functional groups and created a single file for your reference. Last but not the least, we have a section on where you can get additional information to further assist you in your tuning efforts.

Tuning the Export Utility

Prior to Oracle 7.3 there were only a few options for a DBA to choose from when it came to performance tuning the export utility. One was the use of the larger *buffer* size to fetch multiple rows into memory and write to the export dump file; the other was to create a *single-task* executable for the export utility that used less resources.

In Oracle 7.3, a new parameter, *direct*, brought significant performance improvement to export operations. A direct export bypasses the Oracle SGA and writes to the export dump file. This parameter has to be set explicitly because its default value is *n* (meaning no direct export). To run direct mode export, set *direct=y.*

Another parameter, *recordlength*, can be used in conjunction with conventional (which uses the Oracle SGA) or direct path exports. This parameter defaults to the operating system's buffer size (*bufsiz*) and is platform specific. Setting *recordlength* to a value equal to or a multiple of the database block size can increase the performance of exports.

The following table summarizes results from our tests to show how these parameters affect performance. The tests were conducted with an Oracle 8.1.7 database running on an AIX 4.3.3 server. The server had no other users and the database was restarted before each test. All times are averages from three tests using each option. Times were captured using the **timex** command. The table had 4,952,153 rows that were exported.

Options used	Elapsed Time in Seconds	Notes
Conventional (without any options)	412.81	
recordlength=16384	399.65	*recordlength* is set to the value of DB_BLOCK_SIZE

Options used	Elapsed Time in Seconds	Notes
buffer=1048576	251.79	*recordlength* assumed its default value
buffer=1048576 recordlength=16384	248.75	*recordlength* is set to the value of DB_BLOCK_SIZE
buffer=1048576 recordlength=65535	235.38	*recordlength* is set to the maximum value for the platform
direct=y	66.20	*recordlength* assumed its default value
direct=y recordlength=16384	51.85	*recordlength* is set to the value of DB_BLOCK_SIZE
direct=y recordlength=65535	45.60	*recordlength* is set to the maximum value for the platform

As you can see, using the *direct* path method for export provided the fastest performance. And, you can squeeze out a little bit more by using the *recordlength* parameter. However, check the platform-specific maximum values for these parameters. Test what works best in your environment and you can easily make those exports run faster.

Tuning the Import Utility

There are a quite a few things available for a DBA to improve the performance of the import utility. We suggest you always create tables with the proper storage clause before importing its data. Doing so gives you complete control on sizing and placement of the extents. Preallocate extents if required, to minimize dynamic extent allocation during the import process. While importing the data, remember to use the *ignore=y* parameter to ignore any table creation errors due to the existence of the table.

Consider using the *commit=y* setting while importing data. Oracle will issue a commit after every array insert. This reduces the likelihood of rollback segments growing out of control. If you use the default value (*commit=n*), Oracle will not commit data until all rows of the table are imported (inserted). The downside of this setting (*commit=y*) is that if the import fails, you will need either to truncate the table or drop it before restarting the import process, since Oracle does not rollback committed table data.

Do not import indexes along with the data. Set *indexes=n* during the import process (the default is *indexes=y*). You can create all the indexes after the data is imported. This will provide you much better control on the performance of index builds, via adjusting SORT_AREA_SIZE, SORT_AREA_RETAINED_SIZE, using properly configured storage for temporary tablespace and using a locally managed tablespace. You may also consider parallelizing index creations and using the *nologging* or *unrecoverable* attributes to speed things up even further.

Have you ever heard your users complain about slow performance after you had done a good job of reorganizing a table over the long weekend? If the answer is yes, then the *statistics=estimate* default value setting (in Oracle7) or *analyze=y* (in Oracle8 and above) is the culprit. These parameters will estimate statistics on the imported objects with the default sample size. You should use *statistics=none* or *analyze=n* as applicable. This will not only prevent the Monday morning chaos but also improve import performance. You should remember to analyze imported objects using your normal procedures, after the import has successfully completed.

You should also consider increasing the default value of the *buffer* parameter. This is computed using the formula (– number of rows in the insert array times row length). If you have adequate free memory available on the server, then consider assigning some of it to this parameter. In our testing of imports, the *buffer* parameter provided significant improvement in import performance up to a certain threshold.

The following table summarizes results from our tests to show how these parameters affect import performance. The tests were conducted with an Oracle 8.1.7 database running on an AIX 4.3.3 server. The server had no other users and the database was restarted before every test. All times are averages from three tests using each option. Times were captured using the **timex** command. The table had 4,952,153 rows that were imported. The average row size was 65 bytes.

Options used	Elapsed time in seconds	Notes
commit=y indexes=n ignore=y	594.88	
commit=y indexes=n ignore=y buffer=1048576	312.96	Approximately 16,131 rows in the insert array
commit=y indexes=n ignore=y buffer=5242880	289.55	Approximately 80,860 rows in the insert array
commit=y indexes=n ignore=y buffer=10485760	288.12	Approximately 161,320 rows in the insert array

As you can see, increasing the value of *buffer* beyond 5MB for the table in our tests did not increase the performance significantly. However, by using *buffer* we cut the import times by almost half as compared to not using it! We also found that using the *recordlength* parameter did not improve performance significantly.

Tuning the SQL*Loader Utility

Oracle offers two methods to load data into tables using the SQL*Loader utility. One is called the *conventional* method; the other is the *direct* method. In the conventional method, Oracle prepares the data in a bind array to insert using normal *insert* (DML) statements. This method supports SQL functions for data formatting or massaging during the data load process.

In the direct method, Oracle prepares the data in a column array structure to insert and format into data blocks directly written to the data files. The direct method does not use the SGA and always inserts data above the current high water mark of the table. However, you may not be able to use this method to load data for certain data types such as LOB, BLOBS, nested tables, and so on.

The direct method is used when the parameter *direct* is set to TRUE. The *rows* parameter, represents the number of rows that will be inserted into the table at one time, and it affects the frequency of the data save operation. Therefore, it should be set to an appropriate high value to reduce the number of data saves. For large tables (per your definition), you should consider loading in parallel using the *parallel=true* setting. This should be done only if the input data file is segmented into multiple pieces. It is obvious that you will need to run multiple load sessions. If the load operation can be repeated, you should consider using the *unrecoverable* option to further speed up the loading process. If you are loading into partitioned tables that already contain data, you should make the partitioned indexes *unusable* before loading data. This will avoid index maintenance during the load operation.

When using conventional path loading, increasing the value of *rows* is what most DBAs do to improve the load performance. Oracle uses the value of *rows* and *bindsize* to determine the amount of memory to be allocated to the bind array. Every insert operation adds *bind array worth* of records to the table. Another parameter, *readsize*, introduced in Oracle 8.0.5, controls size of the read buffer, which is used to populate the data read from the input file.

The following example shows the last few lines from a SQL*Loader log file with different values for *bindsize* and *readsize*. The confusing part about these two parameters is that if one of them is set to a non-default value, Oracle assigns the same value to the other. In our tests, we let SQL*Loader compute value for ROWS based on the *bindsize* value and the size of a single row. *Bindsize* and *readsize* assumed their default values (65,535 bytes):

```
Space allocated for bind array:                    51084 bytes(2 rows)
Total logical records read:            24063
Total logical records rejected:           30
Run began on Wed Nov 10 18:30:22 1999
Run ended on Wed Nov 10 18:37:18 1999

Elapsed time was:       00:06:56.51
CPU time was:           00:01:34.72
```

When *bindsize* and *readsize* were set to 1,048,576 bytes (1MB):

```
Space allocated for bind array:                 1047222 bytes(41 rows)
Total logical records read:          24063
Total logical records rejected:         30
Run began on Thu Nov 11 00:02:23 1999
Run ended on Thu Nov 11 00:05:06 1999

Elapsed time was:       00:02:42.25
CPU time was:           00:01:14.59
```

Did you notice the difference in the elapsed times and the number of rowsin the bind array in these examples? It is evident that values assigned to *bindsize, readsize,* and *rows* parameters can affect the SQL*Loader performance considerably. This test was performed when we were investigating (and learning) the techniques to improve SQL*Loader performance, way back in 1999.

For a detailed explanation of the aforementioned parameters and to learn a method to compute appropriate values for them, please refer to an article by Stephen Andert, "SQL*Loader: A Case Study in Tuning," available at http://oracle.oreilly.com/news/oraclesqlload_0401.html. Stephen Andert was a technical reviewer for the book *Oracle SQL*Loader: The Definitive Guide,* by Jonathan Gennick and Sanjay Mishra, published by O'Reilly & Associates. We refer you to this book for a thorough understanding of SQL*Loader and how to improve its performance.

Sample Oracle Initialization Parameters

The following is a collection of most of the relevant Oracle initialization parameters discussed in this book. We have segregated them by their function to make it easier to understand the relevant parameters and the functionality they support. Also, the functional groups remind you of the potential system impact (positive or negative) to the specific component when you change them. The values of these parameters are for *reference purposes only* and are *not* to be used *as is* without testing and monitoring your system.

For example, the following listing has DISK_ASYNCH_IO, multiple DBWR_IO_SLAVES, and USE_DIRECT_IO configured. It is not recommended that you utilize all of these at the same time. For a description of any parameter in Oracle, refer the Oracle Reference Guide or query V$PARAMETER and view the Description column in the output.

```
# initMYDB.ora
# ------------
#
# ----------------------------------------------------------------
# Modification History
# --------------------
# Name            Date        Action
# ----            ----        ------
# Kirti           04/16/2001  Created the file
# Gaja            04/17/2001  Cleaned up, added some parameters
# ----------------------------------------------------------------

# Parameters to optimize the Database Buffer Cache and I/O
# --------------------------------------------------------
db_block_buffers = 10000
buffer_pool_keep = (buffers:500, lru_latches:1)     # Oracle8 and above
buffer_pool_recycle = (buffers:1000, lru_latches:2) # Oracle8 and above
db_file_multiblock_read_count = 16
db_writers = 10                             # Oracle 7.3 and below
dbwr_writer_processes = 1                   # Oracle8 and above
dbwr_io_slaves = 10                         # Oracle8 and above
disk_asynch_io = TRUE                       # Oracle8 and above
use_direct_io = TRUE                        # Platform specific
use_ism = TRUE                              # Sun Solaris, Obsolete in 8i
db_files = 200

# Parameters to optimize the Shared Pool Area
# -------------------------------------------
shared_pool_size = 134217728
shared_pool_reserved_size = 10485760
shared_pool_reserved_min_alloc = 5242880 # Obsolete in Oracle 8.1.3
java_pool_size = 20971520                    # Oracle8i and above
large_pool_size = 10485760
large_pool_min_alloc = 8192                  # Obsolete in Oracle 8.1.3
lock_sga = TRUE                              # Platform specific
mlock_sga = TRUE                             # Platform specific
dml_locks = 300
sequence_cache_entries = 100

# Parameters to optimize Hash Joins
# ---------------------------------
hash_area_size = 10485760
hash_multiblock_io_count = 16
hash_join_enabled = TRUE
```

```
# Parameters to optimize Redo Log Buffer, ARCH and LGWR
# ---------------------------------------------------------
log_buffer = 131072
log_archive_dest = /u06/oradata/MYDB/archive
log_archive_format = arch_%s.log
log_archive_start = TRUE
log_archive_buffer_size = 128            # Obsolete in Oracle 8.1.3
log_archive_buffers = 5                  # Obsolete in Oracle 8.1.3

# Oracle8 and Oracle8i introduced a few additional parameters to manage more
# than one log archive destination and conditions for copying log files
# to them. Please refer to Oracle documentation for additional information.

# Parameters to configure Latches
# ------------------------------
log_simultaneous_copies = 8              # Obsolete in Oracle 8.1.3
db_block_lru_latches = 8

# Parameters to optimize Checkpoints
# --------------------------------
log_checkpoint_interval = 0
log_checkpoint_timeout = 1800
log_checkpoints_to_alert = TRUE

# Parameters to optimize Cursors and Library Cache Performance
# -----------------------------------------------------------
cusor_space_for_time = FALSE
row_cache_cursor = 128                   # Obsolete in Oracle 8.1.3
session_cached_cursors = 64
open_cursors = 256

# Parameters to select Optimizer Mode and tune Optimizer
#-------------------------------------------------------
optimizer_mode = choose
optimizer_parallel_percent = 0
optimizer_max_permutations = 79000       # Oracle 8.0.5 and above
optimizer_index_cost_adj = 1            # Oracle 8.0.5 and above
optimizer_search_limit = 1              # Oracle 8.0.5 and above
optimizer_index_caching = 99            # Oracle 8.0.5 and above
partition_view_enabled = true
always_anti_join = HASH

# Parameters to optimize Parallel Query Option
# --------------------------------------------
parallel_max_servers = 16
```

```
parallel_min_servers = 4
parallel_min_percent = 50
parallel_server_idle_time = 5           # Obsolete in Oracle 8.1.3
parallel_automatic_tuning = FALSE       # Oracle8i and above

# Parameters to optimize Sort Performance
# --------------------------------------
sort_area_size = 1048576
sort_area_retained_size = 1048576
sort_direct_writes = TRUE               # Obsolete in 8.1.3
sort_write_buffers = 8                  # Obsolete in 8.1.3
sort_write_buffer_size = 32768          # Obsolete in 8.1.3
sort_multiblock_read_count = 2          # Oracle8i and above

# Pointer to the configMYDB.ora file that stores static parameters
# ----------------------------------------------------------------
ifile = /u01/oracle/admin/MYDB/pfile/configMYDB.ora


# configMYDB.ora
# --------------
db_block_size = 8192
processes = 100
timed_statistics = TRUE

# The following parameter enables public read access to trace files
_trace_files_public = TRUE
global_names = TRUE
compatible = 8.1.6.1
rollback_segments = (rs1,rs2,rs3,rs4)
db_name = MYDB
control_files = (/u03/oradata/MYDB/cntrl1.ctl,\
                 /u04/oradata/MYDB/cntrl2.ctl)
user_dump_dest = /u01/oracle/admin/MYDB/udump
core_dump_dest = /u01/oracle/admin/MYDB/cdump
background_dump_dest = /u01/oracle/admin/MYDB/bdump
service_name = MYDB
```

Additional Resources

For additional information on any of the topics discussed in this book, we refer you to http://www.hotsos.com, http://www.orapub.com, http://technet.oracle.com, and http://metalink.oracle.com. Hotsos LLC and Orapub, Inc., are also home for a variety of downloadable scripts and tools that assist your tuning efforts using the wait interface. In addition, they also offer specialized performance tuning workshops.

For live discussions on various Oracle topics, problems, news, and other fun things, we recommend you join the mailing lists *oracle-l* (moderated by Jared Still) and *lazyDBA* (moderated by Henry O'Keeffe). To join oracle-l send an e-mail to ListGuru@fatcity.com with a subject body *your name*; to join lazyDBA, send a blank e-mail to ORACLEDBA-SUBSCRIBE@LAZYDBA.COM; and for more information visit http://www.lazyDBA.com.

There is also a wealth of information at the Miracle A/S Web site at http://www.miracleas.dk.

APPENDIX C

References

very effort is made to provide you with a list of all the material we have used as references for this book. Any omission from this list is purely unintentional.

- Andert, S. *SQL*Loader: A Case Study in Tuning*. O'Reilly White Paper, 2001. http://oracle.oreilly.com/news/oraclesqlload_0401.html.

- Aronoff, E. *The Oracle Database Block Size – Larger is Better*. White Paper, Proceedings of the International Oracle User Group – Americas, Live 1999, 1999. http://www.ioug.org.

- Aronoff, E., K. Loney., and N. Sonawalla. *Advanced Oracle Tuning and Administration*. Osborne McGraw-Hill, 1997. http://www.osborne.com.

- Cockroft, A. *Sun Performance and Tuning, Sparc & Solaris*. Sun Microsystems, 1997.

- Dudar, E., D. Cook, and C. Shallahammer. *The Ratio Modeling Technique*. White Paper, 1997. http://www.orapub.com.

- Gunther, N. *The Practical Performance Analyst*. McGraw-Hill, 1998. http://www.osborne.com.

- Hewllett-Packard Corporation, *HP-UX Kernel Tuning and Performance Guide*. Tuning Guide, 2000. http://docs.hp.com/hpux/onlinedocs/os/11.0/tuningwp.html.

- IBM Corporation, *Performance Management Guide*. AIX Performance Guide, 2000. http://www.rs6000.ibm.com/doc_link/en_US/a_doc_lib/aixbman/prftungd/toc.htm.

- Lewis, J. *Introduction to the Parallel Query Option*. White Paper, Proceedings of UK Oracle User Group, Spring 1997. http://www.jlcomp.demon.co.uk.

- Lewis, J. *Parallel Query Option in Real Life*. White Paper, Proceedings of UK Oracle User Group, Summer 1997. http://www.jlcomp.demon.co.uk.

- Loney, K. and M. Theriault.*Oracle8i DBA Handbook*. Osborne McGraw-Hill, 1999. http://www.osborne.com.

- Massiglia, P. *RAID for Enterprise Computing*. Veritas Software Corporation White Paper, 2000. http://www.veritas.com/.

■ McDougall, R. *Getting to know the Solaris filesystem, Part 2*. Sun Microsystems White Paper, 1999. http://www.sunworld.com/sunworldonline/swol-06-1999/swol-06-filesystem2_p.html.

■ Millsap, C. *Performance Management: Myths & Facts*. Hotsos White Paper. http://www.hotsos.com.

■ Millsap,C. *Why 99% Cache Hit Ratio Is Not OK*. Hotsos White Paper. http://www.hotsos.com.

■ Millsap, C., C. Shallahammer, and A. Adler. *Predicting the Utility of the Non-unique Index*. Oracle Magazine Article, 1993. http://www.oramag.com.

■ Miracle A/S. *Performance Tools*. http://www.miracleas.dk.

■ Oracle Corporation. *Multiple Articles and Notes related to performace monitoring and tuning at Oracle Support Services* – Metalink. http://metalink.oracle.com.

■ Oracle Technology Network. *Oracle Documentation*. http://technet.oracle.com.

■ Oraperf, Inc., *Online Performance Analyzer*. http://www.oraperf.com

■ Shah, R. *What is RAID? – Details of this popular storage technology*. Sun Microsystems White Paper, 1999. http://www.sunworld.com/swol-06-1999/f_swol-06-connectivity.html.

■ Shallahammer, C. *Total Performance Management (An introduction to the method)*. White Paper, 1995. http://www.orapub.com.

■ Shallahammer, C. *Direct Contention Identification Using Oracle's Session Wait Tables*. White Paper, 2000. http://www.orapub.com.

■ Shome, P. *Using Stored Outlines in Oracle8i for Plan Stability*. Proceedings of Oracle Open World, 1999. http://www.oracle.com/openworld.

■ Sneed, B. *Sun/Oracle Best Practices*. White Paper, Sun Blueprints (TM) Online-January 2001. http://www.sun.com/software/solutions/blueprints/0101/SunOracle.pdf.

■ Vaidyanatha, G. *Implementing RAID on Oracle Systems*. White Paper, Proceedings of the Oracle Open World 2000, 2000. http://www.quest.com/whitepapers.

■ Vaidyanatha, G. *Oracle Performance Management*. White Paper, Proceedings of the Oracle Open World 2000, 2000. http://www.quest.com/whitepapers.

■ Vaidyanatha, G. *System Architecture for Oracle8 VLDBs – A Case Study*. White Paper, Proceedings of the Oracle Open World 1999, 1999. http://www.oracle.com/openworld.

■ Wong, B. *Configuring and Capacity Planning for Solaris Servers*. Prentice Hall, 1997.

■ Wong, B. *RAID: What does it mean to me?* Sun Microsystems White Paper, 1995. http://www.sunworld.com/sunworldonline/swol-09-1995/swol-09-raid5_p.html.

Index

INTERNATIONAL CONTACT INFORMATION

AUSTRALIA
McGraw-Hill Book Company Australia Pty. Ltd.
TEL +61-2-9417-9899
FAX +61-2-9417-5687
http://www.mcgraw-hill.com.au
books-it_sydney@mcgraw-hill.com

CANADA
McGraw-Hill Ryerson Ltd.
TEL +905-430-5000
FAX +905-430-5020
http://www.mcgrawhill.ca

GREECE, MIDDLE EAST,
NORTHERN AFRICA
McGraw-Hill Hellas
TEL +30-1-656-0990-3-4
FAX +30-1-654-5525

MEXICO (Also serving Latin America)
McGraw-Hill Interamericana Editores S.A. de C.V.
TEL +525-117-1583
FAX +525-117-1589
http://www.mcgraw-hill.com.mx
fernando_castellanos@mcgraw-hill.com

SINGAPORE (Serving Asia)
McGraw-Hill Book Company
TEL +65-863-1580
FAX +65-862-3354
http://www.mcgraw-hill.com.sg
mghasia@mcgraw-hill.com

SOUTH AFRICA
McGraw-Hill South Africa
TEL +27-11-622-7512
FAX +27-11-622-9045
robyn_swanepoel@mcgraw-hill.com

UNITED KINGDOM & EUROPE
(Excluding Southern Europe)
McGraw-Hill Education Europe
TEL +44-1-628-502500
FAX +44-1-628-770224
http://www.mcgraw-hill.co.uk
computing_neurope@mcgraw-hill.com

ALL OTHER INQUIRIES Contact:
Osborne/McGraw-Hill
TEL +1-510-549-6600
FAX +1-510-883-7600
http://www.osborne.com
omg_international@mcgraw-hill.com

Knowledge is power. To which we say,

crank up the power.

Are you ready for a power surge?

Accelerate your career—become an **Oracle Certified Professional (OCP)**. With Oracle's cutting-edge *Instructor-Led Training, Technology-Based Training*, and this *guide*, you can prepare for certification faster than ever. Set your own trajectory by logging your personal training plan with us. Go to **http://education.oracle.com/tpb**, where we'll help you pick a training path, select your courses, and track your progress. We'll even send you an email when your courses are offered in your area. If you don't have access to the Web, call us at 1-800-441-3541 (Outside the U.S. call +1-310-335-2403).
Power learning has never been easier.

U n i v e r s i t y

Get Your FREE Subscription to *Oracle Magazine*

Oracle Magazine is essential gear for today's information technology professionals. Stay informed and increase your productivity with every issue of *Oracle Magazine*. Inside each **FREE,** bimonthly issue you'll get:

- Up-to-date information on Oracle Database Server, Oracle Applications, Internet Computing, and tools
- Third-party news and announcements
- Technical articles on Oracle products and operating environments
- Development and administration tips
- Real-world customer stories

Three easy ways to subscribe:

1. Web   **Visit our Web site at www.oracle.com/oramag/. You'll find a subscription form there, plus much more!**

2. Fax   Complete the questionnaire on the back of this card and fax the questionnaire side only to **+1.847.647.9735.**

3. Mail   Complete the questionnaire on the back of this card and mail it to P.O. Box 1263, Skokie, IL 60076-8263.

If there are other Oracle users at your location who would like to receive their own subscription to *Oracle Magazine*, please photocopy this form and pass it along.

☐ YES! Please send me a FREE subscription to *Oracle Magazine*.   ☐ NO

To receive a free bimonthly subscription to *Oracle Magazine*, you must fill out the entire card, sign it, and date it (incomplete cards cannot be processed or acknowledged). You can also fax your application to +1.847.647.9735. Or subscribe at our Web site at www.oracle.com/oramag/

SIGNATURE (REQUIRED)   X _____   **DATE** _____

NAME	TITLE
COMPANY	TELEPHONE
ADDRESS	FAX NUMBER
CITY	STATE POSTAL CODE/ZIP CODE
COUNTRY	E-MAIL ADDRESS

☐ From time to time, Oracle Publishing allows our partners exclusive access to our e-mail addresses for special promotions and announcements. To be included in this program, please check this box.

You must answer all eight questions below.

1 What is the primary business activity of your firm at this location? *(check only one)*
- ☐ 03 Communications
- ☐ 04 Consulting, Training
- ☐ 06 Data Processing
- ☐ 07 Education
- ☐ 08 Engineering
- ☐ 09 Financial Services
- ☐ 10 Government—Federal, Local, State, Other
- ☐ 11 Government—Military
- ☐ 12 Health Care
- ☐ 13 Manufacturing—Aerospace, Defense
- ☐ 14 Manufacturing—Computer Hardware
- ☐ 15 Manufacturing—Noncomputer Products
- ☐ 17 Research & Development
- ☐ 19 Retailing, Wholesaling, Distribution
- ☐ 20 Software Development
- ☐ 21 Systems Integration, VAR, VAD, OEM
- ☐ 22 Transportation
- ☐ 23 Utilities (Electric, Gas, Sanitation)
- ☐ 98 Other Business and Services
  _____

2 Which of the following best describes your job function? *(check only one)*
CORPORATE MANAGEMENT/STAFF
- ☐ 01 Executive Management (President, Chair, CEO, CFO, Owner, Partner, Principal)
- ☐ 02 Finance/Administrative Management (VP/Director/ Manager/Controller, Purchasing, Administration)
- ☐ 03 Sales/Marketing Management (VP/Director/Manager)
- ☐ 04 Computer Systems/Operations Management (CIO/VP/Director/ Manager MIS, Operations)

IS/IT STAFF
- ☐ 07 Systems Development/ Programming Management
- ☐ 08 Systems Development/ Programming Staff
- ☐ 09 Consulting
- ☐ 10 DBA/Systems Administrator
- ☐ 11 Education/Training
- ☐ 14 Technical Support Director/ Manager
- ☐ 16 Other Technical Management/Staff
- ☐ 98 Other _____

3 What is your current primary operating platform? *(check all that apply)*
- ☐ 01 DEC UNIX
- ☐ 02 DEC VAX VMS
- ☐ 03 Java
- ☐ 04 HP UNIX
- ☐ 05 IBM AIX
- ☐ 06 IBM UNIX
- ☐ 07 Macintosh
- ☐ 09 MS-DOS
- ☐ 10 MVS
- ☐ 11 NetWare
- ☐ 12 Network Computing
- ☐ 13 OpenVMS
- ☐ 14 SCO UNIX
- ☐ 24 Sequent DYNIX/ptx
- ☐ 15 Sun Solaris/SunOS
- ☐ 16 SVR4
- ☐ 18 UnixWare
- ☐ 20 Windows
- ☐ 21 Windows NT
- ☐ 23 Other UNIX _____
- ☐ 98 Other _____
- 99 ☐ **None of the above**

4 Do you evaluate, specify, recommend, or authorize the purchase of any of the following? *(check all that apply)*
- ☐ 01 Hardware
- ☐ 02 Software
- ☐ 03 Application Development Tools
- ☐ 04 Database Products
- ☐ 05 Internet or Intranet Products
- 99 ☐ **None of the above**

5 In your job, do you use or plan to purchase any of the following products or services? *(check all that apply)*
SOFTWARE
- ☐ 01 Business Graphics
- ☐ 02 CAD/CAE/CAM
- ☐ 03 CASE
- ☐ 05 Communications
- ☐ 06 Database Management
- ☐ 07 File Management
- ☐ 08 Finance
- ☐ 09 Java
- ☐ 10 Materials Resource Planning
- ☐ 11 Multimedia Authoring
- ☐ 12 Networking
- ☐ 13 Office Automation
- ☐ 14 Order Entry/Inventory Control
- ☐ 15 Programming
- ☐ 16 Project Management
- ☐ 17 Scientific and Engineering
- ☐ 18 Spreadsheets
- ☐ 19 Systems Management
- ☐ 20 Workflow

HARDWARE
- ☐ 21 Macintosh
- ☐ 22 Mainframe
- ☐ 23 Massively Parallel Processing
- ☐ 24 Minicomputer
- ☐ 25 PC
- ☐ 26 Network Computer
- ☐ 28 Symmetric Multiprocessing
- ☐ 29 Workstation

PERIPHERALS
- ☐ 30 Bridges/Routers/Hubs/Gateways
- ☐ 31 CD-ROM Drives
- ☐ 32 Disk Drives/Subsystems
- ☐ 33 Modems
- ☐ 34 Tape Drives/Subsystems
- ☐ 35 Video Boards/Multimedia

SERVICES
- ☐ 37 Consulting
- ☐ 38 Education/Training
- ☐ 39 Maintenance
- ☐ 40 Online Database Services
- ☐ 41 Support
- ☐ 36 Technology-Based Training
- ☐ 98 Other _____
- 99 ☐ **None of the above**

6 What Oracle products are in use at your site? *(check all that apply)*
SERVER/SOFTWARE
- ☐ 01 Oracle8
- ☐ 30 Oracle8*i*
- ☐ 31 Oracle8*i* Lite
- ☐ 02 Oracle7
- ☐ 03 Oracle Application Server
- ☐ 04 Oracle Data Mart Suites
- ☐ 05 Oracle Internet Commerce Server
- ☐ 32 Oracle *inter*Media
- ☐ 33 Oracle JServer
- ☐ 07 Oracle Lite
- ☐ 08 Oracle Payment Server
- ☐ 11 Oracle Video Server

TOOLS
- ☐ 13 Oracle Designer
- ☐ 14 Oracle Developer
- ☐ 54 Oracle Discoverer
- ☐ 53 Oracle Express
- ☐ 51 Oracle JDeveloper
- ☐ 52 Oracle Reports
- ☐ 50 Oracle WebDB
- ☐ 55 Oracle Workflow

ORACLE APPLICATIONS
- ☐ 17 Oracle Automotive
- ☐ 35 Oracle Business Intelligence System
- ☐ 19 Oracle Consumer Packaged Goods
- ☐ 39 Oracle E-Commerce
- ☐ 18 Oracle Energy
- ☐ 20 Oracle Financials
- ☐ 28 Oracle Front Office
- ☐ 21 Oracle Human Resources
- ☐ 37 Oracle Internet Procurement
- ☐ 22 Oracle Manufacturing
- ☐ 40 Oracle Process Manufacturing
- ☐ 23 Oracle Projects
- ☐ 34 Oracle Retail
- ☐ 29 Oracle Self-Service Web Applications
- ☐ 38 Oracle Strategic Enterprise Management
- ☐ 25 Oracle Supply Chain Management
- ☐ 36 Oracle Tutor
- ☐ 41 Oracle Travel Management

ORACLE SERVICES
- ☐ 61 Oracle Consulting
- ☐ 62 Oracle Education
- ☐ 60 Oracle Support
- ☐ 98 Other _____
- 99 ☐ **None of the above**

7 What other database products are in use at your site? *(check all that apply)*
- ☐ 01 Access
- ☐ 02 Baan
- ☐ 03 dbase
- ☐ 04 Gupta
- ☐ 05 IBM DB2
- ☐ 06 Informix
- ☐ 07 Ingres
- ☐ 08 Microsoft Access
- ☐ 09 Microsoft SQL Server
- ☐ 10 PeopleSoft
- ☐ 11 Progress
- ☐ 12 SAP
- ☐ 13 Sybase
- ☐ 14 VSAM
- ☐ 98 Other _____
- 99 ☐ **None of the above**

8 During the next 12 months, how much do you anticipate your organization will spend on computer hardware, software, peripherals, and services for your location? *(check only one)*
- ☐ 01 Less than $10,000
- ☐ 02 $10,000 to $49,999
- ☐ 03 $50,000 to $99,999
- ☐ 04 $100,000 to $499,999
- ☐ 05 $500,000 to $999,999
- ☐ 06 $1,000,000 and over

If there are other Oracle users at your location who would like to receive a free subscription to *Oracle Magazine*, please photocopy this form and pass it along, or contact Customer Service at +1.847.647.9630

Form 5

OPRESS